AUTHORITY, ANXIETY, AND CANON

SUNY Series in Hindu Studies
Wendy Doniger, editor

AUTHORITY, ANXIETY, AND CANON

Essays in Vedic Interpretation

Edited by
Laurie L. Patton

State University of New York Press

The cover illustration is from a manuscript of the *Razm-nāma*, ascribed to kānhā (late sixteenth century). It is reproduced in *Indian Miniatures: The Ehrenfeld Collection*, by Daniel J. Ehnbom; with essays by Robert Skelton and Pramod Chandra (New York: Hudson Hills Press in association with the American Federation of Arts: Distributed by Viking Penguin, 1985), Folio #13, "A brāhmaṇa and his son Medhāvin discourse on the path to salvation."

Published by
State University of New York Press, Albany

Printed in the United States of America

For information, address State University of New York Press,
State University Plaza, Albany, N.Y., 12246

Production by Cathleen Collins
Marketing by Dana Yanulavich

Library of Congress Cataloging in Publication Data

Authority, anxiety, and canon : essays in Vedic interpretation /
edited by Laurie L. Patton.
p. cm. — (SUNY series in Hindu studies)
Includes bibliographical references and index.
ISBN 0-7914-1937-1 (hc). — ISBN 0-7914-1938-X (pb)
1. Vedas—Criticism, interpretation, etc. I. Patton, Laurie L.
II. Series.
BL1112.26.A98 1993
294.5'921—dc20 93-25748
CIP

10 9 8 7 6 5 4 3 2 1

Contents

Preface
WENDY DONIGER vii

Introduction
LAURIE L. PATTON 1

PART ONE
THE VEDAS REFLECT ON THEMSELVES

1 THE MASTERY OF SPEECH
Canonicity and Control in the Vedas
DAVID CARPENTER 19

2 VEDA IN THE BRĀHMAṆAS
Cosmogonic Paradigms and the Delimitation of Canon
BARBARA A. HOLDREGE 35

3 THE VEDA AND THE AUTHORITY OF CLASS
Reduplicating Structures of Veda and *Varṇa*
in Ancient Indian Texts
BRIAN K. SMITH 67

PART TWO
THE VEDAS IN CLASSICAL DISCOURSE

4 PURĀṆAVEDA
FREDERICK M. SMITH 97

5 FROM ANXIETY TO BLISS
Argument, Care, and Responsibility in the
Vedānta Reading of *Taittirīya* 2.1–6a
FRANCIS X. CLOONEY, S.J. 139

6 "WHITHER THE THICK SWEETNESS OF THEIR PASSION?"
The Search for Vedic Origins of Sanskrit Drama
DAVID L. GITOMER 171

PART THREE
THE VEDAS IN MODERNITY AND BEYOND

7 THE AUTHORITY OF AN ABSENT TEXT
The Veda, Upangas, Upavedas, and Upnekhata in European Thought
DOROTHY M. FIGUEIRA 201

8 FROM INTERPRETATION TO REFORM
Dayānand's Reading of the Vedas
JOHN E. LLEWELLYN 235

9 REDEFINING THE AUTHORITY OF SCRIPTURE
The Rejection of Vedic Infallibility by the Brahmo Samaj
ANANTANAND RAMBACHAN 253

10 POETS AND FISHES
Modern Indian Interpretations of the Vedic Rishi
LAURIE L. PATTON 281

Afterword
LAURIE L. PATTON 309

Contributors 317

Index 321

Preface

A FIGHT HAS BEEN RAGING over the ownership of the sacred relic of the body of the *Ṛg-Veda* (and over the question of whether it is, in fact, a corpse) for over a century, from the days of Colebrooke and Wilson, perhaps cresting in 1890, when F. Max Müller published his edition of the Sanskrit text and brought it to the consciousness of Europe. There have been two main warring camps, each consisting of a small, elite group: on this side, German (and British) philologists, in their obsessively neat ranks of scholarship, and on that side, Brahmins, in their equally (but separately) obsessive ranks of ritual. Each has claimed the Veda, for very different purposes and on very different grounds. The anti-Orientalists, following Edward Said, have argued that European scholars have somehow simultaneously inflicted the Veda upon the Hindus and kept it from them; and the subaltern/Marxist coalition, in a parallel rut, have argued that the Brahmins have done the same double damage.

But now a third party has entered the ranks, *academicus ex machina*, to rescue the Veda from the depth of the Ocean of Obfuscation to which those twin demons, European and Brahminical, had abducted it.[1] Now it appears that (if we accept the wise dictum of Antoine de Saint Exupéry's *Petit Prince*, that you can only truly own something that you take care of) the Veda belongs neither to the anal-retentive nor to the sanctimonious, but to the methodological. More precisely, the Veda has attracted the attention of a group of historians of religions in North America, which turns out to be intellectually, if not geographically, midway between Benares and Berlin.

This shift in the center of gravity, this tilting of the *axis mundi*, may be attributed in part to the excitement stirred up in the 1980s by two works by American scholars. First (in 1982) came Jonathan Z. Smith's article on canon, an article that has now itself become canonical in our field: "Sacred Persistence: Toward a Redescription of Canon" (to which several of the chapters in this volume refer, beginning with Laurie Patton in the introduction). In many ways, the ghost in the (methodological) machine of the present volume is not F. Max Müller but Jonathan Z. Smith. Then (in 1989) Brian K. Smith published *Reflections on Resemblance, Ritual and Religion*, a book that took a bold look at the Veda's canonical status within Hinduism and issued in a New Age in the study not merely of the Veda but of the whole religious complex that we call Hinduism.

Laurie Patton, who had already been plowing her own furrow in the rich field of the Vedas, joined with Brian K. Smith and others laboring in other parts of the forest, and they converged on an American Academy of Religion panel in 1990. That panel, in its turn, served as a magnet for yet other scholars with yet other interests in the Veda. The result is this volume.

When I first discussed the possibilities of this series with Bill Eastman (who surely deserves a medal for courageous publishing—perhaps he should be made Knight of the Multiauthored Volume), I said I hoped the series would include both classical studies and the cutting edge of new studies. I did not then imagine that a single volume would do both at once, but this is that volume. For, after all, the Veda is as *Ur* as it gets, while the young scholars who have written this volume represent the *nouvelle vague* in approaches to religious texts. They carry their theoretical assumptions not as shields to protect themselves from unexpected and recalcitrant dirty data (what Mary Douglas called ''matter out of place''), but as awkward backpacks that get heavier with every step, burdens that can neither jettison nor ignore. It is their honest attempt to grapple with the theoretical monkeys on their backs, while still paying careful attention to the Indological tradition before them, that makes these chapters both so solid and so stimulating. Whatever the Veda may or may not be anywhere else (and it is precisely this question that is so hotly debated throughout this volume), it is certainly very much alive and well in these pages.

Wendy Doniger

NOTES

1. An earlier rescue attempt, made, in 1981, not by the traditional Fish avatar, nor even by one of Laurie Patton's fishy rishies, but by a translated Penguin, had met with only moderate success.

Introduction

THE POET KABIR'S WARNING that the one who studies the Vedas "gets entangled and dies therein"[1] is one to be taken quite seriously. Until recently, the study of the Veda has been philologically rigorous yet theoretically moribund. Also until recently, the influence of the Vedic canon on the rest of Indian religious history has been inadequately addressed. One of the few scholars to address the issue, Louis Renou, ends up closing off rather than opening up possibilities for further research in this area. In his small but influential essay, "The Destiny of the Veda in India,"[2] Renou asserts that over time the Vedic canon became a kind of empty icon, signifying various kinds of prestige and power, but little else. According to Renou, in the classical and modern religious traditions of India, only the "outside" of the Veda has survived. Renou concludes rather sadly, "The Vedic world, whose essence has passed. . .was no more than a distant object, exposed to the hazards of an adoration stripped of its textual substance."[3]

The present volume joins other recent Indological scholarship in demuring from such conclusions.[4] The book began as a panel at the American Academy of Religion, held in New Orleans, Louisiana, in late 1990, and continued as a series of informal discussions and conversations well into 1991. The panelists argued that the substance of the Veda is indeed integrated into later traditions. What is more, they demonstrated that Renou has missed the most interesting point of departure: even if it *were* true that only the outside of the Veda survives in later periods, that "outside" itself is not uniformly received. Such a point is simply illustrated by the commonplace fact that the Vedas can refer either to the four earliest collections of verses (the *Ṛg-*, the *Sāma-*, the *Yajur-*, and the *Atharva-Veda*s), or to an aggregate of early Indian works, including the four Vedas, the Brāhmaṇas, and the Upaniṣads. (The chapters in the present volume use both definitions, depending on which historical period is being discussed.) While Renou perceived that the Veda takes on various patterns of influence in different systems of Indian thought, he failed to see how that variety is precisely the reason why inquiry into the vicissitudes of Vedic influence is fruitful.

The chapters in the present volume develop the perspective of that panel, taking up the question of the Vedas from a theoretical as well as a philological and historical basis. In a particularly helpful theoretical essay, "Sacred Persistence," J. Z. Smith asserts that canon is a salutary category in the study of religion because it incorporates questions of authority and innovation simultaneously. In the study of exegesis, one can focus upon both the limiting of canon and the overcoming of that limitation through ingenuity. Smith also suggests that because canons can take the form of ritual objects and spoken words as well as texts, both written and oral media can be taken into account.

Too few scholars have taken up the preliminary challenge that Smith makes to the study of religion, with one notable exception. In his book, *Reflections on Ritual, Resemblance and Religion*,[5] Brian K. Smith, one of our contributors, argues that the amoeba-like cluster of practices and beliefs now called "Hinduism" can be defined as Hinduism precisely by their appeal to the Vedas as their canonical authority. While the question of defining "Hinduism" itself remains open, his suggestive study paves the way for more specific studies to delineate the history of the reception of the Vedas in various genres of discourse and at various points in India's religious history. Indeed, the very element that might define "Hinduism" is also the element that most richly exposes the heterogeneity of Indian religious practices.

In order to incorporate such heterogeneity, each of the chapters in this volume engages a twofold study: the theoretical question of canonicity and the historical question of the continuation, appropriation, or rejection of Vedic authority in different forms of Indian religions. These chapters modify and challenge J. Z. Smith's ideas about limitation and ingenuity in canon formation and exegesis. In doing so, these studies also specify and diversify Brian Smith's more general suggestions about the place of the Veda in Indian religions. For example, in their studies of the Brāhmaṇas, the ritual philosophical works that follow the four Vedas, David Carpenter, Barbara Holdrege, and Brian Smith all argue that the Brāhmaṇas view the Vedas primarily as a form of ritual and cosmological speech (Vāc) that guarantees social status; the Vedas are not collections of oral "texts" that are to be limited or expanded through exegesis. David Gitomer, Frederick Smith, and Francis Clooney all push the definition of canonical exegesis further by inquiring about the Vedic canon's relationship to discourses that are simultaneously "inside" and "outside" the Vedic tradition. While texts from the Purāṇic, Vedāntan, and *Naṭyaśāstra* traditions all claim some kind of development from Vedic origins, their perceptions and methods of maintaining Vedic authority differ radically. Finally, J. E.

Llewellyn, Anantanand Rambachan, Dorothy Figueira, and I take the insider/outsider question one step further—examining how contact with the West affects notions of canonicity. In this period, the Veda is subject to the more strident exegetical strategies of universalization (Llewellyn), rejection (Rambachan), and romanticization, whether in the service of colonialist (Figueira) or anticolonialist (Patton) ends.

As its title suggests, this volume incorporates two themes that are closely related to each other: authority and anxiety. Many of the chapters are concerned with the question of the maintenance and modification of a Vedic authority that has already been established, and remains, to a large extent, unquestioned. The second theme, that of anxiety, addresses explicit tensions about Vedic authority itself—how it is used by non-Vedic traditions, how it is controlled, and how it is overturned. It should be noted at the outset that the distinction between these two sections is one of degree, not of kind. Any tradition that attempts to maintain an authoritative canon necessarily involves some anxiety over the boundaries of that canon, no matter how well accepted they may be. Relatedly, any anxiety about Vedic canon itself involves either a reassertion of Vedic authority or an appeal to another kind of authority.

The chapters move chronologically, delineating varying responses to the Vedic authority in the realm of philosophy, literature and drama, and narrative. Not surprisingly, the volume begins with two chapters dealing with the early Brahmanical interpretation of the four earliest Vedic texts—the *Ṛg-*, *Yajur-*, *Sāma-*, and *Atharva-Veda*s. In his chapter, "The Mastery of Speech," David Carpenter argues that the limitation of Vedic canon is motivated by a kind of uneasiness. The management of canon is achieved far more frequently through narratives depicting the control of oral speech than it is through the precise numbering and cataloguing of the content of the Saṃhitās, or collections, that make up the four Vedas. Carpenter substantiates this suggestion by showing how the Brahmanical appropriation of the goddess of speech, Vāc, is far different from the earlier portrayals of Vāc found in the Sāṃhitās. The later Brāhmaṇas apprehensively depict Speech not as a benevolent muse of poetic eloquence, but as a potential danger to be managed and circumscribed.

In "Veda in the Brāhmaṇas: Cosmogonic Paradigms and the Delimitation of Canon," Barbara Holdrege follows up on Carpenter's "detextualizing" of the Vedic canon. She argues that the Brahmanical tradition's emphasis on the form of the Vedic mantras over their content is integrally connected to the mantras' status as "primordial impulses of speech" that constitute the source and model of creation. Through the actions of the creator Prajāpati, the Veda is cosmologized, so that forms of the Veda correspond to levels of creation.

In his chapter, "The Veda and the Authority of Class," Brian Smith picks up on the cosmological themes introduced by Holdrege and asks about their social meaning. He maintains that the Brāhmaṇa texts have a specific strategy for classifying the Veda according to the *varṇa*, or "social estate" system. Through an analysis of the various hierarchical equivalences (*bandhus*) made in the Brāhmaṇas, as well as through the representation of the Vedas in Brahmanical narratives, Smith shows that the Brāhmaṇas seal the distinctive social scheme of the *varṇa*s as "cosmologically aboriginal" and "authentically Vedic." For Smith, the canonical Vedas are inextricably linked to an idealized form of social hierarchy.

In his chapter, Frederick Smith engages the so-called classical Indian tradition through a close reading of the *Bhāgavata Purāṇa* as a Vedic text. The Purāṇic appropriation of the Vedas involved reshaping the mysterious, mantrically constructed Vedic *puruṣa* into the all-encompassing, sectarian deity *puruṣottama*. In addition, Purāṇic authors manipulated geneaology to align themselves with Vedic sages, and employed contemporary philosophical ideas to prove Vedic infallibility. Finally, Smith argues that the central concern of the Purāṇa was not the performance of Vedic ritual per se. Instead, the *Bhāgavata Purāṇa* used the Vedas and Vedic ritual as a repertory of persuasive invocational and evocational images—shaping the Vedas toward its own theological ends.

The next two chapters take up the classical Indian traditions from the perspective of the philosophy of Vedānta and the aesthetic theories of Sanskrit drama. In his chapter "From Anxiety to Bliss," Francis X. Clooney takes up the question of Vedic interpretation from a dual perspective—that of Vedāntic debate and that of the contemporary Western scholar. While contemporary Vedic exegetes may find their initial enthusiasm giving way to anxiety about the possibility of "right meaning," they can learn a good deal from the Vedāntan perspective. Clooney goes on to provide an example: in pondering a crucial passage from the *Taittirīya Upaniṣad*, the Vedāntans must decide whether or not certain verses refer to *brahman*. In his analysis of what the "right meaning" is to Vedāntan commentators, Clooney discusses not only the ways in which Vedic authority is maintained, but also the specific criteria used within Indian tradition for the "right reading" of Vedic texts. From the perspective of Vedānta, salvation itself is at stake in the interpretive process, and right meaning can only come about through a gradual, temporally attained understanding of the text.

David Gitomer's chapter, "Whither the Sweet Thickness of Their Passion?" provides a detailed analysis of the *nāṭyopatti* myth—the myth of origins of Sanskrit drama. While many Indologists have attempted to ascribe Vedic origins to this myth, Gitomer argues persuasively that the narrative is of a different nature entirely. The story is loosely allegorical, designed to impart priestly prestige to a dramatic profession anxious about its status. Moreover, the *Nāṭyaśāstra*'s appeal to Vedic origins provides a ritual paradigm to set it into a Vedic, and therefore more authoritative, context. Most important, Gitomer argues that the use of such myths is not the unreflective handing down of cosmogonic stories, but a self-conscious use of such cosmogonic motifs to reflect upon the situation of the actors and musicians involved in the drama. Here, Vedic canon is self-consciously used to impute an aura of stature and influence to the less explicitly prestigious realm of dramatic theory.

Dorothy Figueira's chapter, "The Authority of an Absent Text: The Veda, Upangas, Upavedas, and Upnekhata in European Thought," examines Vedic interpretation from an exclusively Western perspective, the contexts of the Enlightenment and Sturm und Drang periods. In these intellectual milieus, the substance of the Vedas as canonical texts was far less significant than the authority the idea of the Vedas engendered as a source of primitive revelation and early monotheist beliefs. Thus, for thinkers like Voltaire, Schlegel, and Herder, the Veda was canonical only in so far as it confirmed their own intellectual and spiritual agendas. Even when Voltaire's *Ezour Veda* was replaced by Rosen's partial translation of the actual Veda in 1838, the interpretations of Max Müller continued in the romanticist vein. As Figueira demonstrates, the text of canon can be "false," or even absent, and the exegetical work continues apace.

Vedic roots were not solely a European concern, however. In his chapter, "From Interpretation to Reform: Dayānand's Reading of the Vedas," John E. Llewellyn argues that Hindu reformer Dayānand Sarasvatī's main reason for founding the Ārya Samāj was to revive the Vedic religion, which embodied the ideal and original spirituality, free from the error of image worship. Llewellyn goes on to trace the development from oral debate to written forms of canonicial interpretation in Dayānand's intellectual life. In this context, Llewellyn also argues that, in his reformist zeal, Dayānand possessed a multilayered interpretive strategy: he was forced to make his canon of Vedic texts narrower and narrower in an effort to exclude those that referred to image worship, and, at the same time, he attempted to wrest the Vedas from brahmin control in order to make canon more universal.

The last two chapters address other aspects—both Euro-American and Indian—of the modern and postmodern interpretation of the Vedas. In his chapter, "Redefining the Authority of Scripture," Anantanand Rambachan argues that the infallibity of the Vedic canon presented a profound dilemma for those defenders of Hinduism to the West. Rambachan analyzes the initial defense of Vedic infallibility by Rammohun Roy, and how, in the midst of controversy between Indian leaders and Christian missionaries, Vedic infallibility aroused consternation and embarrassment. Rambachan goes on to show how the initial rejection of

Vedic authority by Debendranath Tagore was propelled further by Keshub Chandra Sen, who, in the name of antidogmatism, championed the authority of intuitive experience. Thus, the spiritual comprehension held up as principle of Vedic exegesis is the very ground for rejection of the Vedas by Sen and other Brahmo-Samaj leaders.

My own chapter, "Poets and Fishes: Modern Indian Interpretations of the Vedic Rishi," continues the theme of Western influence in the study of the Veda. I examine the work of three modern Indian interpreters of the Veda: C. Kunhan Raja, T. G. Mainkar, and Ram Gopal. These scholars place themselves in the midst of Western scholarly debate, using Western interpretive methods to describe the agents of canon, the rishis who composed the poems of the *Ṛg-Veda*. At the same time, however, these interpreters anticipate later post-Orientalist critique by attacking Western scholars for denigrating the rishis' role as the forebears of Indian tradition. Yet these authors also engage in their own constructions of the significance of the Vedic rishi; to them, the Veda is a repository of early democratic ideals, and the early rishis become the first Indian leaders of the state—egalitarian men of spiritual intuition and political acumen. The Veda becomes a kind of secularized spiritual canon that stands for national unity.

PLURAL VEDAS

The chapters of this volume demonstrate that canon has indeed proved to be a salutary category in the study of Indian traditions, but not only because the study of canon reveals patterns of innovation in the interpretation of a body of knowledge. The study of Vedic interpretation reveals that canonical knowledge can be fixed and fluid in a number of different ways; moreover, canonical knowledge can bestow various kinds of prestige in particular interpretive situations. While Vedic authority may be invoked continuously throughout Indian history, it cannot be said to have a single continuous influence. For the Brahmanical author, the Vedas are interpreted to reinforce the *varṇa* system; for the dramatists, an appeal to the Vedas overcomes the anxiety that they are engaging in a lesser form of discourse; for the modern Indian interpreter, the Vedas "prove" the value of India as a nation. Such diverse exegetical strategies show that Kabir's admonition need not be altogether heeded. While some interpreters of the Vedas may become entangled and die therein, others find in them a vital source of scholarly interest as well as new angles on the study of canon in India and elsewhere.

One of these new angles is a consideration of the integral relationship between the authoritative form of the canon (performed or read, textual or oral, etc.) and the manner in which it is interpreted. It is important to be very clear here: as the subsequent chapters will show, this volume does not suggest that there is fixed, univocal pattern to the relationship between canonical form and canonical commentary. Rather, the authors suggest that certain forms of canon are emphasized in certain interpretive situations, and thus certain forms of canonical commentary are grounded in that dominant form. To interpret the Vedas as a series of canonical utterances, for instance, does not mitigate the fact that there exists a certain textual quality to their highly precise structure and order, even as they are recited in ritual situations. What is more, the Vedas' performative nature does not negate the more devotional and imagistic elements that are clearly present in many of the Vedic hymns—elements that, as we shall see, are emphasized in other forms of Vedic interpretation. Finally, the suggestion of certain situationally-inspired interpretive trends does not in any way establish a kind of rigid historical periodicity. On the contrary, this book suggests that such complex elements in canon can and do interact with each other in all time periods, and thus contribute to the complexity of commentary as well.

Moreover, as Catherine Bell[6] has recently warned us, it would be highly problematic to draw too radical a divide between "performed canon" and "read canon." Such a distinction risks continuing the divide between "action" and "thought" that has plagued ritual theorists for much of the twentieth century. However, discrimination between different kinds of performance (recitation, citation within a debate, etc.) and different kinds of reading (reading individually, reading aloud with a teacher, etc.) is helpful, as long as it is not too rigidly drawn. As we shall see below, the function of these distinctions is not to codify, or to essentialize different kinds of exegesis, but to bring to light more clearly the fascinating combinations of approaches to canonical interpretation over time.

PERFORMING THE VEDIC CANON

Many scholars of religion have noted the distinctive nature of the oral canon,[7] and many Indologists have commented on the "performative," oral nature of the Vedas in early Indian civilization. While debate may still rage about whether one can correctly call the Vedic mantra a "speech act,"[8] and what forms of written texts existed, if any, to aid in the performance of sacrifice, all scholars affirm in various ways that in the first millennium B.C.E., Vedic canon was primarily performed, not read.

The authors of this volume take such issues one step further: they have examined what the impact of the form of canon might be for the authority and the anxiety that inform debates about canonical interpretation in later generations and later contexts. For instance, Holdrege, Smith, and Carpenter show particular ways in which the performative nature of Vedic canon deeply affects its representation in the exegetical works that follow it. As Carpenter suggests, what is being canonized in Vedic India is a system of actions—even a culture itself. As a result, canonical interpretation implies the linking of this system of actions within the sacrifice to the system of actions surrounding and supporting it—in other words, the joining of sacrificial structure and social structure. Brian Smith exemplifies this idea by arguing that canonical exegesis links Veda to *varṇa*. Holdrege and Carpenter both argue that the goddess of speech, Vāc, remains an anxious focus of control for much Brahmanical speculation not because of some mystical theory of eloquence, or because, as one writer on canon puts it, Vedic mantra "acknowledges the music of words."[9] Rather, Vāc is a focus of control because she is performance par excellence: she embodies the canonical language that is being preserved and protected within the sacrifice, and homologized to realms outside it as well. What is more, these authors have also explained why the content of the Vedic canon is "fluid." Such fluidity results not because Vedic exegetes were careless in delimiting their canon, but because the process of limitation itself was centered on the correct performance rather than on the correct textual form.

In this sense, we might argue that commentary on performed canon tends to be both positional and instrumental in nature. I use the term "positional," because while the Brāhmaṇas are comprised of etiological, semantic, and theological elements, these texts' concerns remain fundamentally locative. They tell of bringing speech back from the place to which she has escaped, and positioning her appropriately in relationship to the rest of the sacrificial arena. *Bandhus* position canonical structures, such as syllables and mantras, next to elemental ones (such as Wind, Air, and Fire), social ones (such as Kṣatriyas and Vaiṣyas), and cosmological ones (such as the terrestrial, the middle, and celestial spheres). The location of the Vedic canon tends to be its meaning. Canonical interpretation is enacted in necessarily spatial language—grid-like, or to use Holdrege's term, "blueprint"-like metaphors. Viewed in this way, one might argue that the semantic explanation of canon is not, as many have argued, secondary to formal concerns, but integrally bound up with them: the Vedas' meaning *is* their placement and usage within ritual, and by implication, within the cosmological and social hierarchies connected to the sacrifice. Thus, it is no accident that the relatively late text, the *Laws of Manu* (12.112), requires that an etymologist (whose work is the interpretation of meaning) and a ritual specialist (whose work is the interpretation of performance) be present at any sacrificial assembly.

Yet such locative metaphors are not sui generis. The performers themselves create such comparisons, which leads us to the second aspect of performed canon: its instrumental nature. The interpretive language of proper usage, such as the pronouncing of syllables, the rules of sandhi, and the like, is found throughout the Vedāṅgas and the Brāhmaṇas. These rules and, as Carpenter suggests, these recensions, exist as much for cultural as for conceptual clarity. First, they serve to identify the traditions of recitation in which they place themselves. Second, they establish the performers as primary. The *Laws of Manu* (12.103) states this hierarchy of interpretive modes explicitly: "Those who read the books are better than those who do not know them; those who remember them are better than those who read them; those who understand them are better than those who remember them; and those who put them into action are better than those who understand them."[10]

THE VEDIC CANON OF IMAGES

As if the place of the performed Veda in canonical exegesis were not complex enough, the place of the Veda in devotional literature is even more multilayered. Renou has written that the *Bhagavadgītā* expresses fidelity to the Vedic tradition of ritual while recommending the superiority of devotion (*bhakti*) over such rituals.[11] Yet the chapters in this volume suggest another perspective, consonant with our argument that the form of canon has a significant effect on arguments about canon in subsequent exegetical generations. As Gitomer, Clooney, and Frederick Smith imply, in periods dominated by the more devotionally oriented discourse, interpreters mine the Vedas for their mythic/pictorial resources, not their ritual/procedural resources.

In such an environment, canon becomes illustrative and exemplary through its imagery, not through its sound. It supports and justifies the presence of the deity, who is visually represented. As Frederick Smith argues about the *Bhāgavata Purāṇa*, the sacrificial processes that are the focus of interpretive Vedic schools like Mīmāṃsā give way to sacrificial imagery—the focus of the classical texts. The bird-shaped fire altar becomes Lord Garuda, Viṣṇu's mount, and the *puruṣa* of *Ṛg-Veda* 10.129 becomes *pruṣottama*, Viṣṇu personified. Sacrificial performances themselves become little more than image and list, and canonicity is defined by other, more persuasive theological considerations.

Thus, authority becomes iconic; it is asserted in images whose theological power is magnified and augmented by the Vedas, but not constituted by them. Francis Clooney's chapter, for instance, shows that the salvific power of knowledge is represented and discussed in terms of a Vedic image—the bird. In *Taittirīya Upaniṣad* 2.1, the self is depicted in the form of the bird of the fire altar, and various parts of its body are analogized to various animating elements: the in-breath is the head, the out-breath and middle-breath its wings, and so on. *Brahman*, the great one, is the tail. To be sure, Śaṅkara builds upon this imagery and uses it as his central point of questioning: how can *brahman* be the tail of the bird, a mere member of the self, simply an appendage? However, unlike the Brāhmaṇas' central concerns, the location and use of the sacrificial altar per se is not the issue; it is how the image of the bird can guide this commentatorial meditation as it unfolds.

What, then, happens to the performance emphasis in these approaches? As Frederick Smith also suggests, the performance of sacrifice itself becomes an image—referred to but not elaborated upon to the same instrumentally oriented degree. Moreover, as I have suggested elsewhere, the utterance of a mantra may remain an icon of power, but neither its form nor its semantic content is commented upon with the same vigor. This does not mean that the Vedas become meaningless, or purely "formal" in content.[13] It does suggest, however, that in texts like the Purāṇas, the culturally authoritative mode of interpretation has shifted from performed sound to imagined sound, from uttered mantra to the picture of an uttered mantra.

In addition, classical texts combined image and performance in their interpretation of the Vedas. As Gitomer shows, the *Naṭyaśāstra* was primarily geared toward performance, calling itself the fifth Veda that had been created by Brahma to be *enacted*, like the other Vedas. Yet there is something more to its performance orientation. After the very Vedic-seeming destruction of the performance at the hands of the demons, a playhouse must be constructed in order to safeguard the dramatic action. This structure is replete with the images of deities and demigods; Indra himself is stationed by the side of the stage. Thus, while the *Naṭyaśāstra* is like the Brāhmaṇas in that it focuses instrumentally upon rules of performance, even in this performance mode the self-styled *naṭyaveda* must be protected iconically.

VEDAS AS BOUNDED TEXTS

The question of textuality has, of course, been lurking in the background in both discussions of performance and devotion. As mentioned above, the "textual" nature of the performed Vedic canon is unmistakable; while the number of texts included as Vedic may vary, the verses of the Saṃhitās are relatively frozen in their different recensions. The verses have the aura of the final form, not of a working draft. Mistakes in utterance are viewed in the same way that exegetes of written canon receive "scribal error": such aberrancies change the meaning of the canon in potentially damaging ways. Even more straightforward, the Purāṇas, as texts, referred to themselves as fifth Vedas. They thus "textualize" the image of the Vedas even more directly. And, as Clooney argues, Śaṅkara, Rāmānuja, and others suggest that the act of reading the text of the Vedas in the company of a teacher is salvific. Such a joint textual encounter will eventually result in unity with *brahman*.

Yet these ideas of textuality are not the same as the Enlightenment sense of textuality—one that informs yet another aspect of Vedic interpretation. The Enlightenment text can be viewed as a printed or written source of knowledge to which each individual has access without the mediation of a community. Such an idea of text creates another kind of scenario: the individual rendezvous with the written words, informed either by an autonomous rationality or a romanticized, "intuitive encounter" with the wisdom such written words have to offer. Relatedly, texts also become objects of "discovery," to be catalogued and preserved as artifacts "found" by exploration.

One can see this idea of textuality at work in the various debates about canon in the encounter with the West. As mentioned above, textuality does not exclusively define canon, but exists alongside other attitudes to canon. As Figueira demonstrates, for instance, in the initial Enlightenment encounters with the Vedas, the idea of canon and the actual text of canon were juxtaposed. In a manner that is intriguingly similar to the Purāṇic attitude to the Vedas, Enlightenment and Romantic thinkers in the West were so enthralled by the image of the Vedas that they manufactured a text to conform with that image. Yet unlike much of Purāṇic discourse, questions of "authenticity" and "authority" arise in these debates—questions that form the criteria of argument about Enlightenment canonical texts. And the controversy about the *Ezour Veda* was, if nothing else, a European argument created by Europeans for Europeans.

The question of individual encounter with the text of the Vedas is also central. Even before Müller's edition of the *Ṛg-Veda* in the mid-nineteenth century, the Vedas had become their own "books." Thus, the individual reader could make judgments about them for him- or herself. As Rambachan's chapter intimates, this kind of individual interpretation can also lead to a rejection of canon. The egalitarian access to the Vedas, promoted by many divergent Hindu reformers, including Dayānand, Rammohan Roy, and others, can also mean that the community that mediated canon was no longer forceful enough to overcome doubts as to its authority. Keshub Chandra Sen was just such a reformer, whose anxiety about Hindu authority, as well as faith in the process of intuition, led him to read the Vedas. As a Hindu reformer, Sen's own spiritual inspiration eventually replaced the texts of the Vedas. Yet it was perhaps the very form of the Vedas as bounded, unmediated texts that contributed to their rejection. If Sen had had these doubts in a different milieu from the Hindu reform movements of Calcutta, he may well have appealed to the authority of his teachers. They, in turn, would have explained the texts to him according to their received meaning, and, like Clooney's interpreters of the Upaniṣads, Sen's intuitively based spirituality might have been redirected back toward the canon, instead of away from it.

In the case of Dayānand Sarasvatī, presented by Llewellyn, we can see this kind of textual attitude openly vying for authority over other, performance-oriented attitudes toward canonical interpretation. Despite his vilification of Max Müller, the textual scholar par excellence, Dayānand lived and taught in a world in which the authority of the Veda was the bounded text, accessible to all. To Dayānand, therefore, the Veda existed as its own kind of public document available for reference in the event of controversy. His opponents in the Benares debate, however, were performance-oriented, and saw canonical interpretation as a primarily oral affair. The claim that the Vedas were authoritative was not the question for either party; instead, the central anxiety revolved around exactly which canonical form was most authoritative.

In the twentieth century, the textual attitude prevails in the scholarly worlds of both cultures. Thus, Vedic exegetes are subject everywhere to the same pitfalls as others—the pitfalls of "modern" textual interpretation. In his book, *Validity of Interpretation*,[14] E. D. Hirsch has listed the three dangers of canonical exegesis: (1) radical historicism, which claims that the meaning of a text is "what it means to us today"; (2) psychologization, which claims that the meaning of a text is "what it means to me"; and (3) autonomism, which views the meaning of a text as independent of that which it was intended to mean. While Hirsch did not take into account the different forms that canon could take other than text, his words are consonant with the twentieth century idea of the Vedas as akin to the textual canons of other religious traditions.

My own chapter shows the presence of these three tendencies in both European and Indian canonical exegetes. Western interpreters have historicized the Vedas as being the fountainhead of all civilizations, and Indian interpreters have historicized them through the idea that the Vedas were composed by poets unified in a single nation-state, as was post-Independence India. Both Western and Indian interpreters also psychologized the Vedas, in that they saw them as expressions of Romantic, poetic inspirations, akin to the works of Coleridge and Wordsworth. And finally, both groups of exegetes were susceptible to autonomism, in that they claimed things for the Vedas very different from what they were intended to mean. In dubbing Vedic texts theological twaddle, Western interpreters assumed they were not intended to mean anything at all. In claiming them as egalitarian texts, the Indian exegetes moved away from the obvious intention of many of the poems, to establish a cosmological foundation for *varṇa*, or social hierarchy.

Yet Hirsch wrote from the perspective of modernity, assuming such "pitfalls" of textual interpretation could be avoided. The present volume, on the other hand, takes the more or less postmodern stance that all exegetical strategies are constructions. Some may be perhaps more harmonious with the original language and intent than others, but such harmony itself is a principle imposed by an interpretive community in combination with many other, competing demands that a community makes of its canon. As many other historians and Indologists have recently written, such a stance makes a new kind of intellectual history possible, toward which this volume is just a small beginning.

The editing of this volume has been a testimony to the vitality of scholarly interest in the Vedas. David Gitomer initially persuaded me to embark upon the organization of a panel, and proceeded to insist that I follow through on an edited volume. Wendy Doniger and William Eastman continued this benign form of encouragement, and their support as editors has been crucial. In the final stages of preparation, Dr. William K. Ehrenfeld contributed the artwork that graces the cover of the volume, and my students Annette Reed and Kelly Messerle provided invaluable indexical labor. The faculty and staff of Deccan College, Pune, was kind enough to let me present some of the ideas contained in this volume in one of their seminars, and opened up their libraries to me for invaluable biographical and bibliographical information. My memories of conversations with late twentieth-century Vedic exegetes, conducted in the midst of my editing this volume, are especially vivid.

Finally, the commitment of all the contributors has been invaluable. While they all wrote from very different disciplinary viewpoints, their collective expertise and experience have helped make the project proceed smoothly. What is more, all of the contributors share a commitment to particularizing the study of Indian religions within an articulate theoretical framework. Such a common perspective has made the usually dreaded work of weaving together a set of disparate essays an unusually pleasant and intellectually exciting task.

Laurie L. Patton
Annandale-on-Hudson, New York

NOTES

1. Kabir's *Granthāvalī*, trans. Charlotte Vaudeville (Pondicherry: Institut Francais d'Indologie, 1957), 12:18, 34.

2. Originally written as part of *Études Vêdiques et Paninêènnes*, 17 vols. (Paris: Publications de l'Institut de Civilisation Indienne, 1955–69), Renou's study was translated as *The Destiny of the Veda in India*, ed. Dev Raj Chanana (Delhi: Motilal Banarsidass, 1965).

3. Ibid., 53.

4. However, recent works by scholars not included in this volume should be noted for their theoretical as well as textual sophistication: Wilhem Halbfass' excellent *Tradition and Reflection* (Albany: State University of New York Press, 1991) takes up the question of the significance of the Veda from the persepctive of later philosophical traditions. The present volume might well be seen as a kind of companion piece, written from the perspective of canon-formation. Stephanie Jamison's *Ravenous Hyenas and the Wounded Sun* (Ithaca: Cornell University Press, 1991); Christopher Minkowski's *Priesthood in Ancient India* (Vienna: De Nobili Research Library, 1991); and the various articles of Ellison Banks Findly, most notably, "*Mantra kaviśasta*: Speech as Performative in the *Ṛg-Veda*," in *Mantra*, ed. Harvey Alper, 15–48 (Albany: State University of New York Press, 1989) and Wade Wheelock, (most notably, "A Taxonomy of *Mantra*s in the New and Full Moon Sacrifice," *History of Religions* 19(4) (1980): 349–69; "The Problem of Ritual Language," *Journal of the American Academy of Religion* 50(1) (1982): 49–69; and "The *Mantra* in Vedic and Tantric Ritual," in *Mantra*, ed. Alper, 96–122.

5. *Reflections on Ritual, Resemblance and Religion* (Oxford: Oxford University Press, 1989).

6. See Catherine Bell, *Ritual Theory, Ritual Practice* (Oxford: Oxford University Press, 1992).

7. For more general remarks on properties of oral canons in world religions, see Roger J. Corless, "Sacred Text, Context, and Proof-Text," and Paul Ricoeur, "The Sacred Text and the Community," in *The Critical Study of Sacred Texts*, ed. Wendy O'Flaherty (Berkeley: Graduate Theological Union, 1979); and, finally, J. Z. Smith's essay, "Sacred Persistence," in *Imagining Religion* (Chicago: University of Chicago Press, 1982), extensively quoted throughout this volume. Jack Goody's *The Interface Between the Written and the Oral* (Cambridge: Cambridge University Press, 1987) is also provocative, although his treatment of the Vedas in Chapter Four lacks real engagement with Vedic texts.

8. This debate engages not only the question of mantra, but the entire question of the possibility of meaning. For an approach that posits a certain continuity of mantra usage in the midst of cultural change, see Louis Renou, "Les Pouvoirs de la Parole dans le *Ṛg-Veda*," *Études Vêdiques et paninéènnes* 1 (1955): 1–27; Jan Gonda, *The Vision of the Vedic Poets* (The Hague: Mouton, 1963); "The Indian *Mantra*," *Oriens* 16 (1963): 244–97. For a more mystical, *bhakti*-oriented view of mantra, see Willard Johnson, *Poetry and Speculation in the* Ṛg-Veda (Berkeley: University of California Press, 1980). For a strictly syntactical analysis of mantra usage, see Frits Staal, "The Concept of Metalanguage and Its Indian Background," *Journal of Indian Philosophy* 3 (1975): 315–54; "*Ṛg-Veda* 10:71 on the

Origin of Language," in *Revelation in Indian Thought: A Festschrift in Honour of Professor T. R. V. Murti*, eds. Harold Coward and Krishna Sivaram (Emeryville, Calif.: Dharma, 1977), 3–14; "Ritual Syntax," in *Sanskrit and Indian Studies, Essays in Honour of Daniel H. H. Ingalls*, ed. M. Nagatomi et al., (Boston: D. Reidel: 1980), 119–43; "The Meaninglessness of Ritual," *Numen* 26 (1979): 2–22; "The Sound of Religion," *Numen* 33 (1986): 33–64; "Vedic *Mantras*," in *Mantra*, ed. Alper, 48–95. For a more performative perspective, see Wade Wheelock, "The Ritual Language of a Vedic Sacrifice" (Ph.D. diss. University of Chicago: 1978); "Taxonomy of *Mantras* in the New and Full Moon Sacrifice," 349–69; "Problem of Ritual Language," 49–69; "*Mantra* in Vedic and Tantric Ritual," 96–122; Findly, "*Mantra Kaviśasta*," 15–48; and Laurie Patton, "Vāc: Myth or Philosophy?" in *Myth and Philosophy*, ed. Frank Reynolds and David Tracy (Albany: State University of New York Press, 1990), 183–214.

9. Corless, "Sacred Text, Context, and Proof-Text," 265.

10. Wendy Doniger with Brian Smith, *The Laws of Manu* (London and New York: Penguin, 1991), 288.

11. Renou, *Destiny*, 35ff.

12. See my "The Transparent Text," in *Purāṇa Perennis*, ed. Wendy Doniger (Albany: State University of New York Press, 1993).

13. The historical assumption that, over time, only the "outside" of the Veda becomes known assumes that semantic content originally was the focus, and overlooks the fact that the semantic content of mantras was equally ignored by other schools in the Vedic period itself, more concerned with pronunication than with meaning.

14. E. D. Hirsch, *Validity of Interpretation* (New Haven: Yale University Press, 1967), viii–ix, 39.

PART ONE

The Vedas Reflect on Themselves

1

The Mastery of Speech

Canonicity and Control in the Vedas

DAVID CARPENTER

INTRODUCTION

THE PAST FEW YEARS have witnessed a growing interest in the concept of canon and its usefulness in the study of the religious traditions of South Asia. To an extent this has been due to the influence of Wilfred Cantwell Smith, as well as his students, in arguing for the value of the closely related category of scripture in the comparative study of religions.[1] But much of the interest in canon per se stems from an important article by Jonathan Z. Smith, "Sacred Persistence: Toward a Redescription of Canon," in which he argues for a "redescription" of the category that would make it serviceable not only for non-Western literate traditions, but for so-called primitive, nonliterate traditions as well.[2] Smith's article has already inspired a volume on "traditional hermeneutics" in South Asia,[3] and the influence of the article will be found in the present volume as well. In the specific case of the study of the Vedic tradition of India, the subject of the essays in this book, Smith's influence can be detected in a recent work on the ritual system of Brahmanical India by Brian K. Smith, who invokes the notion of the Vedic canon as a key to defining Hinduism itself.[4]

The utilization of canon as an interpretative category in the study of the religions of South Asia does indeed hold great promise. In the specific and very important case of the Veda, however, a question arises as to the precise meaning that the term might have. As is well known, the Veda was preserved until fairly recently in oral form. If we may assume that the oral tradition of the Veda functioned in some sense as a canon, in what does its canonicity consist? This is a question that must be addressed before we can begin to refer to the role of the Veda as canon in order to clarify other aspects of Indian religious history. The question is a complex one and it is unlikely that a single satisfactory answer can be given to it. The Veda has been different things to different people at different times, as the contributions to this volume make clear.[5] Here I wish to examine the question of the canonicity of the Veda from the perspective of the early Vedic tradition itself, in order to determine where a sense of canonicity first comes into play, and the form that it takes.

I would like to approach this problem from two different perspectives. The first approach will be from the perspective of *content*—from the perspective of canonicity as having to do with specific corpora (whether written or oral) that display the essential features, as J. Z. Smith has noted, of limitation and closure.[6] Are these features found in the early Vedic tradition, and if so, in what context and to what extent? As we shall see, from this perspective we can see part but not all of what is entailed in the problem of the canonicity of "the Veda" as this term is commonly understood. A second approach then becomes necessary, an approach from the perspective not of content, but of *form*. Elsewhere in this volume, Barbara Holdrege argues that the Brahmanical tradition's emphasis on the form of the Vedic mantras is integrally bound up with the mantras' status as transcendent, primordial speech acts that provide a kind of "blueprint" for creation. My own chapter will focus less on the cosmogonic implications of the Vedic canon, than on problems involved in an exclusively literary classification of the Veda as Saṃhitā, or collection. Such a classification ignores the fact that the Veda appears most frequently as a form of speech—speech that is perceived with some anxiety by ritual specialists as a force that must be controlled through ritual mechanisms. From this perspective, less "Western" and more "Indian" perhaps, the canonicity of the Veda will appear to reside more in its form as oral performance than in its content as a well-delimited corpus. The two perspectives are perhaps more complementary than exclusive, but I will argue that from the first perspective alone it is impossible to speak coherently of a Vedic canon. Consequently, our notion of canon must be expanded beyond the dominant Western model, and perhaps even beyond the model suggested by J. Z. Smith, if it is to be applicable to the Vedic material.

IN SEARCH OF CLOSURE: CANON AS CONTENT

In looking for the features of limitation and closure in the oral compositions of the Vedic tradition, the logical place to begin is with the concept of the Saṃhitā, or "collection." A Vedic Saṃhitā would seem to be the closest equivalent to a Vedic canon, in the sense of a collection of compositions that has reached closure, precisely as an authoritative collection. There are at least two problems involved in equating Saṃhitā and canon, however. The first is that there is not one such Saṃhitā but many. Not only are there three, and later four, Vedic Saṃhitās (The *Ṛg, Yajur, Sāman,* and *Atharva*), but there have been multiple recensions of each of these. Second, while the term "Saṃhitā" refers to something that has been joined together or united, the specific reference is to individual *words*, not the individual hymns, formulas, and chants (*ṛcs*, *yajus*es, and *sāmans*) of the Veda. Consequently, the term "Saṃhitā" does not properly refer to a collection of "texts," whether canonical or otherwise, although it is commonly used in this way. Each of these points requires further discussion.

In the case of the *Ṛg-Veda* (and undoubtedly the other Vedas as well) the creation of a Saṃhitā is a rather late achievement. The earliest redaction of the *Ṛg-Veda* for which there is clear evidence appears to have been the redaction of the so-called family books that make up Maṇḍalas 2–7 of the present-day Saṃhitās.[7] There is a regularity in the arrangement of these Maṇḍalas that suggests they were intended to be taken as a whole. What is impossible to know is whether this collection was intended to be canonical by those who created it, in other words, whether its content was intended to be fixed. What is in any case clear is that it did not remain so. Somewhat later additional Maṇḍalas were added—8 and 9, and eventually 1 and 10. The order in which these additions were made is uncertain, but it is clear that closure was not reached before the addition of Maṇḍala 10, which is widely recognized as being quite late, at least in comparison to Maṇḍalas 2–7. It is with the addition of the tenth and final Maṇḍala that the collection of hymns reaches something like a stable form, the *Ṛg-Veda* of ten Maṇḍalas that we know today. But there are complications. The *Caraṇavyūha* mentions five different recensions of the *Ṛg-Veda*: the *Śākala*, *Bāṣkala*, *Āśvalāyana*, *Śāṅkhāyana*, and *Māṇḍūkāyana*. Each of these recensions would presumably display the features of limitation and closure associated with canonicity, although in fact the only recension to have survived is the *Śākala*. Louis Renou has noted that the differences between these recensions were probably minor ones involving the arrangement of the hymns. At least this is true of the differences between the *Śākala* and the *Bāṣkala*, for which we have some information.[8] It remains true, however, that the fact that today we know only one authoritative recension of the *Ṛg-Veda* seems to be more a historical accident than the result of conscious intention.

The same is true of the other two of the original three Vedas: the *Yajur-Veda* and the *Sāma-Veda*. There are five extant Saṃhitās of the *Yajur-Veda*, the *Taittirīya*, *Kāṭhaka*, *Kapiṣṭhala*, and *Maitrāyaṇīya*, together composing the four Saṃhitās of the so-called *Black Yajur-Veda*, and the *Vājasaneyisaṃhitā* or *White Yajurveda*, which itself survives in two different recensions, the *Kāṇva* and the *Mādhyaṃdina*. As for the *Sāma-Veda*, there are three distinct Saṃhitās, the *Kauthuma*, the *Rāṇāyanīya*, and the *Jaiminīya*. Thus, there is no *single* authoritative redaction of either the *Yajur-Veda Saṃhitā* or the *Sāma-Veda Saṃhitā*, but rather multiple redactions, existing side by side, the possessions of separate Vedic schools. More important, there is no provision for combining the three Vedic Saṃhitās, of whichever recensions, into a single corpus that could be dubbed "the" canonical Veda. Rather they have continued to be preserved separately, in distinct traditions. In this sense we can speak perhaps of multiple canons, or of no canon at all.

So the concept of Saṃhitā is not without drawbacks as an equivalent for our notion of 'canon.' Nevertheless, at the level of content, of clearly delimited corpora, there seems little alternative. But there is always the possibility that canonicity in the Vedic context operates at some other level. Perhaps we should look more closely at the context for the creation of the Saṃhitās. Who made them, and what were their functions? There are of course few certainties in this area, but nevertheless some probabilities. The *Śākala* recension of the *Ṛksaṃhitā* is of particular interest in this regard, not only because of its degree of fixity, but also because of what we can surmise about its creator.

The *Śākala* recension is believed to be the work of the Śākalya whom we find mentioned in the *Bṛhadāraṇyaka Upaniṣad* as a contemporary of Yajñavalkya, with whom he debates at the court of King Janaka of Videha. It is noteworthy that this Śākalya is also credited with being the principal inspiration behind the Prātiśākhyas, treatises on the phonetic peculiarities of the different variants of the oral tradition (*śākhās*), and the creator of the *padapātha*.[9] A *padapātha* is a version of the *Ṛg-Veda* (or one of the other Vedas) in which each word is given in its independent form, stripped of the phonetic modifications that occur when the words are recited in a continuous manner. Their form in continuous recitation is precisely what is referred to properly by the term "Saṃhitā." As noted above, what are "united" in a Saṃhitā are not individual compositions but individual words. The concept of a Saṃhitā, then, is logically connected to the concept of a *padapātha*: Saṃhitās reunite what *padapātha*s separate. Hence, it is no surprise that the term "Saṃhitā," as referring to any of the Vedic collections of *rc*s, *yajus*es, and *sāman*s, first begins to appear in the Prātiśākhyas themselves. If in fact Śākalya was the inventor of the *padapātha*, then we can conclude that the very concept of a Saṃhitā, in the specific sense just alluded to, dates from his time as well.

The traditional ascription of both the *Ṛg-Veda Saṃhitā* and the *padapātha* to Śākalya has been accepted by such scholars as Weber, Oldenberg, and Geldner. C. G. Kashikar, who has reviewed the evidence and added some of his own, concludes that Śākalya can be accepted as the compiler of both the Saṃhitā and the *pada* text.[10] Now it is noteworthy that the concern reflected in both of these innovations is not with the meaning of the individual hymns, taken as poetic compositions, but with the proper phonetic form of the individual words. These concerns suggest that the context in which Śākalya worked, and the context to which the "canonical" *Ṛg-Veda* belongs, was one that placed greater emphasis on the form of the words than on their meaning, and this in turn leads us to suppose that the proper context for locating Śākalya's *Ṛg-Veda Saṃhitā* was more ritual than literary.

This is borne out by what little we know about Śākalya's historical context. Geldner has argued, and Kashikar concurs, that Śākalya's redaction of the *Ṛksaṃhitā* took place during the same period that saw the redaction of the *Vājasaneyisaṃhitā*, one of the Saṃhitās of the *Yajur-Veda*.[11] As Gonda has noted, the geographical setting of the *Yajur-Veda* in general is well to the east of that of the *Ṛg-Veda*: "While the Punjab has receded in importance, the Doab, the land of the Kosalas, has come into prominence and the eastern countries of the Magadhas and the Videhas, though not completely aryanized and brahminized, successively make their appearance in the texts."[12] As for the *Vājasaneyisaṃhitā* itself, its name, a patronymic of Yajñavalkya, points to a late origin, something that is borne out by the nature of the collection itself, whose separation of *yajus* from Brāhmaṇa is probably to be seen as a reaction to the more confused organization of the earlier *Yajur-Veda Saṃhitās* such as the *Taittirīya*. These considerations place the redaction of the *Ṛg-Veda* in a fixed or canonical form directly in the context of an attempt to consolidate the oral components of an extensive ritual system. Thus, while the *Ṛg-Veda* as a somewhat fluid collection of hymns is clearly quite early, I would argue that the *Ṛg-Veda Saṃhitā* as a canon, as an authoritative version of the oral tradition that has reached closure, comes late. Furthermore, its canonical form must be understood in relationship to the demands of the ritual system for which it served, whether the hymns that it contains were originally composed for such use or not.

Thus, the problem of canonicity, which is our main concern here, shifts from the question of the redaction of the Saṃhitās taken in isolation, and becomes a question of their redaction as an integral part of the "threefold knowledge" that is an essential component of the *śrauta* sacrificial system, and which is defined, at ŚB 4.6.7.1, for instance, not as a set of three texts, but as three *types* of mantras, the *ṛc*s, the *yajus*es, and the *sāmans*. The context here is not primarily one of texts, but rather one of formulated *speech* as employed in ritual action. When the Saṃhitās are viewed from this perspective, their status as canonical collections looks rather different. Although they remain canonical in the sense of displaying—

precisely as Saṃhitās—a degree of limitation and closure, canonical constraint is exercised not only by closure of the different Saṃhitās as regards their material content (which, as we have seen, for the Veda as a whole remains somewhat fluid), but more importantly by the concern to preserve the correct phonetic form of the individual mantras and by the formal requirements of the ritual in which these mantras, the *ṛcs*, the *yajuses*, and *sāmans*, were to be employed.

This is apparent from the way in which the *ṛcs* of the *Ṛg-Veda*, for instance, are actually incorporated into the sacrificial performance. As Renou has noted, in an article devoted to the place of the *Ṛg-Veda* in the *śrauta* rituals, "the content of the fragments [of the *Ṛg-Veda*] recited is relatively unimportant, once the elementary conditions relative to meter, name of deity, and number have been satisfied." He concludes that

> the employment of the Rgveda in the great ritual does not conform to what one ordinarily expects of citations. Only a minority of the mantras are adapted to a particular act, and then only in limited contexts. The bulk of the selections concern in some cases verses used purely for show. . ., chosen for reasons that are extrinsic to their content and their reference as hymns, and in other cases long recitations in which a superficial fit of meter, attribution of deity, or number prevails.[13]

In other words, it is the formal fit of a specific verse at a given moment in the ritual that matters, not the meaning that the verse, or the hymn to which it belongs, might have had in its original context. Ellison Banks Findly has argued, further, that a shift of emphasis from content to form, from the insight expressed in a verse to the correctness of the verse's pronunciation, can be seen in the later parts of the *Ṛg-Veda* itself, specifically in the concept of mantra, which appears most frequently in the latest portions of the collection, namely, in Maṇḍalas 1 and 10.[14] She quotes with approval Paul Thieme's comment that a "mantra has an effect. . . that is conditioned less through its content than its form, a form that must be safeguarded through scrupulously correct recitation."[15] It was precisely this correct recitation that Śākalya's *padapātha* was designed to guarantee.

The redactors of the Vedic Saṃhitās appear then to have been less litterateurs than specialists in ritual action. Such specialists were responsible for the elaboration of the Vedic tradition in its Indian context, in interaction with the indigenous peoples, and in the new, more sedentary environment of the Doab that made possible the flourishing of Brahminism. Key in this process were the Yajurvedins. As Louis Renou has observed, "It is the Yajurveda that remains the base of the cult and which undoubtedly determined the entire evolution of literary Vedism. It is through this Veda that the notion of *brāhmaṇa*, the category of sūtra, was fixed; through and for this Veda that the schools seem to have been constituted."[16] It is to the views of such ritual specialists on the nature of the Veda that I wish now to turn, views set down in the Brāhmaṇas of the Yajurvedins, and in other Brāhmaṇas as well. It is significant that in the Brāhmaṇas, which presuppose the existence of the content of the Saṃhitās, the Saṃhitās themselves are not represented as such, namely, as fixed collections. Rather their contents appear most frequently as forms of powerful speech, as indeed the offspring of the goddess of speech, Vāc. A closer look at this Brahmanical understanding of speech as a powerful reality, and of Vedic speech in particular, may provide us with the context necessary to appreciate the second aspect of Vedic canonicity to which I alluded earlier, namely, canon as form. One striking example of this view of speech is to be found in the mythology of Vāc herself, to which I now turn.

CANONICITY AND THE MASTERY OF SPEECH

In the Brāhmaṇas the contents of what we know as the Saṃhitās of the Veda appear not as literary corpora but as the "threefold knowledge" (*trayi vidya*), which consists of three types of mantra or formulaic speech: the *ṛcs*, the *yajus*es, and the *sāmans*. These three types of mantra, also frequently referred to as simply "meters" (*chandas*), are all forms of Vāc, or speech. Vāc, the "mother of the Vedas" (TB 2.8.8.4), the "divine speech" (ŚB 10.5.1.1), is personified in the Brāhmaṇas and one can discern an entire cycle of mythology that is devoted to her. A brief look at this cycle of myths, in some ways parallel to the myths of the god Agni, might shed some light on the Brahmanical understanding of speech in general, and Vedic or "canonical" speech in particular. Barbara Holdrege's chapter in this volume addresses the cosmogonic context in which limitless speech is circumscribed through the utterances of the creator, Prajāpati. My own analysis, in contrast, focuses on anxiety about the control of speech within the ritual arena. In many Brahmanical myths, speech is presented as a deeply ambivalent force, potentially disruptive and in need of being controlled. As we shall see, the goddess Vāc, as the personification of speech, is finally "controlled" by being "metered" and integrated into the formal complex of the Vedic sacrifice. This element of the control of speech is but one aspect of the overall interest in ritual control that dominates the late Vedic period and the *śrauta* ritual system. The key to this ritual control is correct form, and I will argue that it is in this concern for correct form as the sine qua non of ritual efficacy and the power it brings that we find an additional and decisively important aspect of canonicity as it is operative in the Vedic context.

The goddess Vāc is probably best known to students of India from the hymns addressed to her in the *Ṛg-Veda*.[17] There she appears as an independent goddess who reveals herself to those fortunate poets whom she herself chooses. This figure of a goddess who acts spontaneously to inspire the Vedic sages has been altered beyond recognition in the Brāhmaṇas. There we find a group of myths that present Vāc as at first united with the chief deity of the Brāhmaṇas, Prajāpati, the personification of the sacrifice, or as in the possession of the gods generally. Then comes a period of separation during which Vāc is located either within elements of the natural cosmos or is in the possession of the demons (Asuras). Finally, she is "won back" through being united with the sacrifice. While still a powerful goddess, as presented in the mythology of the Brāhmaṇas, her power is creative but potentially disruptive and thus must be kept under the control of the sacrifice, personified by Prajāpati. An examination of these myths will help clarify the Brahmanical view of speech as a force that must be controlled, and the role of the sacrifice in exerting this control.

In one basic form of the myth, from the *Kāṭhaka Saṃhitā* (12.5.27.1), Vāc is presented as a consort of Prajāpati, whom she temporarily abandons in order to bring forth the creatures of the world, only to return and be reunited with him: "Prajāpati indeed was this, Speech (Vāc) was his second. He copulated with her. She conceived an embryo. She went away from him. She poured forth these creatures. She returned (*prāvisat*) to him again." A variation of this myth is found at *Pañcaviṃśa Brāhmaṇa* (PB) 20.14.2: "Prajāpati alone was this universe. His Speech (*vāc*) was his own. Speech was his second. He thought 'I would emit this Speech. She will go, manifesting this All.' He poured forth Speech. She went, manifesting this All"—to which the comment is added: "Speech, who was a single syllable, he divided into three" (PB 20.14.5). Somewhat earlier in this same Brāhmaṇa (PB 7.6.1–3) we find a variant that makes it clear that Vāc is here acting as Prajāpati's instrument: "Prajāpati desired, 'I would be many, I would procreate.' Silently he contemplated with his mind. What there was in his mind became *bṛhat*, the Great. He thought, 'This embryo is placed within me. I would procreate it by means of Speech.' He emitted Speech."

Prajāpati's desire to become many requires that he express himself, that a distinction arise between himself and Speech. In these myths, however, Vāc remains obedient to Prajāpati, who is the "lord of Speech" (ŚB 5.1.1.16). She is his instrument, or to use a term borrowed from a later age, she is his *śakti*, and as such is fully under his control. Through her as the "divine Speech" (ŚB 10.5.5.1) Prajāpati creates all beings, chief among which is the Veda itself, the thousandfold progeny of Vāc (ŚB 5.5.5.12).

Speech is not always such a willing instrument of divine purpose, however. This becomes apparent in myths that describe her desertion of the gods, which echo the cosmogonic themes above, but with more of a sense of loss of control: "Vāc went away from the gods, not being willing to serve for the Sacrifice. She entered the trees. She is the voice of the trees, the voice that is heard in the drum, the lute and the flute'' (TS 6.1.4). PB 6.5.10–13 tells a similar story, according to which Vāc deserted the gods and entered the waters, which gave her up for a boon. She then entered the trees, who refused to give her up, and so were cursed by the gods. The trees then divide Vāc into four parts. Sometimes Vāc is described as being originally separate from the gods, as at ŚB 3.2.1.18: ''Now the gods and the Asuras (demons), both sons of Prajāpati, received the inheritance of father Prajāpati: the gods obtained mind and the Asuras Speech. Thereby the gods obtained the sacrifice and the Asuras Speech; the gods obtained that world (heaven) and the Asuras obtained this (earth).'' Here the gods are said to be without Vāc from the very beginning. The Asuras, who are said to possess Vāc, are associated with the earth. Further, their possession of Vāc connects with Vāc's flight to the chthonic elements of water and vegetation, at the farthest remove from heaven.

Another group of myths has a different character. Here the gods are said to have first won Vāc, and her desertion seems to be meant as a single event: ''Once the essence (*rasa*) of Vāc wished to desert the gods who had won it; it tried to creep away along this earth, for Vāc is this earth. Her essence is these plants and trees. By means of this *sāman* they overtook it, and thus overtaken, it returned to them'' (ŚB 4.6.9.16ff.). In another myth (ŚB 3.5.1.21–22), Vāc is slighted by the gods and Asuras and goes away from them angry: ''Having become a lioness, she went on seizing upon (everything) between those two contending parties, the gods and Asuras. The gods called her to them, so did the Asuras.'' Finally, she goes over to the gods in return for a boon.

In a myth preeminent for its connection with the soma sacrifice, the gods intentionally send Vāc away to the Gandharvas to fetch the soma they (the Gandharvas) had stolen. This results in an unintended separation, for although Vāc said that she would return, things develop differently: ''They made Vāc into a woman of one year old, and with her redeemed it (the soma). She adopted the form of a deer and ran away from the Gandharvas; that was the origin of the deer. The gods said, 'She has run from you, she comes not to us; let us summon her' '' (TS 6.1.6). The gods finally win her over by their singing.

Taken as a whole, these myths of Vāc's separation from the gods exhibit her unstable, ambivalent character. The possibility of the loss of Vāc is ever present, and must be countered by attempts to win her back. Several of these attempts have already been alluded to in the course of describing her departure. Thus, the pith of Vāc was seen to have been overtaken by a *sāman* verse, and Vāc is won back after her flight from the Gandharvas in the same manner—by a song. When Vāc had become a lioness, she was won back by a boon: the ghee in the sacrifice reaches her well before it reaches Agni. In these episodes already mentioned, one element stands out: the means by which tht gods win back Vāc are associated with the sacrifice.

The role of the sacrifice is made quite explicit. In one of the myths already mentioned (ŚB 3.2.1.18), the gods were said to have received as their inheritance the sacrifice, whereas the Asuras had received Vāc. But this situation was not intended to be permanent, and the gods employ the sacrifice to win over Vāc: 'The gods said to the Sacrifice, 'That Vāc is a woman; invite her and she will certainly call you.' " After two unsuccessful attempts, the sacrifice manages to win over Vāc for the gods. Having thus won her, "the gods then cut her off from the Asuras; and having taken possession of her and enveloped her in fire, they offered her up as a complete offering, for it was an offering of the gods. And in that they offered her with an *anuṣṭubh*-verse, thereby they made her their own; and the Asuras, being deprived of Speech, crying 'He 'lavaḥ! he 'lavaḥ!', were defeated" (ŚB 3.2.1.19–23). It is through the fire of the sacrifice and the divine Speech of the Veda, the *anuṣṭubh*-verses, or the *sāman*-verses as noted above, that the gods overcame the Asuras. Speech, which had fled, which was in the possession of the Asuras who speak only untruth (SB 9.3.1.13), is restored to the gods, who speak only truth, by the divine words of the sacrifice (or simply by the sacrifice, since the sacrifice is Speech, as the Brāhmaṇas so often affirm). Thus, ŚB 7.4.2.34 becomes intelligible: "By Speech the gods then indeed conquered and drove the Asuras, the enemies, the rivals, from the universe."

CANONICITY AND THE CONTROL OF FORM

These myths concerning the "winning" of Speech present us with a contrast between two types of speech. First, we have one that is unordered, unformed, inarticulate, and out of the control of the gods, the speech of the Asuras and the inarticulate sounds of nature. Second, we have one that is ordered and under control, the sounds of the sacrifice, the measured speech of the Vedic mantras, which are frequently referred to simply as the meters (*chandras*). The conquest of the inarticulate speech of the Asuras is the work of the sacrifice, which sustains the cosmic order of which speech is an integral part. Moreover, this is a conquest of speech by speech, of inarticulate speech by the properly measured speech of the Vedic *ṛc*s and *sāman*s, and by the ritual formulas or *yajus*es. In this concluding section I would like to return to the question of the historical context in which this view of Vedic speech was elaborated, and to the question of the canonicity of the Veda in that context. My point of departure is a passage from the *Śathapatha Brāhmaṇa*, which places the notion of the uncontrolled and inarticulate speech of the Asuras into a more concrete historical context.

I have already referred to the myth, recounted at ŚB 3.2.1.18–23, according to which Vāc was in the beginning in the possession of the Asuras but was won back by the gods through sacrifice, the Asuras being left deprived of Speech, crying "He 'lavaḥ! he 'lavaḥ!" This passage continues as follows: "Such was the enigmatic (*upajijñāsya*) speech which they then spoke. One (who speaks thus) is a *mleccha* (i. e., a barbarian). Therefore let no Brahmin speak barbarous language (*mlecchet*), since such is the speech of the Asuras. Thus indeed he takes away the speech of hateful enemies; and whosoever knows this, his enemies, being deprived of speech, are defeated" (ŚB 3.2.1.24). Paul Thieme has shown that the phrase uttered by the Asuras is an Eastern dialect of the Sanskrit *he 'rayo 'rayaḥ*, or "hail friends!"[18] What is being said here, then, is that no Brahmin should speak the Eastern dialect, but only the formally correct Sanskrit as it is spoken in Aryavarta, the Brahmanical homeland in the region of the Doab, farther West, and the region, as we have seen, which probably saw the compilation of the *Yajur-Veda Saṃhitās*. This tension between the established Brahmanical norms of the Doab and the "barbaric" East is made explicit in another passage from the *Śathapatha Brāhmaṇa* (1.4.1.14–16):

> Mathava, the Videgha, was at that time on the (river) Sarasvatī. Then he [Agni] went toward the east, burning this earth, and Gotama Rāhūgaṇa and the Videgha Mathava followed after him as he was burning along. He burnt over all these rivers. The Sadānīra (= modern Gandak, near Patna), which flows from the northern (Himalaya) mountain, that one he did not burn over. That very river the Brahmins did not cross in former times, thinking, "It has not been burnt over by Agni Vaiśvānara." [15] Nowdays, however, there are many Brahmins to the east of it. At that time (the land east of the Sadānīra) was very uncultivated, very marshy, because it had not been tasted by Agni Vaiśvānara. [16] Nowdays, however, it is very cultivated, for the Brahmins have caused (Agni) to taste it through sacrifices.

Agni Vaiśvānara here of course refers to the fire of sacrifice, the centerpiece of Brahmanical culture. We have here a picture of cultural conquest, with the *śrauta* sacrificial system and the "divine speech" that is inseparable from it, providing both its norm and instrument. Romila Thapar has suggested that the gradual aryanization of language in northern India went hand in hand with the expansion of agrarian village economies. In such a context, the formally "correct" Sanskrit spoken by the Brahmins of Aryavarta would come to serve as an important cultural norm, especially if, as Thapar suggests, this process of expansion included the incorporation of indigenous non-Indo-Aryan speakers into the "Aryan" fold. As she writes:

> The archaeological culture of the PGW [Painted Grey Ware] and its literary counterpart the Later Vedic literature would then be an evolved culture reflecting the indigenous as well as the later elements, and 'aryan' would refer not to an ethnic group but to *a social group identified by status, language and conformity to a particular cultural pattern,* which certainly seems much closer to the connotation of the word 'aryan' as it occurs in the Later Vedic literature.[19]

Recent work on the non-Aryan contributions to the *śrauta* ritual system makes such an interpretation seem quite probable.[20] And if we can accept this view of later Vedic society as a hybrid culture forged out of Indo-Aryan and indigenous (*dāsa*) elements under the aegis of the cultural norm represented by the sacrifice and its language, then I believe we have a way of understanding a dimension of Vedic canonicity that is left unaddressed by the search for textual canons alone. What is being "canonized" here is as much a form of action, and indeed a form of culture, as an authoritative collection of texts. In this historical situation the codification of the Vedic Saṃhitās would have been but one aspect of the codification of the *śrauta* rituals themselves, with both processes intended to establish the normativity of Brahmanical culture. But given what we have seen above concerning the lack of definitive closure of the canon on the level of content, it would appear that the codification of the Vedic Saṃhitās remained subordinate to the codification of the rites themselves, and that therefore the canonical Saṃhitās as such never became independent norms for the Brahmanical community. Whether such a thing is even possible in a nonliterate society is a good question. In the present case it is possible to argue that we have to do not with canonical texts, but with canonical speech, and with the authority of its speakers, both of which are to be defined more by correctness of form—both linguistic and social—than by limitation in content. It was such formal correctness, acting as a norm or "canon," that would have made possible the incorporation of non-Aryan content into the dominant Brahmanical culture through their integration into a common structure.

Given this probable context for the establishment of a "canonical" Veda during the late Vedic period, it becomes possible to understand the apparent lack of concern for *closure* in terms of the *content* of the canon. It would be sufficient if the many Saṃhitās in their many branches (*śākhās*) could be seen to be *formally* correct, and to be in the possession of the proper authorities, namely, the Brahmins. It was in the *form* of the content of the Vedic collections, and in the proper use of that content by the appropriate people, that their power was believed to reside. Thus, in the case of the *Ṛg-Veda Saṃhitā*, for instance, the creation of the Saṃhitā would have been motivated more by the desire to preserve the correct form of the *ṛc*s as powerful mantras than by an interest in canonizing a specific number of hymns. This would help explain why it was possible to employ *ṛc*s in the "canonical" *śrauta* rituals that are not found in the "canonical" *Ṛg-Veda Saṃhitā*,[21] since the existence of such a Saṃhitā would imply merely that all *ṛc*s within it were well formed mantras, and not necessarily that all well-formed mantras are found there and nowhere else. It would also help explain how it was possible to incorporate non-Vedic traditions into the *śrauta* system itself, as extensions to the basic structure. Rather than thinking of the canonical Veda as a fixed collection of texts, then, we might say that the canonical Veda is that which, at a given time, is proper for the dominant learned class, the Brahmins, to use as such. Canonicity then has more to do with formally correct usage in the socially correct context than it does with questions of ultimate origin or authorship, or with questions of limitation and closure.

This lack of fixity, of closure, in the Vedic canon leads us to ask whether it is in fact a canon at all. Individual parts of it, such as the *Ṛg-Veda Saṃhitā* in the *Śākala* recension, display a remarkable degree of fixity over a very long period of time. But no such part, taken in isolation, constitutes *the* Veda, in the sense of incorporating all that is recognized, from the time of the Saṃhitās on, as authentically "Vedic" by the tradition. If we seek in the Vedic tradition a true counterpart of the canonical scriptures of the West, then I believe we will be disappointed. Even the more expansive notion of canon developed by J. Z. Smith, which he believes to be applicable to oral as well as written traditions, nevertheless centers on the essential features of the limitation and closure of content and thus is not fully adequate to the Vedic case.

If, in spite of these problems, we nevertheless wish to speak of the canonicity of the Veda, then we must begin with the recognition that Veda has traditionally been an oral tradition in the exclusive possession of a restricted and authoritative group. As such it is indissolubly united with that group and its historical fortunes. Questions of the canonicity and authority of the Veda thus cannot be separated from questions of the nature of the status of those who preserve it, or from questions concerning the manner in which they employ it. In its traditional context, the Veda has been inseparable from forms of ritual action that have played a central role in the legitimation of a particular social order. That individual parts of the Vedic tradition have survived relatively unchanged over so many generations is an indicator of the extreme conservatism of those entrusted with their preservation. We must not be misled by features that resemble canonical texts as they are known elsewhere into believing that the cases are strictly parallel. While canons everywhere may function as instruments for the creation of identity and the establishment of authority, there remain real differences in the ways in which these things are accomplished in each case, and even in the degree to which they are accomplished. Such differences are worth preserving.

ABBREVIATIONS

PB *Pañcaviṃśa Brāhmaṇa*
ŚB *Śathapatha Brāhmaṇa*
TB *Taittirīya Brāhmaṇa*
TS *Taittirīya Saṃhitā*

NOTES

1. See, for example, Levering, *Rethinking Scripture*; and in particular, Folkert, " 'Canons' of Scripture," 170–79.

2. See Smith, *Imagining Religion*, 36–52.

3. See Timm, *Texts in Context*. In his introduction, Timm refers to Smith's article as "a seminal work read by each author involved in this project, and quoted by many." Although not indebted to Smith's work, mention should also be made here of Bonazzoli's studies of the Purāṇas. See in particular Bonazzoli, "Dynamic Canon of the Purāṇa-s," 116–66.

4. See Smith, *Reflections on Resemblance, Ritual and Religion*.

5. I myself have addressed this question briefly, with reference to the grammarian Bhartṛhari. See Carpenter, "Bhartṛhari and the Veda," 24–27.

6. Smith, *Imagining Religion*, 44–52.

7. For a survey of the evidence on the redaction of the *Ṛg-Veda*, see Gonda, *Vedic Literature*.

8. Renou, *Les Écoles Védiques*, 20–22.

9. Ibid., 22–33.

10. Kashikar, "Problem of the Gaḷantas in the Ṛgveda-padapaṭha," 44.

11. See ibid.; and Pischel and Geldner, *Vedische Studien*, 1:144–46.

12. Gonda, *Vedic Literature*, 336.

13. Renou, "Recherches," 176–77.

14. Findly, "*Mantra kaviśasta*," 15–47.

15. Ibid., 25; Thieme, "Vorzarathustrisches bei den Zarathustriern," 69.

16. Renou, *Les Écoles Védiques*, 9.

17. See in particular RV 10.71. For an in-depth study of this hymn, see Patton, "Hymn to Vāc;" 183–213.

18. Thieme, "Review of T. Burrow," 437–38.

19. Thapar, *Ancient Indian Social History*, 259; emphasis added.

20. See Parpola, "Pre-Vedic Indian Background of the Srauta Rituals," 2:41–75, and *Sky-Garment*.

21. See Renou, "Études védiques," 133–41.

REFERENCES

Bonazzoli, Giorgio

1979 "The Dynamic Canon of the Purāṇa-s." *Purāṇam* 21:116–66.

Carpenter, David

1992 "Bhartṛhari and the Veda." In *Texts in Context*, ed. Timm, 17–32.

Findly, Ellison Banks

1989 "*Mantra kaviśasta*: Speech as Performative in the Ṛgveda." In *Mantra*, ed. Harvey P. Alper, 15–47. Albany: State University of New York Press.

Folkert, Kendall W.

1989 "The 'Canons' of 'Scripture.' " In *Rethinking Scripture*, ed. Levering, 170–79.

Gonda, Jan

1975 *Vedic Literature*. Wiesbaden: Otto Harrassowitz.

Kashikar, C. G.

1946 "The Problem of the Gaḷantas in the Ṛgveda-padapāṭha." *Proceedings and Transactions of the 13th All-India Oriental Conference* 13, 2:39–46.

Levering, Miriam, ed.

1989 *Rethinking Scripture: Essays from a Comparative Perspective*. Albany: State University of New York Press.

Parpola, Asko

1983 "The Pre-Vedic Indian Background of the Śrauta Rituals." In *Agni: The Vedic Ritual of the Fire Altar*, ed. Frits Staal, 2:41–75. 2 vols. Berkeley: Asian Humanities Press.

1985 *The Sky-Garment: A Study of the Harappan Religion and Its Relation to the Mesopotamian and Later Indian Religions*. Helsinki: Finnish Oriental Society.

Patton, Laurie L.

1990 "Hymn to Vāc: Myth or Philosophy?" In *Myth and Philosophy*, ed. Frank Reynolds and David Tracy, 183–213. Albany: State University of New York Press.

Pischel, Richard, and Karl F. Geldner

1889–1901 *Vedische Studien*. 3 vols. Stuttgart: Verlag W. Kohlhammer.

Renou, Louis

1947 *Les Écoles Védiques et la Formation du Veda*. Paris: Imprimerie Nationale.

1952 "Études védiques." *Journal asiatique* 240:133–41.

1962 "Recherches sur le rituel védique: La place du Rig-Veda dans l'ordonnance du culte." *Journale asiatique* 250:176–77.

Smith, Brian K.

1989 *Reflections on Resemblance, Ritual and Religion*. New York Oxford University Press.

Smith, Jonathan Z.

1982 *Imagining Religion: From Babylon to Jonestown*. Chicago: University of Chicago Press.

Thapar, Romila

1978 *Ancient Indian Social History: Some Interpretations*. New Delhi: Orient Longman.

Thieme, Paul

1955 Review of T. Burrow, *The Sanskrit Language* (1955). In *Language* 31:437–38.

1957 "Vorzarathustrisches bei den Zarathustriern und bei Zarathustra." *Zeitschrift der Deutshen Morgenländischen Gesellschaft* 107:69.

Timm, Jeffrey, ed.

1992 *Texts in Context: Traditional Hermeneutics in South Asia*. Albany: State University of New York Press.

2

Veda in the Brāhmaṇas

Cosmogonic Paradigms and the Delimitation of Canon

BARBARA A. HOLDREGE

In discussing the category of canon in the history of religions, Jonathan Z. Smith has suggested that "canon is best seen as one form of a basic cultural process of limitation and of overcoming that limitation through ingenuity."[1] He further suggests that the task of overcoming the limitation posed by a closed canon is accomplished through the exegetical enterprise, in which the task of the interpreter is "continually to extend the domain of the closed canon over everything that is known or everything that exists *without* altering the canon in the process."[2] In order to test the applicability of this model of canon to the case of the Veda in the Brahmanical tradition, two types of questions need to be addressed. First, if indeed the Veda does constitute a closed canon, what are the criteria and mechanisms by which this canon has been delimited? Second, what strategies have been used to overcome this limitation? Are they primarily exegetical in nature? The Veda would appear to conform to at least one aspect of Smith's model in that it functions within the Brahmanical tradition as an encompassing, paradigmatic symbol that is simultaneously delimited and potentially unlimited. At the center of the canon is a fixed corpus of mantras that has been meticulously preserved through oral tradition in strictly unaltered form, syllable for syllable, accent for accent, for over three thousand years: the Vedic Saṃhitās. At the same time the domain of the Veda has been extended through a variety of strategies so that it functions as an open-ended, permeable category within which can be subsumed potentially all texts, teachings, and practices authorized by the Brahmanical elite.

With respect to the mechanisms through which the Vedic canon has been circumscribed, David Carpenter has argued elsewhere in this volume that the canonicity of the Veda can best be defined not in terms of the delimitation of the *content* of a particular corpus of texts, as Smith's model implies, but rather in terms of the delimitation of the correct *form* of speech to be employed in the sacrificial rituals.[3] This chapter suggests that the Brahmanical tradition's emphasis on the form of the Vedic mantras over their content is closely connected to the transcendent status ascribed to the mantras as the primordial impulses of speech that constitute the source and "blueprint" of creation.[4] In this context the strategies for expanding the Veda beyond the domain of the core texts, the Vedic mantras, do not generally involve an extension of content, as Smith's emphasis on the exegetical enterprise would suggest, but rather an extension of status. Irrespective of whether the content of the Vedic mantras is known or understood, their status as transcendent knowledge is acknowledged by orthodox exponents, and it is this status that subsequent texts and teachings seek to acquire through various modes of assimilation.

In order to understand the mechanisms through which the expansion of the purview of the term "Veda" occurred, we need to examine more closely the distinction that is made in the Brahmanical tradition between two categories of sacred texts: *śruti*, "that which was heard," and *smṛti*, "that which was remembered." The core *śruti* texts are the four types of mantras, *ṛcs*, *yajus*es, *sāman*s, and *atharvāṅgiras*es or *atharvan*s, which are collected in the Saṃhitās.[5] The domain of *śruti* was subsequently extended to include not only the Saṃhitās, but also the Brāhmaṇas, Āraṇyakas, and Upaniṣads. Although the canon of *śruti* is technically closed, the category of Upaniṣads has remained somewhat permeable, with new Upaniṣads being added to the traditionally accepted 108 Upaniṣads up to as late as the medieval period.[6] While the domain of *śruti* is thus in principle circumscribed, *smṛti* is a dynamic, open-ended category, which includes the Dharma-Śāstras, Itihāsas, and Purāṇas, as well as a variety of other texts that have been incorporated within this ever-expanding category in accordance with the needs of different periods and groups.[7] The primary criterion for distinguishing between *śruti* and *smṛti* texts is generally characterized by both Indian and Western scholars as an ontological distinction between "revelation" and "tradition."[8] *Śruti* texts—Saṃhitās, Brāhmaṇas, Āraṇyakas, and Upaniṣads—are traditionally understood to have been directly cognized, "seen" and "heard," by inspired "seers" (rishis) at the beginning of each cycle of creation. The formal schools of Vedic exegesis, Pūrva-Mīmāṃsā and Vedānta, maintain that the *śruti* or Vedic texts are eternal (*nitya*), infinite, and *apauruṣeya*, not created by any human or divine agent, while the Nyāya, Vaiśeṣika, and Yoga schools of Indian philosophy view the Vedic texts as the work of God.[9] All other sacred texts are relegated to a secondary status as *smṛti*, for they are held to have been composed by personal authors and are therefore designated as "that which was remembered" rather than "that which was heard." On the basis of this criterion the Itihāsas and Purāṇas are classified as *smṛti* texts, even though they may assimilate themselves to *śruti* by claiming the status of the "fifth Veda."[10]

According to the above definitions, the term "Veda" refers strictly speaking only to *śruti* texts and not to *smṛti* texts. However, Sheldon Pollock has recently brought to light an essential mechanism whereby the domain of the Veda was extended to include not only *śruti* but also *smṛti*. He locates this mechanism in the definition of the terms *śruti* and *smṛti* themselves, which he argues have been incorrectly construed as representing a dichotomy between "revelation" and "tradition." He maintains rather that, according to the etymology derived from the Pūrva-Mīmāṃsā school that is still prevalent among certain traditional Brahmanical teachers, *śruti* refers to the extant Vedic texts that can be "heard" in recitation, whereas *smṛti* is an open-ended category that encompasses any teachings or practices pertaining to dharma that have been "remembered" from lost Vedic texts. Understood in this way Veda becomes a limitlessly encompassing symbol that includes not only *śruti* but also *smṛti*. The meaning of the term "Veda" is extended beyond the circumscribed boundaries of the *śruti* texts—Saṃhitās, Brāhmaṇas, Āraṇyakas, and Upaniṣads—and through a process of "vedacization" comes to include within its purview not only the Itihāsas and Purāṇas, but potentially all śāstric teachings, enshrined in practices as well as texts, that are promulgated by Brahmanical authorities.[11]

While the original etymology of the term *śruti* may be debated, and may indeed be interpreted by certain strands of the Brahmanical tradition to mean "that which is heard" in ongoing recitations of the Vedic texts, it is also clear that the related term *śruta* was used as early as the *Ṛg-Veda* to refer to the cognitions of the rishis[12] and that the term *śruti* itself still retains this association among contemporary Hindu thinkers: Veda as *śruti* is "that which was heard" by the ancient rishis as part of a primordial cognition in the beginning of creation. Moreover, Veda is that which was seen by the rishis, who as "seers" are traditionally designated as *satya-darśins*, "those who see the truth."[13] The transcendent status attributed to the Veda is itself constitutive of the Veda's legitimating authority as the encompassing symbol of the Brahmanical tradition. The core *śruti* texts, the Vedic mantras, are depicted in the mythological speculations of Vedic and post-Vedic texts as having a transhistorical dimension, in which they are conceived to be that eternal, suprasensible knowledge which exists perpetually on the subtle level of creation as the source and blueprint of the universe. The rishis are portrayed as having the ability to station their awareness on that subtle level where they could "see" and "hear" the impulses of knowledge reverberating forth from the Transcendent as the fundamental rhythms of creation. They subsequently "recorded" on the gross level of speech that which they cognized on the subtle level, and in this way the mantras assumed a concrete form on earth as recited texts.[14]

The Vedic mantras are thus granted the status of transcendent knowledge. Any subsequent text or śāstric discourse can participate in that status only by assimilating itself to the Vedic mantras through a variety of strategies, including (1) claiming to form part of *śruti*, the original cognitions of the rishis, in the case of the Brāhmaṇas, Āraṇyakas, and Upaniṣads; (2) claiming the status of the "fifth Veda," in the case of the Itihāsas and Purāṇas; (3) establishing a genealogy that directly links the text's teachings to the Veda or to some form of divine revelation; (4) claiming that the text's teachings derive from lost Vedic texts, a claim that could apply to potentially all *smṛti* texts; or (5) otherwise conforming to the model of the Veda.[15] Brian K. Smith has emphasized that such strategies, including a variety of other modes of assimilation, have been used not only by exponents of the Brahmanical hierarchy but also by non-Brahmanical Hindu groups in order to invest their sacred texts with the transcendent authority of the Veda.[16] Whether the Veda is revered or rejected, appropriated or subverted, it remains a symbol invested with authoritative power that must be contended with by all those who wish to position themselves in relation to the Brahmanical hierarchy.[17] As J. C. Heesterman emphasizes, "The crux of the matter is that the Vedas hold the key to ultimate legitimation. Therefore, even if the Vedas are in no way related to the ways of human life and society, one is still forced to come to terms with them."[18] Heesterman's remark points to an observation often made by Indologists: the authoritative power of the Veda does not lie in the content of the Vedic Saṃhitās themselves, for their content is primarily concerned with sacrificial rituals and is not directly relevant to the teachings and practices of post-Vedic Hinduism.[19] Louis Renou has observed that "even in the most orthodox domains, the reverence to the Vedas has come to be a simple 'raising of the hat', in passing, to an idol by which one no longer intends to be encumbered later on." He further remarks that "the term [Veda] tends to serve as a symbol."[20]

The critical point to be emphasized here is that the Veda serves as a symbol precisely because it transcends the confines of textuality that limit the term to a circumscribed body of texts and comes to represent the totality of knowledge, thus reclaiming its original etymology as "knowledge." Pollock remarks, "As 'Knowledge' *tout court*, as the *śāstra* par excellence, and as the 'omniscient' text (Manu-Smṛti 2.7) and the 'infinite' text (Taittirīya [Brāhmaṇa] 3.10.11.4, et al.), Veda is the general rubric under which every sort of partial knowledge—that is, the various individual *śāstras*—is ultimately subsumed.''[21] The legitimating authority of the Veda is thus inextricably linked to its symbolic function as knowledge—not the ordinary knowledge derived through the powers of human reasoning, but that transcendent, infinite knowledge which is held to be the essence of ultimate reality and the source and foundation of creation.[22] This knowledge is said to have been cognized by the rishis and preserved by them in the form of oral texts, but, as we shall see, certain Brahmanical texts insist that the Veda, the limitless Word, cannot be limited to its finite expressions in the texts preserved by human beings on earth. Moreover, the power of the Veda as embodied in the recited texts is held to lie not in the discursive meaning of the texts, but rather in the sounds through which the primordial impulses of knowledge are expressed. In this view the content of the Vedic Saṃhitās will always be of secondary value, as Indologists have observed, because the primary concern of the Brahmanical exponents of the Vedic recitative tradition is to preserve the purity of the Vedic sounds irrespective of whether their semantic content is understood.[23]

The dual mechanisms by means of which the Veda is identified with the limitless Word or knowledge and at the same time is delimited to a bounded corpus of texts—the Vedic mantras—are already evident in the Vedic texts themselves. In the Saṃhitās, Brāhmaṇas, Āraṇyakas, and Upaniṣads the terms ''Veda,'' ''Vedas,'' and their equivalents are used both in an abstract sense, to refer to ''knowledge'' or ''Word,'' and in a concrete sense, to refer to a circumscribed body of texts. In their discussions of the bounded textual manifestation of the Veda, the Brāhmaṇas, Āraṇyakas, and Upaniṣads tend to focus almost exclusively on the three mantra collections, *ṛcs*, *yajuses*, and *sāmans*,[24] which are generally designated as *trayī vidyā* (''threefold knowledge'')[25] or *traya veda* (''threefold Veda'').[26] The following analysis will focus on the representations of the Veda in the Brāhmaṇas, which present cosmogonic paradigms for the process of delimiting the unlimited Word in which the manifestation of the Vedic mantras is depicted as an integral part of the mechanics of creation.[27]

The discursive framework for the cosmogonic and cosmological speculations of the Brāhmaṇas is the discourse of sacrifice, which is concerned, first, to establish the cosmic import of the sacrifice as the counterpart of the Puruṣa Prajāpati, who is celebrated as the supreme god and creator; and, second, to delineate the role of the sacrificial order in regenerating the cosmic order through enlivening the connections (*bandhus*) between the human, natural, and divine orders.[28] The Veda, both as a cosmological principle embedded in the cosmic order and as the recited texts that form an integral part of the sacrificial order, is granted a pivotal role in this sacrificial discourse. The recitation of the Vedic mantras is represented in the Brāhmaṇas as essential to the world-ordering and maintaining function of the sacrificial rituals. However, the mundane texts recited and studied by human beings on earth are viewed as constituting only a limited manifestation of that infinite (*ananta*) knowledge which is Veda.[29] Just as the sacrifice is held to be the gross counterpart of the cosmic prototype, Prajāpati, so the sound offerings of the sacrifice, the Vedic mantras, are represented as the gross manifestations of the cosmic reality of Veda, which is itself constitutive of Prajāpati. The Veda as a cosmic reality is correlated with the creator Prajāpati as well as with his consort Vāc, speech. Prajāpati is celebrated in the Brāhmaṇas as both expressed (*nirukta*) and unexpressed (*anirukta*),[30] limited (*parimita*) and unlimited (*aparimita*),[31] and Vāc is similarly described as both expressed (*nirukta*) and unexpressed (*anirukta*).[32] The Veda in its correlation with Prajāpati and Vāc is represented as having both unlimited and limited, unexpressed and expressed dimensions even on the cosmic plane.

David Carpenter's chapter in this volume emphasizes the ritual mechanisms described in the Brāhmaṇas through which Vāc, as the consort of Prajāpati and the possession of the gods generally, is transformed from inarticulate speech into the regulated speech of the Vedic mantras.[33] The following analysis, on the other hand, will be concerned primarily with the cosmogonic context of the Brāhmaṇas' representations of Veda and will focus not on the mechanisms through which uncontrolled speech is controlled, but rather on the process through which unlimited speech is delimited through the speech-acts of the creator Prajāpati. As the circumscribed expressions of Prajāpati's speech, the Vedic mantras are allotted a cosmogonic role as the primordial utterances through which the creator brings forth the phenomenal creation and are represented as the subtle blueprint containing the sound correlatives of the concrete realm of forms.

VEDA, PRAJĀPATI, AND VĀC

The Veda as *brahman*, the Word,[34] is described in the Brāhmaṇas as participating in the essence of both Prajāpati and his consort Vāc. The Veda is at times identified with Prajāpati: "In the beginning Prajāpati was the Veda" (*Prajāpatir vedaḥ*).[35] The Veda is described as constitutive of Prajāpati's being, with the Vedic mantras, meters, and various components of the sacrifice forming different parts of his body or self (*ātman*).[36] At the same time the Veda is said to be derived from Prajāpati (*Prājāpatyo vedaḥ*),[37] for it is Prajāpati who brings forth the Veda in the beginning of creation.[38] These two notions—the Veda as constitutive of Prajāpati and the Veda as derived from Prajāpati—are brought together in the *Jaiminīya Brāhmaṇa*, which describes Prajāpati as bringing forth certain *stomas*, *sāmans*, and meters from various parts of his body.[39] The Veda is more specifically represented as the expression of Prajāpati's speech.[40]

As the expression of divine speech the Veda becomes associated with Prajāpati's consort Vāc. Vāc as *brahman*[41] is correlated both with the unexpressed, undifferentiated Word, Veda, and with its expressed, differentiated manifestations as the Vedic mantras. The *ṛcs*, *yajus*es, and *sāmans* are said to be the threefold form of Vāc.[42] From Vāc, who is designated as the "Mother of the Vedas,"[43] the Vedic mantras flow out in the beginning of creation as her "thousandfold progeny."[44] The *Taittirīya Brāhmaṇa* proclaims, "Vāc is the imperishable one (*akṣara*), the first-born of the cosmic order (*ṛta*), the Mother of the Vedas (*vedānām mātā*), the navel of immortality (*amṛta*)."[45] As the progeny of Vāc the Vedas partake of their Mother's infinite, immortal nature and are themselves said to be infinite (*ananta*),[46] immortal (*amṛta*),[47] and imperishable (*akṣita*).[48]

Through correlating the Veda with Prajāpati and Vāc, the Brāhmaṇas are concerned to establish the Veda's primordial status as an inherent part of the two creative principles that are responsible for generating and structuring the cosmic order: the principle of knowledge or mind, and the principle of speech. Prajāpati, as the cosmic intelligence underlying the universe, is the abode of knowledge and is associated in particular with the principle of mind (*manas*),[49] while his consort Vāc represents the principle of speech. Prajāpati is at times identified with the mind,[50] and it is by virtue of his identity with the mind that he knows everything.[51] Prajāpati is described as entering into union with Vāc by means of his mind.[52] *Manas* and *vāc* are consistently paired throughout the Brāhmaṇas as male and female consorts, the human faculties of mind and speech constituting "yoke-fellows" (*yujs*)[53] that represent the microcosmic counterparts of Prajāpati and Vāc, who in their identification with mind and speech are also at times designated as Sarasvat and Sarasvatī.[54] Mind and speech are depicted in the Brāhmaṇas as mutually dependent upon one another. On the one hand, the mind upholds speech, for it is the mind that provides the cognitive content that speech expresses.[55] On the other hand, speech upholds the mind, for it is speech that gives vocalized expression to the cognitive content of the mind.[56] In the Brāhmaṇas the mind is given precedence over speech on both the human and cosmic planes, for while the mind is unexpressed (*anirukta*) and more unlimited (*aparimita*), speech is expressed (*nirukta*) and more limited (*parimita*).[57] On the human plane the mind precedes speech,[58] and on the cosmic plane Prajāpati precedes Vāc. Prajāpati, as the lord of thought (*cit-pati*) and the lord of speech (*vāk-pati* or *vācas-pati*),[59] brings forth Vāc and then unites with her in order to generate the gods and manifest creation.[60]

The Veda is described as emerging in the cosmogonic process as the manifestation of both Prajāpati and Vāc, both mind and speech. *Śatapatha Brāhmaṇa* 7.5.2.52 describes speech as the instrument by means of which the Veda, the threefold knowledge (*trayī vidyā*), is "dug out" from the silent depths of the ocean of mind and given vocalized expression as the Vedic mantras. "Mind (*manas*) is the ocean (*samudra*). From the mind-ocean with speech (*vāc*) for a shovel the gods dug out (root *khan* + *nir*) the threefold knowledge (*trayī vidyā*). . . . Mind is the ocean, speech is the sharp shovel, the threefold knowledge is the offering (*nirvapaṇa*, literally, 'pouring out')." A passage in the *Pañcaviṃśa Brāhmaṇa* depicts Prajāpati meditating silently (*tūṣṇīm*) in his mind and then using speech as the vehicle to bring forth (root *jan* + *pra*) that which is hidden (*antarhita*) in his mind. That which is hidden in Prajāpati's mind becomes the *bṛhat sāman*, and that which is expressed through his speech becomes the *rathantara sāman*.[61] Elsewhere in the *Pañcaviṃśa Brāhmaṇa*, as well as in other Brāhmaṇas, the *bṛhat* is identified with the mind and the *rathantara* with speech.[62] The *bṛhat* and *rathantara* are further equated with the *sāman* and *ṛc*, respectively[63] which are themselves at times identified with mind and speech and portrayed as male and female consorts.[64] The following set of correspondences thus emerges:

Prajāpati	mind	*bṛhat*	*sāman*
Vāc	speech	*rathantara*	*ṛc*

In this schema the *sāman* is correlated with the unexpressed principle of mind, Prajāpati, while the *ṛc* is correlated with the expressed principle of speech, Vāc. However, Vāc is also said to have an unexpressed (*anirukta*) as well as an expressed (*nirukta*) dimension.[65] Moreover, the process through which unexpressed speech becomes expressed as vocalized utterances is itself represented in a number of passages as the means through which creation manifests. In this context the cosmogonic process is described as a two-stage process in which an unmanifest state of undifferentiated unity gives rise to a manifest state of differentiation through a series of discrete speech-acts.

In my reconstruction of the two-phase process of creation, based on several accounts in the Brāhmaṇas, Prajāpati and Vāc both participate in each stage. The division between the first and second stages of the cosmogonic process is demarcated in certain accounts by the measure of time, generally the period of a year. (1) In the first stage the creator Prajāpati has a desire to reproduce and unites with his consort Vāc. The Vāc with which Prajāpati unites at this stage is the unexpressed, transcendent level of speech that is generally identified with the primordial waters.[66] Prajāpati implants his seed in the waters of Vāc and the seed becomes an egg, which represents the totality of the universe in yet undifferentiated form. (2) In the second stage of creation a child, representing the "second self" of Prajāpati, is born and speaks. This speech, which represents the second phase of Vāc, is the expressed, vocalized speech by means of which the creator introduces distinctions in the originally distinctionless totality of creation represented by the egg, dividing it into the three worlds and manifesting various types of beings.[67] The Veda as the undifferentiated Word, *brahman*, is at times correlated with the first stage, while the differentiated Vedic mantras are correlated with the second stage.

One of the most important passages that conforms to this basic pattern is *Śatapatha Brāhmaṇa* 10.6.5.4–5, which also forms part of the *Bṛhadāraṇyaka Upaniṣad*.[68] In the first phase of creation the creator,[69] desiring to have a "second self" (*dvitīya ātman*), enters into union with Vāc by means of his mind (*manas*). The seed becomes the year, which is consistently identified with Prajāpati in the Brāhmaṇas.[70] In the second phase, which is distinguished from the first phase by the period of a year, a child, representing the "second self" of the creator, is born and cries out, producing speech (*vāc*). This speech represents the second phase of Vāc, and it is from this expressed level of speech that the *ṛc*s, *yajus*es, *sāman*s, meters, sacrifices, human beings, and animals are brought forth. It is significant that the Vedic mantras are represented as the first products of the creator's speech, for in other passages, as will be discussed below, the words that the creator first speaks in order to bring forth the phenomena of creation are explicitly identified with the words of the Vedas.

Another variation on this basic pattern of creation is described in *Śatapatha Brāhmaṇa* 11.1.6.1–3. In the first phase of creation the waters alone exist, with no mention of the male creative principle. From the waters a golden egg (*hiraṇmaya āṇḍa*) is produced. In the second phase, which is again separated from the first phase by the period of a year, the Puruṣa Prajāpati is born from the egg, and after another year he speaks (root *hṛ* + *vi-ā*). This expressed level of speech serves as the means by which Prajāpati separates out the earth, midregions, and heaven from the originally undivided totality represented by the egg: "He uttered (root *hṛ* + *vi-ā*) '*bhūḥ*'—that became this earth; '*bhuvaḥ*'—that became the midregions; '*svaḥ*'—that became yonder heaven."[71] Although no mention is made of the Vedas in this creation account, the three *vyāhṛtis* or utterances—*bhūḥ, bhuvaḥ,* and *svaḥ*—are consistently represented throughout the Brāhmaṇas as the essences of the three Vedas—*Ṛg-Veda, Yajur-Veda,* and *Sāma-Veda*—which are correspondingly correlated with the three worlds.[72]

A third variant of this two-stage cosmogonic process appears in *Pañcaviṃśa Brāhmaṇa* 20.14.2–3 and *Jaiminīya Brāhmaṇa* 2.244 and distinguishes in particular between two different levels of Vāc.

> Prajāpati alone was here. Vāc alone was his own; Vāc was second to him. He reflected, "Let me send forth this Vāc. She will spread forth, pervading all this." He sent forth Vāc. She spread forth, pervading all this. She extended upwards as a continuous stream of water (*ap*). [Uttering the sound] "*a*," he split off a third of it—that became the earth. . . . [Uttering the sound] "*ka*" he split off a [second] third—that became the midregions. . . . [Uttering the sound) "*ho*" he cast [the last] third upwards—that became the heaven.[73]

In the first phase, as described in this passage, Vāc is one and undivided as the all-pervading waters. In the second phase she becomes divided, the one Vāc becoming threefold and expressed as three distinct sounds—*a, ka,* and *ho*—through the speech utterances of the creator Prajāpati. The text goes on to describe how Prajāpati uses different parts of his mouth to articulate these three sounds, which are "manifestly speech" (*pratyakṣam vāc*).[74] As in *Śatapatha Brāhmaṇa* 11.1.6.1–3, discussed above, it is by means of three primordial utterances that Prajāpati brings forth the three worlds. The *Pañcaviṃśa Brāhmaṇa* concludes, "Prajāpati indeed divided this Vāc, which was one syllable (*ekākṣara*), into three parts. These became the worlds."[75]

Another variant of the two-phase process of creation is given in *Śatapatha Brāhmaṇa* 6.1.1.8–10, which, like the *Pañcaviṃśa Brāhmaṇa* and *Jaiminīya Brāhmaṇa* accounts, distinguishes between two levels of Vāc—as the undifferentiated waters and as the differentiated expressions of vocalized speech. This passage is of particular significance in that it describes the Veda emerging as part of this process in two stages of manifestation.

> This Puruṣa Prajāpati desired, "May I become many, may I reproduce." He exerted himself; he practiced *tapas*. Having exerted himself and practiced *tapas*, he brought forth first of all *brahman*, the threefold knowledge (*trayī vidyā*). It became a foundation (*pratiṣṭhā*) for him. Hence they say, "*brahman* is the foundation of all this." Therefore, having studied [the Veda] one is established on a foundation, for this *brahman* is his foundation. Resting on this foundation he [Prajāpati] practiced *tapas*. He brought forth the waters out of Vāc, [who was] the world. Vāc alone was his; she was sent forth. She pervaded all this, and because she pervaded (root *āp*) whatever was here, therefore [she is called] water (*ap*); because she covered (root *vṛ*), therefore [she is called] water (*vār*). He desired, "May I reproduce from these waters." He entered the waters together with this threefold knowledge (*trayī vidyā*). Thence arose an egg (*āṇḍa*).

> He came into contact (root *mṛś* + *abhi*) with it. "May it exist, may it exist, may it multiply," thus he spoke (root *brū*). Thence was first brought forth *brahman*, the threefold knowledge (*trayī vidyā*). Hence they say, "*brahman* is the first-born of this all." For even before that Puruṣa, *brahman* was brought forth: it was brought forth as his mouth.

This passage points to two distinct stages of creation in which the Veda, along with Prajāpati and Vāc, participates. (1) In the first stage the Veda as *brahman*, the Word, is brought forth to serve as the foundation not only of the entire creation but of the creator himself. After bringing forth the waters from his consort Vāc, Prajāpati together with the threefold Veda enters the waters—an apparent reference to the process of procreation—from which an egg (*āṇḍa*) is produced. (2) In the second stage, having come into contact with the egg,[76] Prajāpati then speaks (root *brū*) three times—once again three primordial utterances are emphasized—and brings forth the second manifestation of the threefold Veda, which manifests as his mouth.[77]

The first stage in this two-phase process appears to be an unmanifest phase in which the process of differentiation has not yet begun. The Vāc with which Prajāpati unites in this stage is the primordial waters that represent the unexpressed, transcendent level of speech, and the Veda upon which Prajāpati rests as his foundation constitutes the totality of the Word, *brahman*, which although threefold has apparently not yet differentiated into three distinct Vedas. It is only in the second stage of creation that Vāc becomes expressed as vocalized speech, and corresponding to this more expressed level of speech is a more expressed level of Veda—the threefold Vedic mantras, which as the mouth of the creator are intimately associated with his speech. We thus find two levels of Veda corresponding to the two stages of creation: (1) in the first stage the Veda is *brahman*, the Word, which serves as the foundation of the creator and of his creation, while (2) in the second stage the Veda differentiates into the three Vedas, which are connected with the speech of the creator.

The progression from the first stage of creation to the second stage is thus represented as a move from an unmanifest state of undifferentiated unity to a manifest state of differentiation: the primordial waters of Vāc, which represent the unexpressed level of speech, begin to flow out in streams of expressed, vocalized speech that issue forth as discrete utterances; the one Veda divides into the three Vedas; the undifferentiated totality of creation represented by the egg differentiates into the three worlds. The essential elements of these two stages of creation can be schematized as follows:

	MALE PRINCIPLE		FEMALE PRINCIPLE		VEDA		CREATION
STAGE 1	creator Prajāpati	→	waters of Vāc		Veda as *brahman*		undivided egg ↑
STAGE 2	"second self" of Prajāpati	→	vocalized speech	→	three Vedas	→	three worlds

THE VEDAS AS THE SOURCE AND BASIS OF CREATION

In the cosmogonic paradigms discussed above the mechanism through which the unlimited Word becomes delimited as discrete speech utterances is represented as the means through which distinctions are introduced in the primordial unity. Vocalized speech serves as the differentiating principle by means of which the manifold forms of the phenomenal creation are projected into manifestation. The original utterances by means of which Prajāpati brings forth the three worlds are generally identified in the Brāhmaṇas with the three *vyāhṛtis*, the essences of the three Vedas.[78] For example, *Śatapatha Brāhmaṇa* 11.1.6.3, cited earlier, declares, "He uttered (root *hṛ* + *vi-ā*) '*bhūḥ*'—that became this earth; '*bhuvaḥ*'—that became the midregions; '*svaḥ*'—that became yonder heaven." Another passage in the *Śatapatha Brāhmaṇa* describes how Prajāpati's utterance of the three *vyāhṛti*s generates not only the three worlds, but also the three powers that are the essence of the three higher *varṇa*s—*brahman* (→ Brahmins), *kṣatra* (→ Kṣatriyas), and *viś* (→ Vaiśyas)—as well as the self (*ātman*), human beings, and animals.[79]

In a number of passages in the Brāhmaṇas the words that Prajāpati speaks in order to manifest the phenomena of creation are explicitly identified with the words of the Vedic mantras. Prajāpati is portrayed as the primordial rishi who originally "sees" (root *dṛś*) specific *ṛc*s and *sāman*s,[80] as well as the sacrificial rituals in which the mantras are used.[81] He then performs the various sacrifices, assuming the functions of the different priests: as the *hotṛ* priest he recites the *ṛc*s, as the *udgātṛ* priest he chants the *sāman*s, and as the *adhvaryu* priest he utters the *yajus*es.[82]

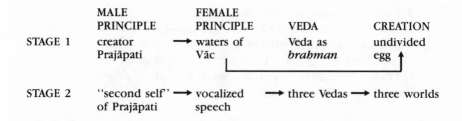

The *Aitareya Brāhmaṇa*, in accordance with its perspective as a *Ṛg-Veda* Brāhmaṇa, emphasizes Prajāpati's role as the *hotṛ* priest.[83] For example, *Aitareya Brāhmaṇa* 2.33 depicts the *hotṛ* Prajāpati as bringing forth all beings through a series of twelve utterances, which are identified with the twelve lines of the *nivid* ("proclamation"), a prose formulary that is inserted at specified points in the recitation of certain Ṛg-Vedic hymns of praise (*śastra*s).[84] "In the beginning Prajāpati alone was here. He desired, 'May I reproduce and become many.' He practiced *tapas*. He restrained (root *yam*) speech. After a year he uttered (root *hṛ* + *vi-ā*)

twelve times. The *nivid* has twelve lines (*padas*). He uttered this, indeed, the *nivid*. Through that all beings were brought forth." As in several of the passages discussed earlier, it is only in the second stage of creation, demarcated from the first by the period of a year, that the creator Prajāpati utters vocalized speech in order to bring forth the differentiated forms of creation. In the first stage speech is restrained, indicating that although Vāc exists, it is not yet expressed.

The *Pañcaviṃśa* and *Jaiminīya Brāhmaṇas*, as the Brāhmaṇas of the *Sāma-Veda*, give precedence to the role of Prajāpati as the *udgātṛ* priest[85] who in the primeval sacrifice chants *sāmans* and *stotras* in order to bring forth creation. In *Pañcaviṃśa Brāhmaṇa* 6.9.15, and the corresponding variant in *Jaiminīya Brāhmaṇa* 1.94, Prajāpati is depicted as chanting the words of a *sāman* (SV 2.180 = RV 9.62.1) in order to bring forth not only the gods, human beings, ancestors, and other beings, but also various aspects of the sacrificial order, including the Soma libations, *stotras* chanted by the *udgātṛ*, and *śastras* recited by the *hotṛ*.

> [Saying] "*ete*" ("these") Prajāpati brought forth the gods; [saying] "*asṛgram*" ("have been poured out") he brought forth human beings; [saying] "*indavaḥ*" ("Soma drops") he brought forth the ancestors; [saying] "*tiraḥ pavitram*" ("through the filter") he brought forth the [Soma] libations; [saying] "*āśavaḥ*" ("swift") he brought forth the *stotra*; [saying] "*viśvāni*" ("all") he brought forth the *śastra*; [saying] "*abhi saubhagā*" ("for the sake of blessings") he brought forth the other beings.[86]

In *Pañcaviṃśa Brāhmaṇa* 7.5.1 Prajāpati is described as bringing forth beings by means of the *āmahīyava sāman*,[87] while in *Jaiminīya Brāhmaṇa* 1.104 he produces beings through chanting the words of the *bahiṣpavamāna stotra*.[88]

Prajāpati's recitation of the Vedic mantras, like the sacrificial rituals in which the mantras are used, is portrayed not only as an instrument of creation, but also as an instrument of rectification by means of which he establishes an ordered cosmos.[89] For example, in the *Pañcaviṃśa* and *Jaiminīya Brāhmaṇas* Prajāpati is portrayed as chanting certain *sāmans* in order to subdue and domesticate his unruly creatures and to provide them with rain and food.[90]

The Vedic mantras, as the expressions of the divine speech of the creator Prajāpati, are depicted in the Brāhmaṇas as part of the very fabric of reality and as reflective of the structures of the cosmos. The realm of concrete phenomena is held to have been brought forth through the sound impulses contained in the Vedic mantras, and thus the Vedic words are viewed as the subtle correlatives of the forms of creation. In this context the three Vedas—*Ṛg-Veda, Yajur-Veda,* and *Sāma-Veda*—are incorporated into the Brāhmaṇas' cosmological system as part of an elaborate set of correspondences (*bandhus*) that, building upon the speculations of the *Puruṣa-Sūkta* (*Ṛg-Veda* 10.90), correlate the various orders of reality—sacrificial order, human order, natural order, and divine order. Brian K. Smith's chapter in this volume emphasizes the manner in which the Brāhmaṇas' cosmological system provides transcendent legitimation for the hierarchical social order through correlating the structure of the *varṇa* system with the structure of the Veda, which is itself represented as reflecting the structures of the cosmic order.[91] It is the Brāhmaṇas' representations of the Veda's role as the cosmic blueprint, in which correspondences are established between the realm of sound and the realm of form, that are of particular significance for the present analysis.

At the basis of this system of correspondences are the three primordial utterances or *vyāhṛtis—bhūḥ, bhuvaḥ, svaḥ*—which constitute the seed syllables of creation corresponding to the three worlds—earth, midregions, and heaven[92]—and which are identified, respectively, with the *Ṛg-Veda, Yajur-Veda,* and *Sāma-Veda,* representing their essences (*śukras* or *rasas*).[93] With these three primordial utterances, as discussed above, Prajāpati brings forth not only the three worlds, but also other aspects of creation.[94] A number of passages in the Brāhmaṇas establish correspondences between the three *vyāhṛtis*, *bhūḥ, bhuvaḥ, svaḥ*; the three Vedas, *Ṛg, Yajur,* and *Sāma*; the three worlds, earth, midregions, and heaven; and the three elements fire, wind, and sun, together with their presiding deities, Agni, Vāyu, and Sūrya/Āditya.[95] This system of homologies is at times extended to include certain human faculties, as will be discussed below.

A passage in the *Jaiminīya Upaniṣad Brāhmaṇa* describes Prajāpati as uttering the three *vyāhṛtis* in order to extract the essences of the three Vedas, from which in turn the three worlds and the three elements along with their deities are produced.

> Prajāpati indeed conquered this [universe] by means of the threefold Veda (*traya veda*). . . . He reflected, "If the other gods sacrifice thus by means of this Veda they will certainly conquer this conquest that is mine. Well then let me extract the essence (*rasa*) of the threefold Veda." [Saying] "*bhūḥ*," he extracted the essence of the *Ṛg-Veda*. That became this earth. The essence of it that streamed forth became Agni, fire, the essence of the essence. [Saying] "*bhuvaḥ*," he extracted the essence of the *Yajur-Veda*. That became the midregions. The essence of it that streamed forth became Vāyu, wind, the essence of the essence. [Saying] "*svaḥ*," he extracted the essence of the *Sāma-Veda*. That became yonder heaven. The essence of it that streamed forth

> became Āditya, the sun, the essence of the essence. Now of one syllable (*akṣara*) alone he was not able to extract the essence: Om, of that alone. That became this Vāc.[96]

While in the above passage the three *vyāhṛtis* are depicted as the primal utterances that represent the essences of the three Vedas from which the three worlds are produced, in other passages—in a typical Vedic paradox of mutual creation—the three utterances are described as being drawn forth as the essences of the three Vedas after the three worlds have already been produced. The *Śatapatha Brāhmaṇa*'s account is representative.

> In the beginning Prajāpati alone was here. He desired, "May I be, may I reproduce." He exerted himself; he practiced *tapas*. From him who had exerted himself and practiced *tapas* the three worlds—earth, midregions, and heaven—were brought forth. He infused warmth into these three worlds. From those heated [worlds] three lights were produced: Agni, fire; he who purifies here [Vāyu, wind]; and Sūrya, the sun. He infused warmth into these three lights. From those heated [lights] the three Vedas were produced: the *Ṛg-Veda* from Agni, the *Yajur-Veda* from Vāyu, and the *Sāma-Veda* from Sūrya. He infused warmth into these three Vedas. From those heated [Vedas] three essences (*śukra*s) were produced: *bhūḥ* from the *Ṛg-Veda*, *bhuvaḥ* from the *Yajur-Veda*, and *svaḥ* from the *Sāma-Veda*.[97]

The *Aitareya Brāhmaṇa,* in a parallel passage outlining the same progressive series of correspondences, goes on to describe how from the three *vyāhṛtis—bhūḥ, bhuvaḥ,* and *svaḥ*—three sounds (*varṇa*s) are in turn produced—*a, u,* and *m*—which Prajāpati subsequently combines to form the syllable Om.[98] Om is generally described in the Brāhmaṇas as the most concentrated essence of the Veda, which cannot be further pressed out[99] and which represents truth (*satya*).[100]

In the accounts of the Brāhmaṇas, it is only after Prajāpati draws forth the three Vedas and their essences, the *vyāhṛti*s, that he brings forth the sacrifice, establishing a further set of correlations between the three Vedas, the three *vyāhṛti*s, and various aspects of the sacrificial order: the three priests—*hotṛ, adhvaryu,* and *udgātṛ*—and the three sacrificial fires—*gārhapatya, āgnīdhrīya* or *dakṣiṇa,* and *āhavanīya*.[101] The sacrificial order is pivotal to the Brāhmaṇas' system of correspondences, for the regenerative power of the sacrifice is held to be the essential means of enlivening the connections between the human, natural, and divine orders. These connections are not thought to be arbitrary, but are rather considered to be actual intrinsic relations that exist between the different orders of reality. In the Brāhmaṇas' tripartite taxonomy the three constituent sounds of the syllable Om, the three *vyāhṛti*s, and the three Vedas constitute an essential part of the cosmic order as the expressions of divine speech, which are incorporated in the sacrificial order as particularly potent words of power that are recited as part of the sacrificial rituals. The natural order in this schema is represented by the three worlds—earth, midregions, and heaven—and by the three elements—fire, wind, and sun—while the divine order is represented by the presiding deities of these elements—Agni, Vāyu, and Sūrya/Āditya. A final link is established between the macrocosm and the microcosm by correlating these different parts of the natural and divine orders with certain human faculties. The standard tripartite schema generally correlates the *ṛc, yajus,* and *sāman* with speech, breath, and the eye, respectively,[102] although alternative schemas are also presented. While the *ṛc* is consistently identified with speech, the *sāman* is at times identified with the mind, as discussed earlier, as well as with the breath (*prāṇa*). The *yajus* is also sometimes correlated with the mind.[103]

UTTERANCES/ SACRIFICIAL ORDER			NATURAL ORDER		DIVINE ORDER	HUMAN ORDER
a	*bhūḥ*	*Ṛg-Veda*	earth	fire	Agni	speech
u	*bhuvaḥ*	*Yajur-Veda*	midregions	wind	Vāyu	breath/mind
m	*svaḥ*	*Sāma-Veda*	heaven	sun	Sūrya/Āditya	eye/mind/breath

This tripartite taxonomy establishes a series of correlations between, on the one hand, the realm of sound, represented by the primordial utterances, and, on the other hand, the realm of form, represented by the human, natural, and divine orders. Implicit in this schema, as well as in the more general Vedic conception of the creative power of the divine speech, is the notion that an intrinsic relation exists between the Vedic word and the object that it signifies, between the name (*nāma*) and the form (*rūpa*) that it designates. In this conception *bhūḥ* is not simply a conventional designation; it is the natural name of the earth and thus represents the subtle correlative that contains the "reality" of the earth within its structure. The primordial utterances *bhūḥ, bhuvaḥ,* and *svaḥ* are like potent seeds containing the entire tree of creation about to sprout. These three seed syllables represent the concentrated essences of the divine speech, which are in turn elaborated in the three Vedas.

The Vedas in this perspective contain the primordial sounds from which the phenomenal creation is structured. *Taittirīya Brāhmaṇa* 3.12.9.1–2 describes the *ṛc*s, *yajus*es, and *sāman*s as the sources of form (*mūrti*), motion (*gati*), and light (*tejas*), respectively, and then declares, "All this (*sarvam idam*) indeed was brought forth through *brahman*

[Veda]." A passage in the *Śatapatha Brāhmaṇa* depicts the three Vedas as containing the entire universe in potential form.

> He [Prajāpati] then surveyed all existing things. He beheld all existing things in the threefold knowledge (*trayī vidyā*), for therein is the self (*ātman*) of all meters, of all *stomas*, of all breaths, and of all the gods. This indeed exists, for it is immortal, and that which is immortal exists, and this [also contains] that which is mortal. Prajāpati reflected, "Truly all existing things are in the threefold knowledge. Well then let me construct for myself a self (*ātman*) that is the threefold knowledge."[104]

The passage goes on to describe how, through putting the threefold Veda into his own self, the creator Prajāpati becomes the soul animating the body of the universe, encompassing all existing things.[105]

While the three Vedas together correspond to the creation in its entirety, each Veda separately, in its correlation with one of the three worlds, represents the plan for that particular world. It is perhaps in this sense that the *Śatapatha Brāhmaṇa* establishes a direct identity between the three Vedas and the three worlds, declaring that the *ṛc*s are the earth, the *yajus*es are the midregions, and the *sāman*s are the heaven,[106] for the sounds of each Veda are held to reveal the underlying structure of the corresponding world.

The role of the Veda in the process of creation is thus twofold: the Veda, as the undifferentiated Word, *brahman*, serves as the foundation of creation, while the three Vedas, as the differentiated impulses of knowledge contained in the primordial expressions of divine speech, constitute the sound correlatives of the three worlds.

FORM OF VEDA	LEVEL OF CREATION
Veda as *brahman*, undifferentiated Word	undifferentiated totality of egg
Ṛg-Veda	earth
Yajur-Veda	midregions
Sāma-Veda	heaven

In the cosmogonic and cosmological speculations of the Brāhmaṇas the Veda thus assumes a multidimensional role as (1) the foundation of the creator Prajāpati and his creation, (2) the constitutive elements of the body and self of the creator, (3) the primordial impulses of the creator's speech from which the three worlds and their manifold forms are structured, and (4) the oral texts recited by Brahmin priests as part of the sacrificial order. The sacrificial order is represented in the Brāhmaṇas as subsuming all of these levels, for the sacrifice is held to be the counterpart of the creator Prajāpati and the means through which, in the beginning, he brings the process of creation to fruition. The creator Prajāpati is portrayed as bringing forth the sacrifice and assuming the functions of the various priests, reciting the *ṛcs*, chanting the *sāmans*, and performing the sacrificial actions with the aid of the *yajuses*. The Brahmin priests are represented in this context as the earthly counterparts of Prajāpati, who reproduce the cosmogonic activities of the creator every time they perform the sacrificial rituals.[107] Just as Prajāpati set the universe in motion by means of a particular sacrifice, so those who perform the sacrifice set the universe in motion.[108] Just as Prajāpati brought forth all beings by means of the sacrifice,[109] so those who reenact the primordial sacrifices are ascribed the power to produce beings: "Prajāpati indeed is that sacrifice which is being performed here and from which these beings were produced, and in the same manner are they produced thereafter even to the present day."[110]

The creative power of the sacrifice is linked not only to the priests' performance of the sacrificial actions, but also to their recitation of the Vedic mantras. For example, *Jaiminīya Brāhmaṇa* 1.94, discussed above, which depicts Prajāpati as bringing forth the gods, human beings, ancestors, and other beings through chanting the words of a particular *sāman*, concludes, "Having become Prajāpati, he who, knowing thus, chants with this opening produces beings."[111] Moreover, just as Prajāpati used particular Vedic mantras or sacrifices not only to bring forth creation, but also to establish an orderly cosmos through subduing his unruly creatures, providing them with rain and food, and so on, so "he who knows thus" and replicates the activities of Prajāpati is correspondingly ascribed the power to obtain comparable ends.[112]

The Brāhmaṇas thus present a variety of cosmogonic paradigms for delimiting the Vedic canon and investing it with transcendent authority. The creator himself is represented as circumscribing the potentially limitless domain of Vāc through his own speech-acts, in which he uses certain discrete utterances to manifest the phenomenal creation. These primordial utterances—in particular the three *vyāhṛtis* and their more elaborated expression in the *Ṛg-Veda, Yajur-Veda,* and *Sāma-Veda*—are represented as the sound correlatives of the realm of form, reflecting the structures of the human, natural, and divine orders. It is this circumscribed set of utterances that is granted the status of the blueprint of creation, and thus the Vedic canon would appear to be closed. The primordial mantras that constitute this blueprint are fixed and are to be preserved with scrupulous precision by the earthly counterparts of Prajāpati, the Brahmin priests. At the same time the Brāhmaṇas provide a strategy for extending the purview of Veda beyond this bounded domain. For while the primordial Word might have found its quintessential expression in the *ṛcs*, *yajus*es, and *sāmans*, it is not considered to be limited to that expression. Beyond its bounded, differentiated manifestation as the Vedic mantras, the Veda is celebrated as the unbounded, undifferentiated Word. While the domain of the threefold Veda is closed, the domain of the infinite Veda remains open. The mechanisms are thus established whereby later Brahmanical texts may claim a place within the limitless purview of Veda by assimilating themselves to the core texts that retain their authoritative status at the center: the Vedic mantras.

ABBREVIATIONS

AB	*Aitareya Brāhmaṇa*
ArthaS	*Artha-Śāstra*
BAU	*Bṛhadāraṇyaka Upaniṣad*
BP	*Bhāgavata Purāṇa*
CU	*Chāndogya Upaniṣad*
JB	*Jaiminīya Brāhmaṇa*
JUB	*Jaiminīya Upaniṣad Brāhmaṇa*
KB	*Kauṣītaki Brāhmaṇa*
KU	*Kauṣītaki Upaniṣad*
Maitri	*Maitri Upaniṣad*
Mbh	*Mahābhārata*
PB	*Pañcaviṃśa Brāhmaṇa*
Ram	*Rāmāyaṇa*
RV	*Ṛg-Veda Saṃhitā*
SadvB	*Ṣaḍviṃśa Brāhmaṇa*
SB	*Śatapatha Brāhmaṇa*
Skanda	*Skanda Purāṇa*
SV	*Sāma-Veda Saṃhitā*
TB	*Taittirīya Brāhmaṇa*
TS	*Taittirīya Saṃhitā*
TU	*Taittirīya Upaniṣad*

NOTES

1. Smith, "Sacred Persistence," 52.
2. Ibid., 48.
3. See Carpenter, "Mastery of Speech," in this volume.
4. Even though the term "blueprint" is obviously a modern designation for which no literal equivalent can be found in Sanskrit, I have nevertheless chosen to use the term at times when discussing images

of the Veda as the plan of creation in order to connote the plan's association with the architect of creation.

5. As will be discussed below, the earliest references to the Veda(s) in Vedic texts generally focus on the triad *ṛcs*, *yajus*es, and *sāman*s, which are designated as the "threefold knowledge" (*trayī vidyā*) or "threefold Veda" (*traya veda*). The Vedic corpus was subsequently expanded to incorporate the *atharvāṅgiras*es or *atharvan*s as part of the "four Vedas" (*catur veda*). See n.24.

6. Many of the later Upaniṣads are highly sectarian, and thus this phenomenon represents one of the strategies used by sectarian movements to legitimate their own texts through granting them the nominal status of *śruti*.

7. See Coburn, "'Scripture' in India," for an illuminating discussion of the relationship between *śruti* and *smṛti* in Hindu conceptions of scripture.

8. See, for example, Renou and Filliozat, *L'Inde classique,* vol. 1, 381, 270; Radhakrishnan and Moore, eds., *Source Book in Indian Philosophy,* xix; Dandekar, "Dharma, The First End of Man," 217; Gonda, *Die Religionen Indiens,* vol. 1, 107; Basham, *Wonder That Was India,* 112–13; Botto, "Letterature antiche dell'India," 294. For a discussion and critique of such characterizations of *śruti* and *smṛti* as a distinction between "revelation" and "tradition," see Pollock, "'Tradition' as 'Revelation.'" Pollock's views will be discussed below.

9. In opposition to the view of the Mīmāṃsakas and Vedāntins that the Vedas are eternal and *apauruṣeya,* the exponents of the Nyāya, Vaiśeṣika, and Yoga schools use a variety of arguments to establish that the Vedas are noneternal (*anitya*) and *pauruṣeya,* created by the personal agency of Īśvara.

10. See Mbh 1.57.74; Mbh 12.327.18; Ram 1.1.77; BP 1.4.20; BP 3.12.39; Skanda 5.3.1.18; ArthaS 1.3.1–2. The *Bhāgavata Purāṇa* (1.4.20), for example, declares that "the four Vedas, termed *Ṛg, Yajur, Sāma,* and *Atharva,* were separated out [from the one Veda], and the Itihāsa-Purāṇa is called the fifth Veda (*pañcamo veda*)." As early as the Upaniṣads we find the notion that the Itihāsa and Purāṇa are "the fifth" among sacred Brahmanical texts and sciences, although they are not explicitly referred to as the "fifth Veda." See CU 7.1.2,4; CU 7.2.1; CU 7.7.1, which enumerate "the *Ṛg-Veda,* the *Yajur-Veda,* the *Sāma-Veda,* the *Atharvaṇa* as the fourth (*caturtha*), Itihāsa-Purāṇa as the fifth (*pañcama*)."

11. See Pollock, "'Tradition' as 'Revelation'"; idem, "From Discourse of Ritual to Discourse of Power in Sanskrit Culture," 322–28.

12. See, for example, RV 8.59.6.

13. Among contemporary Hindus this position is articulated, for example, by the philosopher-yogi Śrī Aurobindo Ghose (1872–1950) in

his *On the Veda,* 11: "The Rishi was not the individual composer of the hymn, but the seer (*draṣṭā*) of an eternal truth and an impersonal knowledge. The language of Veda itself is *śruti,* a rhythm not composed by the intellect but heard, a divine Word that came vibrating out of the Infinite to the inner audience of the man who had previously made himself fit for the impersonal knowledge."

14. For a detailed analysis of the cosmogonic and epistemological paradigms associated with the Veda in the mythological speculations of Vedic and post-Vedic texts, see Holdrege, *Veda and Torah,* chaps. 1 and 3.

15. A number of these modes of assimilation are discussed by Pollock in "From Discourse of Ritual to Discourse of Power in Sanskrit Culture," 332.

16. See Smith, *Reflections on Resemblance, Ritual, and Religion,* 3–29, esp. 20–29. Smith goes so far as to claim that "the Veda functions as a touchstone for Hindu orthodoxy" and that Vedic authority is constitutive of "Hinduism" itself, including not only the Brahmanical tradition but also devotional sects and Tantric movements: "Hinduism is the religion of those humans who create, perpetuate, and transform traditions with legitimizing reference to the authority of the Veda" (ibid., 26, 13–14). Jan Gonda similarly defines Hinduism as "a complex of social-religious phenomena, which are based on that authority of the ancient corpora, called Veda" (*Change and Continuity in Indian Religion,* 7). For statements by other Indologists concerning the authority of the Veda as the decisive criterion of Hindu orthodoxy, see Smith, *Reflections on Resemblance, Ritual, and Religion,* 18, n. 45.

17. The paradigmatic function of the Veda is evidenced in the way in which certain devotional sects have sought to imitate the Veda by elevating their own vernacular texts to a quasi-*śruti* status. For example, the Tamil hymns of the *Tiruvāymoḷi* by the poet Nammāḷvār (ca. ninth century C.E.), a low caste exponent of the Vaiṣṇava Āḷvārs, are said to represent the four Vedic Saṃhitās and are designated as the "Dravidian Veda" or "Tamil Veda." See Reddiar, "Nālāyiram as Drāvida Veda." The *Rāmcaritmānas* of the poet Tulsīdās (ca. sixteenth century C.E.), a Hindi version of the *Rāmāyaṇa* popular throughout North India, has been granted a similar status as the "fifth Veda" or "Hindi Veda" that is said to represent the concentrated essence of all the Hindu scriptures. For a discussion of the "vedacization" of the *Rāmcaritmānas*, and of *Mānas* recitation rituals in particular, see Lutgendorf, "Power of Sacred Story." See also Lutgendorf's *Life of a Text.*

While some devotional sects have thus sought to legitimate their texts through assimilating them to the Veda, certain *bhakti* and Tantric movements have responded to the Veda by rejecting or subverting its authority. For example, the *vacana* poets of the Vīraśaiva sect, which originated in the Kannada-speaking region of South India in the tenth century C.E., were leaders of a protest movement that rejected the Vedic texts and rituals because of their association with the caste system and other Brahmanical institutions. See Ramanujan, trans., *Speaking of Śiva,* 19–55. Certain left-handed Tantric sects such as the Kashmir Śaivas have not only rejected Vedic authority, but they have treated the Veda as a symbol to be subverted by actively adhering to teachings and practices that directly transgress orthodox Brahmanical traditions. Abhinavagupta (tenth century C.E.), the most famous exponent of Kashmir Śaivism, asserts: "The wise *sādhaka* [Tantric practitioner] must not choose the word of the Veda as the ultimate authority because it is full of impurities and produces meager, unstable, and limited results. Rather, the *sādhaka* should elect the Śaivite scriptures as his source. Moreover, that which according to the Veda produces sin leads, according to the left-handed doctrine, promptly to perfection. The entire Vedic teaching is in fact tightly held in the grip of *māyā* (delusional power)." *Tantrāloka* 37.10–12; cf. 15.595–99. Cited in Muller-Ortega, "Power of the Secret Ritual," 49.

18. Heesterman, "Veda and Dharma," 92–93.

19. See, for example, Brian K. Smith's remark:

> The great paradox of Hinduism . . . is that although the religion is inextricably tied to the legitimizing authority of the Veda, in post-Vedic times the subject matter of the Veda was and is largely unknown by those who define themselves in relation to it. Its contents (almost entirely concerning the meaning and performance of sacrificial rituals that Hindus do not perform) are at best reworked (being, for example, reconstituted into ritual formulas or mantras for use in Hindu ceremonies), and [in] many cases appear to be totally irrelevant for Hindu doctrine and practice. (*Reflections on Resemblance, Ritual, and Religion,* 20)

Paul Younger has similarly noted that "in spite of the acknowledgment of its authority, the content of the *Veda* does not seem to be used very directly in guiding the later development of the Religious Tradition" (*Introduction to Indian Religious Thought*, 71).

20. Renou, *Destiny of the Veda in India*, 2, 1. Renou's study provides a useful survey of the different attitudes, beliefs, and practices that the major texts, philosophical schools, and sects of the Indian tradition have adopted with respect to the Veda in the course of its history. J. L. Mehta has challenged some of Renou's perspectives on the "destiny of the Veda" and suggests that the Veda may possess an inherent potency, or *svadhā*, which has enabled it to create its own destiny in spite of the perils of history. See Mehta, "Hindu Tradition." See also Wilhelm Halbfass's

discussion of the role and "destiny" of the Veda in traditional Hindu self-understanding in his *Tradition and Reflection*, esp. 1–22.

21. Pollock, "From Discourse of Ritual to Discourse of Power in Sanskrit Culture," 332. See also Robert Lingat's suggestion that "in reality, it seems that when a Hindu affirms that *dharma* rests entirely upon the Veda, the word Veda does not mean in that connection the Vedic texts, but rather the totality of Knowledge, the sum of all understanding, of all religious and moral truths" (*Classical Law of India,* 8).

22. While Brian K. Smith, as discussed in n. 16, views the authority of the Veda as pivotal to his definition of Hinduism, he declines from including "the orthodox claim that the Veda is a body of transcendent and super- or extra-human knowledge" as part of his definition, for "from the standpoint of the academic and humanistic study of religion, the Veda, like all other canonical literatures, was entirely composed [by] human beings" (*Reflections on Resemblance, Ritual, and Religion*, 19). I would of course agree with Smith that as scholars of religion we are not ourselves in a position to adopt the traditional Brahmanical view of the Veda as transcendent knowledge. I would nevertheless argue that the authority that the Veda holds in the Brahmanical tradition—if not in all Hindu traditions—is directly predicated on its status as transcendent knowledge. If the Veda were stripped of that status, it would thereby lose its legitimating function as a *transcendent* source of authority.

23. J. Frits Staal's studies of Vedic recitation and ritual have provided important insights into the oral-aural character of the Vedas, in which priority is given to phonology and syntax over semantics. See particularly his *Nambudiri Veda Recitation* and "The Concept of Scripture in the Indian Tradition." For a more recent formulation of Staal's theories, see his *Rules Without Meaning*, esp. 191–311.

24. This prevalent emphasis in the Vedic texts on the threefold Veda, *Ṛg-Veda, Yajur-Veda,* and *Sāma-Veda*, suggests that it took some time before the *Atharva-Veda* was accorded an equivalent status as the fourth Veda. The *atharvāṅgiras*es or *atharvan*s are rarely mentioned along with the other three mantra collections. See, for example, TB 3.12.9.1; SB 11.5.6.4–7; CU 3.1–4; TU 2.3. Even when the formal designations *Ṛg-Veda, Yajur-Veda,* and *Sāma-Veda* are used for the other three Vedas, the expressions *atharvāṅgiras*es or *atharvan*s are used to refer to "the fourth" of the Vedas. See CU 7.1.2,4; CU 7.2.1; CU 7.7.1, which list "the *Ṛg-Veda*, the *Yajur-Veda*, the *Sāma-Veda*, the *Atharvaṇa* as the fourth." Cf. BAU 2.4.10; BAU 4.5.11; BAU 4.1.2; Maitri 6.32. The term *Atharva-Veda* does not occur until the Sūtra period.

25. See, for example, AB 5.32–33; KB 6.10–12; TB 3.10.11.5–6; SB 1.1.4.2–3; SB 4.6.7.1; SB 6.1.1.8,10; SB 6.3.1.20; SB 7.5.2.52; SB 10.4.2.21–22,27,30; SB 10.5.2.1–2; SB 11.5.4.18; SB 11.5.8.4,7; JB 1.357–58; JUB 1.18.10; JUB 1.23.5–6; JUB 1.45.3; JUB 1.58.2; JUB 3.15.9; JUB 3.19.4–6; KU 2.6.

26. The expression *traya veda* appears less frequently than *trayī vidyā*. See, for example, SB 5.5.5.9–10,12, where the designation *traya veda*, "threefold Veda," is juxtaposed with the expression *trayī vidyā*, "threefold knowledge." Cf. AB 5.32; TB 2.3.10.1; SB 11.5.8.3–4; JB 1.358; JUB 1.1.1–2; JUB 1.8.1,3–4,10; JUB 3.19.2.

27. While the following discussion will focus primarily on the Brāhmaṇas, occasional reference will also be made to Āraṇyakas such as the *Jaiminīya Upaniṣad Brāhmaṇa* that expand upon the speculations of the Brāhmaṇas.

28. With respect to the representation of the sacrifice as the counterpart of Prajāpati, see, for example, SB 11.1.8.3: "Having given his self (*ātman*) to the gods, he [Prajāpati] then brought forth that counterpart (*pratimā*) of himself which is the sacrifice (*yajña*). Therefore they say, 'The sacrifice is Prajāpati,' for he brought it forth as a counterpart of himself." For other references in which Prajāpati is identified with the sacrifice, see AB 2.17; AB 6.19; KB 13.1; KB 26.3; TB 3.2.3.1; TB 3.7.2.1; SB 4.2.4.16; SB 4.5.5.1; SB 4.5.6.1; SB 4.5.7.1; SB 5.1.4.1; SB 1.1.1.13; SB 1.2.5.12; SB 1.7.4.4; SB 2.2.2.4; SB 3.2.2.4; SB 5.2.1.2; SB 5.2.1.4; SB 5.4.5.20–21; SB 6.4.1.6; SB 11.1.1.1; SB 14.1.2.18; SB 14.2.2.21; SB 14.3.2.15; PB 7.2.1; PB 13.11.18; JB 1.135. As Brian K. Smith has emphasized, the initial generative act of Prajāpati, as described in the creation accounts of the Brāhmaṇas, generally results in a chaotic creation rather than an ordered cosmos. It is only by creating the counterpart of himself, the sacrifice, that Prajāpati obtained the "instrument of cosmic healing and construction" that was necessary in order to structure an ordered cosmos as well as to revitalize his own disintegrated being. See Smith, *Reflections on Resemblance, Ritual, and Religion*, 50–81, esp. 67.

The sacrifice is at times described not only as the instrument of reparation but also as the instrument of creation by means of which Prajāpati sets in motion the entire universe and brings forth all beings. See PB 25.6.2; PB 25.17.2; AB 4.23; KB 6.15; KV 5.3; SB 2.5.1.17; SB 2.5.2.1; SB 2.5.2.7; SB 2.6.3.4; PB 6.1.1–2; PB 8.5.6; PB 4.1.4; PB 22.9.2; JB 1.67. Thus, every time human beings reenact the primeval sacrifice on earth, they participate in the creative process of constructing an orderly cosmos. See below, 52.

29. See, for example, TB 3.10.11.3–6. A similar conception is found in the *Taittirīya Saṃhitā* (7.3.1.4): "The *ṛc*s are limited, the *sāman*s are limited, and the *yajus*es are limited, but of the Word (*brahman*) there is no end."

30. SB 6.5.3.7; SB 7.2.4.30; SB 14.1.2.18; SB 1.1.1.13; SB 1.6.1.20; SB 6.4.1.6; SB 12.4.2.1; SB 14.2.2.21; SB 14.3.2.15; KB 23.2; KB 23.6; KB 29.7; PB 7.8.3; PB 18.6.8.

31. SB 6.5.3.7; SB 7.2.4.30; SB 14.1.2.18; AB 2.17; KB 11.7; JUB 1.46.2.

32. For references, see n. 65.

33. See Carpenter, "Mastery of Speech."

34. For the identification of the Veda with *brahman*, see in particular SB 6.1.1.8,10, which will be discussed below. See also JUB 4.25.3; SB 10.2.4.6.

35. JUB 1.46.1.

36. See, for example, SB 10.4.2.26; SB 10.3.1.1; SB 6.2.1.30; AB 2.18; PB 13.11.18; TB 3.3.9.11; cf. SB 12.1.4.1–3; SB 12.6.1.1; KB 6.15. For the identification of the threefold Veda with Prajāpati's counterpart, the sacrifice, see SB 1.1.4.3; SB 5.5.5.10; SB 3.1.1.12; JB 1.358.

37. TB 3.3.2.1; TB 3.3.8.9.

38. See, for example, AB 5.32; KB 6.10; TB 2.3.10.1; SB 6.1.1.8–10; SB 10.6.5.5 [= BAU 1.2.5]; SB 11.5.8.1–3; JB 1.68–69; JB 1.357; PB 7.8.8–13; SadvB 1.5.7; JUB 3.15.4–7; JUB 1.23.1–5.

39. JB 1.68–69; cf. PB 6.1.6–11. These passages build on earlier conceptions found in the Saṃhitās, in particular RV 10.90, the *Puruṣa-Sūkta*, and TS 7.1.1.4–6.

40. Relevant passages will be discussed below.

41. See, for example, SB 2.1.4.10; AB 2.15; AB 2.17; JB 1.82; JB 1.102; JB 1.115; JB 1.140; JB 1.178; JUB 2.9.6; JUB 2.13.2; JUB 3.39.2.

42. SB 6.5.3.4; SB 10.5.1.2,5; cf. AB 5.33; PB 10.4.6,9.

43. See, for example, TB 2.8.8.5. Cf. PB 7.8.8–13, in which Prajāpati creates the *pṛṣṭha sāmans* out of the womb (*yoni*) of the *gāyatrī* meter. In post-Vedic texts Gāyatrī is hypostatized as a feminine principle who is identified with Vāc and is the consort of the creator. Like Vāc, Gāyatrī is called in post-Vedic texts the "Mother of the Vedas."

44. See, for example, SB 5.5.5.12; SB 4.6.7.1–3; cf. SB 4.5.8.4.

45. TB 2.8.8.5.

46. See, for example, TB 3.10.11.4.

47. See, for example, SB 10.4.2.21.

48. SB 12.3.4.11.

49. For a discussion of the relationship between Prajāpati and *manas*, see Gonda, "Creator and His Spirit (Manas and Prajāpati)."

50. See, for example, KB 26.3; TB 2.2.6.2; TB 3.7.1.2; JB 1.68; JB 2.174; JB 2.195; JUB 1.33.2.

51. See, for example, JB 1.314.

52. See, for example, SB 6.1.2.6–9; SB 10.6.5.4; cf. SB 6.3.1.12.

53. SB 1.4.4.1–7. See also JUB 4.27.15–16, where mind and speech are referred to as a "couple" (*mithuna*).

54. See, for example, SB 7.5.1.31; SB.11.2.4.9; SB 11.2.6.3. For the identification of Sarasvatī with Vāc, see also AB 2.24; AB 3.1; AB 3.37;

AB 6.7; KB 5.2; KB 10.6; KB 12.8; KB 14.4; SB 2.5.4.6; SB 3.1.4.9; SB 3.9.1.9; SB 5.2.2.13–14; SB 5.3.4.25; SB 5.3.5.8; SB 5.4.5.7; SB 13.1.8.5; SB 14.2.1.12; SB 14.2.1.15; PB 6.7.7; PB 16.5.16; JB 1.82.

55. See, for example, SB 1.4.5.9,11; SB 3.2.4.11; SB 12.9.1.13; AB 2.5; JB 1.19; JB 1.320; JUB 1.58.3–4; JUB 1.40.5.

56. See, for example, SB 1.4.5.10; SB 4.6.7.5; SB 12.9.1.13; JUB 1.58.3–4; JUB 1.40.5.

57. SB 1.4.4.5–7; cf. KB 26.3; JUB 1.47.5. While in relationship to the mind the expressed dimension of speech is emphasized, in other passages, as will be discussed below, speech is also represented as having an unexpressed dimension.

58. See, for example, SB 1.4.5.8–11; SB 3.2.4.11; AB 2.5; JB 1.19; JB 1.128; JB 1.320; JB 1.323; JB 1.329; JUB 1.59.14.

59. See, for example, SB 3.1.3.22; SB 5.1.1.16.

60. See, for example, PB 20.14.2; JB 2.244; SB 6.1.1.8–10; SB 6.1.2.6–9; SB 7.5.2.21; SB 10.6.5.4–5 [= BAU 1.2.4–5]. Cf. SB 10.5.3.1–4, which describes the mind, which was neither existent (*sat*) nor nonexistent (*asat*), as existing alone in the beginning and desiring to become manifest, after which it produced speech.

61. PB 7.6.1–3.

62. See, for example, PB 7.6.17; JB 1.128; JB 1.329; AB 4.28.

63. See, for example, JB 1.128; JB 1.133.

64. See, for example, JB 1.326; JUB 1.53–54; JUB 1.56–57; AB 3.23; SB 8.1.3.5. The correlation of the three Vedas with various human faculties will be discussed further below.

65. See, for example, JB 1.102; JB 1.260; SadvB 2.1.26, which distinguish between the expressed (*nirukta*) and unexpressed (*anirukta*) aspects of speech. See also SB 4.1.3.16–17, which, citing RV 1.164.45, refers to the four quarters of Vāc, three of which are hidden while the fourth is expressed through the speech of human beings. Cf. JUB 1.7.3–5.

66. For the association of Vāc with the waters, see in particular PB 20.14.2; JB 2.244; SB 6.1.1.9, discussed below. Cf. SB 6.3.1.9; PB 7.7.9; PB 6.4.7; JB 1.70.

67. This two-stage process of creation conforms in its essential features to the two stages delineated by F. B. J. Kuiper in his reconstruction of the Vedic cosmogonic myth. (1) In the first stage the primordial world is "an undivided unity, a *rudis indigestaque moles*," which consists of the primordial waters and the undifferentiated totality of the cosmos—frequently represented by the image of the cosmic egg—floating on the surface of the waters. (2) In the second stage heaven and earth are separated out of the originally undifferentiated unity, either through an autonomous process of division or through the demiurgic act of a god. See Kuiper, "Cosmogony and Conception."

68. BAU 1.2.4–5.

69. The creator is designated in this passage as death, which is identified with Prajāpati elsewhere in the *Śatapatha Brāhmaṇa*. See, for example, SB 10.4.3.1–3.

70. AB 1.1; AB 1.13; AB 2.17; AB 4.22; AB 4.25; AB 6.19; KB 6.15; SB 1.2.5.12; SB 1.6.3.35; SB 2.2.2.4; SB 2.3.3.18; SB 3.2.2.4; SB 5.1.3.2; SB 5.2.1.2; SB 5.2.1.4; SB 5.4.5.20–21; SB 6.1.2.18; SB 6.2.2.12; SB 7.4.2.31; SB 8.4.3.20; SB 10.4.2.1–2; SB 10.4.3.3; SB 11.1.1.1; SB 11.1.6.13; PB 16.4.12–13; JB 1.135; JB 1.167. For a discussion of the significance of the identification of Prajāpati with the year, see Gonda, *Prajāpati and the Year.*

71. Cf. SB 2.1.4.11–13.

72. Relevant passages will be discussed below.

73. PB 20.14.2. This passage appears almost verbatim in JB 2.244.

74. PB 20.14.3.

75. PB 20.14.5; cf. JB 2.244.

76. It is not entirely clear how the verb, root *mṛś* + *abhi,* "to touch, come in contact with," is to be understood in this context.

77. Fragments of this creation account are repeated in SB 6.3.1.9–10, which mentions how after the waters (*ap*) went forth from Vāc, Prajāpati entered the waters with the threefold Veda (*trayī vidyā*).

78. See, however, PB 20.14.2 and JB 2.244, discussed above, in which Prajāpati brings forth the three worlds through the sounds *a, ka,* and *ho.*

79. SB 2.1.4.11–13. Cf. JB 1.101, which mentions only the creation of the earth from the utterance *bhūḥ.*

80. See, for example, AB 2.16; PB 7.5.1; JB 1.116; JB 1.117; JB 1.128; JB 1.148; JB 1.160.

81. See, for example, AB 4.23; KB 5.3; KB 12.8; PB 4.1.4; PB 6.1.1; PB 6.3.9; PB 18.7.1.

82. See, for example, AB 5.32; KB 6.10.

83. See, for example, AB 2.15; AB 2.16; AB 2.33.

84. *Nivid* is the technical term used to designate eleven prose formularies, derived from the period of the *Ṛg-Veda*, that are composed of a series of short sentences addressed to a particular deity or group of deities. A *nivid* generally begins with an invitation to the deity to partake of the Soma libation, followed by various epithets and short invocations and concluding with a prayer for help.

85. For references identifying or relating Prajāpati and the *udgātṛ* priest, see PB 6.4.1; PB 6.5.18; PB 7.10.16; JB 1.70; JB 1.85; JB 1.88; JB 1.259; cf. SB 4.3.2.3.

86. PB 6.9.15; cf. JB 1.94. The verse cited from the *Ṛg-Veda* (9.62.1) reads,

ete asṛgram indavas tiraḥ pavitram āśavaḥ |
viśvāny abhi saubhagā ||
"These swift Soma drops have been poured out through the filter for the sake of all blessings."

87. Cf. JB 1.117.

88. The *bahiṣpavamāna stotra* is the first *stotra* chanted at the morning pressing of the *agniṣṭoma* sacrifice. The *stotra* is composed of nine verses from the *Ṛg-Veda*: RV 9.11.1–3; RV 9.64.28–30; and RV 9.66.10–12. JB 1.104 cites sections of RV 9.66.10–11 as the words with which Prajāpati creates beings. Cf. JB 1.99.

89. See n. 28.

90. See, for example, PB 7.10.13,15; PB 7.5.1–2; PB 13.5.13; JB 1.148; JB 1.160; JB 1.116; JB 1.117–18; cf. PB 11.5.10.

91. See Smith, "The Veda and the Authority of Class," in the present volume.

92. See, for example, SB 8.7.4.5.

93. The three *vyāhṛti*s are at times directly identified with the three Vedas. See, for example, JUB 2.9.7; JUB 3.18.4. However, they are more often described as their essences. See AB 5.32; KB 6.10–11; SB 11.5.8.1–4; SadvB 1.5.7–10; JB 1.357–58; JB 1.363–64; JUB 1.1.2–5; JUB 1.23.6; JUB 3.15.8–9.

94. See, for example, SB 11.1.6.3; SB 2.1.4.11–13, discussed earlier. See also JUB 1.1.3–5, cited below, and SadvB 1.5.7.

95. AB 5.32; KB 6.10; SB 11.5.8.1–4; JB 1.357; JUB 1.1.1–7; JUB 3.15.4–9; JUB 1.23.1–8; cf. SB 4.6.7.1–2; SB 12.3.4.7–10; SadvB 1.5.7–10; SadvB 5.1.2; JB 1.363–64.

96. JUB 1.1.1–7; cf. SadvB 1.5.7.

97. SB 11.5.8.1–4. For parallel accounts, see AB 5.32; KB 6.10; JB 1.357; JUB 3.15.4–9; JUB 1.23.1–8. The account in JUB 1.23.1–8 begins with Prajāpati pressing Vāc, the essence of which becomes the worlds, from which Agni, Vāyu, and Āditya are brought forth, and so on. The rest of the passage follows the standard sequence.

98. AB 5.32. JUB 1.23.1–8 similarly concludes with the syllable Om emerging as the essence of the three *vyāhṛti*s.

99. JB 1.322; JB 1.336; JUB 1.18.10; JUB 1.8.1–13; JUB 3.19.2–7; JUB 1.1.6; cf. KB 6.12. However, see JUB 1.23.8–1.24.1–2, in which Prajāpati succeeds in pressing the syllable Om, and its essence (*rasa*) flows forth (root *kṣar*) and is not exhausted (root *kṣi*). Hence Om is called *akṣara* and *akṣaya*.

100. JB 1.323; JUB 1.10.11. In post-Vedic cosmogonies Om constitutes the primal sound from which the three sounds *a, u, m,* the three *vyāhṛti*s, the three Vedas, and the three worlds progressively unfold.

101. AB 5.32–34; KB 6.10–12; JB 1.357–58; SB 11.5.8.1–7; cf. SadvB 1.5.7–10; SadvB 5.1.2; JUB 3.15–17.

102. See, for example, SB 12.3.4.7–10; cf. JB 1.249. These correlations build upon those established earlier in the *Puruṣa-Sūkta*. See RV 10.90.13.

103. See, for example, JB 1.326; JUB 1.53.2; JUB 1.9.2; JUB 3.34.1; JUB 1.25.8–10; JUB 1.57.7–8. The *sāman* and the *yajus* are thus associated with both mind and breath, which are intimately related in the speculations of the Brāhmaṇas. See, for example, SB 7.5.2.6, which describes the mind as the first of the *prāṇa*s and identical with all the *prāṇa*s.

104. SB 10.4.2.21–22. Cf. JB 1.332, in which the Vedic meters are identified with "all *stoma*s, all animals, all gods, all worlds, all desires."

105. SB 10.4.2.27.

106. SB 4.6.7.1–2; cf. SadvB 1.5.7–10; SadvB 5.1.2.

107. As mentioned above, the *Aitareya Brāhmaṇa* identifies Prajāpati with the *hotṛ* priest, while the *Pañcaviṃśa* and *Jaiminīya Brāhmaṇa*s associate the creator with the *udgātṛ*. See, for exampie, AB 2.15; AB 2.16; PB 6.4.1; PB 6.5.18; PB 7.10.16; JB 1.70; JB 1.85; JB 1.88; JB 1.259; cf. SB 4.3.2.3.

108. PB 25.6.2; PB 25.17.2.

109. See, for example, AB 4.23; KB 6.15; KB 5.3; SB 2.5.1.17; SB 2.5.2.1; SB 2.5.2.7; SB 2.6.3.4; PB 6.1.1–2; PB 8.5.6; PB 4.1.4; PB 22.9.2; JB 1.67.

110. This formula is frequently repeated in the *Śatapatha Brāhmaṇa*. See, for example, SB 4.2.4.16; SB 4.5.5.1; SB 4.5.6.1; SB 4.5.7.1. Cf. AB 2.33; AB 4.23.

111. Cf. JB 1.99; JB 1.104; PB 7.5.1,4.

112. With respect to the recitation of certain *ṛc*s or *sāman*s for specific purposes, see, for example, PB 7.10.13–17; PB 7.5.1–3; PB 13.5.13; JB 1.148; JB 1.160; JB 1.116; JB 1.117–18. With respect to the performance of certain sacrifices to obtain particular ends, see KB 5.3; KB 12.8; PB 4.1.4–5; PB 6.1.1–3; PB 6.3.9–10; PB 22.9.2–3.

REFERENCES

Basham, A. L.

1967 *The Wonder That Was India: A Survey of the History and Culture of the Indian Sub-continent before the Coming of the Muslims.* 3d rev. ed. London: Sidgwick and Jackson.

Botto, Oscar

1969 "Letterature antiche dell'India." In *Storia delle Letterature d'Oriente,* ed. Oscar Botto, 3:5–350. Milan: Casa Editrice Dr. Francesco Vallardi, Società Editrice Libraria.

Coburn, Thomas B.

1984 " 'Scripture' in India: Towards a Typology of the Word in Hindu Life." *Journal of the American Academy of Religion* 52:435–59. Reprinted in *Rethinking Scripture: Essays from a Comparative Perspective,* ed. Miriam Levering, 102–28. Albany: State University of New York Press, 1989.

Dandekar, R. N.

1958 "Dharma, The First End of Man." In *Sources of Indian Tradition,* ed. Wm. Theodore de Bary et al., 216–35. New York: Columbia University Press.

Ghose, Aurobindo

1956 *On the Veda.* Pondicherry: Sri Aurobindo Ashram Press.

Gonda, Jan

1960 *Die Religionen Indiens.* Vol. 1, *Veda und älterer Hinduismus.* Stuttgart: W. Kohlhammer.

1965 *Change and Continuity in Indian Religion.* Disputationes Rheno-Trajectinae, vol. 9. The Hague: Mouton.

1983 "The Creator and His Spirit (Manas and Prajāpati)." *Wiener Zeitschrift für die Kunde Südasiens* 27:5–42.

1984 *Prajāpati and the Year.* Amsterdam: North Holland.

Halbfass, Wilhelm

1991 *Tradition and Reflection: Explorations in Indian Thought.* Albany: State University of New York Press.

Heesterman, J. C.

1978 "Veda and Dharma." In *The Concept of Duty in South Asia,* ed. Wendy Doniger O'Flaherty and J. Duncan M. Derrett, 80–95. New Delhi: Vikas.

Holdrege, Barbara A.

1994 *Veda and Torah: Transcending the Textuality of Scripture.* Albany: State University of New York Press.

Kuiper, F. B. J.

1970 "Cosmogony and Conception: A Query." *History of Religions* 10(2): 91–138. Reprinted in F. B. J. Kuiper, *Ancient Indian Cosmogony,* ed. John Irwin, 90–137. New Delhi: Vikas, 1983.

Lingat, Robert

1973 *The Classical Law of India.* Trans. J. Duncan M. Derrett. Berkeley: University of California Press.

Lutgendorf, Philip

1990 "The Power of Sacred Story: *Rāmāyaṇa* Recitation in Contemporary North India." In *Ritual and Power*, ed. Barbara A. Holdrege, *Journal of Ritual Studies* 4(2):115–47.

1991 *The Life of a Text: Performing the Rāmcaritmānas of Tulsidas.* Berkeley and Los Angeles: University of California Press.

Mehta, J. L.

1984 "The Hindu Tradition: The Vedic Root." In *The World's Religious Traditions: Current Perspectives in Religious Studies. Essays in Honour of Wilfred Cantwell Smith*, ed. Frank Whaling, 33–54. Edinburgh: T. and T. Clark.

Muller-Ortega, Paul E.

1990 "The Power of the Secret Ritual: Theoretical Formulations from the Tantra." In *Ritual and Power*, ed. Barbara A. Holdrege, *Journal of Ritual Studies* 4(2):41–59.

Pollock, Sheldon

1990 "From Discourse of Ritual to Discourse of Power in Sanskrit Culture." In *Ritual and Power*, ed. Barbara A. Holdrege, *Journal of Ritual Studies* 4(2):315–45.

[forthcoming]
" 'Tradition' as 'Revelation': *Śruti, Smṛti,* and the Sanskrit Discourse of Power." In *Lex et Litterae: Essays on Ancient Indian Law and Literature in Honour of Oscar Botto*, ed. Siegfried Lienhard and Irma Piovano. Turin: CESMEO.

Radhakrishnan, Sarvepalli, and Charles A. Moore, eds.

1957 *A Source Book in Indian Philosophy.* Princeton: Princeton University Press.

Ramanujan, A. K., trans.

1973 *Speaking of Śiva.* Harmondsworth, Middiesex, England: Penguin.

Renou, Louis

1965 *The Destiny of the Veda in India.* Trans. Dev Raj Chanana. Delhi: Motilal Banarsidass.

Renou, Louis, and Jean Filliozat

1947–1949 *L'Inde classique. Manuel des études indiennes.* 2 vols. Paris: Payot.

Smith, Brian K.

1989 *Reflections on Resemblance, Ritual, and Religion.* New York and Oxford: Oxford University Press.

Smith, Jonathan Z.

1982 "Sacred Persistence: Toward a Redescription of Canon." Chapter 3 of his *Imagining Religion: From Babylon to Jonestown*, 36–52. Chicago and London: University of Chicago Press.

Staal, J. Frits

1961 *Nambudiri Veda Recitation*. Disputationes Rheno-Trajectinae, vol. 5. The Hague: Mouton.

1979 "The Concept of Scripture in the Indian Tradition." In *Sikh Studies: Comparative Perspectives on a Changing Tradition,* ed. Mark Juergensmeyer and N. Gerald Barrier, 121–24. Berkeley: Graduate Theological Union.

1989 *Rules Without Meaning: Ritual, Mantras and the Human Sciences.* New York: Peter Lang.

Subbu Reddiar, N.

1977 "The Nālāyiram as Drāvida Veda." Chapter 26 of his *Religion and Philosophy of Nālāyira Divya Prabandham with Special Reference to Nammāḷvār,* 680–93. Tirupati: Sri Venkateswara University.

Younger, Paul

1972 *Introduction to Indian Religious Thought.* Philadelphia: Westminster.

3

The Veda and the Authority of Class

Reduplicating Structures of Veda and *Varṇa* in Ancient Indian Texts

BRIAN K. SMITH

INTRODUCTION

WHILE THERE ARE OBVIOUS and important differences between the way Hindus use the Veda and the way others use "holy books" such as the Bible, the Torah, and the Qur'an, the Veda may nevertheless be regarded as the functional equivalent of the canonical works that form the heart of other religious traditions. Constituting a canon (a finite set of "texts," oral or written, which are regarded as foundational and absolutely authoritative),[1] constructing a mechanism for its transmission, and establishing the means for its infinite interpretability (so that the canon will perpetually be "relevant" as well as authoritative)[2] generate the conditions of possibility for what we call a "religious tradition."[3] The Veda has been so constituted as the canon for those traditions that make up what we might call "orthodox Hinduism," comprised of people holding various beliefs and practices who "create, perpetuate, and transform their traditions with legitimizing reference to the authority of the Veda."[4]

Like other canons, the Veda was deemed canonical retroactively by religious traditions (those we call "Hindu") who defined themselves as "orthodox" through this very act of allegiance to the authority of the Veda. Unlike most other canons in world religions, however, the Veda also represented itself (and was not only represented later) as the summation of all truth, the unassailable wisdom of the ages. The canonical status of the Veda was first established, self-referentially and tautologically, in Vedic texts. The absolute truth and authority of the Hindu canon were posited from its Vedic inception and reasserted in its later reception.

The three Vedas or "triple wisdom"[5] are declared, in the Veda itself, equal to *satya* or "truth" (ŚB 9.5.1.18), or to *vāc*, "speech" or "the word" also in the sense of "truth." *Vāc* is the "mother of the Vedas" (TB 2.8.8.5) and is divided into three forms which are none other than the three Vedas.[6] Alternatively, the Vedas are equated with the *brahman*, the universal principle that is the ground and end of all knowledge.[7] The Vedas, it is said in the Veda, are "endless" like great mountains while human knowledge of them is likened to mere handfuls of dirt (TB 3.10.11.3–5).

The Veda frequently wrote itself into its own accounts of the creation of the world; the canon is not only absolutely authoritative but also primeval. In some texts, it is even claimed that the universe in its totality was originally encapsulated in the three Vedas and was generated out of them.[8] The structure of the cosmos as a whole is thus patterned on the structure of the Veda.[9] Conversely, the very tripartite *form* of the Veda is proof of the eternal verity of its contents since it produces and reproduces the form of world.

The interpretation of the Veda thus begins in the Veda itself, especially in the interpretive portion of the Vedas called the Brāhmaṇas. As Barbara Holdrege has demonstrated elsewhere in this volume, these texts established the authority of the Vedas—as absolutely true and as coeval with or even generative of the creation of the cosmos—even as the Vedas were being composed.

Furthermore, the authors of the Veda, members of the Brahmin class, also appropriated to themselves the absolute authority they had posited for their compositions. The Veda became the sanctifying source of a hierarchical social order in which the Brahmins are placed at the summit. The theoretical basis for the later Indian caste system entails a division into three or four classes or *varṇa*s: Brahmin priests, Kṣatriya rulers and warriors, Vaiśya commoners, and later including Śūdra or servants. As we shall see, this framework for the caste system is laid out in the Veda itself. Caste and Brahmin privilege thus derive at least part of their subsequent endurance and persuasiveness in India from the fact that they have canonical authorization; unlike many other Hindu beliefs and practices that claim Vedic legitimacy, caste and the superiority of the Brahmins actually are ordained in the Veda.

The prestige of the Brahmin class within the social hierarchy was thus underwritten by the Brahmin authors of the canonical Veda. The varṇa scheme, like the Vedas themselves, is traced back in the Vedic texts to the dawn of time: canon and social classification are both part of creation itself according to Vedic cosmogonies. Canon and class are not only primordial; both are also represented in the Veda as structurally reduplicative of a generalized cosmic pattern and are therefore both supposedly part of the "natural order of things." Finally, because both Veda and *varṇa* are predominantly regarded as divisible into three components, canon and class are isomorphic. Thus, in addition to the legitimation the social structure receives by being part of the *content* of the Veda, the *formal authority* of the structure of the canon (which is also the structure of the universe as a whole) is lent to a vision of society also comprised of three principal parts.

The social system presented in the Veda is structurally reduplicative of the tripartite form of the canon, which is in turn itself a mirror image of the structure of the cosmos. Society becomes merely one expression of a universe created in the image of the Veda. Because of the *bandhu*s or connections that govern Vedic philosophy,[10] the two tripartite structures of Vedas and *varṇa*s are regarded as transformations of one another, reduplicative manifestations of the fundamental triadic form.

Although direct equations between the Vedas and *varṇa*s were usually not drawn,[11] the absence of explicit connections equating the three Vedas and the three social classes does not mean that such homologies were not implied or even presupposed. It is, in fact, possible that direct connections between the Vedas and *varṇa*s were not articulated for a reason. As Bruce Lincoln has pointed out in another context, "social stratification can well be—and often is—expressed by implication alone. . . . In ways, that which is unsaid can be far more powerful than that which is openly asserted, for by being left mute it is placed beyond question or debate."[12]

The Vedas and the *varṇa*s share mutual linkages to components of other realms—metaphysical, spatial, temporal, ontological, theological, ritual, anatomical, zoological—which are their analogues. Canonical and sociological classes can thus be interrelated by tracking the connections they have in common, and one can assume that these homologies were so well known to the Brahmin theologians that they, just as we, could easily extrapolate from them to conjoin scripture and society.

In what follows, I will delineate two ways in which Vedas and social classes are implicitly represented in Vedic texts as homological transformations of one another.

First, the three Vedas are often metonymically represented by their essential kernels, the three *vyāhṛti*s or utterances: "The *vyāhṛti*s are *bhūḥ, bhuvaḥ*, and *svaḥ*," one text explains, "and they are the three Vedas. *Bhūḥ* is the *Ṛg-Veda*, *bhuvaḥ* is the *Yajur-Veda*, and the *svaḥ* the *Sāma-Veda*" (AitĀ 1.3.2; cf. TU 1.5.3). Furthermore, the three *vyāhṛti*s are also names for the three worlds of Vedic cosmology, earth (*bhūḥ*), atmosphere (*bhuvaḥ*), and sky (*svaḥ*),[13] and the worlds are regularly associated with the three social classes: earth = Brahmins, atmosphere = Kṣatriyas, and sky = Vaiśyas. If the Vedas = the three worlds, and the social classes = the three worlds, then the Vedas = the social classes.

The second mode of indirectly equating Vedas and society centers around the various meters (*chandas*es) in which the Veda was composed. Particular meters are, *inter alia*, explicitly connected to particular social classes, the "elemental powers" that are the essences of each *varṇa* (i.e., the *brahman, kṣatra*, and *viś*), and certain distinctive metaphysical qualities (e.g., *tejas* or "fiery luster" for the Brahmin meter, "power" or *indriya* for the meter of the Kṣatriya class, and a certain animal nature characteristic of Vaiśyas). Furthermore, the meters are connected to components of various realms that are also direct analogues of the Vedas (e.g., the three worlds). We are therefore again led to logical, although unstated, equations of the social classes and the Vedas: if the meters = the *varṇa*s = the worlds = the Vedas, then the *varṇa*s = the Vedas.

THE CREATION OF THE VEDAS AND THE UNIVERSE

We may begin to fill out this algebraic skeleton of one corner of Vedic homological thought by turning to some myths of orgins.[14] The following cosmogonic tale has many repetitions and variants in Vedic texts:

> In the beginning, Prajāpati was the only one here. He desired, 'May I be, may I reproduce.' He toiled. He heated up ascetic heat. From him, from that one who had toiled and heated up, the three worlds—earth, atmosphere, and sky—were emitted. He heated up these three worlds. From those heated [worlds], three lights (*jyoti*s) were born: Agni the fire, he who purifies here [Vāyu the wind], and Sūrya the sun. He heated up these three lights. From those heated [lights], three Vedas were born: from Agni, the *Ṛg-Veda*; from Vāyu the *Yajur-Veda*; and from Sūrya, the *Sāma-Veda*. He heated up those three Vedas. From those heated [Vedas], three essences (*śukra*s) were born: *bhūḥ* from the *Ṛg-Veda*, *bhuvaḥ* from the *Yajur-Veda*, and *svaḥ* from the *Sāma-Veda*. (ŚB 11.5.8.1–3)[15]

Four different orders of things and beings, each order divided into three parts, are here depicted as coeval: the three cosmological worlds of earth, atmosphere, and sky (the spatial order); three natural elements or "lights" (fire, wind, and sun), which are identical to three deities (Agni, Vāyu, and Sūrya/Āditya);[16] the three Vedas; and the three verbal essences of the Vedas (*bhūḥ, bhuvaḥ,* and *svaḥ*). The Vedas and their verbal essences are thus situated within a primordial nexus of connections to other cosmological, natural, and superhuman realms. The three chains of associations[17] that co-order the cosmological worlds, natural elements/gods, scriptures, and sacred utterances are thus:

- earth = fire/Agni = *Ṛg-Veda* = *bhūḥ*
- atmosphere = wind/Vāyu = *Yajur-Veda* = *bhuvaḥ*
- sky = sun/Sūrya = *Sāma-Veda* = *svaḥ*

A close variant of this text goes on to add the three principal sacrificial fires of the Vedic sacrificial cult—the centerpiece of ancient Indian religion—to the three associative chains:

> The gods said to Prajāpati, 'If there should be a calamity in our sacrifice due to the verse (*ṛk*, i.e. the *Ṛg-Veda*), or due to the formula (*yajus*, the *Yajur-Veda*), or due to the chant (*a sāman*, the *Sāma-Veda*), or due to unknown causes, or a total miscarriage, what is the reparation?' Prajāpati said to the gods, 'If there is a calamity in your sacrifice due to the verse, offer in the *gārhapatya* fire saying '*bhūḥ*'; if due to the formula, in the *āgnīdhrīya* fire [in soma sacrifices] or, in the case of *havir* sacrifices, in the *dakṣina* fire saying '*bhuvaḥ*'; if due to the chant, in the *āhavanīya* fire saying '*svaḥ*.'; and if due to unknown cases or a total miscarriage, offer only in the *āhavanīya* fire saying all consecutively—'*bhūḥ*,' '*bhuvaḥ*,' '*svaḥ*'. (AitB 5.32; cf. 5.34; KB 6.12; ChU 4.17.1–8)

And in yet another version of the establishment of these same basic linkages, the appropriate priests are added to the chains:

> [Prajāpati] heated up these three worlds. From this world he emitted Agni, from the world of the atmosphere Vāyu, from the sky Āditya. He heated up these three lights. From Agni he emitted the verses, from Vāyu the formulas, from Āditya the chants. He heated up the threefold wisdom. He spread out the sacrifice. He recited with the verse, he proceeded with the formula, he chanted with the chant. Then he developed the essence of fiery luster (*tejas*) for this threefold wisdom, for the healing of these Vedas. He developed *bhūḥ* from the verses, *bhuvaḥ* from the formulas, and *svaḥ* from the chants. . . . It is by means of the verse that the *hotṛ* priest becomes *hotṛ*, by the formula that the *adhvaryu* priest becomes *adhvaryu*, by the hymn that the *udgātṛ* priest becomes *udgātṛ*. (KB 6.10,11)

Combining the components of these two texts to those established above, the scheme now looks like this:

- earth = fire/Agni = *Ṛg-Veda* = *bhūḥ* = *gārhapatya* fire = *hotṛ* priest
- atmosphere = wind/Vāyu = *Yajur-Veda* = *bhuvaḥ* = *āgnīdhrīya* or *dakṣina* fire = *adhvaryu* priest

- sky = sun/Sūrya/Āditya = *Sāma-Veda* = *svaḥ* = *āhavanīya* fire = *udgātṛ* priest

Still other triads from other arenas fill out these three sets of homologies even further. At ŚB 12.3.4.7–11 three metaphysical qualities—"light," "might," and "fame"—are depicted as the primary generative categories. Components from the cosmological, theological, scriptural, and bodily realms[18] are then asserted as analogues:

> This world is light (*bharga*), the atmospheric world is might (*mahas*), the sky is fame (*yaśas*), and what other worlds there are, that is everything (*sarva*). Agni is light, Vāyu is might, Āditya is fame, and what other gods there are, that is everything. The *Ṛg-Veda* is light, the *Yajur-Veda* is might, the *Sāma-Veda* is fame, and what other Vedas there are, that is everything. Speech is light, breath is might, sight is fame, and what other breaths there are, that is everything. One should know this: 'I have put into myself all the worlds, and into all the worlds I have put myself. I have put into myself all the gods etc. . . . , all the Vedas etc. . . . , all the breaths etc. (ŚB 12.3.4.7–10)

In this text, light, might, and fame generate the three worlds (earth, atmosphere, and sky), the three naturalistic deities (Agni the fire, Vāyu the wind, and Āditya the sun), the three Vedas (*Ṛg*, *Yajur*, and *Sāma*), and three physical functions (speech, breath, and sight).[19] The passage may be compared to the following text from AitĀ 3.2.5 (cf. ŚānĀ 8.8), where the categorical system proceeds from an analysis of speech (a.k.a. recited Sanskrit) into mutes, sibilants, and vowels:

> And now for this secret teaching (*upaniṣad*) concerning all speech. . . .The consonants are the earth, the sibilants the atmosphere, and the vowels the sky. The consonants are Agni (or fire), the sibilants Vāyu (or air), the vowels Āditya (or the sun). The consonants are the *Ṛg-Veda*, the sibilants the *Yajur-Veda*, the vowels the *Sāma-Veda*. The consonants are the eye, the sibilants the ear, the vowels the mind. The consonants are the inhalation, the sibilants the exhalation, the vowels the circulatory breath.

The constituent parts of the Sanskrit language in which the Veda was composed are here equated to that tripartite Veda, among other cosmic components. Note here also the addition of three breaths to the triads which include, as in other passages already encountered, the three worlds, the three gods/natural forces, and the three Vedas. Corresponding to the *Ṛg-*, *Yajur-*, and *Sāma-Veda*s, however, are in this instance different bodily organs: the eye, the ear, and the mind, respectively, as opposed to speech, breath, and sight as one of the tests cited above argues.

The tripartite Veda is, in sum, depicted in many Vedic texts as created in the beginning as part of the cosmos in which we live. The three worlds, three natural elements, three deities (or types of deities), the ritual components of three fires and three principal priests, three qualities (light, might, and fame), three bodily parts or functions, three aspects of speech, three kinds of breaths—all are homologized to the three Vedas and their verbal essences. We thus arrive at a composite tripartite structure, here reconfigured in order to present the three Vedas first:

- *Ṛg-Veda* = earth = fire/Agni = *bhūḥ* = *gārhapatya* fire = *hotṛ* priest = light = speech or eye = mutes = inhalation
- *Yajur-Veda* = atmosphere = wind/Vāyu = *bhuvaḥ* = *āgnīdhrīya* or *dakṣina* fire = *adhvaryu* priest = might = breath or ear = sibilants = exhalation
- *Sāma-Veda* = sky = sun/Sūrya/Āditya = *svaḥ* = *āhavanīya* fire = *udgātṛ* priest = glory = sight or mind = vowels = circulatory breath

It will be noted that nowhere in the texts cited thus far are there specific social attributions given to the Vedas or their analogues; the social classes, in other words, are not mentioned in any of these cosmogonies. From other associations found elsewhere in the Veda, however, we may assume what the authors of these texts undoubtedly did. Though unstated in the texts above, each chain of resemblances includes a social component too.

Light, might, and fame, for example, may be regarded as ideal qualities of the three social classes (Brahmin priest, Kṣatriya warrior, and Vaiśya commoner respectively) or as transformations of the three elemental metaphysical powers that are the essences of the three Aryan social classes: *brahman, kṣatra*, and *viś*. The three worlds are also regularly associated with the three groups comprising society. The earth belongs to the Brahmin *varṇa*, the atmosphere to the Kṣatriyas, and the sky to the Vaiśyas.[20] The deities included in the three chains are also *varṇa*-encoded: Agni and the Vāsus are Brahmin deities; Vāyu, Indra, and the Rudras are Kṣatriyas; and Āditya, Sūrya, Varuṇa, and the Ādityas are Vaiśya gods.[21]

Evidence of a similar kind comes from the ChU (3.1–5). That text associates the *Ṛg-Veda* with the east, the south is linked to the *Yajur-Veda*, and the west is connected to the *Sāma-Veda*.[22] As we shall see below, the cardinal directions are regularly given *varṇa* attributions, with the east being the Brahmin direction, the south the Kṣatriya quarter, and the west (or north) belonging to the Vaiśyas. The directions thus also serve as mediators linking Vedas and social classes: *Ṛg-Veda* = east = Brahmins; *Yajur-Veda* = south = Kṣatriyas; and *Sāma-Veda* = west (or north) = Vaiśya.

The *Ṛg-Veda*, we may conclude, is the Brahmin Veda, for typically Brahmin components such as the earth, Agni, speech, and the east are regularly associated with it. We can infer on the same grounds that the *Yajur-Veda* is that of the Kṣatriyas, and the *Sāma-Veda* belongs with the Vaiśyas. These conclusions regarding the social correlates for each of the three Vedas are corroborated when we isolate one triadic set of the structure, the three *vyāhṛtis* or syllabic essences of the Vedas, which are also, as we have observed, the three worlds of Vedic cosmology.

At ŚB 2.1.4.11–13 these metonymical representatives of the Vedas are directly correlated with the three *varṇas* (portrayed in the form of neuter elemental powers) and also to cosmological and ontological triads:

> Prajāpati generated this [world by saying] '*bhūḥ*,' the atmosphere [by saying] '*bhuvaḥ*,' and the sky [by saying] '*svaḥ*.' As much as these worlds are, so much is this all. . . . Prajāpati generated the *brahman* power [by saying] '*bhūḥ*,' the *kṣatra* power [by saying] '*bhuvaḥ*', and the power of the *viś* [by saying] '*svaḥ*'. As much as the powers of the *brahman, kṣatra*, and *viś* are, so much is this all. . . . Prajāpati generated the Self (*ātman*) [by saying] '*bhūḥ*,' the human race [by saying] '*bhuvaḥ*', and the animals [by saying] '*svaḥ*'. As much as these Self, human race, and animals are, so much is this all.

This text confirms what we have assumed above—that connections can be drawn between the Vedas (since the three *vyāhṛtis* are equated with the three Vedas) and the three *varṇas* (which are here also correlated to the *vyāhṛtis*). Because the *vyāhṛtis* are also the names for the worlds which, as we have seen, are said to have *varṇa* attributes, the text formulates the equation between the Vedas and the *varṇa* through the mediation of the three worlds: Vedas = worlds = social classes.

It should also be noted that we have explicitly stated here what in other texts might seem less apparent: the establishment of a hierarchical ranking for each of the three strings of associations. The hierarchy is indicated by the order in which the chains are presented; the components comprising the chain that includes within it the Brahmins are invariably first, those aligned with the Kṣatriya second, and those connected to the Vaiśya third. But hierarchy is also enunciated in terms of the ontological entities that are located within each string. The Brahmin category contains within it the all-encompassing *ātman* or cosmic Self, the summation and essence of all beings. The Kṣatriyas are linked to the lower ontological class of humans, and the Vaiśyas here, as elsewhere, are associated with animals.[23] So too, we may conclude, are the three Vedas similarly hierarchically ranked in the eyes of the Vedic classifiers (and this despite a certain amount of disputation over which is the "higher" Veda, largely driven by competition between members of the different schools of transmission): the *Ṛg*, *Yajur*, and *Sāma* correspond to the Brahmin (and the Self), Kṣatriya (and humans), and Vaiśya (and animals), and in that order.[24]

METERS AND SOCIAL CLASSES

The Veda is also analyzable into the meters (*chandas*es) in which the Vedic verses (*ṛk*s), formulas (*yajus*es), and chants (*sāman*s) are composed. The meters are even given the same primordial standing as the three Vedas themselves: "From that sacrifice in which everything was offered," one reads in the famous creation hymn, "the verses (i.e., the *Ṛg-Veda*) and chants (the *Sāma-Veda*) were born, the meters were born from it, and from it the formulas (the *Yajur-Veda*) were born" (ṚV 10.90.8).[25]

Linkages between certain meters and the social classes are regularly forged in Vedic texts, most notably in those places where the ritual mantras are modified according to the class of the sacrificer.[26] Each of the meters is supposed to embody a power or quality that is particularly characteristic of the inborn and ritually actualized traits of one or another of the three *varṇa*s. In one rite that entails taking the sacrificial fire forward from one fireplace to another (see AitB 1.28), a *gāyatrī* verse (a triplet consisting of eight syllables in each verse) is recited if the sacrificer is a Brahmin, for "the Brahmin is connected with the *gāyatrī*. The *gāyatrī* is fiery luster (*tejas*) and the splendor of the *brahman (brahmavarcasas)*, and with those he makes him prosper." If the sacrificer is a Kṣatriya, a different verse in the *triṣṭubh* meter (a quartet of verses each containing eleven syllables) is used, for "the Kṣatriya is connected with the *triṣṭubh*. The *triṣṭubh* is force (*ojas*), power (*indriya*), and virility (*vīrya*); truly thus with force, power, and virility he makes him prosper." Alternatively, in the case of a Vaiśya sacrificer the verse is composed in the *jagatī* meter (a quartet with each verse comprised of twelve syllables), for "the Vaiśya is connected with the *jagatī* and animals are connected with the *jagatī*. Truly thus with animals he makes him prosper."

In the initiation or *upanayana* described in the Gṛhya Sūtras,[27] the *sāvitrī* verse (ṚV 3.62.10: "We contemplate the excellent glory of the divine Savitṛ; may he inspire our intellect!") was imparted to the boy to inaugurate his period of Veda study. The verse is to be composed in different meters for members of the different classes. Brahmins were to learn the verse in the *gāyatrī* meter, Kṣatriya in the *triṣṭubh*, and Vaiśya in the *jagatī*.[28] The adjustment was not only in order to match the boy's *varṇa* to the meter that bore the proper power. The syllabic composition of the meters (eight syllables for each line in the *gāyatrī* meter, eleven in the *triṣṭubh*, and twelve in the *jagatī*) was also reduplicative of the respective ages for initiation of boys from different classes (eight for the Brahmin, eleven for the Kṣatriya, and twelve for the Vaiśya).[29]

Other examples of the ritual uses of the meters "according to *varṇa*" (*yathāvarṇa*) could be cited.[30] In all instances, the meters were thought to embody and instill certain properties that were characteristic of the ontology of members of the different social classes. *Varṇa*-encoded properties were ritually injected into the appropriate person through the metrical medium.

The Brahmin meter, the *gāyatrī*, was supposed to hold within it typically Brahmin traits. The text cited above, which connects this meter to the powers of fiery luminosity (*tejas*) and the splendor of the *brahman* (*brahmavarcasas*), is not alone in making such a claim.[31] Other texts regard the *gāyatrī* as the representative of speech or the mouth (TS 5.4.10.4; 7.2.8.1; KB 11.2; JUB 4.8.11); of light (KB 17.6); of the sacrifice (ŚB 4.2.4.20); of perfection (ŚānĀ2.15); or as the bearer of the elemental metaphysical power invigorating the Brahmin class called the *brahman*.[32]

Furthermore, the *gāyatrī*, like other Brahmin entities, is regarded as the primary and foremost member of its realm. When the priest puts a kindling stick on the fire with a *gāyatrī* verse, "He thereby kindles the *gāyatrī*; the *gāyatrī*, when kindled, kindles the other meters; and the meters, when kindled, carry the sacrifice to the gods" (ŚB 1.3.4.6). At PB 8.4.2–4, the *triṣṭubh* and *jagatī* are said to have been created from the primordial *gāyatrī*. The Brahmin meter, like other Brahmin components of the universe, is prior to and generative of others.

The Kṣatriya meter, the *triṣṭubh*, is the meter of force (*ojas*), power (*indriya*), and virility (*vīrya*), as we have observed above. Elsewhere similar attributes such as physical strength (*bala*) as well as the elemental *kṣatra* power itself are said to be inherent in that meter.[33] The eleven-syllabled verses of the *triṣṭubh* are also homologized to Indra's great weapon, the thunderbolt or *vajra*, and thus replicate the coercive force of that cosmic armament within the ritual.[34]

The *jagatī* is frequently associated with the Vaiśya (TB, 1.1.9.7; TĀ 4.11.1–2) and with animals who are, in turn, connected to the commoner class.[35] An etymological basis for the correlation is also sometimes encountered: "He offers [oblations] with *jagatī* verses, for animals are mobile (*jagata*). By means of the *jagatī* he thus obtains animals for him."[36] In at least one text (ŚB 8.3.3.4), the Vaiśya meter is connected to both animals and food, the latter also a typical designation of the commoners vis-à-vis the higher social "eaters."[37] The meter of the third *varṇa* is also said to be weaker than the other two, just as Vaiśya are supposedly weaker (although numerically larger) than the Brahmin and Kṣatriya elites: "The *gāyatrī* and the *triṣṭubh* are the strongest among the meters. In that these are on either side and the *jagatī* is in the middle [in this chant], thereby, he encompasses the animals with the strongest of the meters'' (PB 20.16.8).

Creation stories for the three meters explain why each belongs to one or another of the social classes and the parts of the day (morning, midday, and evening) correlative to each of those classes. One myth tells how the *gāyatrī* flew to heaven and procured the soma:

> What she [the *gāyatrī* in the form of a bird] grabbed with her right foot became the morning pressing [of the soma plant at the soma sacrifice]. The *gāyatrī* made that her own home, and therefore they regard it as the most perfect of all the pressings. He who knows this becomes foremost, the best; he attains preeminence. And what she grasped with her left foot became the midday pressing. That crumbled off and thus did not match the former pressing. The gods wanted to fix this, so in it they put the *triṣṭubh* from the meters and Indra from the deities. With that [in it] it became equal in strength to the first pressing. He who knows this becomes successful with both pressings of equal strength and equal in relationship. That which she grabbed with her mouth became the third pressing. While flying she sucked out its sap. With its sap sucked out it did not equal the two previous pressings. The gods wanted to fix this. They saw it in domestic animals. When they pour in an admixture [of milk], and proceed with the [offering of] butter and the animal [offering], with that it became of equal strength with the previous two pressings. He who knows this becomes successful with pressings of equal strength and equal in relationship. (AitB 3.27)

Hierarchy and inequality—with the Brahmin *gāyatrī* and the morning pressing presented as ''perfect,'' and the other two pressings as defective in various ways—are transformed into pressings of ''equal strength'' and ''similar quality'' through supplementation: the *triṣṭubh* meter and the warrior god Indra beef up the midday, while different symbols for animals bring the third pressing up to par. The Brahmin components of morning and the *gāyatrī* meter are thus depicted as self-contained, primary, and preeminent, the ''womb'' of the others.[38]

A variant also assumes original inequality but tells the story somewhat differently:

> [Originally] the *gāyatrī* was composed of eight syllables, the *triṣṭubh* of three, the *jagatī* of one. The eight-syllabled *gāyatrī* carried the morning pressing upward. The three-syllabled *triṣṭubh* was unable to to carry the midday pressing upward. The *gāyatrī* said to her, 'I will come [to the midday pressing]. Let there

> be something here for me too.' 'Okay,' replied the *triṣṭubh*. 'Add these eight syllables to me.' 'Alright,' [the *gāyatrī* said]. She added herself to her. Thus at the midday [pressing] the last two [verses] of the introductory verse dedicated to Indra Marutvat and the response belong to the *gāyatrī*. She (the *triṣṭubh*) became eleven-syllabled and carried up the midday pressing. The *jagatī* had one syllable and was unable to carry the third pressing upward. The *gāyatrī* said to her, 'I will come [to the evening pressing]. Let there be something here for me too.' 'Okay,' replied the *jagatī*. 'Add these eleven syllables to me.' 'Alright,' [the *gāyatrī* said]. She added herself to her. Thus at the third [pressing] the last two [verses] of the introductory verse dedicated to the Viśva Devas and the response belong to the *gāyatrī*. She (the *jagatī*) became twelve-syllabled and carried up the third pressing. This is how the *gāyatrī* became eight-syllabled, the *triṣṭubh* eleven-syllabled, and the *jagatī* twelve-syllabled. He who knows this becomes successful with pressings of equal strength and equal in relationship. (AitB 3.28)

The Brahmin *gāyatrī* meter of eight syllables is once again represented as perfect and self-sufficient, capable of "supporting" on its own the morning pressing to which it is assigned. The Kṣatriya and Vaiśya representatives are, as in the other version, originally smaller and thus unable to carry out their functions. But in this account they are not supplemented by other props; rather, they are infused with the *gāyatrī*'s eight syllables in order to attain their proper syllabic strength, and thus all the meters are made "of equal strength and of equal quality."[39] The myth, in sum, belies its own overt message of equality among the meters, the parts of the day, and (implicitly) the *varṇa*s by arguing that such equality was achieved by the incorporation of the *gāyatrī* (i.e., Brahmin) component into those representing the Kṣatriya and Vaiśya.

The connections made in the texts above between the morning and the *gāyatrī*, midday and the *triṣṭubh*, and evening and the *jagatī* are extremely common.[40] These three meters, which are sometimes said to be the very "forms" (*rūpa*s) of the three parts of the day,[41] are also here and elsewhere routinely assigned to the Brahmins, Kṣatriya, and Vaiśya. The linkages to the three parts of the day are, therefore, yet another transformation of the *varṇa* of the meters.

The meters, no less than the social classes they signify, are clearly structured in a hierarchical fashion. The Brahmin meter, like the Brahmin class, is the "first" of the meters—hierarchically and chronologically—and also the meter of the fewest syllables, just as the elite Brahmin social class is numerically small: "The *gāyatrī*, while being the smallest meter, is the meter yoked first on account of its strength (*vīrya*)'' (ŚB 1.8.2.10). The ''larger'' Kṣatriya and Vaiśya meters, on the other hand, are displayed as subsequent to and the inferior offspring of the *gāyatrī*. Less, indeed, is more.

The *gāyatrī*, like the social class it represents, is simultaneously said to encompass all the other meters. This notion is ritually put into play in the following text, where the well-known code of morning = *gāyatrī*, midday = *triṣṭubh*, and evening = *jagatī* is tapped in order to efficiently and efficaciously collapse the soma sacrifice into a single rite:

> They complete the entire sacrifice at the morning pressing only. . . . He presses [the soma] eight times. The *gāyatrī* consists of eight syllables and the morning pressing is connected to the *gāyatrī*. Thus this [pressing of the soma eight times] is made to be the morning pressing. . . . He then presses [the soma] eleven times. The *triṣṭubh* consists of eleven syllables and the midday pressing is connected to the *triṣṭubh*. Thus this [pressing of the soma eleven times] is made to be the midday pressing. . . . He then presses [the soma] twelve times. The *jagatī* consists of twelve syllables and the evening pressing is connected to the *jagatī*. Thus this [pressing of the soma twelve times] is made to be the evening pressing. (ŚB 4.1.1.7–12)

All three of the day's ritual pressings of soma are symbolically condensed into the morning pressing through manipulating the number of syllables of the three meters.[42] The Brahmin-encoded morning encompasses within it all other parts of the day and the *gāyatrī*, which is the meter of the morning pressing, thus also contains all other meters within itself.

The *varṇa* codes for the three meters are exemplified somewhat differently in the fragmentary tripartite classification scheme of the following text:

> The animals have Vāyu [the god of wind] as their leader, and Vāyu is breath; the animals are animated by means of breath. He [Vāyu] departed from the gods together with the animals. The gods prayed to him at the morning soma pressing, but he did not return. They prayed to him at the midday soma pressing, but he did not return. They prayed to him at the afternoon soma pressing. . . . If he had returned at the morning soma pressing, the animals would be among the Brahmins; for the *gāyatrī* is the morning soma pressing, and the *brahman* is the *gāyatrī*. And if he had returned at the midday soma pressing, the animals would be among the Kṣatriya for the midday soma pressing concerns Indra [the king of the gods], and the *kṣatra* is Indra.

> And since he returned at the evening soma pressing—the evening soma pressing concerns the Viśva Devas ("All the Gods"), and this all is the Viśva Devas—therefore the animals are everywhere here. (ŚB 4.4.1.15–16,18)

The *gāyatrī* meter is here equated to the morning pressing of soma, the Brahmin social class, and the metaphysical power of the ***brahman***. The midday pressing is connected to the Kṣatriya, but then, instead of following the order of the first series of associations (which would require at this point the appropriate meter), the text conjoins midday and Kṣatriya to the deity Indra before returning to the expected order and supplying the metaphysical power called the ***kṣatra***. The connections issuing from the evening pressing are limited to the related divinity (the Viśva Devas) and the animals (an ontological component).

The missing links can be identified, and the holes in the text filled, by comparing the associations posited here to others made in other texts. The first category presented here (morning = Brahmins = *gāyatrī* = ***brahman***) is the most complete in the text, but unlike the other two it fails to mention the deity belonging to the series. Correlative to the Kṣatriya Indra and the Vaiśya Viśva Devas is Agni for the Brahmin category, as we will have occasion to observe below. The second set (midday = Kṣatriya = Indra = ***kṣatra***) omits the meter of this category corresponding to the *gāyatrī* meter in the first set; the ***triṣṭubh***, which is obviously called for given the other homologies, is here left implicit. The third and least filled-out category (evening = Viśva Devas = animals) neglects the appropriate social class, meter, and metaphysical power of the chain. But, again, as we know from other regularly formulated homologies, the Vaiśya, *jagatī*, and power of the ***viś*** can be supplied. Furthermore, as we have seen above ("Prajāpati generated the Self [by saying] '***bhūḥ***,' the human race [by saying] '***bhuvaḥ***,' and the animals [by saying] '***svaḥ***' "), the ontological correlates for the Vaiśya "animals" are the Brahmin Self or *ātman* and humans for the Kṣatriyas. A reconstructed tripartite framework of the text would look like this:

- morning = Brahmins = Agni = *gāyatrī* meter = the ***brahman*** = the Self
- midday = Kṣatriya = Indra = ***triṣṭubh*** meter = the ***kṣatra*** = humans
- evening = Vaiśya = Viśva Devas = *jagatī* meter = the ***viś*** = animals

The linkage of the *gāyatrī*, ***triṣṭubh***, and *jagatī* meters and three *varṇa*-encoded deities (usually Agni, the divine priest; Indra, the deified exemplar of the warrior; and the Viśva Devas, the "masses" among the gods;[43] or the three groups called the Vāsus, Rudras, and Ādityas[44]) is also well attested. This series of correlates between meters and divinities can include within it the Brahmin morning, the Kṣatriya midday, and the Vaiśya evening: "Prajāpati assigned to the gods the sacrifice and the meters in portions. He allotted the *gāyatrī* at the morning pressing to Agni and the Vāsus, the *triṣṭubh* to Indra and the Rudras at the midday (pressing), the *jagatī* to the Viśva Devas and the Ādityas at the third pressing" (AitB 3.13; cf. ŚB 14.1.1.15ff.).

Numerological explanations are put forward to explain the particular bonds between meters and deities. The connection between the three meters (containing verses with eight, eleven, and twelve syllables respectively) and the Vāsus, Rudras, and Ādityas is explicated in one passage which declares that there are thirty-three gods who drink soma, "eight Vāsus, eleven Rudras, twelve Ādityas, Prajāpati and the *vaṣat* call" (AitB 2.18). Furthermore, in some texts the deities that are elsewhere connected to the meters and the three parts of the day are conjoined with the meters and the three worlds:[45] meters (*gāyatrī*, *triṣṭubh*, and *jagatī*), gods (Agni and/or the Vāsus; Indra and/or the Rudras or Maruts; and one or more of the Vaiśya deities), space (earth, atmosphere, and sky), and time (morning, noon, and evening) are thus brought together in triadic equations.

In the realm of anatomy, the *gāyatrī* is, unsurprisingly, assimilated to the head (and "the head means excellence," comments ŚB 4.2.4.20) or the mouth, the usual Brahmin body parts; the *triṣṭubh*, like the Kṣatriya, was created from the chest or arms of the Cosmic Man; and the Vaiśya meter, the *jagatī*, is connected to the hips (e.g., ŚB 8.6.2.6–8; 10.3.2.1–6), belly, or penis. Indeed, in several texts (PB 6.1.6–11; TS 7.1.1.4–6; JB 1.68–69), the meters and the social classes are produced from these distinctive body parts of the creator, as are deities (Agni, Indra, and the Viśva Devas), seasons (spring, summer, and rains), and animals (goat, horse, and cow).[46] In yet other cosmogonies (ŚB 5.4.1.3–5; 8.1.1–2; TS 4.3.2.1–3; 5.5.8.2–3), the expected cardinal directions are added to the chains of connections (east, south, and west for the Brahmin and *gāyatrī*, Kṣatriya and *triṣṭubh*, and Vaiśya and *jagatī* respectively).[47]

Vedas and social classes can thus also be indirectly related through the mediation of the meters, just as we have seen they can be through the mediation of the *vyāhṛtis*. The meters are explicitly equated to the three social classes, the metaphysical qualities that are so often definitive of each *varṇa* (e.g., fiery luster, force and power, and animality), as well as to parts of the day, deities, worlds, parts of the body, seasons, animals, and directions that are all class-encoded. As a comparison of Chart 1 (which maps the analogues of the three Vedas) and Chart 2 (surveying the analogues of the three meters) demonstrates, the shared connections

CHART 3.1 The Three Vedas and Their Analogues

	ṚG-VEDA	YAJUR-VEDA	SĀMA-VEDA
SOCIAL CLASS	Brahmin	Kṣatriya	Vaiśya
ELEMENTAL POWER	*brahman*	*kṣatra*	*viś*
QUALITY	splendor	greatness	fame
COSMOLOGICAL WORLD	earth	atmosphere	sky
SEASON	spring	summer	rainy
PART OF DAY	morning	midday	evening
CARDINAL DIRECTION	east	south	west
NATURAL ELEMENT	fire	wind	sun
DEITY	Agni, Vāsus	Vāyu, Indra, Rudras	Sūrya/Āditya, Varuṇa, Ādityas
ONTOLOGICAL ENTITY	Self	humans	animals
BODY PART	eye	ear	mind
PHYSICAL FUNCTION	speech	breath	sight
BREATH	inhalation	exhalation	circulatory
SACRIFICIAL FIRE	*gārhapatya*	*āgnīdhrīya/ dakṣina*	*āhavanīya*
PRIEST	*hotṛ*	*adhvaryu*	*udgātṛ*
LINGUISTIC COMPONENT	mutes	sibilants	vowels

are so numerous that we may surmise from these connections, ourselves employing the homologic typical of the Veda, that each of the meters is an analogue of one of the three Vedas (*gāyatrī* = *Ṛg-Veda*, *triṣṭubh* = *Yajur-Veda*, and *jagatī* = *Sāma-Veda*). Since the meters are given *varṇa* attributions and are implicitly connected to the Vedas, the Vedas are thus in this way too analogues of the social classes.

CHART 3.2 The Three Meters and Their Analogues

	GĀYATRĪ	*TRIṢṬUBH*	*JAGATĪ*
SOCIAL GLASS	Brahmin	Kṣatriya	Vaiśya
ELEMENTAL POWER	*brahman*	*kṣatra*	*viś*
QUALITY	fiery luster, splendor of the *brahman*,	force, power, virility	animals, food
COSMOLOGICAL WORLD	earth	atmosphere	sky
SEASON	spring	summer	rainy
PART OF DAY	morning	midday	evening
CARDINAL DIRECTION	east	south	west
DEITY	Agni, Vāsus	Indra, Rudras, Maruts	Varuṇa, Viśva Devas, Āditya, Ādityas
ONTOLOGICAL ENTITY	Self	humans	animals
BODY ORGAN	head, mouth	chest, arms	hips, belly, penis
ANIMAL	goat	horse	cow

CONCLUSION

One of the questions that remains unaddressed is why particular Vedas were correlated to particular *varṇa*s. For this I do not claim to have definitive answers but feel compelled to offer some speculations.

The *Ṛg-Veda* is often accorded a status above that of the other two scriptures. Like the Brahmins in the social realm, the morning or spring in temporal categorizations, and the eastern direction in spatial structures, the *Ṛg-Veda* is the "first" or "primary" member of its class. Moreover, as the Veda of the *hotṛ* priest who is the "reciter" of verses in the sacrifice, it is also connected to speech. Since the Veda as a whole, as we have also noted, is sometimes said to be the summation of all speech, the *Ṛg-Veda* might have been regarded as the metonymical placeholder for the Veda qua creative, sacred speech. As such it stands in the same relation to the other Vedas as the Brahmin (the fullest representative of the human being) does vis-à-vis the lesser social classes.

The *Yajur-Veda*, the Veda of the *adhvaryu* priest or the officiant who is charged with much of the actual ritual maneuvers, is appropriately classified with the Kṣatriyas, the social class noted for physical activity. Other associations—with might, force, power, and virility; with the turbulent realm of the atmosphere; and with Vāyu the wind and the microcosmic anatomical equivalent, breath—are in keeping with the "active" nature of both the Kṣatriya *varṇa* and the *Yajur-Veda*.

Finally, the connection between the *Sāma-Veda* and the Vaiśya would seem to follow from the fact that both are characterized by multiplicity. The *Sāma-Veda* is used by the *udgātṛ* priest in the soma sacrifices in which he is employed accompanied by a group of supporting chanters or singers. Just as the sky is the analogue of the *viś* in cosmology (owing to the countless heavenly orbs), and just as the dappled or spotted animal belongs to the Vaiśya because of its multiple markings,[48] so too, it would seem, do the *Sāma-Veda* and the multitude of priests connected with it indicate a connection to the commoner class. Furthermore, the third place given to the *Sāma-Veda* in these structures may also be attributed to the fact that the *Sāma-Veda* is derivative: all its chants are reworkings of the hymns of the *Ṛg-Veda*.

More important than the specifics of the equations forged between the Vedas and the social classes is the fact that such homologies are made at all, albeit in a roundabout way. The canonical powers of the Veda—as a supposedly authorless (*apauruṣeya*) text outside of the realm of particular individual or social interests; as primordial and eternal, and therefore not subject to the contingencies and quirks of historical time; and as unquestionable, and therefore not subject to contestation—all these canonical powers are brought to bear on the hierarchical social order of the *varṇa*s.

The caste system (or at least caste *in nuce*) can thus be presented as canonical: the authority of caste derives from the authority of Veda, but more than that caste is made to appear as a social transformation or reduplication of canon. The legitimacy, or even indisputability, of the distinctive social scheme of historical and contemporary India rides piggyback on the unquestionable truth of the Veda, and both are part of the eternal cosmic order of things.

Because of this series of homologies, any challenge to either the sociological or the scriptural structure could be debunked as obviously "unnatural" and false—one reason, perhaps, why the Brahmin class that composed the Veda and located themselves at the top of the social hierarchy the Veda legitimated have maintained such an entrenched position of privilege in India over the course of several millennia. The first interpreters of the Veda were the Brahmin authors of the Veda, and they interpreted these texts in such a way that both the canonical status of their compositions and their own standing within India society would be established and guaranteed for generations to come.

ABBREVIATIONS

AitĀ	*Aitareya Āraṇyaka*
AitB	*Aitareya Brāhmaṇa*
BĀU	*Bṛhadāraṇyaka Upaniṣad*
BDhS	*Baudhāyana Dharma Sūtra*
ChU	*Chandogya Upaniṣad*
GB	*Gopatha Brāhmaṇa*
JB	*Jaiminīya Brāhmaṇa*
JUB	*Jaiminīya Upaniṣad Brāhmaṇa*
KB	*Kauṣītaki Brāhmaṇa*
KGS	*Kāṭhaka Gṛhya Sūtra*
KU	*Kauṣītaki Upaniṣad*
MGS	*Mānava Gṛhya Sūtra*
Manu	*Manu Smṛti*
MU	*Maitrāyaṇī Upaniṣad*
PB	*Pañcaviṃśa Brāhmaṇa*
PGS	*Pāraskara Gṛhya Sūtra*
PU	*Praśna Upaniṣad*
ṚV	*Ṛg-Veda Saṃhitā*
ṢaḍB	*Ṣaḍviṃśa Brāhmaṇa*
ŚānĀ	*Śānkhāyana Āraṇyaka*
ŚB	*Śatapatha Brāhmaṇa*
ŚGS	*Śānkhāyana Gṛhya Sūtra*
TĀ	*Taittirīya Āraṇyaka*
TB	*Taittirīya Brāhmaṇa*
TS	*Taittirīya Saṃhitā*
TU	*Taittirīya Upaniṣad*
VGS	*Varāha Gṛhya Sūtra*

NOTES

My thanks to Bruce Lincoln, Laurie Patton, and Katherine E. Fleming for their suggestions upon reading earlier drafts of this chapter.

1. For the etymological history of the term "canon" (originally "rule" or "measure," later "list"), see Graham, *Beyond the Written Word*, 52–53. Graham prefers the word "scripture" to denote a religiously authoritative text: "A book is only 'scripture' insofar as a group of persons perceive it to be sacred or holy, powerful and portentous, possessed of

an exalted authority, and in some fashion transcendent of, and hence distinct from, all other speech and writing'' (5). ''Canon,'' as I use the term here, avoids the literary connotations of ''scripture'': nonliterate groups can and do have the oral equivalent of a written canon (a set of myths, stories of origins, legends, histories, etc.), not to mention the case of the Veda, which was preserved only orally until recently.

2. ''Where there is a canon, it is possible to predict the *necessary* occurrence of a hermeneute, of an interpreter whose task it is continually to extend the domain of the closed canon over everything that is known or everything that exists *without* altering the canon in the process. . . . [A] canon cannot exist without a tradition and an interpreter'' (Smith, *Imagining Religion*, 48–49).

3. ''Canon'' or ''scripture'' thus does not exist apart from the perception of it as such by a community and a tradition. One cannot but agree with Graham when he writes that ''neither form nor content can serve to distinguish or identify scripture as a general phenomenon or category. . . . [F]rom the historian's perspective, the sacrality or holiness of a book is not an a priori attribute of a text but one that is realized historically in the life of communities who respond to it as something sacred or holy. A text becomes 'scripture' in active, subjective relationship to persons, and as part of a cumulative communal tradition. No text, written or oral or both, is sacred or authoritive in isolation from a community'' (*Beyond the Written Word*, 5). On the other hand, religious traditions and communities come into existence only when they assign to themselves a point of origins (to which they endlessly return) and absolute authority—that is, a canon.

4. This formulation I have offered as a working definition of that nebulous entity we call ''Hinduism.'' See Smith, *Reflections on Resemblance, Ritual and Religion*, 13–14. Cf. idem, ''Exorcising the Transcendent,'' 32–55.

5. The three principal Vedas are the *Ṛg, Yajur,* and *Sāman*. The fourth Veda, the *Atharva*, attained its status relatively late in the scheme of things and became one example of adding an inferior fourth to a prior triad. The other principal instance of this phenomenon is, coincidentally enough, the addition of the Shūdra or servant class to the basement of the previously tripartite *varṇa* structure. For the much more common tendency to place a ''transcendent fourth'' on top of an inferior triad in Hinduism (e.g., *mokṣa* to the three *puruṣārthas*), consult Organ, ''Three into Four Hinduism,'' 7–13.

6. For the three Vedas as the three forms of *vāc*, see ŚB 6.5.3.4; 10.5.5.1,5; and PB 10.4.6,9 (with Sāyaṇa's commentary). The three (or four in the case of the *Atharvavedic* GB, e.g., 1.5.28) Vedas are also equated with the sacrifice, another all-encompassing entity in Vedic

thought. See, e.g., JB 1.35; ŚB 1.1.4.3; 3.1.1.12; 4.6.7.13; and esp. 5.5.5.10 ("The whole sacrifice is equivalent to that threefold Veda."). This chain of connections also entails the linkage of speech (*vāc*) and sacrifice, for which consult Thite, *Sacrifice in the Brāhmaṇa-Texts*, 288–90.

7. E.G., ŚB 10.1.1.8; 10.2.4.6; JUB 4.25.2. For connections between *vāc* and the *brahman*, see ŚB 2.1.4.10; AitĀ 1.1.1; BĀU 4.1.2.

8. E.g., ŚB 10.4.2.21–22, where it is said that in the beginning Prajāpati (the Lord of Creatures) "surveyed all beings and perceived all beings in the triple wisdom. For in that [Veda] is the essence (*ātman*) of all meters, of all hymns of praise, of all breaths, and of all the gods. This indeed exists for it is immortal, and what is immortal exists; and this (contains also) that which is mortal. Prajāpati reflected to himself, 'Truly all beings are in the triple wisdom.' "

9. This notion continues into recent history. The nineteenth-century Hindu apologist Haracandra Tarkapancanana could declare that "If there is to be faith in a book, let it be in the Veda, since it has prevailed on earth from the time of creation onward." Cited and translated in Young, *Resistant Hinduism,* 99. Swami Dayānanda Sarasvatī, the founder of the nineteenth—century organization called the "Arya Samaj," similarly argued that the Vedas were superior to Christian scriptures because they lie outside of or before history and do not refer to historical persons or events or to geographical locales. See Jordens, *Dayānanda Sarasvatī*, 271–72.

10. For a survey of the Vedic philosophy of universal resemblance and interconnection, see Smith, *Reflections on Resemblance, Ritual, and Religion*.

11. The only exception to this rule I have encountered is provided by TB 3.12.9.2: "They say that the Vaiśya class is born from the verses (*ṛks*, i.e., the *Ṛg-Veda*). They say the *Yajur-Veda* is the womb of the Kṣatriya. The *Sāma-Veda* is the procreator of the Brahmins." The Vedas associated here with Brahmins and the Vaiśyas are inverted in comparison to the usual homologies, as we shall see. The fact that the passage does indeed directly connect the *varṇa*s and the Vedas, however, is significant in itself. It demonstrates that such *bandhu*s were not only theoretically possible but actually articulated.

12. Lincoln, "Tyranny of Taxonomies," 16–17.

13. In most Vedic taxonomies, the heaven of Vedic salvation and the sky of Vedic cosmology were conceived differently, although the difference was often assumed and implicit. That such a distinction was indeed made by some Vedic writers is borne out by the following passage, in which in a quadripartite cosmology an explicit division between "yonder world" or the sky, on the one hand, and heaven on the other is formulated: "By nine (verses) the *maitravaruṇa* [priest] carries him from this world to the world of the atmosphere; by ten from the world

of the atmosphere to yonder world, for the world of the atmosphere is the longest; with nine from yonder world to the world of heaven" (AitB 6.9). For heaven (*svarga*) as the "fourth" world, beyond the cosmological "world of the sky" (*divi loka, svar, dyaus*), see Gonda, *Loka*, 91; and Bodewitz, "Waters in Vedic Classifications," 49, n. 27: "Heaven, regarded as the 'beyond' rather than as the sky of the day time, was also described as boundless (*ananta*)."

14. I have analyzed Vedic cosmogonies and the *varṇa* system from a different angle elsewhere. See Smith, "Classifying the Universe," 241–60.

15. Variants include ŚB 4.6.7.1–2; JB 1.357; AitB 5.34; KB 6.12; JUB 1.1.1–4; 16.1.23.1–6; 3.15.4–9; PU 5.3–5.

16. Manu 1.23 also connects Agni (fire), Vāyu (wind), and Āditya (the sun) with the *Ṛg-Veda, Yajur-Veda*, and *Sāma-Veda* respectively. ChU 3.6–10, alternatively, associates the *Ṛg-Veda* with Agni and the Vasus, the *Yajur-Veda* with Indra and the Rudras, and the *Sāma-Veda* with Varuṇa and the Ādityas (and goes on to connect Soma and the Maruts with the *Atharva-Veda*, and Brahmā and the Sādhyas with the Upaniṣhads).

17. Lincoln, in his "Tyranny of Taxonomies," prefers the term "module" for what I will call "chains of associations" to refer to a set of elements (or "analogues") capable of being homologized to one another.

18. KU 1.7 anomalously connects the *Yajur-Veda* and the belly, the *Sāma-Veda* and the head, and the *Ṛg-Veda* and "form," while JUB 4.24.12 regards the various parts of the right eye as analogues of the various Vedas.

19. Cf. JUB 1.25.8–10 where *Ṛg-Veda* = speech, *Yajur-Veda* = mind, and *Sāma-Veda* = breath.

20. E.g., ŚB 2.1.4.11–13; 11.5.8.1–4; 12.3.4.7–11; KB 6.10,11; 22.1–3; JB 1.18; JUB 1.1.1–4; 1.8.1ff; 3.15.4ff; ChU 4.17.1–6. This scheme is obviously hierarchical even though the spatial correlates for each of the *varṇa*s are vertically inverted: the "lowest" world, earth, is associated with the "highest" of the social classes, the Brahmins; and the "highest" spatial world is connected with the "lowest" of the three *varṇa*s. The earth, like the Brahmins, is from this perspective logically prior, primary, and foremost; the other two worlds and the *varṇa*s that characterize them are, concomitantly, presented as subsequent, secondary (and tertiary), and derivative. The atmosphere is the cosmic realm which, because of its natural characteristics, suggests the tempestuous warrior on the rampage. The countless stars in the sky, together with the other planets, sun, and moon, perhaps suggested the great numbers that comprise the commoner class, the "masses" of ancient India.

21. For the *varṇa* assignments of the principal deities of Vedism, see, e.g., BĀU 1.4.11–15.

22. The text goes on to connect the *Atharva-Veda* (and the *itihāsa* and *purāṇa* literature) to the north, and the Upaniṣhads are associated

with the zenith. Cf. TĀ 2.3, which declares the *Yajur-Veda* the head (= east) of the fire altar regarded as a person; *Ṛg-Veda* the right side (= south); *Sāma-Veda* the left side (= north); and *Atharva-Veda*, the lower part, the foundation (= west).

23. For the Vaiśyas as animals, consult Smith, "Classifying Animals and Humans in Ancient India," 323–41.

24. One wonders whether a hierarchy of the Vedas is also being posited in a post-Vedic text that works with slightly different ontological correlates (gods, men, and ancestors, respectively): "One should never recite the recitations (*ṛcs*) or formulas (*yajuses*) when there is the sound of chants (*sāmans*)," says Manu, for "The *Ṛg-Veda* is known to be sacred to the gods, the *Yajur-Veda* to men, and the *Sāma-Veda* to the ancestors. Therefore the sound of the latter is impure (*asuci*)" (Manu 4.123–24). Elsewhere, however, one encounters passages where the *Sāma-Veda*, and not the *Ṛg-Veda*, is exalted as the "highest Veda." See, e.g., ŚB 12.8.3.23 where "the *sāman*" is said to be "the essence of all the Vedas." Alternatively, a Kṣatriya connection for the *Sāma-Veda* is suggested at ŚB 13.4.3.14; 14.3.1.10; AitB 3.23; and especially ŚB 12.8.3.23: "He then sings a *sāman*. The *sāman* is the *kṣatra* power. With *kṣatra* he thus sprinkles him [i.e., consecrates a king]. And the *sāman* is imperial rule. With imperial rule he thus brings him to imperial rule." These kinds of "inconsistencies" have led scholars, past and present, to ignore the overwhelming number of "consistencies" in the connections drawn in the Brāhmaṇas, some of which are traced in this chapter.

25. The hymn from which this citation is taken, the famous "*Puruṣa Sūkta*," provides the best known example of the Vedic claim that the Vedas and *varṇas* were created together at the beginning of time. Following the verse already cited we read: "His mouth became the Brahmin, his arms were made into the Kṣatriya, his thighs the commoners, and from his feet the Shūdras were born" (ṚV 10.90.12).

26. The phenomenon is in general called *mantra ūha*, the details of which are described in Chakrabarti's *The Paribhāṣās in the Śrautasūtras*, 132–36, 154–65.

27. For the following, see also Smith, "Ritual, Knowledge, and Being," 65–89.

28. ŚGS 2.5.4–7; MGS 1.22.13; PGS 2.3.7–9; BDhS 1.2.3.11. According to other texts (VGS 5.26; KGS 41.20; cf. MGS 1.2.3), wholly different Vedic verses, each in the appropriate meter, were to be imparted to initiates of different classes. See also Mookerji, *Ancient Indian Education (Brahmanical and Buddhist)*, 182; and Kane, *History of Dharmaśāstra*, 2:300–304.

29. The difference between these ages and the last ages possible for performing the *upanayana* for members each class (also eight, eleven,

and twelve respectively) numerologically strengthened the bond between the *varṇa*s and the meters.

30. For the correlation of the three meters and the three social classes when the *adhvaryu* priest puts firesticks into the fire within the ritual of setting up the sacred fires for a new *āhitāgni*, consult the texts brought together in Dandekar, ed., *Śrautakośa*, 1:16, 20, 24. For similiar mantra adjustments in the *agnicayana* ritual, see, e.g., TS 5.1.4.5; 5.2.2.4.

31. See also KB 17.2; 17.9; TS 5.1.4.5; AitĀ 1.1.3; ŚB 4.1.1.14; PB 6.9.25; 12.1.2.

32. For the equation of the *gāyatrī* and the *brahman*, see AitB 3.5; 3.34; 7.23; KB 7.10; AitĀ 1.1.3; ŚB 4.1.1.14; JUB 1.1.8; 1.6.6; 1.33.11; 1.34.2.

33. TS 5.4.1.5; AitB 3.5; 4.3; 6.21; 7.23; 8.2; AitĀ 1.1.3; KB 7.10; 8.7; 10.5; 11.2; 16.1; 16.2; 17.2; 17.9; 18.6; 30.11; TB 3.3.9.8; PB 18.10.7; JUB 4.8.1.

34. ŚB 10.2.3.2; cf. 7.5.2.24; 8.5.1.10–11; 9.2.3.6; AitB 2.2; 2.16.

35. AitĀ 1.1.3; KB 16.2; 17.2; 17.9; 18.6; ŚB 8.3.3.3; 13.1.3.8; 13.2.6.6; 13.6.2.5; TS 2.5.10.1; 6.1.6.2; 3.2.9.4; AitB 3.18; 3.25; 3.48; 4.3; PB 18.11.9–10. See also Smith, "Classifying Animals and Humans in Ancient India."

36. ŚB 12.8.3.13; cf. ŚB 1.2.2.2; 1.8.2.11; 3.4.1.13; TB 3.8.8.4; KB 8.7.

37. See Smith "Eaters, Food, and Social Hierarchy in Ancient India," 201–29. For an exception to the association of the *jagatī* and these obviously Vaiśya powers, see KB 11.2 where the meter is connected to the ordinarily Kṣatriya virtues of physical strength and virility (*bala* and *vīrya*).

38. Cf. AitB 6.9: "He recites verses in the *gāyatrī* meter [for] the morning pressing is connected to the *gāyatrī*. He recites nine small [verses] at the morning pressing. Seed is spurted into that which is small. He recites ten [verses] at the midday pressing. When the seed which is spurted into that which is small reaches the woman's midsection it becomes that which is most broad. He recites nine small [verses] at the third pressing [for] children are born from that which is small."

39. Yet another version of the story (ŚB 4.3.2.7–11) starts with the opposite premise: the meters were originally equal. The conclusion, however, is identical to those reached in variants that begin differently. Originally equal, the *varṇa*-encoded meters are soon rendered unequal, only to be made again equal—but as slightly transformed versions of the all-encompassing Brahmin meter. Here, as elsewhere, the *gāyatrī* is, mythically, the meter not only of the morning soma pressing but of them all, for "all the soma pressings are connected to the *gāyatrī*."

40. Other tests that draw homologies between these three meters and the three day parts include ŚB 4.1.1.15–18; 4.2.5.20; 4.5.3.5; 14.1.1.17; AitB 3.12; 6.12; KB 14.3; TB 3.8.12.1–2; PB 7.4.6.

41. E.g., TB 3.8.12.1–2; AitB 3.12; KB 14.3; ŚB 4.2.5.20; 4.5.3.5; PB 7.4.6.

42. For some different symbolic uses to which the syllabic content of the meters are put, see AitB 6.2; ŚB 1.7.3.22–25; TB 3.2.7.4–5; KB 10.1; JUB 4.2.1–10; ChU 3.16. In other passages, however (e.g., KB 25.3; 26.8; AitB 6.21; 6.30; PB 4.4.8; ŚānĀ 1.2; ŚB 1.8.2.13), the ritualists warn against recitations in meters inappropriate to the time of the pressing.

43. ŚB 11.5.9.7; KB 14.3; 14.4; 30.1; AitB 8.6. For other correlations between the meters and individual gods, see ŚB 10.3.2.1–6 (*gāyatrī* = Agni, *triṣṭubh* = Indra, and *jagatī* = Āditya); ŚB 5.4.1.3ff.; TS 4.3.2.1ff.; TS 5.5.8.2ff. (*gāyatrī* = Agni, *triṣṭubh* = Indra, and *jagatī* = the Maruts); AitB 3.47 (*gāyatrī* = Anumati, *triṣṭubh* = Rāka, *jagatī* = Sinīvālī); KB 7.10 (*triṣṭubh* = *kṣatra* = Varuṇa; *gāyatrī* = *brahman* = Bṛhaspati); KB 10.5 (*gāyatrī* = Agni, *triṣṭubh* = Soma = *kṣatra*).

44. E.g., ŚB 6.5.2.3–5; 12.3.4.1–6; 13.2.6.4ff.; JB 1.239; 1.283–84; JUB 1.18.4–6; 4.2.1–9; ChU 3.16.1–5. Cf. KB 22.1ff., where the deities of the three chains are Agni and the Vāsus, Indra and the Maruts, and Varuṇa and the Ādityas respectively.

45. E.g., KB 8.9 (Agni = *gāyatrī* = earth; Soma = *triṣṭubh* = atmosphere; Viṣṇu = *jagatī* = sky); KB 14.3 (with the respective deities being Agni, Vāyu, Āditya); ṢaḍB 2.1.9ff.; JB 1.102; 1.270 (the gods here being Agni, Indra, Sūrya); and KB 22,1–9 (Agni and the Vāsus; Indra and the Maruts; and Varuṇa and the Ādityas). For an inversion of the usual pattern, see ŚB 14.3.1.4–8 (*gāyatrī* = sky, *triṣṭubh* = atmosphere, *jagatī* = earth).

46. These texts actually form quadripartite structures: "From his feet, from his firm foundation, he emitted the twenty-one-versed (*ekaviṃśa*) hymn of praise; along with it he emitted the *anuṣṭubh* among the meters, not a single one among the gods, the Śūdra among men. Therefore the Śūdra has abundant animals but is unable to sacrifice, for he has no deity which was emitted along with him. Therefore he does not rise above simply the washing of feet, for from the feet he was emitted. Therefore the twenty-one-versed among the hymns of praise is a firm foundation, for it was emitted from the firm foundation" (PB 6.1.11; cf. TS 7.1.1.5–6; JB 1.69, where the fourth chain is feet/firm foundation = twenty-one-versed hymn of praise = *anuṣṭubh* meter = *yajñayajñiya* chant = no god = Śūdra = sheep = washing feet).

47. These texts go on to add chains of homologies for the north and the zenith as well, e.g., ŚB 5.4.1.6–7: "Ascend to the north! May the *anuṣṭubh* (meter) impel you, the *vairāja* chant, the twenty-one-versed hymn of praise, the autumn season, fruit (*phala*) the power. Ascend to the zenith! May the *pankti* (meter) impel you, the *śākvara* and *raivata* chants, the twenty-seven- and thirty-three-versed hymns of praise, the

winter and cool seasons, splendor (*varcas*) the power." For the equation of the *gāyatrī* and the east, *triṣṭubh* and the south, *jagatī* and the west, *anuṣṭubh* and the north, and *paṅkti* and the zenith, see also ŚB 1.2.5.6–7; 8.3.1.1,12; 8.3.2.9; 8.3.3.1; etc. For four-part equations (leaving out *paṅkti* = zenith), consult TB 3.2.9.6–8. For six-part structures that include meters and cardinal directions (together with zenith and nadir), see KB 22.1–23.8; MU 7.1–6.

48. For such connections, see, e.g., TS 2.1.3.2–3; ŚB 5.1.3.3; 5.3.1.6; 5.5.2.9; 8.7.3.21.

REFERENCES

Bodewitz, H. W.
1982 "The Waters in Vedic Classifications." *Indologica Taurinensia* 10:49, n. 27.

Chakrabarti, S. C.
1980 *The* Paribhāṣās *in the Śrautasūtras*. Calcutta: Sanskrit Pustak Bhandar.

Dandekar, R. N., ed.
1958 *Śrautakośa (English Section)*. Vol. 1, pt. 1:16, 20, 24. Poona: Vaidika Saṃśodhana Maṇḍala.

Gonda, Jan
1966 *Loka: World and Heaven in the Veda*. Amsterdam: N.V. Noord-Hollandsche Uitgevers Maatschappij.

Graham, William A.
1987 *Beyond the Written Word: Oral Aspects of Scripture in the History of Religion*. Cambridge: Cambridge University Press.

Jordens, J. T. F.
1978 *Dayānanda Sarasvatī: His Life and Ideas*. Delhi: Oxford University Press.

Kane, P. V.
1974 *History of Dharmaśāstra*. Vol. 2, pt. 1:300–304. Poona: Bhandarkar Oriental Research Institute.

Lincoln, Bruce
1985 "The Tyranny of Taxonomies." Center for Humanistic Studies Occasional Paper, no. 1. Minneapolis: University of Minnesota.

Mookerji, R. K.
1947 *Ancient Indian Education (Brahmanical and Buddhist)*. London: Macmillan.

Organ, Troy

1973 "Three into Four in Hinduism." *Ohio Journal of Religious Studies* 1:7–13.

Smith, Brian K.

1986 "Ritual, Knowledge and Being." *Numen* 33(1):65–89.

1987 "Exorcising the Transcendent: Strategies for defining Hinduism and Religion." *History of Religions* 27(1):32–55.

1989 *Reflections on Resemblance, Ritual and Religion*. New York: Oxford University Press.

1989 "Classifying the Universe: Ancient Indian Cosmogonies and the Varṇa System." *Contributions to Indian Sociology* (n.s.) 23(2):241–60.

1990 "Eaters, Food, and Social Hierarchy in Ancient India: A Dietary Guide to a Revolution of Values." *Journal of the American Academy of Religion* 58(2):201–29.

1991 "Classifying Animals and Humans in Ancient India." *Man (The Journal of the Royal Anthropological Institute)* (n.s.) 26:323–41.

Smith, Jonathan Z.

1982 "Sacred Persistence: Toward a Redescription of Canon." In *Imagining Religion: From Babylon to Jonestown*. Chicago: University of Chicago Press.

Thite, G. U.

1975 *Sacrifice in the Brāhmaṇa-Texts*, 288–90. Poona: University of Poona.

Young, Richard Fox

1981 *Resistant Hinduism: Sanskrit Sources on Anti-Christian Apologetics in Early Nineteenth-Century India*. Vienna: Publications of the De Nobili Research Library.

PART TWO

The Vedas in Classical Discourse

4

PURĀṆAVEDA

FREDERICK M. SMITH

THE VĀYU PURĀṆA EMPLOYS the term *purāṇaveda* not only in its literal sense of "ancient knowledge" or "ancient Veda," but also to define the Veda as Purāṇa,[1] a Veda that is not fixed in time but is continually renewed.[2] This sense of the renewal of knowledge is shared by virtually all Purāṇas and represents a continuity of vision found in the *Mahābhārata* as well as in certain texts of the early Vedic canon. As prominent in the Purāṇas as the idea of Veda as Purāṇa, and usually as explicitly stated, is the reverse: the idea of Purāṇa as Veda. The Purāṇa envisioned itself as bearing the message of the Vedas and, with good reason, as responsible for the transmission of this message to the general public.

The primary aim of this chapter is to study the mechanisms through which the images of the Vedas were transmitted and transformed in the Purāṇas, focusing primarily on the *Bhāgavata Purāṇa.* In this way we hope to gain at least a taste of the Vedic identity of the Purāṇas. The method will be largely text-critical, at the same time hoping to minimize flat retelling and analysis of mythology, encyclopedic summaries of sacrifices reported in the Purāṇas, and so on.[3] After enlarging on the methodological approach, I shall engage three topics: (1) the infallibility of the Veda in the Purāṇas, (2) the treatment and transformation of Agni and Soma, and (3) the manner in which sacrifice was transformed. Finally, I shall offer a few conclusions pertaining to the reinterpretation of the Vedas in the Purāṇas, the Purāṇas as Vedic canonical text, and the nature of Vedic orthodoxy.

Among the Purāṇas the *Bhāgavata* (BhP) has arguably maintained the highest profile through the last millennium and a half,[4] a period during which "devotional" paradigms have maintained ascendancy. There are obvious reasons for this. First, the BhP contains the definitive account of the life and exploits of the devotionally archetypal deity Kṛṣṇa (earlier accounts such as that found in the *Mahābhārata* notwithstanding). Second, no other Purāṇa has managed to usurp or even adequately share this territory. Many Purāṇas describe the grandeur of Śiva, Viṣṇu, the Goddess, or other deities, but in none is the Purāṇa's vitality so fully consumed by a single burst of originality as the Kṛṣṇa cycle expressed in the *Bhāgavata.* And rarely is any single Purāṇic deity so estimably beyond the boundaries of Vedic discourse than is Kṛṣṇa, as will be evident by his relative absence from this chapter. It is well known that Śiva, as Rudra, as well as the Goddess reside at the peripheries of Vedic mythology and ritual; more central is Viṣṇu. But nowhere in the Vedas is Kṛṣṇa mentioned, at least in any form that could predict his future course on the subcontinent.[5] Nevertheless, in spite of a near absence of references to the Vedas in the life of Kṛṣṇa as presented in the tenth book of the BhP, the Purāṇa, taken as a whole, is saturated with references to Vedic deities, sages, rituals, and myths.

Without the practically anomalous tenth book, the BhP shares much with other (particularly Vaiṣṇava) Purāṇas in that it glorifies Viṣṇu, using either that name or the names Nārāyaṇa and Hari. In other words, the differentiation of Viṣṇu from Kṛṣṇa, while always a minor current in the Purāṇa, does not burst forth until the tenth book. The integration of that book with the remainder of the work is, then, somewhat problematic. Because of the difficulties encountered in trying to introduce explicit Vedic material into the tenth book, the author(s) attempted to equalize its Vedic content in other ways, notably through the grammar, which was forcibly, though literately, archaized.[6]

Ludo Rocher, in his book *The Purāṇas,* provides an excellent summary (pp. 13–17), to which the reader should profitably refer, of the different views within both the Indian and Western scholarly traditions concerning the relationship of the Vedas and the Purāṇas. In brief, within both communities there is considerable disagreement, some holding that there is no relationship, others contending that they are identical. An extreme example of the latter view is the notion that the BhP is nothing more than an interpretation of the Vedic Gāyatrī mantra.[7] Similar to the term *purāṇaveda* is the term *purāṇasaṃhitā,* found at the end of the *Matsya Purāṇa,* which refers to the Purāṇa itself as superior to all the *śāstra*s, as the true path of dharma, *artha,* and *kāma.*[8] This term also occurs in the BhP (8.21.2), in which the personified *purāṇasaṃhitā*[9] bows to the feet of Viṣṇu Trivikrama. In similar fashion, the Purāṇas often claim to be the fifth Veda, surely not an unimportant assertion in their quest for canonical recognition.[10]

Such claims are not usually taken seriously by modern scholarship. The reasons are simple and clear: the Vedas are generally considered to be a specific body of literature beginning with the *Ṛg-Veda* and ending with the Upaniṣads, while the Purāṇas are organized and conceptualized along demonstrably different lines. Nevertheless, a serious reading of the Purāṇas could just as well bear out a Vedic identity. In the first instance, we must consider the claim simply because it is made; whatever differences in belief and ritual we might locate from reading the respective texts, the authors and compilers of the Purāṇas envisioned a continuity. Furthermore, a serious reading of any Purāṇa reveals, as already noted, a myriad of references to the Vedas. In order for the assertion of the Purāṇas to be comprehensively demonstrated, the notion and parameters of Vedic tradition must be reevaluated, and quite likely taken beyond the boundaries set upon it by modern scholarship. While that is not the task of the present chapter, we can consider the way a single very important Purāṇa addresses this continuity. Thus, using a limited number of examples I shall try to show how the BhP takes both the Veda and Vedic ritual and reshapes them to meet its own ideological and ritual needs. Thus, the question of the "canonicity" of the Purāṇa will be a constant subtext. In the context of other studies in this volume, it will be clear that despite formal descriptions of what constitutes Vedic literature, the fact is that in India the Veda was no closed canon.[11] The Purāṇas regarded themselves as Veda and canonical, and constantly employed previous versions to serve their own purposes.

INFALLIBILITY OF THE VEDA

One of the guiding notions throughout the history of Indian religious thought has been that the Veda is infallible. Essentially this means that the word of the Veda contains absolute validity and that the pursuit of the four *puruṣārtha*s or goals of life—dharma, *artha, kāma,* and *mokṣa*—must be carried out in accordance with this word. Yet from the very outset a major problem arose: very few knew or understood the words of the Veda. Nevertheless, this did not prevent massive attempts at its interpretation. This problem has been addressed by paṇḍits and scholars alike for thousands of years with little agreement except that a few basic principles of interpretation must be established that can confer upon the Vedas relevance to life as it is usually experienced in this world. These principles were largely configured around injunction and prohibition, and were taken up largely by the Pūrvamīmāṃsā and the Dharmaśāstra. Disregarded very early on in this search for interpretative standards were the Saṃhitās of the *Ṛg-Veda* and *Atharva-Veda,* whose language was almost entirely unintelligible and whose mythology and doctrines, such as they could be discerned, were largely irrelevant. What emerged was the *notion* of Veda as an interpretive category, to a great extent apart from the canon of texts consisting of Saṃhitās, Brāhmaṇas, Āraṇyakas, and Upaniṣads. The Veda became a symbol for pure and divine origins, which is to say an abstract signifier of transcendence, and a tool for the exercise of current interpretive ideas.[12] With relevance to the principal text in question, the BhP says, "just as the waking and sleep states (retain their authority) during dreaming, likewise the injunctive and prohibitive force (of the sacred texts retain their authority in any situation)" (7.15.61).[13]

The Purāṇas employed several strategies to prove this authority or infallibility: (1) they tried to demonstrate that the Veda was identical with the primary deity of the Purāṇa; (2) they employed unlikely varieties of genealogy to demonstrate that the Vedas themselves were part of a lineage that included the sages of the Vedas and Purāṇas; (3) they employed current theological or philosophical ideas, particularly the doctrine of *śabdabrahman,* to logically prove the Veda's infallibility. Because the notion of *śabdabrahman* is predicated on the idea of the gradual manifestation of sound, that is of the Veda, this strategy also involved a genealogy of sorts: a genealogy of sound.

The very first verse of the BhP (1.1.1) says that the Vedas, which bewilder even the greatest sages, were revealed to Brahmā by the mere intention (*hṛd*) of Viṣṇu.[14] Thus, the primary deity of the BhP generates the Veda, a position scrupulously denied by the supposed progenitors of "Vedic orthodoxy," the Mīmāṃsakas beginning with Śabara. According to the Pūrvamīmāṃsā, the Veda is self-created and eternal; it is without an external creator, even God.[15] An intermediary position, admitting both the idea of creation and the priority of the gods over the Vedas, is found in the *Mahābhārata,* where it is said in the *Śāntiparvan* that "the Vedas were created here by the self-existent one in order to praise the gods."[16] In philosophical discourse, however, the position of the Mīmāṃsakas was accepted by most of the influential Vedānta schools, most notably the *advaita* of Śaṅkara. Thus, the question naturally arises: were these *advaitin*s any more "orthodox" because of this view than the Paurāṇikas who argued that God created the Vedas?[17] Certainly not, as orthodoxy could be found in many stripes.[18] In any event, the Vedas were rendered no more or less infallible for their self-manifestation (*apauruṣeyatva*) as they were for being created by God.

This is enlarged in the BhP where Nārāyaṇa is equated with the original person (*ādipuruṣa*) and is thus the subject of inquiry of the inspired sages and even of the Veda itself (5.22.3).[19] We shall encounter many instances of the Vedic *puruṣa* becoming the Purāṇic *puruṣottama.* In the BhP the Lord is praised as the Veda itself (*sarvavedamayo hariḥ,* 7.11.7). In a common Purāṇic image of the *puruṣottama,* the BhP reconfigures the cosmological duties of Puruṣa and Prajāpati of the Vedas[20] by equating significant attributes to Viṣṇu's body parts: "Asceticism is my heart; mantra (*brahman*) is my body; knowledge assumes the shape of my activity; sacrifices are (my) limbs, the dharma born (from those sacrifices) is (my) essence (*ātman*), the gods are (my) various breaths'' (6.4.46).[21] More specifically borrowing the imagery of the *Ṛg-Vedic puruṣa,* the BhP states that ''the Brāhmaṇa (caste) and the (sacred) fire are the mouth of Viṣṇu, (which is) the essence (*ātman*) of all the Vedas'' (8.16.9).[22]

From body parts, it is a short step to identifying the Veda as the very body of the Lord (BhP 11.16.13, MatsyaP 8.4). Thus, Vedic deities and other elements of creation emerge from the body of Bhagavān, as the supreme *puruṣa* (BhP 3.6.12–40). Combining his Vedic form with his spiritual attributes and authority, the BhP states: "Through (your) body in the form of the threefold (Veda), with the knowledge of the four groups of priests, you weave the seven threads [soma sacrifices]. You are the One, the Self of embodied beings, without beginning or end, infinite, the inspired sage (*kavi*), the inner controller'' (7.3.30).[23] Infallibility, then, is due to the Lord's identity with the Vedic *puruṣa*. A more specific identity with the Vedic ritual occurs in the form of a riddle, part of an old tradition going back to *Ṛg-Veda* 1.164: ''Hail (to you), endowed with two heads, three feet, four horns, seven arms, the one presiding over the sacrifice, the one whose essence is the threefold knowledge'' (BhP 8.16.31).[24]

These attributes and functions of Viṣṇu are taken over by Kṛṣṇa during his instruction of Uddhava in the eleventh book of the BhP. For example, Kṛṣṇa as *puruṣa* is identified with Viṣṇu and the Veda while imparting knowledge of the duties of the four *varṇa*s (BhP 11.17).[25] Finally Kṛṣṇa declares his instruction to Uddhava to be Veda (BhP 11.14.3). Because the identification Viṣṇu/Kṛṣṇa has become so thorough, Kṛṣṇa's instruction in the Purāṇa, pointedly his devotional lessons, becomes equally ''Vedic,'' thus rendering their container, the Purāṇa, equally infallible. In one revealing instance referred to earlier (BhP 8.21.2), the Vedas and Upavedas come to prostrate at the feet of the Trivikrama form of Hari.[26]

Infallibility is also traced through genealogies. This strategy, taken from the Brāhmaṇa texts themselves,[27] both divinizes the cosmos and the Veda and establishes an interdependence between them and the Lord and his agents, the sages. This is both manifestation and proof of an ancient Indian notion of connectedness and continuity in all aspects of nature, even if it was essentially unfathomable. In the BhP, the divine origins of ritual and time are known from their ancestry, in which they are either divinized descendants or descended from deities specifically known from the Vedas for their ritual associations (6.18.1–4).

One of the conceptual identities of the Vedas and the Purāṇas is that the entire cosmos is conceived as divine. The difference is that the Vedas make little coherent attempt to unify or organize this conception through a single deity and generally maintain a distinct dualism of gods and divine demons, while the Purāṇas, with their decidedly sectarian bias, attempt to focus all creative (and destructive) activity through a single deity, even to the extent of denying the dualism of the demons and the supreme deity. For example, in the passage cited above (6.18.1–4), Pṛśni, the wife of Savitṛ, bore several children including Sāvitrī, the deity presiding over the Gāyatrī mantra; Vyāhṛti, who presides over the three sacred syllables *bhūḥ, bhuvaḥ,* and *s(u)vaḥ* (*vyāhṛti*[28]); Trayī, who presides over the ritual knowledge of the threefold Veda; and the deities Agnihotra, Paśu, Soma, Cāturmāsya, and the (Five) Great Sacrifices.[29] Also, the four wives of Dhātā, the seventh son of Aditi, named Kuhū, Sinīvālī, Rākā, and Anumati, who as deities preside over the fourteenth day of the dark fortnight, the new moon day, the fourteenth day of the bright fortnight, and the full moon day, respectively, gave birth to the deities Sāyam (Evening), Darśa (New Moon), Prātaḥ (Morning), and Pūrṇamāsa (Full Moon).

In spite of genealogy containing an assortment of notions and life forms, all deities and sacrifices are ultimately resolved in the character of Viṣṇu, even as they are responsible for his creation. The BhP recognizes this interdependence: "Viṣṇu, sacrifice personified and the embodiment of dharma, has his origin in the rites of the twice born. He is the refuge of the gods, rishis, ancestors, and other beings, as well as of dharma (itself)" (7.2.11).[30] Even beyond this, Viṣṇu as both manifest and unmanifest is known from the Veda.[31]

Another guarantor of the infallibility of the Veda lies in its own genealogy, broadly defined as both familial origin and lines of direct transmission or authority. The BhP relates the following (1.4.19–29). Originally the Veda was one. This was subsequently divided by Vedavyāsa into four Saṃhitās, with Itihāsa and Purāṇa as the fifth Veda. These were passed on to his pupils Paila, Jaimini, Sumantu, Vaiśampāyana, and Romaharṣaṇa, who learned the *Ṛg-Veda, Sāma-Veda, Atharva-Veda, Yajur-Veda,* and Itihāsa and Purāṇa, respectively. The first four then divided their Vedas into various rescensional branches (*śākhā*), so that "they could be maintained (even) by the dull-witted" (*durmedhair dhāryante,* 1.4.24).[32] Vedavyāsa then composed the *Mahābhārata* in order to reveal the import of the Vedas to women, fallen Brahmins, Śūdras, Kṣatriyas, and Vaiśyas.

The BhP contains the following, from Kṛṣṇa to Uddhava, explaining how the Vedas became so diverse and confused: "In time, this word (*vāṇī*), designated 'Veda,' was lost during the cosmic dissolution. At the beginning (of the next creation) I declared to Brahmā this dharma, whose purpose is to maintain Me as the object. He taught this to his eldest son Manu, and the seven great seers associated with the Veda (*brahmamaharṣayaḥ*) received it from him. From these fathers, (it was transmitted to) their progeny: the gods, demons who directly oppose the gods (*dānava*), Guhyakas, men, Siddhas and Gandharvas, along with Vidyādharas and

Cāraṇas, men of other continents [comm. on *kiṃdevāḥ*], Kinnaras, Nāgas, ordinary demons (*rakṣas*), Kiṃpuruṣas,[33] and others. Their natures are all different, born of the three fundamental qualities of *sattva* (clarity, purity), *rajas* (energy, activity, passion), and *tamas* (inertia, darkness). As a result of this, in accordance with their nature, beings and their ideas differ; thus flow diverse interpretations of the Vedas'' (11.14.3–7).[34] It should be noted that all these beings, good or evil, accept the authority of the Veda. The most wicked of them all in the BhP, Kaṃsa, who killed Kṛṣṇa's brethren believing each of them to be Kṛṣṇa, implicitly recognizes the supremacy of the Veda, the cow, Brahmins, asceticism, and sacrifices. Because their presence is prerequisite to the appearance of Viṣṇu, he vows to kill all Brahmins who are knowers of the Veda, all ascetics, cows that give milk for sacrifice, and so on. Kaṃsa is aware of Kṛṣṇa's nature and of his own role, and through recognition of the inevitable failure of his mission he admits the infallibility of the Veda (BhP 10.4.38–40).

Again, with respect to the transmission of the Vedas by the Manus, the BhP explains that the Manus, Indras, and other gods are under the command of *puruṣa* (*puruṣaśāsana*) (8.14.1–10). This *puruṣa*, understood as Viṣṇu (viz., *puruṣa* manifested as sacrifice, Yajña personified), directs the Manus to administer the universe. "At the end of each cycle of four *yugas*, the rishis, through their asceticism, saw the collections of *śrutis* swallowed up by time, after which the eternal (*sanātanaḥ*) dharma (was re-established).''[35] Then instructed by Hari, the Manus themselves propagated the dharma. Eventually the BhP states that ''in every *yuga* the Lord imparts pure knowledge by assuming the form of *siddhas*, imparts knowledge of ritual by taking the form of rishis, and transmits knowledge of yoga by taking the form of Lords of Yoga.''[36] Thus, the Lord himself is responsible for the generation of the Veda and consequent sacred knowledge through his various manifestations and agents.

Another type of Vedic genealogy is that of phonetics, the genealogy or origin of the Veda in primal sound, acknowledged by the BhP as *śabdabrahman.* The BhP, of course, is not the ideal source for this doctrine,[37] but it is mentioned in several places and neatly summarized twice, in the eleventh and twelfth books.[38] The final book describes the tripartite nature of the syllable *om* and the subsequent descent of the *guṇas*, the sounds *bhūr, bhuvaḥ, s(u)vaḥ,* Brahmā, the alphabet (*akṣara*), and finally, through Brahmā, the four Vedas with the four chief ritual officiants.[39] After this sequential manifestation, Brahmā taught the Vedas to his sons, and finally, at the end of the *dvāparayuga,* they were divided into the four divisions of Saṃhitā, Brāhmaṇa, Āraṇyaka, and Upaniṣad (12.6.36–47). The passage in the eleventh book begins by declaring that the Vedas deal with the subject of the Self as *brahman* (*vedā brahmātmaviṣayāḥ*) and that ''*śabdabrahman,* extremely difficult to

PLATE 4.1. Manifestation of the Vedas in the Purāṇas: the four Vedas salute Viṣṇu after their rescue from the depths of the cosmic ocean by Matsya Avatāra. (Chamba school, ca. 1780, from the private collection of Wayne and Vimala Begley).

understand, consists of vital breath (*prāṇa*), the ability to apprehend (*indriya*), and the mind (*manas*).'' The Vedas, through *śabdabrahman,* are manifested by Kṛṣṇa (*mayopabṛṃhitam*) like a spider spinning forth a web from its heart through its mouth. In the same way the *prāṇa* moves from the heart through the mind, possessed of the sound *om,* materializing the various syllables.[40] Ultimately the Vedic meters are produced, at least those that increase in syllable count in increments of four, beginning with the eight-syllabled Gāyatrī, and, most interestingly, other, presumably vernacular, languages (*vicitrabhāṣāvitatām,* 11.21.40).

Finally, says the narrator—none other than Kṛṣṇa himself—all of sacred sound, which is the Veda, including injunction, mantras, ritual, deities, and spiritual knowledge, is none other than He Himself (BhP 11.21.35–43). Ultimately, this explication of *śabdabrahman* is integrated into an anticipated theistic framework: ''Such is the meaning of all the Vedas: the Veda (*śabda*), after becoming established in Me, posits difference as mere illusion and (then) denies it, in the end becoming quiescent'' (11.21.43).[41] Along the same lines but more simply, the BhP declares that Brahmā brought forth from his four mouths, each of which faces one of the four primary directions, the four Vedas and Upavedas. Then he discharged (*sasṛje*) the Itihāsa and Purāṇa, the fifth Veda, from all his mouths simultaneously (3.12.37–39).[42] In one passage (6.16.51) the BhP speaks explicitly of the Veda as *śābdabrahman* and identifies it as the body of Bhagavān.[43]

Commenting on these interpretive notions, Wilhelm Halbfass writes:

> The theistic traditions. . .view the Vedas as the word of God, and as a stage in an open-ended process of revelation. In this view, they are susceptible to, and even call for, continued revisions, explications, adaptations, and other forms of divine supplementation and renewal. Furthermore, there is also room for the idea that the present Vedas are not the Veda per se, that is its true and real archetype. The 'real' and original Veda is thus contrasted with the extant Vedic texts and invoked against their 'orthodox' and inflexible guardians, and a dynamic sense of tradition is brought into confrontation with a static and archival one.[44]

Halbfass supports this statement with a citation from BhP (9.14.48): *eka eva purā vedaḥ praṇavaḥ sarvavāṅmayaḥ*: "Previously there was only one Veda, the syllable 'om', that constituted all speech."[45] The passage continues that there was also only one god, Nārāyaṇa, as well as only one fire and one *varṇa.* Then the Purāṇa states that the threefold Vedic knowledge was brought into being by Purūravas at the beginning of the *tretayuga.* I need add to Halbfass' perceptive comments only that this passage is also employed by the BhP to justify the "static and archival" Veda, to locate it in a certain familiar, indeed familial or genealogical, context in order to bring it, warts and all, into the realm of infallibility.

The question may be asked, as van Buitenen did more than twenty-five years ago, why it was necessary for the BhP to carry this cumbersome baggage of Vedic infallibility.[46] Van Buitenen posits that under pressure from the Smārta Brahman community of South India, following attacks by Śaṅkara and others,[47] the minority Bhāgavatas were forced to prove their orthodoxy: "The Bhāgavata's point is: I am not only orthodox in the Vedic tradition, I even sound like the Veda."[48] Perhaps more to the point is that it is natural in most of Indian intellectual tradition to attempt to authenticate the present by resorting to the authority of the past. Van Buitenen writes that, "For us, to put it briefly, knowledge is something to be *discovered,* for the Indian knowledge is to be *recovered.*"[49] Just as generations later a family can retain the name of an ancient ancestor, the Purāṇa harks back to its highly revered ancestor, the Veda, for a continuity of revelation, though the form of the revelation might have significantly altered. More explicitly, the baggage of Vedic infallibility was also the baggage of Purāṇic infallibility: the Veda must be proven infallible in order for the Purāṇa to assert its infallibility In other words, Vedic infallibility was an important strategy in the Purāṇa's quest for status as part of the Vedic canon.

Despite donning this cloak of Vedic infallibility, the Purāṇa still maintains an uncomfortable distinction between Purāṇa and Veda by reminding us constantly that in practice devotion to the Lord is more important than the personal fulfillment of Vedic injunction. Yet, transgressing Vedic injunction, at least to the extent that it also contravened Bhāgavata dharma, risked grave consequence. The BhP reminds us that transgressors of the Veda are subject to severe afterlife punishments for illegal soma drinking, sacrificing animals, and so on (5.26.25ff.). However, the transcendent value of devotion to the Lord was a constant resource—we can call it a "canonical resource"[50]—that proved to work well with the *notion* of the Veda and its infallibility. Perhaps the most glaring testimony to this is the story of Ajāmila (BhP 6.1–2), a Brahmin characterized as ideal in his truthfulness, service, self-control, virtue, and knowledge of the Veda (6.1.56–58). Despite living fully in accord with the Veda, he falls from his pedestal (naturally a woman of low caste is involved), ruining himself and his family. Finally, in a drunken stupor he cries out, with little clarity but great sincerity, the name of his son, Nārāyaṇa. The Lord, hearing his own name called, releases Ajāmila from his foolishness, restores him to a life of virtue, and ultimately welcomes him into Vaikuṇṭha, his highest abode. In spite of his knowledge of the Vedas, Ajāmila, otherwise a prime candidate for afterlife punishment, was "at once completely liberated by taking the Lord's name" (*sadyo vimukto bhagavānnāma gṛhṇan,* 6.2.45).

AGNI AND SOMA

Agni and Soma, the two principal deities of the Vedic sacrifice, are brought into the Purāṇic orbit through many of the same strategies that were applied to the notion of infallibility. On these two deities in general, the *Ṛg-Veda* (ṚV) says, "Agni and Soma, joined together in sacrifice, you have put these shining lights in heaven" (1.93.5). In their joint operation, they represent the two poles of the Vedic universe: fire and ambrosia, heat and cold, consumption and continuity, sustenance in this world and deliverance to the next.[51] This is borne out in a variety of texts that bear on mythology, ritual, and medicine. While this chapter is not the proper place to fully demonstrate this point—it would take a major book—I shall try to show how the Vedic conceptions of Agni and Soma are reflected and transformed in the Purāṇas.

In the Vedas, Agni is the center of the ritual, the mediator between man and deity who existed independently as well as within man and deity. As fire and god of fire, he is both the earthly representative of the sun and the one who draws together the terrestrial and celestial realms. But his form is not simple and univalent: forms of Agni proliferate as his functions expand.[52] This ontology persists in the Purāṇas. The *Brahmāṇḍa Purāṇa* recognizes both the connection between the sun and fire and the distinction and connection between Agni as deity and Agni as fire that is forged in the Agnihotra ritual as described in the earlier Brāhmaṇa texts: the luster of the sun, after sunset, enters the fire. As a result of this, the fire shines from afar. When the sun rises again the luster reenters it.[53]

Like the Vedas, the Purāṇas distinguish aspects of Agni. While the Vedas recognize dozens of aspects or forms of Agni,[54] the Purāṇas deal almost exclusively with three of the most important ones: Agni Pavamāna ("the Purifying"), Agni Pāvaka ("the Purifier"), and Agni Śuci ("the Resplendent"), three deities who are often invoked in this order and offered oblations of rice flour cakes (*puroḍāśa*) in the Vedic ritual, usually in rituals of expiation and reparation (*prāyaścitta*).[55] For example, the *Kūrma Purāṇa* (1.12.14ff.) knows the fire as Rudra, the son of Brahmā. From the union of this Rudrāgni with Svāhā were born three sons: Pavamāna, Pāvaka, and Śuci. The fire produced from churning is Pavamāna; lightning is Pāvaka; Śuci is the fire that shines in the sun.[56] In the *Brahmāṇḍa Purāṇa* (1.2.11.4–6) Agni's three forms are Kavyavāhana, the son of Pavamāna, the bearer of oblations to the deceased ancestors; Saharakṣas, the son of Pāvaka, the fire of the Asuras; and Havyavāhana, the son of Śuci, who carries oblations to gods. The BhP says that Agni has forty-nine forms: himself, his three sons by Svāhā—Pavamāna, Pāvaka, and Śuci—and their forty-five sons (who are not named), and adds that all are invoked in sacrifices (4.1.60–66).[57] Though the BhP notes that the names of Pṛthu's grandsons, Pāvaka, Pavamāna, and Śuci, are born as a result of the order of Agni's names in the sacrifice (4.24.4), the fact is that the BhP is aware that a conceptual transformation of the Vedic proliferation of forms or aspects of Agni has taken place. This is certain because the complete list of forty-nine names, from which the BhP passage must have been summarized, is given in other Purāṇas, namely, in the *agnivaṃśa* chapters of the *Vāyu* (ch.29) and *Matsya* (ch.51) *Purāṇa*s. In these Purāṇas most of the family names are of fires or fireplaces. Thus, Pavamāna, Pāvaka, and Śuci, who receive offerings in the Vedic ritual as aspects of the deity Agni, serve in the Purāṇas as the Vedic link to a list of names of fires.

The question thus arises: is Agni reduced in the Purāṇas from multifaceted deity to mere multifaceted fire? Though most of the names of Agni in the Purāṇas are names of fires and fireplaces, several names of Agni as deity do occur, many of them not mentioned in the Vedas. For example, the *Brahmāṇḍa Purāṇa* says that the fire is called Paśupati (Lord of Animals): Agni is the archetypal sacrificial animal and protects all others as well (*pāti paśūn,* 1.2.10.47). Other names of Agni as deity predate the Purāṇas but are sometimes not found in the ṚV or the primary ritual texts. For example, the BhP mentions Hutāśana ("Oblation Eater"), Havyavāhana ("Oblation Carrier"), and Vahni ("Conveyer [of Oblations]") (1.15.8, 8.4.21, etc.). Hutāśana occurs only in the late Vedic literature,[58] while Havyavāhana is often found in the ṚV (e.g., 1.36.10, 1.44.2),[59] as is Vahni (e.g., ṚV 1.3.9, 1.14.6). More revealing is a passage in the BhP that contains a list of the names of the ten sons of Priyavrata, himself a son of Manu (5.1.25). All ten are said to be names of Agni, yet only two are taken from the Vedic literature (Ghṛtapṛṣṭa and Kavi).[60] It is important to note that these are not members of Agni's lineage of fires and fireplaces, but are names of Agni himself, though the Purāṇas do not assign any ritual significance to these names.

In this way the Purāṇas, including the aggressively Vaiṣṇava *Bhāgavata,* expanded Agni's domain through both the construction of genealogies (*agnivaṃśa*) and the assignation of names that recalled the Vedic Agni. Agni, like other deities, was substantialized through name. With respect to genealogy, the Purāṇas tell of an original fire giving rise to many, usually with the help of a rishi.[61] Rarely does Agni reproduce on his own volition. It is a natural process only to the extent that it is mediated, thus squarely in the tradition of the Veda. Though not as anthropomorphised as many other deities, Agni in the Veda is given various genealogies. He "arises from strength" (ṚV 6.48.5), doubtless a reference to the ritual churning of fire. Thus, he is born of wood (ṚV 6.3.3, 10.79.7), as the embryo of plants (ṚV 2.1.14, 3.1.13). He also originates in celestial waters (as Apāṃ Napāt) and is the embryo of these waters (ṚV 7.9.3, 1.70.3). He is born in the highest heavens (ṚV 1.143.2, 6.8.2), on the other side of the air (ṚV 10.187.4,5). Perhaps most important for our purposes, Agni is called, in one passage of the *Ṛg-Veda,* the sun rising in the morning (ṚV 10.88.6). This is the earliest recorded formulation of the Brāhmaṇic and Purāṇic notion noted above of the continuity of the nocturnal fire and the diurnal sun. Agni is the son of heaven and earth who nevertheless generates these same two worlds (ṚV 1.96.4, cf. 7.5.7). With respect to the role of sages or semidivine figures mediating the birth of Agni in the Veda, Mātariśvan, the messenger of Vivasvat, is said to have "kindled the oblation-bearer who was concealed" (ṚV 3.5.10, cf. 3.2.13). By churning he brought the hidden Agni from the world of the gods (ṚV 3.9.5, cf. 1.71.4, 1.141.3, 1.148.1).

In the Purāṇas Agni's conception and birth occur by methods and into families hardly recognized in the Vedas. The *Brahmāṇḍa Purāṇa* (2.3.66.19) says that the original fire was named Aila, the son of Ilā. The sage Purūravas, possessor of this fire, then divided it into the three principal sacred *śrauta* fires: *āhavanīya, dakṣiṇa,* and *gārhapatya.* In

PLATES 4.2, 4.3. Agni Bhagavān emerging from the sacred fire: Two images of Ṛśyaśṛṅga, the deer-horned sage (on the left of the fire), offering an oblation for the purpose of producing a son (namely Rāma) for King Daśaratha. The photo on the top clearly depicts Ṛśyaśṛṅga. The photo below depicts Agni emerging from the fire. (Hazari-Ram Temple, Vijayanagara. Photos by the author.)

another story, the *Skanda Purāṇa* (5.3.22.2ff.) reports that Agni was a mind-born son of Brahmā, and that his wife was Svāhā, the daughter of the sage Dakṣa.[62] From the union of Agni and Svāhā were born the three fires. Sometime later Agni propitiated Śiva on the bank of the Narmadā and requested as a boon that the sixteen rivers become his wives. Two elements are of importance here: first, the union of fire with the personified exclamation Svāhā, the daughter of a rishi. The Purāṇa here recognizes the impulsion and manifestation through ritual sound, thus man-made, of Agni's position as link between man and deity. In addition, this passage demonstrates a balance—actually Agni's plea for balance—between heat and cold, fire and water, the latter being the sixteen rivers, thus Agni and Soma: as if Agni or heat requires for his/its sustenance Soma or coolness, with the transposition in the Purāṇa of soma to water.[63]

The three *śrauta* fires are also assigned family relationships. Not unrelated in spirit to the Purāṇas, *Manusmṛti* (2.231) states that the *gārhapatya* is the father, the *dakṣiṇāgni* the mother, the *āhavanīya* the guru.[64] The Vedas provide no precedent for this and the Smṛti no explanation. In the Vedic ritual the offerings to the wives of the gods are made in the *gārhapatya,* the offerings to the ancestors—who are the Vedic gurus[65]—are made in the *dakṣiṇa,* and the offerings to the gods—almost invariably male—are made in the *āhavanīya.* Elsewhere in the Purāṇas the *gārhapatya* is Brahmā, the *dakṣiṇa* is Śiva (*trilocana*),[66] and the *āhavanīya* is Viṣṇu (*GaruḍaP* 1.205.66). In the *Vāyu Purāṇa* (29.12–15), the two additional *śrauta* fires, the *sabhya* and *āvasathya* (recognized by the texts and traditions of the *Śuklayajurveda*), are said to be the sons of Śaṃsya, while the *āhavanīya*, rather than Agni himself, marries the sixteen rivers.[67]

In addition to his unique family and ancestry, Agni is associated with certain terrestrial and celestial places. According to one passage he had his own celestial domain, which was visited by Arjuna in search of a dead child of a Brahmin of Dvāraka (BhP 10.89.44). In this world, the Sarasvatī River, visited by Vidura, is sacred to Agni (BhP 3.1.22).[68] Likewise he is worshiped in Kuśadvīpa (BhP 5.20.2), and has a *tīrtha* or sacred bathing place assigned to him, called Agnitīrtham, on the southern bank of the Yamunā (MatsyaP 108.27). In the Veda, and throughout ancient India the fire itself was held sacred. Thus, until the habit of commemorating sacred places with the performance of sacrifices and the construction of temples was developed in the epics and Purāṇas, it was not necessary to assign Agni any particular sacred place. It seems rather redundant to do so, as if the Purāṇas regarded the sanctity of the deity Agni differently than the sanctity of the fire. As deity rather than fire, hymns of praise are sung to him (e.g., VāyuP 21.71ff.), occasionally as a manifestation of another deity, such as Viṣṇu (BhP 4.24.37). As a deity he shows his pleasure with a devotee of Kṛṣṇa (BhP 10.41.13). Similarly, he can confer boons or curses, and on one occasion he even curses elephants (BhP 4.14.26–27). Yet he can also be impetuous and ignorant, behaving like wildfire. Due to Viṣṇu's *māyā,* Agni sometimes knows not what he does (BhP 6.3.14–15). After burning women and children in Tripura, he pleaded that he was not a free agent, but only carrying out orders (MatsyaP 188.29–57). Because of such behavior, he was considered not as powerful as a Brahmin, even a corrupt one (BhP 10.64.32).

Soma, like Agni, underwent a transformation in the Purāṇas. The *Ṛg-Veda* states that Mātariśvan brought Agni from the sky, while the eagle brought Soma from the rock (ṚV 1.93.6), probably a reference to a mountain in the Himālayas called Mūjavant.[69] Whatever their origins, in the later Vedic literature Agni came to be regarded as a terrestrial deity while Soma became identified with the moon.[70] Soma, like Agni, is an agent of purification. While Agni purifies through heat, Soma does so through coolness. In one exceptional instance in the *Atharva-Veda* (18.3.6–7), Agni cools and refreshes the spot he has scorched. Thus, some crossover, or, better, expansiveness, is evident in the personality of Agni; but cooling is more characteristic of Soma. The purifying and exalting properties of Soma are adduced by Soma's capacity to convey the ritualist to the world of the gods and to empower the gods themselves. The curative, hence purifying, power of Soma is frequently spoken of in the Veda: for example, Indra is said to have drunk his beloved *amṛta* (*priyam amṛtam apāyi*), which is of course none other than soma (ṚV 6.44.16). Further, the ṚV says that *amṛta* is found in the waters (*apsv antar amṛtam*) and that medicine is also found in the waters (*apsu bheṣajam*).[71]

A verse from the BhP (4.15.17) demonstrates the assumption of this proximity, indeed identity, with little distinction drawn between Soma the deity overseeing the moon, Soma the moon itself, and soma as the cooling and curative nectar (derived from the moon). Pṛthu, a part manifestation of Viṣṇu, was installed as king and honored by Brāhmins and gods, including Soma. In the verse in question, Rudra presents Pṛthu with a sword inscribed with ten marks of the moon while the goddess (Ambikā) presents him with a sword inscribed with a hundred moons. Soma is next in line to present a gift to Pṛthu, a juxtaposition intended to illustrate his position as the deity presiding over the moon. He presents as tribute a hundred horses of immortality (*amṛtmayān aśvān*).[72] Rudra and the goddess are known for their heroic and destructive exploits; thus the presentation of swords is perhaps their natural gift. The fact that they are inscribed with ten and a hundred moons signifies that they regard the moon, that is to say the multifaceted Soma, as empowering their swords. Thus, Soma's gift of undying horses, signifying eternality and strength, not only substantiates but also validates the gift of swords.

Soma's nourishing lunar life-giving coolness is succinctly illustrated in the BhP (4.30.14). Soma, here king of herbs, ameliorates the distress of the hungry and crying infant, Māriṣā, by placing his index finger (a mere digit, or fifteenth part, of the moon [*kalā*] is sufficient), dripping with nectar (*pīyūṣa*), on her mouth. The ability of Soma and the moon to create nectar is shown once more in the *Vāyu Purāṇa* (51.14–21). Soma, that is to say the moon, feeds rivers by causing rain. Soma's dedication to keep the cosmos operating smoothly by supplying a constant flow of nectar is also shown by his eternal battle with Rāhu, the head of the demon that chases and occasionally eats up the moon, causing eclipses (e.g., BhP 8.10.31).

Regarding Soma's ancestry, the BhP (4.1.15,33; 4.14.26; cf. ViṣṇuP 1.10.8) claims he is a part manifestation of Brahmā, the son of Atri and Anasūyā. The *Brahmāṇḍa* and *Matsya Purāṇa*s expand this to say that Soma, here the moon, was born from the eyes of Atri, and honored at birth by Śiva and Umā. Because of his identity as the crescent moon emerging from the crown of Śiva's head, Soma was a one-eighth manifestation of Śiva. He was later carried for three hundred years by the four directions, and upon his release became a part manifestation of Brahmā. Brahmā then transported him in his Vedic chariot borne by a thousand horses to his realm, where brahmarishis worshiped him as their king and praised him with mantras.[73] Elsewhere the BhP (6.18.1) supplies a different genealogy: Soma was the son of Savitṛ and Pṛśni. Certain other Purāṇas record still different ancestry: many say Soma was a Vasu, the son of Dharma and Sudevī.[74]

As for marriage and family, he conquered the three worlds and took Tārā (Star), Bṛhaspati's wife, by force. Soma then impregnated her and, through the intervention of Brahmā, returned her to Bṛhaspati. The offspring was Budha, the planet Mercury (BrahmāṇḍaP 3.65.28–44).[75] The relationship between the moon and Mercury, often noted in astrological literature, is, in the Purāṇas, one of mind begetting intellect. The word ***budha*** itself means intelligent or wise, and in the BhP Soma, praised by Brahmā as the food, strength, and life of the gods, the ruler of plants, and the progenitor of created beings, is declared to be the mind of Viṣṇu (8.5.34).

One of Soma's important jobs—and one not lacking in occupational hazards—is king of the plant kingdom. This role is linked to his identity as the moon, and is one in which he is often associated with other celestial bodies. In a very fine story illustrating this, he appealed to the ten Pracetases not to destroy trees that had overgrown their domain (BhP 6.4.6–16).[76] As part of his appeal (or deal), Soma, in his role as ruler of plants, offered Vārkṣī, "Daughter of the Trees," in marriage to them. They accepted, a union that ultimately produced Dakṣa, who himself eventually sired sixty daughters, among whom twenty-seven were betrothed to Soma (BhP 6.6.2). Of these twenty-seven, identified as the lunar mansions or constellations (*nakṣatra*), Soma's favorite was Rohiṇī. This partiality disturbed Dakṣa, who wanted his daughters treated equally. Thus, Dakṣa cursed Soma with a wasting disease (*yakṣma*) so that he would be childless. Though he propitiated Dakṣa and recovered by taking parts or digits (*kalā*) from the waning moon, he nevertheless remained childless (BhP 6.6.23–24).[77] Though without genetic offspring, Soma was far from impotent, as demonstrated by his nourishing and curative powers.

As with other deities he was occasionally worshiped as the highest. According to the BhP Soma was worshiped largely in Śālmalidvīpa (5.20.11–12), where he is praised as the soul of the universe, the Veda personified (*bhagavantaṃ vedamayaṃ somam ātmānam,* v. 11). The four *varṇas* of Śālmalidvīpa worship Soma with the following verse: "May Soma, the lord of all creatures, who, by means of his rays, distributes his nourishment to the gods and ancestors during both the bright and dark fortnights, reside with us on all sides."[78]

Thus, while Soma—or the moon—is equal to other gods; is capable of curing, enlivening, and empowering others; is called Rājā, the lord of plants, Brahmins,[79] and constellations; is worshiped in order to obtain a life of fullness and enjoyments; and sired the planet Mercury, he remains ever alone, always unstable.[80]

SACRIFICE

That ritual exists for purposes beyond its prescribed efficacy can be argued from even a cursory examination of the representation of the Vedic ritual in the *Mahābhārata* and the Purāṇas. In these later texts, ritual was discussed and glorified not in order to teach it, but for more imaginative and didactic purposes that lay at its peripheries: to provide a culturally credible apparatus of imagery or to illustrate human and divine possibility. The two prongs of Vedic orthodoxy, as noted above, were expressed in the Pūrvamīmāṃsā and the Purāṇas. The former argued that the cosmic or ritual process, rather than the individual, was the epicenter of the universe. Conversely, the epics and Purāṇas argued that the goal of ritual is the manifestation of the deity for salvific purposes. Often the deity is one who is not even invoked in the rituals (such as Kṛṣṇa), or who manifests in spite of or in opposition to the performance of ritual.

That said, it must be emphasized that the Purāṇas, including the BhP, are thoroughly immersed in Vedic ritual: in references to ritual detail, ritual mythology, ritual morality, and ritual mysticism. In the BhP and other Purāṇas, sacrifice is the very hypostasis of Viṣṇu, a major argument for recognition of the Purāṇas as a late genre of Vedic literature. Thus, short of repeating most of the entire Purāṇa, I will restrict my comments to summarizing a few areas of ritual discourse in the BhP.[81]

One of the primary areas of saturation is in the Purāṇa's literary imagery of invocation and evocation, which is (outside most of the tenth book) largely sacrificial. Viṣṇu and his *avatāras* Varāha, Vāmana, Narasiṃha, and even Kṛṣṇa, are very often praised as the sacrifice incarnate. Indeed, Viṣṇu depends on sacrifice for his very existence (BhP 7.2.11), while the sacrifice is effective only through Viṣṇu.[82] Viṣṇu is addressed several times as Yajña, once counted as the seventh of Viṣṇu's twenty-one *avatāras* (BhP 1.3.12),[83] and again as a partial manifestation (BhP 6.8.18).[84] One who desires fame should worship or sacrifice to Yajña (*yajñaṃ yajet,* BhP 2.3.7). Yajña is Viṣṇu, whose parts are the four *yugas*, who directs the rule of the Manus over the universe, who takes the form of rishis in order to teach proper ritual (BhP 8.14.3–10). In Viṣṇu's three strides resides the sacrifice itself (BhP 8.20.28). One of the passages that epitomizes the Purāṇic reformulation of the Vedic *puruṣa* describes the ritually constructed cosmic *puruṣa* as the body of Viṣṇu composed of regions from characteristically Purāṇic geography (such as Pātāla and Rasātala), Vedic deities (such as Indra and the Aśvins), moral attributes, the rivers, time, clouds, the constituent elements (*tattva*) of Sāṃkhya, and various animals, with the unmanifest as his heart and the Veda itself as the crown of his head (BhP 2.1.23–39). Indeed, the modeling, or dressing, of the cosmic *puruṣa,* the *puruṣottama,* with different universal constituents is a relatively common Purāṇic theme (see also, for example, BhP 3.6).

Three examples of sacrificial imagery in the BhP will suffice to illustrate the ways in which the Vedic ritual is adapted to suit the temperament of the Purāṇa. The first takes a ritual form, namely, the bird-shaped fire altar, and imbues it with salvific potency. The passage reads: "May Lord Garuḍa, praised as *stotra* and *stobha,* the Veda (*chandas*) personified, protect me" (6.8.29). Garuḍa, Viṣṇu's mount, here recollects the sunbird as the cosmic *puruṣa* constructed in the Agnicayana. Garuḍa's elevation to personal savior, albeit of limited scope, is assisted by the ritual chanting of the *Sāma-Veda,* with its sung verses (*stotra*) and chanted interjections (*stobha*). The second example illustrates the Purāṇic technique of constructing a supreme *puruṣa,* a *puruṣottama,* by reidentifying the sacrifice as the Lord. The passage contains a description of the Lord, none other than a mass of pure consciousness (*viśuddhavijñānaghanaḥ*), manifested as the form of sacrifice (*adhvaraḥ*) with all its accessories including substances, qualities, actions, and intentions (BhP 6.8.29).[85] The third example illustrates how typically Purāṇic verse absorbs Vedic imagery. Prince Āgnīdhra, son of Priyavrata, in a swoon recites several verses to a lovely Apsaras, sent by Brahmā to rouse him from his extended meditation (BhP 5.2.9,13). One verse (5.2.9) contains two metaphors reminiscent of classical Sanskrit poetry (which in fact it is). The first compares the humming of bees hovering nearby to the continuous glorification of the Lord through the singing of the *Sāma-Veda* in its esoteric mode (*sarahasyam*). The second compares the bees gravitating toward flowers that have fallen from her hair, to the attraction of multitudes of rishis to their traditional Vedic texts (*ṛṣigaṇā iva vedaśākhāḥ*), meaning that it is as natural for bees to go to a flower as it is for rishis to recite the Veda. Another verse (5.2.13) compares the fragrance of recently eaten food on her breath to the aroma of oblations poured into the sacred fire. Dozens, if not hundreds, of other examples could be culled to demonstrate this connection.

In addition to well-adapted Vedic imagery, the Purāṇas adapt the genealogies of Vedic sacrifice to their own needs. According to the BhP, Yajña was born along with a twin sister named Dakṣiṇā to Ākūti and Ruci, but was adopted by his grandfather Svāyambhuva Manu (4.1.4–5).[86] Despite their shared ancestry, Yajña and Dakṣiṇā together sired twelve sons who were known as Yāmas in the period of Svāyambhuva (BhP 4.1.6–8). All textual evidence points to a metaphysical and ritual rather than to a suggestively incestuous significance of this pairing. The simplicity of the structural complementarities will be clear if we consider that the feminine *dakṣiṇā* was almost certainly paired with the masculine *yajña* for no other reason than because of her gender. Nevertheless, *dakṣiṇā* is in fact essential to the sacrifice, though in the Veda it is much more than a simple fee rendered for services performed,[87] which is what it was reduced to in the later conception. In this passage of the Purāṇa, at least, the pair Yajña and Dakṣiṇā are the two gendered aspects or principles of an original unitary androgynous whole from whom the manifest creation descended. Beyond the use of this image as a convenient cipher for a decidedly post-Vedic original unity pressed into service by the requirements of ritual discourse, I see no further sexual significance.

One of the most interesting tales of the emergence of the sacrifice occurs in the ninth book (9.14.42–49), when the sage Purūravas, after searching fruitlessly in the forest for his missing love Urvaśī, returned home at night and began meditating on her. In his meditation, knowledge of Vedic ritual dawned on him, whereupon he returned to the forest and created the ritual out of churning sticks (*araṇi*), the upper one visualized as himself, the lower as Urvaṣī, and the middle one connecting them as their offspring. From this was created the sacred fire (*jātavedas*), the three fireplaces, and even the threefold Veda (*Ṛg, Sāma, Yajur*) whose purpose was the organizing of the ritual.[88]

In the Purāṇas, sacrifice is celebrated practically without interruption—its idea, its prescribed details, and its event. One of the striking features of the BhP is that the tenth book, which relates the life and exploits of Kṛṣṇa, is relatively free of such references in spite of the fact that Kṛṣṇa himself is said in the ninth book to have studied the Vedas along with his brother Balarāma, and performed sacrifices himself in order to popularize his own path among the people.[89] Otherwise, with striking regularity, Vedic gods, if not battling with demons over sacrificial viands, are busy consuming oblations, while kings and rishis are performing sacrifices. Hanging in the balance for men, gods, and demons is the future of the kingdom, a visit to more glorious realms, immortality in the body, a life of worldly enjoyments, victory over enemies, fame and the acquisition of territory, or the creation and destruction of entire universes.

According to the BhP (7.14.14ff.), sacrifice, regardless of its form, is offered to the supreme Lord; and it is regarded as the duty of all (cf. ViṣṇuP 3.8.22). It consists of dharma and mantra, and as its result the sacrificer or *yajamāna* ascends to heaven (VāyuP 32.16). Success of the sacrifice depends not only on ritual exactitude and the blessing of the gods, who give rain when pleased (ViṣṇuP 1.6.8), but according to the BhP (8.18.29ff.) the presence of a saint makes the sacrifice successful. This old tradition, observed in the *Mahābhārata* by Yudhiṣṭhira, who performed his Rājasūya only after taking the permission of Kṛṣṇa, who then served as one of the chief officiants (*sadasya,* BhP 10.74.18–29), is maintained today in practically all major sacrifices, which are either performed under the advisement of the *yajamāna*'s guru or visited by various saints.

Several other subjects must be dealt with in order to convey the breadth of the transition from Vedic to Purāṇic ritual ideology and discourse. These subjects include the animal sacrifice, the concept of dharma, the role of women in the rituals, varieties of sacrificial performances, and the all important final ritual bath (*avabhṛtha*).

One of the major features of the sacrifice that continually troubled post-Vedic ritualists was the prescribed presence of a sacrificial animal.[90] From at least the time of the Buddha, *ahiṃsā* or nonviolence increasingly became part of "orthodox" ethics. In fact, the BhP describes the killing of animals for food as both enervating and to be restricted to what is necessary (4.26.6,10). Regarding animal sacrifice the *Matsya Purāṇa* (143.13) says, "This is not dharma, this is in fact *adharma*; such violence cannot be called *dharma*."[91] Indeed the Purāṇas often considered rituals as useless (e.g., BhP 4.25.1–5), as mere engagement of the three *guṇa*s, (*traividyam*), thus inferior to and opposed to *bhakti*,[92] or as intended only as inducement to better or more productive practices (BhP 11.21.23ff.). The BhP speaks of sacrifices made horrible by the killing of animals (4.27.11[93]), of the animal's revenge (4.25.7–8, 4.28.26), and of the prohibition of meat in rites honoring the ancestors (*śrāddha*, BhP 7.15.7–14).

In one passage Kṛṣṇa suggests the limits of permissibility in sacrifice by conspicuously avoiding mention of sacrifice in which animals are immolated, including soma sacrifice: "A forest dweller should offer at the prescribed times cooked gruel (*caru*) and flour cakes (*puroḍāśa*) prepared from wild grains; but he should not offer a Vedic animal sacrifice to me. Vedic authorities have enjoined for the ascetic (*muni*) the normative Agnihotra, New and Full Moon sacrifices, as well as the Cāturmāsyas" (BhP 11.18.7–8).[94] Nevertheless, in a pinch, Viṣṇu, as Śipiviṣṭa, the one who resides in the sacrificial animal, will accept offerings (BhP 4.13.35).

Animal sacrifice was also prohibited in *kaliyuga,* though as a rule this and most other prohibited actions had passed into history by the time of their interdiction.[95] The BhP (12.3.21,23) says that in *tretayuga* and *dvāparayuga* people performed Vedic rites as well as austerities, but in *kaliyuga bhakti* should prevail. In one passage, the BhP even says that in *kaliyuga* the Vedas, symbolized by Garuḍa, do not shine (12.11.19, cf. 10.20.8).[96] Elsewhere, however, a bit more generous to the notion of the infallibility of the Vedas, the BhP says that the Vedas enjoin both sacrifice (*pravṛtta dharma*) as well as asceticism and devotion (*nivṛtta dharma*) (4.4.20, 7.15.48–49).

Turning to the notion of dharma, it is clear that on the whole, perhaps with a good measure of added populism, the dharma espoused in the Purāṇas is consistent with the received Dharmaśāstra tradition, and followed the same alignments of ritual power:[97] Brahmanical purity, puritanism and supremacy (BhP 11.5.4–18). A single brief example should suffice. The BhP says, "Only the smelling of wine is sanctioned (in the Sautrāmaṇi);[98] also an animal is to be taken (only) in sacrifice, not violently (*paśor ālambhanaṃ na hiṃsā*). Similarly, sexual intercourse (*vyavāya*) is for procreation, not for enjoyment. They do not understand their pure dharma" (11.5.13).

Regarding women, the BhP states that they—especially wives of sacrificers (*yajñapatnī*)—should engage in uninterrupted devotion to the Lord (10.23.25ff.) or should approach the Lord by associating with saintly people (*satsaṅga,* 11.12.2ff.). In another typical passage, preparatory to a rite performed for bearing of a son (*puṃsavana*), the sage Kaśyapa strongly denounces women and at length enjoins restrictions on them, ostensibly for the sake of the vow in question. In fact, however, his remarks are intended for women in general (6.18.38ff., 6.19).[99] Another passage (BhP 8.19.38–43) warns that truth is of the greatest value,[100] but that falsehood is not to be condemned when addressed to women.[101] Typically, Śūdras are accorded the same treatment as women (or vice versa): they have no eligibility for sacrifice or the repetition of mantras (*amantra-yajña,* 7.11.24).[102]

Many sacrificial performances dealt with in the Vedas or *Mahābhārata* are treated extensively in the BhP. It may not be without interest simply to list some of the most interesting and important among them, at least to show that largely they are the sacrifices that were later forbidden during *kaliyuga*.[103] In this way their importance was progressively dissipated, providing a platform for the legitimation of Purāṇic *bhakti*. As examples of these, we find the sacrifices performed by Dakṣa (discussed in virtually all Purāṇas), including his Vājapeya and Bṛhaspatisava (4.2–7); Yudhiṣṭhira's Rājasūya (10.75.1ff.); Hariścandra's Viśvajit sacrifice (9.7); the hundred Aśvamedhas and Viśvajit soma sacrifices of Vāmana's demonic adversary Bali (8.15ff.); the hundred Aśvamedhas performed by both Pṛthu (4.19–20) and Uśanas (9.23.34); the Aśvamedhas of Janamejaya (9.22.37) and King Sāgara (9.8.7ff.); King Aṅga's frustrated attempt to perform an Aśvamedha (4.13.25ff.); and Antardhāna's Sattra (4.24.6ff.).

Other noteworthy Vedic ritual sacrifices mentioned in the BhP were Vāmana's Upanayana, in which the *avatāra* of Lord Viṣṇu was initiated into Vedic study by all the various gods and rishis (8.18.13ff.); Nanda's many (unidentified) sacrifices (10.84.42ff.); Rāma's daily Agnihotra, which he performed for 13,000 years, observing celibacy throughout (9.11.18); and King Nābhi's soma sacrifice (5.3), in which Viṣṇu appeared during the performance of one of the Pravargyas, a complicated rite to be performed at least six times before the soma pressing. These are important because Vedic ritual is employed in the service of Purāṇic agendas. Nanda, as the father of Kṛṣṇa, who had little use for Vedic ritual, must be shown to perform sacrifices, if only to locate him within the elite reaches of orthodoxy, thus extending maximum religious authority to his son. Rāma extended the notion of celibacy from its limited place in the Vedic ritual to a general consideration. The Vedic Saṃhitā and Brāhmaṇa texts prescribe celibacy only on the evening before the new and full moon sacrifices (Darśapūrṇamāsa), and during other major rituals including soma sacrifices, but never as a daily prescription. Implicit in Rāma's exemplary celibacy is an appeal for adherence to a more classical morality, with its pronounced ambiguity between householder and renunciate. The mention of Viṣṇu appearing at King Nābhi's Pravargya, a sacrifice in which Viṣṇu is not invoked, is clearly a device designed to illustrate Viṣṇu's supremacy over the sacrifice.

Similarly, the sacrificial career of Bharata (BhP 5.7.5–6, cf. 9.20.24ff.) is important in that it describes Bharata's characteristically Purāṇic attitude during the ritual proceedings. While the officiants were offering the various oblations, Bharata mentally transformed the dharma of the sacrifice, called *apūrva* (the future reward of the present sacrifice), into offerings to the supreme sacrificial deity, Vāsudeva.[104] It is this attitude, with different sectarian biases, that ritualists of all beliefs and sects have attempted to replicate up to the present day.[105] It is also important because it recognizes the two sides of orthodox ritual practice, the process-oriented Mīmāṃsā and its opposite, the human- or deity-centered sacrifice, with the latter emerging supreme.

The final bath (*avabhṛtha*), always one of the most spectacular rites of a soma sacrifice, assumed extraordinary significance in the epics and Purāṇas. Great religious merit and spiritual power were generated by being present at the *avabhṛtha,* because the public was allowed to bathe with the sacrificer and his ritual officiants in waters in which the final important oblations (including the remains of the soma stalks and rice flour cakes) were offered. This was significant not just because of relatively unguarded access to the sacrificer, whose vows of privacy and austerity were more or less dropped during the *avabhṛtha,* and because, signaling the end of a long and arduous ritual process, it possessed a celebratory quality to it. In addition, it was due to the nature of water itself. Water was regarded as the most purifying substance that the body could safely contact (fire burned). Thus, merit, power, and blessing were readily conducted by the sacrificer through water shared during the bath.

The *avabhṛtha* was not the only rite from the *śrauta* ritual emphasized in the Purāṇas. The BhP stresses the significance of the offerings to the wives of the gods (*patnīsaṃyāja*) in at least two places (10.75.8–24, 10.84.53). The reason for this is not stated, but it may be due to the unique importance of the wives of the two sacrificers mentioned in these passages: Draupadī, spouse of Yudhiṣṭhira, and the wives of Nanda, father of Kṛṣṇa.[106]

Two highly condensed stories among many interesting possibilities will serve to illustrate ways in which shifts from Vedic to Purāṇic ritual discourse served oddly paradigmatic and didactic ends. In the first, Vaivasvata Manu sacrificed to Mitra and Varuṇa (*mitrāvaruṇayor iṣṭam*) in order to obtain a son. But Manu's wife, Śraddhā, requested the chief officiant in charge of ṚV recitation (*hotṛ*) to change a mantra in order to give birth to a daughter. Thus a daughter, Ilā, was born. But on Manu's protest she was changed into a son, Sudyumna, the foremost among men (9.1.13–22). This demonstrates both the power of the sacrifice and the inevitability of the patriarchal order.

Another familiar story containing lengthy ritual narration is the battle between Indra and Vṛtra (6.7–13). One point here will suffice to illustrate a distinction between Purāṇic and Vedic thought. In both the Purāṇic and Vedic accounts (e.g., BhP 6.9, cf. *Taittirīya Saṃhitā* 2.5.2) Indra slew Tvaṣṭṛ's three-headed son Viśvarūpa, a Brahmin. The resultant stain of brahminicide (*brahmahatyā*) was then distributed to women, water, trees, and the earth. Tvaṣṭṛ then sacrificed in order to produce an enemy for Indra. Because of his purpose he failed to invite Indra, who is integrally involved in the sacrifice. According to the Purāṇa, out of the *dakṣiṇāgni* fire emerged a frightful demon, Vṛtra, whose physical horror was embellished well beyond its Vedic prototypes. In the Veda, Vṛtra arose from the *āhavanīya* after Tvaṣṭṛ cast into it the remains of the soma. The shift of fires is unexplained, but, as noted above, oblations to deceased ancestors are offered into the *dakṣiṇāgni,* while the *āhavanīya* receives offerings to the gods. Why, again, would Vṛtra, a demon equal to the gods, emerge from the *dakṣiṇāgni*? With no explanation forthcoming from the Purāṇa, I tentatively suggest a twofold reason: first, the Purāṇic obsession with supplying genealogies to its dramatis personae is better effected from the *dakṣiṇāgni,* and, second, a desire to separate the genesis of the gods from that of the demons renders the *dakṣiṇāgni* an appropriate point of origin for Vṛtra. Ultimately in the Purāṇa, unlike in the Veda, Vṛtra delivers a lecture on dharma, and after he is vanquished his soul merges with the Lord as it issues forth from his body in a field of light (6.12.35).

CONCLUSIONS

Several points should be clear from the foregoing. First, one can detect the strategies whereby the Vedic *puruṣa* became the Purāṇic *puruṣottama* by "incorporating" expanding realms of objects, entities, and notions that developed through intervening centuries of ritual and philosophical thought.[107] In the same way that conceptually different entities and notions were constantly brought together by the Brāhmaṇa texts in various "codes of connections,"[108] sums or equations greater than their parts because they comprised higher ontological and ritual realities, the Purāṇas, including the *Bhāgavata,* brought them together in the unimaginable and supremely powerful, yet comparatively unambiguous, *puruṣottama.* Immersed in that figure were all realms and worlds; all gods, demons, sages, and kings with their crossbred genealogies; all rituals and vows; all truth and falsehood; all philosophical notions and worldly actions; all Vedic mantras, meters, and chants. The shadowy, mantrically constructed conceptualizations of the Vedic ritual as *puruṣa* assumed a more directly recognizable raiment on the body of the sectarian deity. The *puruṣottama* was not just a sheep in wolf's clothing, as in Arjuna's terrifying vision of Kṛṣṇa in the eleventh chapter of the *Bhāgavad Gītā,* but he could take on the entire zoo, so to speak, simply, comprehensively, and at once. Rarely is an image less than all-inclusive. To provide a relatively circumscribed example, the BhP describes the path of Sūrya's chariot as encompassing the primary Vedic meters. Both the chariot and the meters represent all the Vedas and all there is to know, including, in their respective but contiguous paths and dimensions, infinite expanses of space (5.21.10ff.).

By reshaping or refocusing the vision of the Vedas through the personality and body of the *puruṣottama,* the Purāṇas, which in turn embodied that *puruṣottama,* extended infallibility first to the *puruṣottama* and finally to themselves. From complicated ritual production or philosophic investigation, the salvific act became the simple remembrance of sacred name (*smaraṇa*), whether ritually or informally produced and controlled.[109] Salvation could even be achieved through the reverence of the book itself.[110] As consciously engendered canon, the Purāṇa appropriated the territory held by the Veda. Though it conceived of itself as both divine and human creation rather than *apauruṣeya,* it claimed the latter as part of its realm, a realm inhabited by both word and image. Except among a decreasing number of learned scholars (as continues to be the case), the Veda was known only orally, through the word. The visual dimension that added flesh to the bones of the Veda and ignited the imagination of first- and second-millennium India was supplied by the epics and Purāṇas. As Thomas Coburn writes, "India, it would appear, wants both the *literal preservation* and the *dynamic recreation* of the Word."[111]

Thus, the Purāṇas transformed Vedic context and authorship. In important ways, however, the Veda readily lent itself to such transformation. The splintered segments of ritual and myth presented both in the hymns of the *Ṛg-Veda* and in the more discursive texts of the *Yajur-Veda* were perfect for cutting and pasting. Like television today, particularly news, which believes that it "has the power to transmit the experience itself rather than information about the experience,"[112] the Purāṇas represented packages of Vedic "reality" in the (often rather copious) interstices of more contemporary and immediate religious dialogue and concern. Though it may be argued that selecting, cutting, and pasting a limited set of images misrepresented and altered the original experience, the fact was that the images themselves were significant and evocative—significant *because* evocative. Thus, through the power of imagination and recontextualization a new image was secured and a fresh experience was induced.[113]

Genealogy figures most prominently in the foregoing discussions. We do not need the Purāṇas to inform us that pedigree was an important consideration in ancient India. What the Purāṇas tell us is how far into conceptualized reality genealogy burrowed. It became a mechanism for investigating the mysterious origins of all name and form, a prism for viewing history and all of its objective and subjective contents. All objects, entities, beings, and notions had origins, roots that stretched into the indeterminate past. Eventually they all became bound up with each other, creating the warp and woof of the *puruṣottama.* Genealogy was also a mechanism for the preservation of the Purāṇic universe. Yet it was a highly dynamic universe, open to freshly conceived name, form, deity, and concept. As genealogies became increasingly inclusive, they began to cover their futures as well as their pasts. In the same way as the Veda entered into the Purāṇa, or was absorbed into the Purāṇa, there emerged just as little distance between the Veda, which is to say the Purāṇaveda, and the Tantra. As if incorporating additional genetic information, the BhP on at least half a dozen occasions proclaims the equality of the Veda and Tantra, thus acknowledging and sanctioning what must have been an increasingly evident mixture of both ritual and philosophy.[114]

All of this suggests that the canonicity of the Veda was not negated by the Purāṇic hermeneuts, but transformed by the introduction of concepts that stretched the limits of the canon. For example, most of the spectacular sacrifices that helped define the early Vedic canon including the Aśvamedha, Rājasūya, Agnicayana, and Viśvajit, along with animal sacrifice, were prohibited by the later Dharmaśāstras after occupying an intermediate position as antiquarian or rhetorical devices in the *Mahābhārata* and Purāṇas. Was the change in the position of these sacrifices crucial to the positioning of the Purāṇas as canonical, or did this occur due to other factors? Probably the latter, as these sacrifices became little more than image and list.[115] Canonicity was determined by other, more pervasive theological and moral considerations, such as the importance of the *puruṣottama* and the imperatives of *bhakti* and personal purity. It is these other concerns that provided limits, legitimization, definitions of orthodoxy, ideals, and archetypes, within which "canonical resources," such as injunction or prohibition of certain sacrifices, were simply grist for the mill.

One further point should be discussed in closing: that the Purāṇas were not alone in antiquity in appropriating and reconfiguring the Veda, and in defining and establishing orthodoxy. As noted, an obligatory locus of comparison is the Pūrvamīmāṃsā (PM), which did essentially the same thing, though with radically different strategies, goals, and audience. Both the PM and the Purāṇas embraced the Veda and reassessed it systematically. Where the PM developed a highly specialized exegetical vocabulary, the Purāṇa did not. In fact, I might venture to say that the development of a technical vocabulary, perhaps as much as anything else, separated "philosophy" from "religion" in classical India, if I may be permitted to draw such a dubious distinction. Whatever philosophy or dharmaśāstra was eventually written into the Purāṇas, they were never regarded by the native academic elite as *śāstra*.

The PM dealt with process, with the primacy of action, specifically ritual action, and its unity with word and purpose. Like the Purāṇas, the Mīmāṃsā sought to explain things and actions by placing them in a correct matrix of relationship, though the entities constituting the relationship differed.[116] Relative to the Mīmāṃsa discourse, at least, the Purāṇas were consciously historical; they dealt with worlds and eras; with the lives of deities, celestial beings, sages, and kings; with morals, renunciation, and yoga; with all aspects of life and human purpose. The primary relationship in the Purāṇas is of the individual and his or her involvement with these entitites and notions, for example, one's relationship with the Lord. The Veda, including the deities Agni and Soma, the details and institution of sacrifice, and the issue of its infallibility, is, as we have seen, but a single element in this grand matrix of human history and purpose, placed in the service of higher organizing principles. The consciously ahistorical PM, on the other hand, dealt with the Veda as the *only* true authority, the centrality of which was the sacrifice. The Veda, the sacrifice, and the universe dependent on it stood outside history. The infallibility of the Veda and its deities was expressed in terms of the sacrifice, which itself lay at the center, "beyond ordinary human purposes."[117]

Like the PM, a conscious concern of the Purāṇas, from the mid-first millennium on, became the preservation of the Veda. At the same time, however, the Purāṇas threatened to capsize the entire project. Preservation to the Purāṇic hermeneuts was of image and essence rather than word and substance. The ascendancy of Kṛṣṇa was so antithetical even to their own conceived image and essence of the Veda that the Purāṇa itself occasionally attempted to disguise it. Kṛṣṇa's identification with Viṣṇu, the *puruṣottama,* which assisted his ascendancy, was finally superseded by his own dominance. This resulted, probably fairly rapidly, in the final three books of the BhP graciously burying the first nine. Kṛṣṇa assumed Viṣṇu's *māyā* (e.g., he satisfied 16,000 *gopi*s at once, BhP 10.32–33; cf. 10.59.42); he slaughtered demons; he healed, purified, and sacrificed (BhP 9.24.66). Through his identification with Viṣṇu he embodied the *puruṣottama,* hence the Veda, the gods, and the sacrifice. In spite of his bucolic origins, he possessed the right pedigree (he studied the Veda and his father, Nanda, performed sacrifices). What set him apart from his lordly predecessors was the fact that he embraced and embodied both the Veda and the sentiments of ordinary people, which is to say devotees.

NOTES

1. Purāṇavedo hy akhilas tasmin samyak pratiṣṭhitaḥ. "The entire ancient knowledge (or ancient Veda, or Veda as Purāṇa) is correctly established in this (text)" VāyuP 1.18 (Ānandāśrama edition) Cf. Rocher, *Purāṇas,* 15. Consistent with this, VāyuP 1.54 says that the Purāṇa was remembered first by Brahmā, then the Vedas issued forth from his mouths. A well-known traditional etymology of the word *purāṇa* is *purā hi anati idam,* "this breathes from former times" (VāyuP 1.183).

2. Rocher writes, "The most salient feature of items described as *purāṇá* in the RV is that they do more than continue to exist in the present; while being 'ancient', they are, at the same time, also 'new, young'. . . . being *purāṇá* involves existence from time immemorial together with repeated renewal and rejuvenation" ("The Meaning of *Purāṇá* in the Ṛgveda," 12). "[I]n most occurrences in the RV the constant repetition and identical renewal of things ancient, implied by the term *purāṇá,* are not determined by men; they are governed by rules laid down by supernatural powers or by the necessities of cosmic order" (ibid., 20).

3. Wendy O'Flaherty's *Hindu Myths* is an especially fine example of tracing Vedic mythology in the Purāṇas. For particularly uninspiring recent examples, see P. M. Upadhye, "Sacrifice in the Purāṇic Tradition" (121–26), and S. G. Kantawala, "Sacrificial Element in the Purāṇic Vows" (127–32), in Dange, ed., *Sacrifice in India.*

4. Arguments could also be made for the *Skanda* and *Śiva Purāṇas*.

5. See Majumdar, *Kṛṣṇa in History and Legend.*

6. See Meier, "Der Archaismus in der Sprache des Bhāgavata Purāṇa"; also Renou, *Histoire de la Langue Sanskrite,* 120–21; Biswas, *Bhāgavata Purāṇa.* For a more general study, see Prasad, *Bhāgavata Purāṇa,* 65ff. However, the BhP, like other early and relatively early Purāṇas, was largely written in an epic-purāṇic vernacular, *ārṣa* Sanskrit, with literary and stylistic features shared with the *Rāmāyaṇa* and *Mahābhārata*; cf. Salomon, "The Viṣṇu Purāṇa as a Specimen of Vernacular Sanskrit."

7. Rukmani, *Critical Study of the Bhāgavata Purāṇa,* 172–73. More reasonable are the views of Bhattacharya, "Paurāṇic Tradition, Is It Vedic?": "The set of traditions propagated by the Purāṇas is basically founded on the Vedic heritage" (132–33); and Kane, "Vedic Mantras and Legends in the Purāṇas": "the Purāṇas try hard to build on the foundations of the Vedic tradition" (5; both cited by Rocher, *Purāṇas,* 14, n. 5).

8. MatsyaP 290.20,25, 291.1,36; cf. *MatsyaP* 292 (entire) the last chapter of this Purāṇa is a *phalaśruti* (see n. 10); also VāyuP 6.8.12., in which the Purāṇa is said to follow the Vedic tradition. Also see Agrawala, *Matsya Purāṇa—A Study,* 30ff. for discussion of passages that assert that the Purāṇas preceded the Vedas.

9. Also BrahmāṇḍaP 2.34.21, ViṣṇuP 3.6.15, VāyuP 60.21; cf. Hazra, *Studies in the Purāṇic Records on Hindu Rites and Customs,* 5 and n. 26 glosses *purāṇasaṃhitā* as "original Purāṇa"; also Kane, *History of Dharmaśāstra,* vol. 5.2: 858, n. 1392. This compound was probably not intended as a *dvandva,* referring to the eighteen Purāṇas and the sectarian Saṃhitās such as the Pāñcarātra and the Brahmā; see the Gita Press translation by C. L. Goswami, vol. 1, 914.

10. E.g., BhP 1.4.20, itihāsapurāṇaṃ ca pañcamo veda ucyate; SkandaP 5.3.1.18, purāṇaṃ pañcamo vedaḥ.

11. Cf. Smith, *Imagining Religion,* 44. I shall not attempt to replicate the valuable work of Coburn, "Study of the Purāṇas and the Study of Religion"; and " 'Scripture' in India." In the first paper, Coburn summarizes the meanings of the word *purāṇá* in a number of Vedic and Purāṇic texts and describes the academic and religious preconceptions that condition the notion of a "critical" edition of an Indian text. In the later paper, he devises typologies of scripture and discusses issues such as the distinction between revelation and scripture. Also I shall not deal with developmental aspects of text construction, as does Bonazzoli in a growing oeuvre, largely appearing in the journal *Purāṇa*; see, e.g., "Dynamic Canon of the Purāṇa-s"; and "Schemes in the Purāṇas."

12. In fact, in North India today, people mean the *Bhāgavatam* when they speak of the Veda. (I am grateful to Philip Lutgendorf for this observation.)

13. jāgratsvāpau yathā svapne tathā vidhiniṣedhatā.

14. tena brahma hṛdā ya ādikavaye muhyanti yat surayaḥ.

15. See the *Pūrvamīmāṃsāsūtra* of Jaimini 1.1.27–32 and commentaries.

16. *Mahābhārata* 12.328.50: stutyartham iha devānāṃ vedāḥ sṛṣṭāḥ svayambhuvā.

17. This was also the position of the Nyāya and Vaiśeṣika schools of philosophy; see Halbfass, *Tradition and Reflection*, 25 and references.

18. In any case, as Staal points out, "orthopraxy, not orthodoxy, is the operative concept in India" (*Agni,* xiv); on such distinctions Gonda also writes: "The opposition between Viṣṇuists and Śivaists [is] ritual and sociological in nature rather than dogmatic or philosophical" ("Indian Mantra," 279–80).

19. sa eṣa bhagavān ādipuruṣa eva sākṣān nārāyaṇo . . . kavibhir api ca vedena vijijñāsamānaḥ.

20. Note that Prajāpati of, for example, the *Śatapatha Brāhmaṇa,* book 10, was already reconfigured from the *puruṣa* of *Ṛg-Veda* 10.90. On the sources of the *Ṛg-Vedic púruṣa,* see Brown, "Sources and Nature of *púruṣa* in the Puruṣasūkta (Ṛg Veda 10.90)."

21. tapo me hṛdayaṃ brahmaṃs tanūr vidyā kriyākṛtiḥ / aṅgāni kratavo jātā dharma ātmāsavaḥ surāḥ //

22. brāhmaṇo'gniś ca vai viṣṇoḥ sarvevedātmano mukham /

23. tvaṃ saptatantūn vitanoṣi tanvā trayyā caturhotrakavidyayā ca / tvam eka ātmātmavatām anādir anantapāraḥ kavir antarātmā //

24. namo dviśīrṣṇe tripade catuḥśṛṅgāya tantave / saptahastāya yajñāya trayīvidyātmane namaḥ // Following the commentary of Śrīdhara, two heads: the *prāyaṇīya* and *udayanīya,* the rites of entering and

and exiting the sacrificial arena at the beginning and end of a soma sacrifice; three feet: the three sessions of a soma sacrifice; four horns: the four Vedas; seven hands: the seven primary Vedic meters (*gāyatrī, triṣṭubh, anuṣṭubh, bṛhatī, paṅktī, jagatī, uṣṇik*).

25. Cf. also 11.20.1–4, where Uddhava praises his word (*vacas*) as the form of the Veda. Also 11.29.49, where Kṛṣṇa is addressed as *nigamakṛt,* "author of the Vedas."

26. Along with *purāṇasaṃhitā,* see above, n. 9. Cf. BhP 10.87.14–41, in which the *śrutis* sing a hymn of praise to the Lord.

27. E.g., *Taittirīya Saṃhitā* 2.5.1 explains that Indra killed Viśvarūpa, the son of Tvaṣṭṛ. Men are also descended from gods, e.g., Bhṛgu from Varuṇa (*Aitareya Brāhmaṇa* 3.34.1, *Jaiminiya Brāhmaṇa* 1.42, *Taittirīya Upaniṣad* 3.1).

28. The primal sounds representing the three worlds: the earth, the midregion constituted of space, and the solar region, respectively.

29. Cf. *Manusmṛti* 3.70–71: brahmayajña, pitṛyajña, daivayajña, bhūtayajña, nṛyajña.

30. *viṣṇur dvijakriyāmūlo yajño dharmamayaḥ pumān / devarṣipitṛbhūtānāṃ dharmasya ca parāyaṇam //*

31. BhP 7.9.47: *rūpe ime sadasat tava vedasṛṣṭe*. . .

32. The genealogy is greatly expanded in BhP 12.6.48–66. This section provides names of different sages and Saṃhitās, and briefly recounts the origin of the *Taittirīya Saṃhitā* from the vomit of Yājñavalkya. Cf. BrahmāṇḍaP 2.34.2,12–30; 2.35.116–26; 3.10.69; 4.1.30; 6.64; MatsyaP 14.16, where it is related that the Vedas, originally one, were rearranged by the twenty-eight Vedavyāsas *manvantaras*. They were then edited into four sections by Parāśara's son. *ViṣṇuP* 3.3.20, 3.4.7–9 tells another story: at some point the Vedas were lost in a flood, after which they were discovered by Viṣṇu, who taught them to Brahmā, who divided them into three and taught them to his sons. This threefold division of the Vedas conveys the truth of *brahman* and *ātman* in which Viṣṇu manifests. According to MatsyaP 53.5, 83.8, 172.50, they were restored by Matsya after the deluge. For further information on Vedic *śākhās* in the Purāṇas, see Rai, *Introduction to the Vedic Śākhās.*

33. The classical conception of a *kiṃpuruṣa* was of a demigod with a horse's head and human body; a *kinnara* was reversed. For the Vedic conceptions and their developments, see Parpola, "Dravidian Solution to the Problem of *kiṃpuruṣa / kinnara*," 24–25, 166–67.

34. kālena naṣṭā pralaye vāṇīyaṃ vedasaṃjñitā / mayādau brahmaṇe proktā dharmo yasyāṃ madātmakaḥ //3// tena proktā ca putrāya manave pūrvajāya sā / tato bhṛgvādayo 'gṛhṇan sapta brahmamarṣayaḥ //4// tebhyaḥ pitṛbhyas tatputrā devadānavaguhyakāḥ / manuṣyāḥ siddhagandharvāḥ savidyādhara-cāraṇāḥ //5// *ki*ḍevāḥ kinnarā nāgā rakṣ aḥ-

kiṃpuruṣādayaḥ / bahvyas teṣāṃ prakṛtayo rajassattvatamobhuvaḥ //6// yābhir bhūtāni bhidyante bhūtānāṃ matayas tathā / yathāprakṛti sarveṣāṃ citrā vācaḥ sravanti hi //7//

35. BhP 8.14.4: caturyugānte kālena grastāñ chrutigaṇān yathā / tapasā ṛṣayo 'paśyan yato dharmaḥ sanātanaḥ//

36. BhP 8.14.8: jñānaṃ cānuyugaṃ brute hariḥ siddhasvarūpadhṛk / ṛṣirūpadharaḥ karma yogaṃ yogeśarūpadhṛk //

37. The Śaiva Tantras of the tenth century on are the most complete sources, though accounts are also found in Vaiṣṇava Āgamas and elsewhere. The doctrine is first enunciated clearly in the *Vākyapadīya* of Bhartṛhari of the fourth or fifth century B.C.E. The best account of the doctrine of *śabdabrahman* is Padoux, *Vāc.*

38. It is possible that this discussion can be used in dating at least part of this Purāṇa.

39. MatsyaP 93.129, the face of the Veda is in the shape of *om* accompanied by *sūkta, brāhmaṇa,* and mantra.

40. The commentators interpret this as identical to the evolution of sound through the four levels of speech; see Padoux, *Vāc,* 175ff.

41. etāvān sarvavedārthaḥ śabda āsthāya māṃ bhidām / māyāmātram anūdyānte pratiṣiddhya prasīdati //

42. Cf. MatsyaP 2.13., 3.2, 4.7, 285.8.

43. śabdabrahma paraṃ brahma mamobhe śāśvatī tanū. That is, the Lord has two eternal bodies, one is *śabdabrahman,* the other is the highest *brahman,* here assumed to be something other than *śabdabrahman* or the Veda.

44. Halbfass, *Tradition and Reflection,* 4.

45. Ibid., 19, n. 11.

46. Van Buitenen, "On the Archaism of the Bhāgavata Purāṇa," 23–40, 215–217.

47. See. e.g., Śaṅkara on *Brahmasūtra* 2.2.42–45. See Gambhirananda, *Brahma-Sūtra Bhāṣya of Śaṅkarācārya,* 439ff.

48. Van Buitenen, "On the Archaism of the Bhāgavata Purāṇa," 31.

49. Ibid., 35.

50. Smith, *Imagining Religion,* 51.

51. Both, however, are masculine. For another conception of the Vedic ritual world divided along gender lines, see Smith, "Indra's Curse, Varuṇa's Noose, and the Suppression of the Woman in the Vedic *Śrauta* Ritual," 17–45.

52. For basic mythology, see the following classical accounts, still useful: Macdonell, *Vedic Mythology,* 88ff.; Hillebrandt, *Vedic Mythology* (English translation), 48ff.; Oldenberg, *Religion of the Veda* (English translation), 61ff.; Keith, *Religion and Philosophy of the Veda and*

Upaniṣads, 154ff., 285ff. An updated general treatment of Vedic mythology, a truly daunting task in view of the explosion of Vedic lexical and mythological study in the last century, remains a desideratum.

53. BrahmāṇḍaP 1.2.21.56: prabhā hi saurī pādena hy astaṃ gacchati bhāskare / agnim āviśate rātrau tasmād dūrāt prakāsate // Cf. *Śatapatha Brāhmaṇa* 2.3.1.2–5, *Kāṭhaka Saṃhitā* 6.5, Aitareya Br*āhmaṇa* 8.28, *Jaiminīya Brāhmaṇa* 1.7–8. The clearest exposition of this doctrine in the Vedas is to be found in Bodewitz, *Jaiminīya Brāhmaṇa 1–65,* 35ff. and *passim.*

54. Cf. Smith, "Names of Agni in the Vedic Ritual."

55. See, e.g., Smith, *Vedic Sacrifice in Transition,* 384ff.; Caland, *Altindische Zauberei,* para. 89, 90.

56. Agrawala (*Matsya Purāṇa,* 155ff.) has nicely summarized the corresponding discussion in the MatsyaP. He further notes (213f.) that chapter 128 "refers to the principle of Agni causing the movements of Sun, Moon, planets and stars." Within this process is a variation on the threefold *pāvaka, pavamāna,* and *śuci.* In this case the self-born Lord (*svayambhūr bhagavān*, MatsyaP 128.4) discovered Agni hidden within himself. He gathered up this Agni in three forms: *pācaka* (following the Venkateshwar Steam Press edition; cf. Agrawala's reading *pāvaka,* following the Ānandāśrama edition) from the earth, used for cooking; *śuci* from the sun, for general heat; and *vaidyuta agni,* lightning or electrical fire, present in the belly (*jaṭhara*), for digestion.

57. Cf. Vi*ṣṇuP* 1.10.15–17.

58. RV khila 3.10.7 (Vaidika Saṃśodhana Maṇḍala edition, 4:946), *Āgniveśyagṛhyasūtra* 2.6.7.

59. In the *Mahābhārata* (e.g., 3.220.5), *havyam* and *kavyam* are not names but idioms for offerings to the gods and to the ancestors.

60. The names are Āgnīdhra (a ritual officiant), Idhmajihva ("Fuel's Tongue"), Yajñabāhu ("Arm of the Sacrifice"), Mahāvīra ("Great Hero"), Hiraṇyaretas ("Golden Semen"), Ghṛtapṛṣṭa ("Ghee-Backed"; cf. *ṚV* 1.13.5, 5.4.3, etc.), Savana ("[Soma]-Pressing"), Medhātithi ("Whose Guest Is Intelligence"), Vītihotra ("Beckoned to a Feast"), and Kavi ("Inspired Sage"; cf. RV 1.12.6, 6.16.30, etc.).

61. One need not worry, of course, about "tracing correctly the true genealogy of Agni" (Mani, *Purāṇic Encyclopaedia,* 10).

62. Cf. BhP 4.1.48, VāyuP 1.76, BrahmāṇḍaP 2.9.56, 2.12.1.

63. Other lines of descent may be briefly noted. According to VāyuP 29.1, Agni is the eldest, as well as mind-born, son of Brahmā in the Svāyambhuva Manvantara. VāyuP and MatsyaP also provide lineages for specialized Agnis. For example, the Agni that digests food, called Jaṭharāgni, is the son of Hṛdaya (Heart); and the Agni produced by friction that consumes the bodies of all beings, called Saṃvartaka, is the son of

Agni Manyumān (MatsyaP 51.28–29, VāyuP 29.31,33). According to ViṣṇuP 1.10.14, Agni was born of Brahmā's austerities. According to MatsyaP 4.38,43, 196.9, he was the son of Āgneyī and Ūru, of Ārṣeya *pravara.* Also his daughter Suchāyā married Śiṣṭa, the son of Dhrūva. BrahmāṇḍaP 2.13.23 says he was also known as Ṛta, the son of Saṃvatsara. BhP 6.6.11,13 says he is one of the eight sons of Vasu, his wife is Dhārā, and his sons are Draviṇaka and others. According to the ŚivaP (3.13.14–15), Vaiśvānara Agni emerged from Gṛhapati, the son of the rishi Vaiśvānara, as a boon of Śiva. The ritual fire is not ignited, but is born, and like its human progenitors only after proper sacraments of conception (*garbhadhāraṇa* and *puṃsavana*) are performed on the altar or *vedi*. According to the AgniP (309.14, 311.17–19, cf. GaruḍaP 1.28.51–67), the fireplace should be in the shape of female genitalia. The usual practice in Tāntric *homa* is to inscribe a *yoni* in red *kumkum* or *aṣṭagandha* powder, the latter a mixture of eight fragrant essences, on a rim of the fireplace (which itself can assume many different shapes) away from the side (usually west) on which the person making the offerings sits (facing east).

64. Also *Āpastamba Dharmasūtra* 1.3.44, *Viṣṇusmṛti* 31.8.

65. In that the Veda is transmitted through either parentage or *gotra.* We are not here speaking of guru-disciple initiation in the classical sense; for the evolution of this from the Veda, see Gonda, *Change and Continuity in Indian Religion,* 315–462.

66. Perhaps originating in a related set of ideas, namely, Śiva as representing darkness and destruction. BhP 10.66.30ff. records that the *dakṣiṇāgni* can be useful in *abhicāra* if properly worshiped. In fact in the voluminous texts on Vedic ritual, particularly on *kāmya* rites (see, e.g., *Śrautakośa,* vol. 1, English section, pt. 2, 539–645; Caland, *Altindische Zauberei*), designed to fulfill worldly desires, all the fires are used.

67. Among other family origins and relations in the Purāṇas are the following: he married Vikeśi, father of the Ūrja clan of Apsaras as well as of Nala and Aṅgāraka, who later became the planet Mars (*BrahmāṇḍaP* 2.24.91, 3.7.21, 229). He was an Ātreya, a descendent of Atri, one of the seven sages of the Tāmasa age (BrahmāṇḍaP 2.36.47; MatsyaP 9.15; VāyuP 62.41). Agni was the name of a class of Maruts (MatsyaP 171.52). His son was Manu Svārociṣa (BhP 8.1.19). Another classification of Agnis or, more reasonably, fires is their origin as *divyam* (celestial), *abyoni* (watery), and *pārthivam* (earthly) (BrahmāṇḍaP 2.24.6, 2.21.53,56; VāyuP 53.5).

68. The location of the Sarasvatī remains problematic. Evidence points to the Ghaggar in western India. See "Short Bibliography on the Sarasvati River," compiled by Gregory L. Possehl, with sixty-four entries. Two fine recent studies are: Dalal, "Short History of Archaeological

Exploration in Bikanir and Bahawalpur along the 'Lost' Saraswati River''; and Ghose et al., ''Lost Courses of the Sarasvati River in the Great Indian Desert.'' This topic is currently under study by C.Z. Minkowski. Doubtless, celestial correspondences exist (see Witzel, ''Sur le chemin du ciel'').

69. Yāska, *Nirukta* 9.8, on RV 10.34.1.

70. See Gonda's carefully argued article, ''Soma, Amṛta, and the Moon,'' in *Change and Continuity in Indian Religion,* 38–70.

71. Gonda, *Change and Continuity,* 61–62.

72. daśacandram asiṃ rudraḥ śatacandraṃ tathāmbikā / somo 'mṛtamayān aśvāṃs tvaṣṭā rūpāśrayaṃ ratham //

73. BrahmāṇḍaP 3.65–1–20. MatsyaP 23.4–15.

74. MatsyaP 5.21, 171.46, 203.3.

75. According to MatsyaP 5.23 he had one son, Varcas, ''Illumination''; ViṣṇuP 1.15.110, 112 says Soma is a Vasu, the son of Bhagavān Varcas.

76. If environmentalists seek a Sanskrit verse in support of their work, BhP 6.4.15ab is one, spoken by Soma to the ten Pracetases: *alaṃ dagdhair drumair dīnaiḥ khilānāṃ śivam astu vaḥ,* ''Add no more to the number of trees (already) burnt, distressed as they are, and let the remaining ones enjoy your auspicious protection.''

77. In another conclusion to the story in the same Purāṇa, Soma cured his consumption by bathing in the Prabhāsā River (BhP 11.6.36).

78. svagobhiḥ pitṛdevebhyo vibhajan kṛṣṇaśuklayoḥ / prajānāṃ sarvāsāṃ rājā 'ndhaḥ somo na āstv iti // The comm. glosses *andhaḥ* as *annam* and acknowledges the metric irregularity.

79. Brāhmins protect the Veda, Hari's body (BhP 7.14.26,41). A *somapa* (''soma-drinker'') is a soma sacrificer (therefore almost exclusively Brahmin) who enjoys the lunar world (BhP 3.32.3).

80. See BhP 8.18.15, 10.84.47, 11.16.16, 2.3.9, 9.1.35; BrahmāṇḍaP 3.65.46.48; MP 11.53.54.

81. It should be noted, however, that the BhP gives far less attention to explicitly ritual instruction than many other Purāṇas, such as the *Śiva, Skandha, Matsya,* and *Agni Purāṇa*s.

82. BhP 5.19.26ff. In describing the genesis of Varāha, both Viṣṇu and Varāha are indistinguishably praised as *yajñaliṅga, yajñeśvara, yajñabhagavān,* and *yajñavarāha* (BhP 3.13.13,23,33ff.); also *yajñasūkara* (BhP 3.19.9); cf. 4.13.4, 4.25.29, 5.17.1, 8.17.8. Yajñavarāha is a very common representation of the boar as the parts of the Veda or the sacrifice; e.g., BhP 3.13.34: *yad romagarteṣu nililyur adhvarās tasmai namaḥ kāraṇasūkarāya te,* ''Homage to you, to the boar of (unique) purpose, in the pores of whose bristles sacrifices lie hidden''; cf. 5.18.34f., 6.8.15; VāyuP 6.11–23. More directly, Viṣṇu himself states: *aṅgāni kratavo jātā dharma ātmāsavaḥ surāḥ,* ''Sacrifices are (my) limbs, the dharma born (from those sacrifices) is (my) body (*ātmā*), the

gods are (my) various breaths (*āsu*)'' (BhP 6.4.46). Also find Nārāyaṇa as *yajñavīrya* (BhP 6.9.31).

83. Also BhP 3.19.13, 8.1.6.

84. An amusing reference: yajñaś ca lokād avatāj janāntāt, ''(Lord) Yajña, guard me against public scandal.''

85. asāv ihānekaguṇo 'guṇo 'dhvaraḥ pṛthag vidhadravyaguṇakriyoktibhiḥ / sampadyate 'rthāśayaliṅganāmabhir viśuddhavijñānaghanaḥ svarūpataḥ //

86. According to ViṣṇuP 3.1.36–40 Yajña was born of Viṣṇu and Ā kūti in the Svāyambhuva era (*manvantara*), of Tuṣitā in Svārociṣa, of Satyā in Uttama, of Havya in Tāmasa, and of Sambhūti in Raivata.

87. See Charles Malamoud, ''Terminer le sacrifice. Remarques sure les honoraires rituels dans le brahmanisme,'' in Biardeau and Malamoud, eds., *Le sacrifice dans l'Inde ancienne,* 155–204.

88. One passage containing imagery on sacrificial genealogy may shed light on the history of a certain South Indian ritual tradition. The South Indian BhP (4.13.15–16) mentions the names of the twelve sons of Cakṣu, the Manu of the sixth Manvantara, and his consort Naḍvalā. They are Puru, Kutsa, Trita, Dyumna, Satyavān, Ṛta, Vrata, Agniṣṭoma, Atirātra, Pradyumna, Śibi, and Ulmuka. Among these are the names of (only) two sacrifices, Agniṣṭoma and Atirātra. This mention may reflect that the ritual practice now observed only by the Nambudiris of Kerala, of performing only the Agniṣṭoma and the Atirātra (with Agnicayana), among soma sacrifices, dates back at least to the composition of the BhP and may have once had wider distribution.

89. BhP 9.24.66: puruṣaḥ kratubhiḥ samīje ātmānam ātmanigamaṃ pathayañ janeṣu.

90. For a brief recounting of how ritualists have dealt with this from the Śrauta Sūtras to the present day, see Smith, *Vedic Sacrifice in Transition,* 73f., 255ff.

91. nāyaṃ dharmo hy adharmo 'yaṃ na hiṃsā dharma ucyate; see Agrawala, *Matsya Purāṇa,* 227f. *ahiṃsā paramo dharmaḥ* was often repeated by Bhāgavatas, *dravyātmakayajña* (sacrifice characterized by grain and other nonflesh offerings) replaced *hiṃsātmakayajña* (sacrifice characterized by violence), and moral attributes, especially *tapas,* replaced sacrifice (MatsyaP 143.40–41; Agrawala, ibid.).

92. BhP 6.2.24, 11.19.18,23; cf. *Bhagavad Gītā* 2.42–45.

93. īje ca kratubhir ghorair dīkṣitaḥ paśumārakaiḥ.

94. vanyaiś carupuroḍāśair nirvapet kālacoditā / na tu śrautena paśunā mām yajeta vanāśramī // agnihotraṃ ca darśaś ca pūrṇamāsaś ca pūrvavat / cāturmāsyāni ca muner āmnātāni ca naigamyaiḥ // Cf. BhP 7.12.19.

95. See Smith, *Vedic Sacrifice in Transition,* 38ff.; Kane, *History of Dharmaśāstra,* 3:929–68.

96. Perhaps reflecting the antiquity of the dispute over animal sacrifice, the VāyuP (57.86ff.) says that the dispute over the inclusion of violence in the sacrifice began when the sacrifice itself originated during the *tretayuga.*

97. Cf. Pollock, "From Discourse of Ritual to Discourse of Power in Sanskrit Culture." Pollock deals primarily with the Pūrvamīmāṃsā (PM). Though most of the *śāstra* of PM was contemporaneous with the Purāṇas, the latter had little use for the PM. However, they were allies—though not conspiratorial ones—in the consolidation of Brahmanical power.

98. The Vedas explicitly enjoin the drinking of a very potent wine (*surā*) during the performance of the Sautrāmaṇi, a long and complicated animal sacrifice to be performed as expiation after certain soma sacrifices including the Rājasūya, Vājapeya, and Agnicayana. The *surā* was prepared from parched grain, pulverized grass, unripened barley, cooked rice, milk, and other substances, fermented for three days then topped off with hair of lion, tiger, and wolf. If ever a substance were eligible for prohibition, this is it (cf. Smith, *Vedic Sacrifice in Transition,* 40). Nevertheless, after offering most of it, the remains were to be consumed by a Brahmin (who was paid to drink it), or by the sacrificer himself. Alternately it was to be dumped down a termite mound, a standard receptacle for impure or defiled offerings (cf. *Āpastamba Śrautasūtra* 19.3.3–5).

99. Cf. Kane, *History of Dharmaśāstra,* 550ff.; also see Menski, "Marital Expectations as Dramatized in Hindu Marriage Rituals," 47–67, and Leslie, "Śrī and Jyeṣṭhā," 107–27, both in *Roles and Rituals for Hindu Women,* ed. I. J. Leslie.

100. The passage adds that whatever statement is begun with the utterance of *om* is inherently true.

101. Or while joking, during marriage ceremonies, in obtaining one's livelihood, for saving one's life, in protecting cows and Brahmins, or to avert violence.

102. However, Brahmins can earn their livelihood (*vṛtti*) by performing sacrifices for Śūdras (see Smith, *Vedic Sacrifice in Transition,* 178; also *Manusmṛti* 11.24 and commentaries).

103. See n. 93.

104. sampracaratsu nānāyāgeṣu viracitāṅgakriyeṣv apūrvaṃ yat tat kriyāphalaṃ dharmākhyaṃ pare brahmaṇi yajñapuruṣe. . .

105. See Smith, *Vedic Sacrifice in Transition,* 47ff.

106. E.g., 10.75.19: patnīsaṃyājāvabhṛthaiś caritvā te tam ṛtvijaḥ / ācāntaṃ snāpayāṃcakruḥ gaṅgāyāṃ saha kṛṣṇayā // "After performing the *patnīsaṃyāja*s and the *avabhṛtha,* (Yudhiṣṭhira) sipped water and, directed by the officiants, bathed in the Gaṅgā along with Kṛṣṇā (Draupadī)."

107. Gonda, in his article "Vedic Cosmogony and Viṣṇuite Bhakti," traces the development of the notion of *puruṣa* from the *puruṣasūkta* (*ṚV* 10.90) through various later Vedic texts and the *Bhagavad Gītā.*

108. Heesterman, *Ancient Indian Royal Consecration,* 6.

109. E.g., *prātaḥsmaraṇa, nāmasmaraṇa*; see Gonda, *Notes on Names and the Name of God in Ancient India.* Elsewhere, Gonda provides verses from the RV that demonstrate the presence of *bhakti* in the Veda; cf. "Indian Mantra," 251ff.

110. See Brown, "Purāṇa as Scripture," on the growing importance of the written word in India, on "the holy book as the form of God" (82), and on the *phalaśruti,* or closing verses of a hymn or text (often added later) that glorify its religious and spiritual value.

111. " 'Scripture' in India," 450.

112. Reuven Frank, former president of NBC News, quoted in *The New York Times Book Review,* May 3, 1992, 7.

113. Thus, I would hesitate to accept Frits Staal's assertion that the rise in importance of the Gāyatrī mantra (RV 3.62.10) was totally arbitrary and accidental ("Sound of Religion," 55ff.). I am inclined to think that this deserves further investigation.

114. BhP 4.24.62, 8.6.9; 11.3.28,46,47; 11.11.37. The value of all scriptures is praised in BhP 11.8.10. Vedic, Tantrik, and mixed ritual is recognized in BhP 11.27.6,7, at least with respect to the consecration of an image. One passage (BhP 11.25.36–41) mentions rites specific to the *śrauta iṣṭi* (e.g., New and Full Moon Sacrifices), namely, *āghāras* and *ājyabhāgas* (the first, offerings of ghee to Prajapāti and Indra; the second, to Agni and Soma; all into the *āhavanīya*; cf. Kane, *History of Dharmaśāstra,* 1050f., 1059f.), but with Kṛṣṇa as the recipient.

115. Cf. Smith on the role of lists, in *Imagining Religion*: "The only formal element that is lacking to transform a catalog into a *canon* is the element of closure: that the list is held to be complete" (48).

116. See Clooney, *Thinking Ritually,* for a balanced view of PM.

117. Ibid. 134.

REFERENCES

Agnipurāṇam

1874 Ed. Rājendralāla Mitra. Bibliotheca Indica, no. 306 (NS). Calcutta: Asiatic Society of Bengal.

Āgniveśyagṛhyasūtra

1940 Ed. L. A. Ravi Varma. University of Travancore, Trivandrum Sanskrit Series, no. 142. Trivandrum.

Agrawala, V. S.

1963 *Matsya Purāṇa—A Study.* Varanasi: All-India Kashiraj Trust.

Āpastambadharmasūtram, Apastamba's Aphorisms on the Sacred Law of the Hindus
1892, 1932 Ed. with notes and extracts from Haradatta's commentary Ujjvalā, by George Bühler. Bombay Sanskrit and Prakrit Series, nos. 49, 50. Bombay: Department of Public Instruction.

Āpastambaśrautasūtra, vol 3
1902 Ed. Richard Garbe. Bibliotheca Indica Series, no. 92. Calcutta: Asiatic Society of Bengal.

Bhāgavata Purāṇa of Kṛṣṇa Dvaipāyana Vyāsa, with Sanskrit commentary Bhāvārthabodhinī of Śrīdhara Svāmin
1983 Ed. Ācārya Jagadīśalāla Śāstrī and J. L. Shastri. Deihi: Motilal Banarsidass.

Bhattacharya, Viman Chandra
1957–58 "Paurāṇic Tradition, Is It Vedic?" *Journal of the Ganganath Jha Research Institute* 15:109–33.

Biardeau, Madeleine, and Charles Malamoud
1976 *Le sacrifice dans l'Inde ancienne.* Paris: Presses Universitaires de France.

Biswas, Asutosh Sarma
1968 *Bhāgavata Purāṇa: a Linguistic Study, Particularly from the Vedic Background.* Dibrugarh [Hoshiarpur: Vishveshvaranand Book Agency].

Bodewitz, H. W.
1973 *Jaiminīya Brāhmaṇa 1–65.* Leiden: Brill.

Bonazzoli, Giorgio
1979 "The Dynamic Canon of the Purāṇa-s." *Purāṇa* 21.(2): 116–66.
1982 "Schemes in the Purāṇas." *Purāṇa* 24.(1):146–89.

Brahmaṇḍapurāṇam
1973 Ed. Ācārya Jagadīsa Śāstrī and J. L. Shastri. Delhi: Motilal Banarsidass.

Brown, Cheever Mackenzie
1986 "Purāṇa as Scripture: From Sound to Image of the Holy Word in the Hindu Tradition." *History of Religions* 26.(1):68–86.

Brown, W. Norman
1931 "The Sources and Nature of *púruṣa* in the Puruṣasūkta (Ṛg Veda 10.90)." *Journal of the American Oriental Society* 51:108–18. (Reprint: *India and Indology: Selected Articles by W. Norman Brown,* ed. Rosane Rocher, 5–13. [Delhi: Motilal Banarsidass], 1978).

Buitenen, J. A. B. van.

1966 "On the Archaism of the Bhāgavata Purāṇa." In *Krishna: Myths, Rites, and Attitudes,* ed. Milton Singer, 23–40, 215–17. Honolulu: East-West Center Press. (Reprint: *Studies in Indian Literature and Philosophy: Collected Articles of J. A. B. van Buitenen,* ed. Ludo Rocher, 223–42. [Delhi: AIIS and Motilal Banarsidass, 1988]).

Caland, Willem

1908 *Altindische Zauberei: Darstellung der altindischen "Wunschopfer."* Amsterdam: Johannes Müller.

Clooney, Francis X.

1990 *Thinking Ritually: Rediscovering the Pūrva Mīmāṃsā of Jaimini.* Vienna: Publications of the De Nobili Research Library, vol. 17.

Coburn, Thomas

1980 "The Study of the Purāṇas and the Study of Religion." *Religious Studies* 16.(3):341–52.

1984 " 'Scripture' in India: Towards a Typology of the Word in Hindu Life." *Journal of the American Academy of Religion* 52:435–59.

Dalal, Katy Feroze

1980 "A Short History of Archaeological Exploration in Bikanir and Bahawalpur along the 'Lost' Saraswati River." *Indica* 17)1):3–40.

Dange, S. S.

1987 *Sacrifice in India: Concept and Evolution.* Aligarh: Viveka.

Gambhirananda, Swami

1972 *Brahma-Sūtra Bhāṣya of Śaṅkarācārya.* Calcutta: Advaita Ashrama.

Ghose, Bimal, Amal Kar, and Zahid Husain

1979 "The Lost Courses of the Sarasvati River in the Great Indian Desert: New Evidence from Landsat Imagery," *The Geographical Journal* 145(3): 446–51.

Gonda, Jan

1963 "The Indian Mantra." *Oriens* 16:244–97.

1965. *Change and Continuity in Indian Religion.* Leiden: Brill.

1970 *Notes on Names and the Name of God in Ancient India.* Amsterdam and London: North-Holland.

1977 "Vedic Cosmogony and Viṣṇuite Bhakti." *Indologica Taurinensia* 5:85–111.

Goswami, C. L.
1971 *Śrimad Bhāgavata Mahāpurāṇa* [English translation]. Gorakhpur: Gita Press.

Halbfass, Wilhelm
1991 *Tradition and Reflection: Explorations in Indian Thought.* Albany: State University of New York Press.

Hazra, R. C.
1940 *Studies in the Purāṇic Records on Hindu Rites and Customs.* Dacca: University of Dacca.

Heesterman, J. C.
1957 *The Ancient Indian Royal Consecration.* The Hague: Mouton.

Hillebrandt, Alfred.
1980 *Vedic Mythology.* Trans. Sreeramula Rajeswara Sarma. Delhi: Motilal Banarsidass.

Kane, P. V.
1946 "Vedic Mantras and Legends in the Purāṇas." *C. Kunhan Raja Commemoration Volume.* Madras, 5–8.
1974, 1974a, 1962 *History of Dharmaśāstra.* Vols. 2.2, 3, 5.2. Poona: Bhandarkar Oriental Research Institute.

Keith, A. B.
1925 *The Religion and Philosophy of the Veda and Upaniṣads.* Harvard Oriental Series, no. 31. Cambridge: Harvard University Press.

Leslie, I. Julia
1991 "Śrī and Jyeṣṭhā: Ambivalent Role Models for Women." In *Roles and Rituals for Hindu Women,* ed. I. J. Leslie, 107–27. London: Pinter.

Macdonell, A. A.
1897 *Vedic Mythology.* (*Grundriss der Indo-Arischen Philologie und Altertumskunde* 3.1.A.) Strassburg: Trübner. (Many Indian reprints, e.g., Varanasi: India Book House, 1963.)

Majumdar, Bimanbehari
1969 *Kṛṣṇa in History and Legend.* Calcutta: Calcutta University.

Mani, Vettam
1975 *Purāṇic Encyclopaedia.* Delhi: Motilal Banarsidass.

Manusmṛtiḥ, with the commentary by Kullukabhaṭṭa entitled Manvarthamuktāvalī
1970 Ed. Paṇḍita Gopāla Śāstrī Nene. Kāśī Sanskrit Series, no. 114. Varanasi: Chowkhamba Sanskrit Series Office.

Matsya Mahāpurāṇa
1984 Ed. Dr. Pushpendra. New Delhi: Meherchand Lachhmandas.

Meier, F. J.
1931. "Der Archaismus in der Sprache des Bhāgavata Purāṇa." *Zeitschrift für Indologie und Iranistik* 8: 33–79.

Menski, Werner
1991 "Marital Expectations as Dramatized in Hindu Marriage Rituals." In *Roles and Rituals for Hindu Women*, ed. Leslie, 47–67.

O'Flaherty, Wendy
1975 *Hindu Myths.* Harmondsworth: Penguin.

Oldenberg, Hermann
1988 *The Religion of the Veda.* Trans. Shridhar B. Shrotri. Delhi: Motilal Banarsidass.

Padoux, Andre
1990 *Vāc: The Concept of the Word in Selected Hindu Tantras.* Trans. Jacques Gontier. Albany: State University of New York Press.

Parpola, Asko
1979 "A Dravidian Solution to the Problem of *kiṃpuruṣa / kinnara.*" *Fourth World Sanskrit Conference, Selected Papers.* New Delhi, 1979: 24–25, 166–67.

Pollock, Sheldon
1990 "From Discourse of Ritual to Discourse of Power in Sanskrit Culture." *Journal of Ritual Studies* 4.(2):315–45.

Possehl, Gregory L.
1991 "A Short Bibliography on the Sarasvati River." Privately distributed.

Prasad, Sheo Shanker
1984 *The Bhāgavata Purāṇa: A Literary Study.* Delhi: Capital.

Rai, Ganga Sagar
1990 *An Introduction to the Vedic Śākhās.* Varanasi: Ratna.

Renou, Louis
1956 *Histoire de la Langue Sanskrite.* Lyon: Editions IAC.

Ṛgveda-Saṃhitā with the commentary of Sāyaṇācārya, vols. 1–5.
1933–51 Ed. C. K. Kashikar and N. S. Sontakke. Poona: Vaidika Saṃśodhana Maṇḍala.

Rocher, Ludo
1977 "The Meaning of *Purāṇá* in in the Ṛgveda." *Wiener Zeitschrift für die Kunde Sudasiens,* 20:6–24.
1986 *The Purāṇas.* Wiesbaden: Otto Harrassowitz.

Rukmani, T. S.

1970 *A Critical Study of the Bhāgavata Purāṇa (with special reference to Bhakti).* Chowkhamba Sanskrit Studies, no. 77. Varanasi: Chowkhamba Sanskrit Series Office.

Salomon, Richard

1986 "The Viṣṇu Purāṇa as a Specimen of Vernacular Sanskrit." *Wiener Zeitschrift für die Kunde Sudasiens* 29:39–56.

Smith, Frederick M.

1985 "Names of Agni in the Vedic Ritual." *Annals of the Bhandarkar Oriental Research Institute* 64:219–26.

1987 *The Vedic Sacrifice in Transition: A Translation and Study of the Trikāṇḍamaṇḍana of Bhāskara Miśra.* Poona: Bhandarkar Oriental Research Institute.

1991. "Indra's Curse, Varuṇa's Noose, and the Suppression of the Woman in the Vedic *Śrauta* Ritual." In *Roles and Rituals for Hindu Women,* ed. Leslie, 17–45.

Smith, Jonathan Z.

1982 *Imagining Religion: From Babylon to Jonestown.* Chicago: University of Chicago Press.

Śrautakośa: Encyclopaedia of Vedic Sacrificial Ritual, vol. 1, English section, part 2

1962 R. N. Dandekar. Poona: Vaidika Saṃśodhana Maṇḍala.

Staal, Frits

1983 *Agni: The Vedic Ritual of the Fire Altar.* Berkeley: Asian Humanities Press.

1985 "The Sound of Religion." *Numen* 33.(1): 33–64, 33.(2): 185–224.

Taittirīyasaṃhitā with the commentary of Sāyaṇācārya

1900–1908 Ed. Kāśīnāth Śāstrī Āgāśe. Ānandāśrama Sanskrit Series, no. 42. Poona: Ānandāśrama.

Vāyu Purāṇa

1905 Ānandāśrama Sanskrit Series, no. 49. Poona: Ānandāśrama.

Viṣṇupurāṇa with Sanskrit Commentary of Śrīdharācārya

1986 Ed Pt. Thāneś Candra Upreti. Delhi: Parimal.

Witzel, Michael

1984 "Sur le chemin du ciel." *Bulletin d'Etudes Indiennes* 2:231–77.

5

From Anxiety to Bliss

Argument, Care, and Responsibility in the Vedānta Reading of *Taittirīya* 2.1–6a

FRANCIS X. CLOONEY, S.J.

WHEN BLISS TURNS INTO ANXIETY

IT IS COMMONPLACE TODAY to observe that texts do not yield single, definite meanings, either in their parts or as wholes. This indeterminacy pertains also—and perhaps especially—to classic religious texts that have endured in significance over many generations. Although such texts clearly make claims about the way the world "really is" and impose demands on the lives of those who hear or read them, today one ordinarily takes for granted that such claims on truth and moral practice are of historical rather than of current pertinence or, at best, options rather than potential obligations. Even the options are thought to be meditated differently for each of the various potential audiences: room is left too for those who understand the texts correctly but simply fail to find any larger truth or guidance there, and also for those who may find even classic texts useful primarily for some extrinsic purpose—to prove some unrelated thesis or to display one's interpretive skills in the context of an interesting example.

The Vedas are not exempt from this treatment, nor are those texts that stand at the end of the Vedic period, the Upaniṣads. These are treated as ambiguous, open to multiple interpretations, and more curious than compelling, despite the fact that for millennia they have been appreciated, defended as embodying definite truths and as making great demands upon engaged readers. Throughout their history the several Vedānta schools defended the cognitive and moral claims of the Upaniṣads, argued for their own interpretation of those claims, and did not hesitate to state that divergent interpretations were in fact wrong—examples of inept reading or ill will.

When contemporary scholars choose to join such debates, their contributions are at least oblique. Philologists, cultural historians, and scholars of religion all bring to their reading of the Upaniṣads refined interpretive skills, detached carefulness, and, in some ways, an expertise that is better equipped to identify the meaning of classic texts in their original settings than are the methods of the traditional Vedānta teachers. Contemporary scholars are for the most part content with modest contributions to the understanding of the original, contextual meaning of such texts and with a concomitant dismissal of various erroneous, overly exegetical or theological interpretations; they decline to affirm or deny the larger truth value such texts might hold for those who study them carefully with open minds. Frequently skeptical and even dismissive of the theological interpretations with which the Vedāntins invested the Upaniṣads, and reluctant to take sides in debates that begin from the premise that truth and moral implication can be identified, scholars are often in the position of knowing a great deal about the great texts, and of being able to catalogue quite skillfully various actual and possible interpretations, while nevertheless remaining comfortably distant from categories such as "true meaning," "right interpretation," and "the right way to live one's life according to the text." Though a scholar may know a great deal about a text and about why others thought it important, she or he may have little to say about whether it is, or ought to, be important today in any way that stands in recognizable continuity with the tradition.

I submit that despite important distinguishing factors, the detachment and skepticism that mark contemporary scholarship were in a certain sense already taken into account by the traditions that identified canonical texts worth knowing and preserving. Just as the Upaniṣads were given a privileged and well-defined status in the traditions of Vedānta, these same traditions also elaborated protective rules that surrounded the canonized texts and identified right ways of reading, interpreting, and defending these texts. They likewise established a set of expectations about the ways in which potential readers became ready to read and were inevitably transformed during the long and patient process of right reading. The bare fact of canon—a set of texts put forward as in some way privileged, to be distinguished from other texts, to be read and interpreted by special standards—was thought by the Vedāntins to be in itself insufficient; also required were what one might call "the extended canon of right practice"—right reading by right readers. By such extended traditional standards, scholarship that precludes the discussion of truth and right reading and ignores the possibility of the transformation of the reader is at best incomplete scholarship, and possibly merely naive virtuosity: anxious busyness, yielding no fruit.

This chapter explores the connections between the textual canon and the extended canon of right practice. It traces some key Vedānta arguments about the meaning of one text from the important *Taittirīya Upaniṣad*, and thereby explores the claims made by the Vedāntins as they sought to ensure that the bare fact of the Upaniṣadic canon was always accompanied by an extended regulatory and practical canon. I will suggest that contemporary scholarship has little excuse for avoiding, and much to gain from, a conversation with its ancient counterpart that is based not merely on attention to the same texts, but also on critical openness to the possibility of appropriating the extended canonical practices as well—to the possibility of having one's mode of scholarship and identity as scholar modified in the course of one's research. To be sure, these traditions present formidable barriers to the modern reader—technical terms, stylized forms of argument, unexpected choices in interpretation, heated and occasionally wearisome debates over points the modern scholar either takes for granted or cannot fathom. In time, however, these same complexities turn out to be the materials of a grammar and a pedagogy of interpretation, the means by which one can make a judicious entry into that community's tradition, bartering a measure of independence for the sake of a more comprehensive and vital understanding of the classic religious texts.

A defense of this confidence requires that we read more, get involved more and not less deeply in the complexities of reading the Upaniṣads as they have been and are read in the Indian tradition. In this project we approach the master readers of the Upaniṣads, the Vedāntins, as guides to the proper reading of the *Taittirīya* and other such texts. Though writing considerably after the Upaniṣadic period, Vedāntins such as Bādarāyaṇa (fifth century C.E.), Śaṅkara (eighth century C.E.), and Rāmānuja (eleventh century C.E.) and their disciples brought to bear on the Upaniṣads an intense array of practices of reading, argument, practical application, and systematization. They produced these in a way that successfully combined the requisite elements of a three-way dialectic among careful reading, the arguable and defensible truth of what one reads, and both of these in creative tension with the effects they may have on their reader.

Through attention to Vedānta we learn to place firmly together our arguments about the right meaning of a text, our patient practices of reading the text, and our achieved vulnerability to be educated by what we read. We learn, in brief, to maintain the strong connections among apologetics, exegesis, and ethics. In the Vedānta commentaries careful reading, argument as preparatory to and about what is read, and application to the life of the reader are inseparable: to read well requires that one be able to argue; to argue requires that one be invested in the stakes of the argument, as applied to oneself.

By this view, the contemporary student of the Upaniṣads cannot remain in a qualitatively different position. Readers ancient and contemporary engage in a dialectic between the theoretical positions that preceded reading and that reading itself; both may discover in the texts sufficient evidence of the positions required and, thereafter, may devise ways in which to appropriate the texts read and truth argued. In the process, then and now, the text remains the chosen vehicle of the articulation of positions, the clarification of thought and communication, and, finally, of the transformation of the reader.[1]

THE VEDĀNTA READING OF *TAITTIRĪYA* 2.1–6a

Let us first review the relevant portion of the *Taittirīya Upaniṣad* 2.1-6a.[2] Probably in replication of the patterning of certain Vedic fire altars, the passage is structured according to the description of five birds as patterns for increasingly interior layers of the self. Each bird forms a complex arrangement of components, accessible only when the prior bird form has been understood; together they constitute the complex self of the human person: the self consisting of the essence of food (*annarasamaya*); the self consisting of vital breath (*prāṇamaya*); the self consisting of mind (*manomaya*); the self consisting of knowledge (*vijñānamaya*); and the self consisting of bliss (*ānandamaya*). In teaching about the self through a presentation of these five bird forms, the passage expends considerable effort in order to say something about ***brahman***, while at the same time regulating how what is said is to be received by the reader. Here is the text:

> 1. One who knows ***brahman*** reaches the highest. About that there is this verse:[3]
>
> > "*Brahman* is reality, knowledge, infinite; he who knows it concealed in the cavity of the heart and in the highest space, attains all wishes, along with omniscient *brahman*."
>
> Out of this self, indeed, emerges ether, out of ether wind, out of wind fire, out of fire water, out of water earth, out of earth plants, out of plants food, out of food man. This one, indeed, consists of the food-sap (*annarasamaya*); in him this is the head, this is the right wing, this the left wing, this the self, this the tail, that on which it rests. About it, there is this verse:
>
> > 2. "Out of food are born creatures, all these that are on earth; therefore, through food they have their life. Into

> this food they enter at last. Food is the oldest of beings; that is why it is called all-healing. They obtain all food who adore *brahman* as food. That is why it is called all-healing. Beings originate out of food. Through food, they grow. It eats beings, and beings eat it: that is why it is called food."

Different from this one consisting of the food-sap is the inner self (*ātman*) which consists of vital breath (*prāṇamaya*). With it this one is filled. This now is the human form, and according to its human formation, it is the human form. In it the in-breath is the head, the intermediate breath the right wing, the out-breath the left wing, the ether the self, the earth the tail, that on which it rests. About it, there is this verse:

> 3. "According to this vital breath breathe the gods, men and animals. Breath is indeed the life of beings; that is why it is named the all-animating."

Who adores *brahman* as the breath comes to the full duration of life; that is why he is named the all-animating. Thus he is the embodied self of that one which is before [the self consisting of food]. Different ftom this one consisting of vital-breath is the inner self which consists of mind (*manomaya*). With it this one is filled. This now is the human form, and according to its human formation, it is the human form. In it, the *yajus* is the head, the *ṛg* the right wing, the *sāman* the left wing, the directives the self, the *atharva* and the *aṅgirasa* chants the tail, that on which it rests. About it, there is this verse:

> 4. "Before this, words turn back, not reaching it with the mind; he who knows the bliss of *brahman* dreads nothing, now or ever."

Thus he is the embodied self of that one which is before [the self consisting of vital breath]. Different from this one consisting of mind there is the inner self consisting of knowledge (*vijñāna-maya*). With it this one is filled. This now is the human form, and according to the human formation, it is the human form. In it faith is the head, justice the right wing, truth the left wing, yoga the self, the great one the tail, that on which it rests. About it, there is this verse:

> 5. "He sets forth knowledge as the sacrificial offering, he sets forth knowledge as the rites. All the gods adore *brahman* as knowledge, the oldest of all. He who

> knows *brahman* as knowledge and does not deviate from it leaves evil behind in his body and attains all that he wishes."

Thus he is the embodied self of that one which is before [the self consisting of mind]. Different from this one consisting of knowledge, there is the inner self consisting of bliss (*ānanda-maya*). With it this one is filled. This now is the human form, and according to its human formation, it is the human form. In it, what is dear is the head, joy the right wing, cheerfulness the left wing, bliss the self, *brahman* the tail, that on which it rests (*brahma puccham pratiṣṭha*). About it, there is this verse:

> 6. "He who knows *brahman* as non-existent becomes as it were non-existent; he who knows *brahman* as existent, him they know as existent."

The metaphorical birds are ordered according to the directions, each having a head in the east, a right (south) wing, a left (north) wing, a central "self" (*ātman*), and a tail to the west. The general pattern is thus:

	head	
south wing (right)	trunk	north wing (left)
	tail	

Each of the five bird forms is identified according to a domain appropriate to its name:

FOOD		food	
	food	food	food
		food	
BREATH		in-breath	
	intermediate breath	air	out-breath
		earth	
MIND		*yajus*	
	ṛg	*brāhmaṇa*	*sāman*
		mantras	
KNOWLEDGE		faith	
	justness	yoga	truth
		might	
BLISS		the pleasing	
	joy	bliss	great joy
		brahman	

The meaning of each is illuminated by a mantra, as cited above: mantras that speak of the nature and importance of food (2.2), or of the limits of verbal and conceptual knowledge (2.4), or of the relationship between knowledge and existence (2.6).

Each bird form has a fuller significance by its location within the sequence of five. Each is located as interior to the one before it on the list, and presumably is reached after one has encountered and passed through the preceding, exterior one. Only by tracing each form one after the other does one proceed along the interior path and gradually achieve insight into the structure of the person thus layered and, through this self-analysis, self-composition, and self-appropriation, attain to the locus of the self of bliss, to knowledge of *brahman*.

Though complex and rich in meaning(s), and already self-interpreted in the interplay of prose and mantra passages, *Taittirīya* 2.1–6a does not decisively fix its meaning(s). Though the subsequent portion of *Taittirīya* 2 contributes to a possible decision by delineating a corresponding cosmology (2.6–7) and by a demythologizing analysis that equates a detached knowledge of texts with each traditional level of bliss (2.8), the point of the text is practical and is not rendered merely available by simple declaration: one must work one's way through the five forms in order to know what is thereby achieved. It is as if to say, "Is *brahman* the self of bliss, or beyond it? Find out for yourself."

In particular, *Taittirīya* 2 seems neither to ask nor to answer the key question posed to it by the Vedānta tradition in its classical treatment of *Taittirīya* 2.1–6a in the *Uttara Mīmāṃsā Sūtra* (henceforth UMS) of Bādarāyaṇa 1.1.12-19:[4] is *brahman* the fifth form, that which consists of bliss, or is it yet farther beyond that fifth form? Let us introduce briefly this Vedānta approach to the text by spelling out Bādarāyaṇa's position, and in light of this reflect upon the presuppositions the Vedānta brings to its reading of the Upaniṣad.

ARGUING THE TEXT: BĀDARĀYAṆA

The Vedāntins were, and are, committed to finding the meaning of texts primarily in them as we "see" them—in their literal meaning, on their surface. As a commentarial tradition, the Vedānta was (and remains) committed to the establishment of meaning in texts themselves, and expects them to yield coherent meanings. Each text's significance is constituted as a whole; the parts cohere and signify together, and in theory meanings cannot be picked and chosen by a selection of some of what is said. In their interaction the parts of what is said constitute the set of markers and codes by which right understanding is able to be achieved, signaled and then communicated. A reduction of the text to one or another coherent theme deprives it of its textual energy, as this increases in the event of the interaction of text and reader.

This commitment is enacted only within the framework of a concomitant responsibility for the right exterior framing of meaning: "where" texts are located helps us to know how to read what they mean on their inner surfaces. In practice, this exterior space is mapped in a series of increasingly broader locations within a tradition of texts and learning. Their reading, however careful, does not occur in a vacuum, but only in specific settings that are in important ways determinative of that reading. Even before we make much out of the determinations of meaning offered by the various Vedāntins, the way any Upaniṣadic text is to be read is already significantly set, as it is made into a locus for exegetical argument in the larger context of a systematization of the Upaniṣads. As such, the effort to read them occurs only in the context of the project of *samanvaya* (coherence, harmony), the defense of which is the major project undertaken in the first *adhyāya* of the UMS. The interpretive practice of *samanvaya* has as its goal the fixing of the meaning of all the debated and controversial texts of the Upaniṣads that pertain to knowledge and salvation. *Brahman* alone is the object of salvific knowledge, and other purported objects of knowledge—the human self, Sāṃkhya's *pradhāna*, the Vaiśeṣika atoms—must be ruled out. Let us now put UMS 1.1.12–19, where *Taittirīya* 2.1–6a is examined, in context.

The UMS is an extended effort to systematize the practices, experiments, and theories that comprise the *Taittirīya* and other old Upaniṣads. The UMS is divided into four major parts (*adhyāyas*), each of which is divided into *pādas*; each of these is in turn divided into *adhikaraṇas*, "places" for the interpretation and arguing of key Upaniṣadic verses. The major divisions of the UMS are these:

Adhyāya 1: The harmonization of scripture (*samanvaya*)

- 1.1.11–11 Introduction: The object of Advaita, the source of its right knowledge, and its claim about the single, identifiable meaning of the Upaniṣads
- 1.1.12–14 Treatment of scripture texts that are unclear on first reading, in order to show that the important major texts unanimously point to *brahman* as source of the world, major goal of knowledge, etc.

Adhyāya 2: The removal of contradiction (*virodha*)

- 2.1 The coherent, reasonable nature of the Advaita system
- 2.2 The incoherence and unreasonableness of other systems
- 2.3–4 The consistency of the Advaita view of the cosmos

Adhyāya 3: Meditation as the means to liberation (*sādhana*)
- 3.1 The cosmology of meditation
- 3.2 The nature of the self, *brahman*, and the connection of the two
- 3.3 The use of the Upaniṣads in meditation
- 3.4 The implications of the progress of the Advaitin in meditation; the discourse of the renunciant

Adhyāya 4: The result of meditation (*phala*)
- 4.1 The liberationof the self
- 4.2 The process of dying
- 4.3 Analysis of the postdeath ascent
- 4.4 Analysis of the results-end points of the ascent

UMS 1.1.12–19, the twelve *sūtra*s devoted to an analysis of *Taittirīya* 2.1–6a, occur in the first *adhyāya*, and thus in the section devoted to *samanvaya*, the identification and harmonization of the primary content of the Upaniṣads.

Bādarāyaṇa presents the argument as to why the self consisting of bliss is indeed *brahman*. Taken alone, these *sūtra*s are not readily communicative; indeed, without amplification it is not possible even to translate them intelligibly. I render each somewhat freely, and to each I append a brief comment, drawn for the most part from the first of Śaṅkara's two elucidations of the *sūtra*s of the *adhikaraṇa*:

> 12: On account of repeated references to "bliss," the "one consisting of bliss" must be *brahman*.
>
> According to Bādarāyaṇa, *ānanda* ("bliss") is frequently repeated in *Taittirīya* 2 and 3, and so can be identified as its key thematic word.[5] When cited, it is connected with *brahman*, which is key in *Taittirīya* 2.1–6a because "*brahman*" is mentioned at its beginning (2.1) and end (2.5–6a); hence, it is reasonable to assume that the referent of the conclusive, *ānandamaya*, "consisting of bliss," is *brahman*, bliss.
>
> 13: If one objects that *brahman* cannot be *ānandamaya* because "*-maya*" implies liability to change, we say the objection does not hold, since "*-maya*" can also mean "abundant in."
>
> Bādarāyaṇa's point is that *-maya* ("consisting of") does not always indicate what is changeable and quantifiable, but can also mean "abundance"; it may therefore be applied to *brahman* without implying that it is composed of measurable quantities.

14: Moreover, *brahman* is mentioned as the cause of bliss.

This *sūtra* notes that in *Taittirīya* 2.7 *brahman* is said to "make [others] blissful"; it is reasonable for this bliss-maker to have already been called "*ānandamaya*."

15: The same *brahman* mentioned in the mantra portion is also mentioned in the Brāhmaṇa portion.

According to Bādarāyaṇa's analysis, both the text's first prose (rubrical) section (Brāhmaṇa)—"one who knows *brahman* reaches the highest"—and its first mantra section—"*brahman* is reality, knowledge, infinite"—refer to *brahman*. The concluding mantra section also refers to *brahman*: "He who knows *brahman* as non-existent becomes as it were non-existent." It is therefore appropriate that the concluding Brāhmaṇa section, which deals with the self of bliss, concludes similarly by referring to *brahman*. Therefore, "consisting of bliss" refers to *brahman*.

16: It is implausible to think that the alternative, the human self, consists of bliss.

If *brahman* were not the one "consisting of bliss," Bādarāyaṇa says, the prime alternative would be the human self; but an examination of the plight of the human self shows that it cannot be plausibly identified with bliss.

17: Moreover, the difference between the self and *brahman* is clearly taught.

Bādarāyaṇa notes that a subsequent part of the text (*Taittirīya* 2.7)—"Them, when one receives this essence, he becomes full of bliss"—makes it clear that humans acquire bliss. Therefore, they cannot be bliss.

18: Because desire is explicitly mentioned, we cannot depend on inference to draw a conclusion.

In the latter half of *Taittirīya* 2.6 (not cited above) the one "consisting of bliss" is said to desire: "He desired, may I become many." But desire involves anticipation, and so the one who desires must be able to anticipate, that is, to be intelligent. Therefore, Bādarāyaṇa concludes, the unintelligent material principle (*pradhāna*) cannot be the one "consisting of bliss."

19: In the Upaniṣad, the union of this self and that *brahman* is clearly taught.

> Finally, Bādarāyaṇa notes that *Taittirīya* 2.7 teaches that knowledge of the self consisting of bliss leads to release; but *brahman* is the only object of knowledge that leads to release; moreover, one cannot be already what one is going to unite with.

The very fact Bādarāyaṇa's posing the question transforms the text by using it newly and differently. The effort to fix its right meaning relocates it within an interpretive and systematic framework in which the text is subject to precise determination. As the subject matter of an *adhikaraṇa*, this relocation gives it a purpose and function that reach beyond those of meditation. However resolved, this interrogation formalizes and makes the conclusion of meditation available in a new way.

Bādarāyaṇa's scrutiny of *Taittirīya* 2.1–6a leads to these conclusions. First, "*brahman*" is the primary content of this section of the Upaniṣad, in both its prose and mantra sections. Second, that which is blissful must be other than the human self, and must be superior, efficacious. Third, there is nothing in the passage that indicates any other "self of bliss," nor that discounts *brahman* as that self. We may conclude that according to Bādarāyaṇa, *Brahman* consists of bliss, is the fifth and final self, and may be reached by an inward journey according to the steps marked in this text.

This *adhikaraṇa*, the first in the series in which the principle of *samanvaya* is applied, shows that *Taittirīya* 2.1–6a has a proper Vedānta meaning, and coheres with all the other rightly understood Upaniṣadic texts surrounding it in UMS1: it is a text about *brahman*, not merely about the self of the meditator.[6]

For the Vedāntins, the meaning of *Taittirīya* 2 cannot reside merely in the text, and they make this (in today's context) commonplace claim an important and explicit factor in their reading. They understood that an Upaniṣad's meaning is constituted in the act of systematization and theological commentary, by its inclusion in the UMS, within a planned set of exegeses and all the commentarial refinements that occur thereafter: its authority, in other words, is dependent in part on its establishment as canon. To know the text properly requires that one also know the general system of the UMS, share the Vedānta confidence in and defense of a single, coherent meaning expressed in all the Upaniṣads, and accept the ways in which that "system of the text" binds its committed readers to read within at least provisionally fixed boundaries. The specific debate over the text presumes a commitment to the need to regularize the meaning of the whole body of texts. Moreover, it is only a short step from the practical composition of *samanvaya* to the articulation of a doctrine about *brahman*, a subsequent, informative use of language that deserves the assent of its hearers, even if the words are not simply those of the Upaniṣad itself.[7]

The *Taittirīya* is therefore transformed; a text for meditation, it becomes a resource for a teaching about ***brahman***, and then also an important contributor to a full doctrine of ***brahman***, its words liable to formalization as a truth about the world and ***brahman***, a truth that can be argued, shown to be in conformity with reason and experience. Thus, in part because of the authority that is attributed to the *Taittirīya* text, one can finally declare that it is true that ***brahman*** consists of bliss, or, depending on how one reads, that it is true that ***brahman*** is beyond what consists of bliss.

The transition to formal doctrine is both the possibility and result of the decision by the various schools of Vedānta to invest a great deal of energy in arguing, on the basis of *Taittirīya* 2, the relationship of ***brahman*** and the human self. They—come to, choose to—believe that the question of ***brahman*** and the self is implied by the serial move from the "food-self" to the "bliss-self" and possibly beyond, and that this implication needs to be made explicit through a proper exposition, in the UMS.

The process of relocation with the UMS and the subsequent doctrinalization can be most broadly described as the conscious location of the text in a tradition. Such a tradition is comprised of a number of elements: 1) a series of readings, accompanied by the teachings and rules that govern them; 2) a set of commentaries which serve as exegetical, doctrinal, and pedagogical loci; 3) a set of accumulated loyalties to the smaller and larger choices made by one's own teachers and their teachers—choices about topics such as patterns of language, the norms and precedents of argument, and the idea of tradition itself. All of this is involved in the establishment of the Vedānta canon as a practical endeavor. Moreover, the establishment of this canon does not mark the termination of argument, but rather the establishment of the possibility of vigorous argumentation. Let us now see how this occurs in the dispute between Śaṅkara and Rāmānuja on the reading of the text.

CARE IN READING: ŚAṄKARA AND RĀMĀNUJA

Because of, and not despite, the fact of their shared recognition of the authority of the *Taittirīya* text, the close readings to which Śaṅkara and Rāmānuja submit the text can be compared and shown, as it happens in this case, to be in disagreement; because they have accepted the canonical framework with all its implications, they find argument worthwhile, and do in fact argue. In both their interpretations, *Taittirīya* 2.1–6a as a resource for meditation is reconstituted as a location on which the nature of ***brahman*** can be expounded positively—even if its ineffability is part of this exposition. In neither Śaṅkara's nor Rāmānuja's position, however, does a clear and significantly predetermining doctrinal commitment lessen the commitment to read. Both insist on the articulation of doctrine and on the careful reading of texts: indeed, the latter is the material basis of the former.

The Vedāntins seek to determine the meaning of *Taittirīya* 2.1–6a as exactly as possible, following every clue in every part of the text, in order to decide what the text as a whole says. On that basis, they will determine whether ***brahman*** is the self consisting of bliss, or still beyond it. Though, as we have seen, this reading is in part determined by prior questions brought to the text as it is read in Vedānta, this partial predetermination does not diminish the Vedānta commitment to the discovery of meaning in the text. Let us now examine examples of the readings of the text as an UMS ***adhikaraṇa*** in the Advaita school of Śaṅkara and the Viśiṣṭādvaita school of Rāmānuja.

Śaṅkara

As I acknowledged earlier, my assessment of Bādarāyaṇa's position as it is set forth in the *sūtras* depended on Śaṅkara's first exposition of the ***adhikaraṇa***, and we may recount that first position briefly, as a replication of Bādarāyaṇa's. For Śaṅkara, there are three main clues in the *Taittirīya*, and a problem to be resolved. The clues are these:

1. The text does not mention any self beyond that which consists of bliss (2.5): what is the import of this abrupt termination of the series?
2. "***Brahman***" is said to be the "tail" (2.5): does the fact that ***brahman*** is the tail of the self consisting of bliss mean that ***brahman*** is not that self, or rather that it is the "tail," in the sense of "that on which everything rests"?
3. The passage begins and ends with references to the importance of knowledge of ***brahman*** (2.1, 2.6a): is it significant that these references do not mention the self that consists of bliss, but only ***brahman***?

None of these clues is decisive in itself, and all three, along with others, must be simultaneously introduced in order to achieve the desired persuasiveness. Nevertheless, they, and others like them, remain the basis on which right meaning is constructed.

The problem to be resolved is this:

4. It is evident in regard to each of the prior selves that "consisting of" (*-maya*) has a quantitative aspect, and indicates a certain materiality, measure; it therefore marks the finitude of the self thus composed. If "consisting of" continues to function in this way in

regard to the "self consisting of bliss," then the latter will be a measured, finite self, and not *brahman*. Or does "consisting of" also mean "abundance," "fullness without limitation"?

In his first interpretation, in keeping with Bādarāyaṇa's reading, Śaṅkara makes these corresponding decisions:

1. The lack of mention of a self beyond the self consisting of bliss is not a clue to indicate that the self consisting of bliss is final, though one may take it as a clue that it is not said explicitly that self consisting of bliss is the goal.
2. The mention of "*brahman* the tail" after the mention of "the self which consists of bliss" is meant to distinguish the two.
3. Because the framing verses praise knowledge of *brahman* and not of *ānandamaya*, we can infer a distinction between the two.
4. "Consisting of" can mean either "quantitatively composed of" or "abundant in." The former meaning applies to the first four selves, and the latter to the last of the five.

Śaṅkara then offers a second, contrary interpretation, according to which *brahman* is not the self consisting of bliss; this too is legitimated on textual grounds. In effect, he reevaluates the first conclusion—that "consisting of bliss" indicated *brahman*—into an only incompletely correct position, in need of further refinement, in order to show that the self consisting of bliss is certainly not *brahman*, and that this reading is well supported by the text. He puts forth his second reading without any effort to conceal the earlier view, and without any apology for it.[8]

In it, he is guided by the same concern to show the propriety and traditional roots of interpretation, and without any diminishment in his commitment to a meticulous explanation of each *sūtra*. I note four of his revised readings here, in approximate correspondence with the preceding four points:

1. Although the self consisting of bliss is last among the five, and no self is mentioned beyond it, the text does not actually state that this self is the supreme reality, *brahman*. Rather, it states that *brahman* is its support: "bliss the self, *brahman* the tail, that on which it rests." (*Taittirīya* 2.5) The mere fact of being last in the series does not determine conclusively that the self consisting of bliss is *brahman*.
2. Similarly, the text clearly says that *brahman* is the "tail"; in Śaṅkara's reading, this must mean, "like a tail," "a support." But *brahman* cannot be both the self consisting of bliss that has a support, and the support itself.[9]

3. Even if knowledge of the self consisting of bliss does not equal knowledge of *brahman*, its salvific purpose is preserved, since *brahman* is the foundation of that self, its support; therefore, the salvific import of the text is not lost if we decide that "consisting of bliss" does not refer to *brahman*.[10]
4. Regarding Bādarāyaṇa's *sūtra* 13: *-maya* does mean "consisting of," and is so used regarding each of the first four selves and so has a quantitative meaning. If so, one can hardly suggest that it suddenly comes to mean "abundant in" when the fifth self is reached. For the sake of consistency, we must assume that *ānandamaya* means "consisting of bliss" in a quantitative sense, and so refers to a self that is not *brahman*, some finite reality such as the individual self.[11]

On the basis of these (and other) arguments the previously firm conclusion—"*brahman* is the self consisting of bliss"—is returned to a state of tentativeness and a new conclusion is fashioned: "*brahman* is not the self consisting of bliss, but lies yet deeper inside that."

It is most striking that both interpretations put forward by Śaṅkara, and the eventual argument between the proponents of each, are worked out on the strictest of textual grounds. All sides of the argument agree that if the text poses difficult questions for the educated reader, the text is *the* place where answers are to be found. Advaita desires precision, and considers the definition of a correct meaning as an attainable goal. But precision and rightness of meaning occur only through exact and proper reading. Argument and the refutation of one's opponents are essentially textual matters, in which the texts are both the vehicle of larger arguments and the constitutive possibility of those arguments.

Though prolific in their amplification of Śaṅkara's arguments, the later Advaita commentators—Vācaspati, Amalānanda, and Appaya Dīkṣita—do not question either Śaṅkara's first or second interpretation. Rather, accepting one and then the other, they read the Upaniṣad, the *sūtras*, and Śaṅkara's comments ever more closely. Just as they dutifully explained Śaṅkara's first presentation, they dutifully confirm the second. Their careful refinements give precision to Śaṅkara's arguments, elaborating a broad set of subsequent questions the novice Advaitin must consider, thereby sharpening ever more finely his ability to question and read properly. This pedagogical, literary mode of extended argumentation allows us to understand their commentarial project; the fruit is increasing refinement, not correction or novelty.[12]

Rāmānuja

Now let us turn more briefly to the Viśiṣṭādvaita interpretation of the *adhikaraṇa*, as presented by Rāmānuja and his successors; here the same mutual dependence of argument and reading is evident. Rāmānuja's view conforms closely to Bādarāyaṇa's, as the latter is presented in Śaṅkara's first interpretation: "*ānandamaya*" refers to *brahman* and not to the individual self. I highlight three major points.

If Śaṅkara's interpretation is most vividly marked by his juxtaposition of two readings of the text, Rāmānuja's reading is marked by a grand aside. Into the middle of his interpretation of the first *sūtra* in the *adhikaraṇa*, he inserts a lengthy exposition[13] of the claim that the *Taittirīya* text cannot be read as equating the self consisting of bliss with *brahman* on the grounds that from scripture and reason we (already) know that *brahman* and the human self are not identical. The *adhikararṇa* thus becomes the place in which Rāmānuja chooses to detail his position on the difference between *brahman* and the human self; within that doctrinal context, *Taittirīya* 2.1–6a is read in support of this position, as follows.[14]

First, in Rāmānuja's exegesis of the text and *sūtras*, as in Śaṅkara's, much is made of the range of meanings attributable to "consisting of" (*-maya*). On the one hand, there is an important distinction between "consisting of knowledge" (*vijñānamaya*, in 2.4) and "knowledge" (2.1,6): the former indicates the human self, which is not pure knowledge, while the latter indicates something higher, the Self, *brahman*.

On the other hand, there are also instances where "consisting of" does not mark a distinction between "x" and that which "consists of x." For example, that which "consists of vital breath" (the *prāṇamaya*) cannot be different ftom "vital breath." That which "consists of bliss" (*ānandamaya*) is like the *prāṇamaya* and not like the *vijñānamaya*, and so can legitimately be interpreted as referring to that which is pure bliss, *brahman*:

> The regard for consistency [in the usage of *-maya* as meaning a modification] already has to be set aside in the case of the "*prāṇamaya*" [consisting of vital breath]; for in that term *-maya* cannot denote "made of." The *prāṇamaya* Self can only be called by that name in so far as air with its five modifications has (among others) the modification called vital breath, breathing out, or because among the five modifications or functions of air vital breath is the "abounding, prevailing one." (UMS1.1.14)[15]

Second, the mantra, "Before this, words turn back, not reaching it with the mind; he who knows the bliss of *brahman* dreads nothing, now or ever" (*Taittirīya* 2.4), cannot be used as a proof of the idea that there is a self beyond all qualities, Advaita's *brahman* without qualities (*nirguṇa brahman*). The ample exposition of *brahman* in *Taittirīya* 2 would be rendered futile were 2.4 to declare almost all of the exposition fruitless. Rather, "what the clause really means is that if one undertakes to state the definite amount of the bliss of ***brahman***. . .words and thought have to turn back powerless, since no definite amount can be assigned" (UMS1.1.17).

Third, another text, *Bṛhadāraṇyaka Upaniṣad* 3.9.28, "knowledge, bliss, is ***brahman***," shows that "bliss" and "made of bliss" both refer to ***brahman***, that there are no grounds for designating "bliss" alone as referring to "***brahman***" (UMS1.1.20).

On the basis of his reading of the Upaniṣad and the *sūtras*, Rāmānuja concludes that the succession of selves must be read as culminating in one that is qualitatively different—***brahman***, which is made of bliss. This difference, he claims, is attested by the text itself, which proceeds by a differentiated use of "made of" and has in various ways signaled the difference of the fifth self. Though the reading is in conflict with Śaṅkara's, and though there are differences in what is counted as pertinent in reading the *Taittirīya* text, careful reading remains in all cases the basis for decision.[16]

Let us review our position at this point. The possibility of argument within the Vedānta context—arguing the meaning of texts with other Vedāntins, as a Vedāntin—requires that one believe that it is possible to know precisely the meaning of a text and on that basis to make one's point. This requires that one be able to read them properly, to sort out a complex set of arguments and counterarguments. One must be able to reassess that entire set against the backdrop of still other arguments—and yet be able to see more simply then, transformed by mastery of a portion of the text. The determination of the right meaning of the *Taittirīya* text is a matter of skill, judgment, and persuasion. For the decision regarding right meaning depends on how one reads the text, what one takes for clues and how one assesses them, and how one brings to bear on that reading other clues, drawn ftom other sources.

There is a mutually dependent and corrective relationship between careful reading and argument about the nature of the self, the world, and ***brahman***. Argument and the consequent articulation of what matters in regard to human liberation contribute to the identification of which texts matter, and what one is to look for in reading them. But patient, persistent, careful reading of those texts is the vehicle of progress in the comprehensive judgment of what constitutes liberation, its bliss, its means.

TAKING SIDES: GETTING INVOLVED IN THE ARGUMENT

As texts are canonized and their authority becomes increasingly productive and assertive, the stakes are raised, the arguments become more heated, the simple objectivities of detached scholarship become increasingly labored. If Śaṅkara and Rāmānuja show us what kind of reading was practiced in the tradition, can the contemporary scholar engage seriously in careful reading, of that kind or another, and at what cost?

On a philological level careful reading is surely possible, and requires little explanation; on certain grounds one may even argue that contemporary Indologists read the Upaniṣads better than did the Vedāntins.[17] One may wonder, though, if the reader who does not share with Vedānta its presuppositions about the salvific status of the whole text—as a coherent, complete whole in which nothing is superfluous, nothing lacking—will in fact read with the same kind of careful and confident attention to the whole that characterizes the Vedānta reading; one may suspect that at least some contemporary readers will be inclined to appeal rather quickly to factors such as the probable redaction of the text, to explain (away) elements that do not fit, or to relegate others to the category of "etc." Since wholeness of reading is intrinsic to its full argument about texts such as *Taittirīya* 2, the selective, at least mildly reductionist contemporary reader may remain burdened with a fragmentary reception of the text and a slightly arbitrary set of arguments to be put forward.

Although we need not apologize for our inability to examine every commentarial refinement of every argument, the enormous and forbidding mass of exegesis, complexly intertwined with doctrine, compels us to recognide the practical implications of our omissions: we are making a choice about just how much we want to become skilled in Vedānta, how much Vedānta we want to actually know, and so declining to pursue further our education as Uttara Mīmāṃsakas. Since the fruit of the Vedānta lies in its commentarial fullness, a recognition of the Advaita Vedānta decision that *brahman* is not the *ānandamaya* is only a small step toward mastery of the *adhikaraṇa*. The conclusion is important, but so is the set of practices by which one gets there. We can choose to become part of the Vedānta argument, but the price is a willingness to put on a certain kind of argumentative attitude—just as one began by becoming willing to learn Sanskrit, to follow the protocols of *adhikaraṇa*, to proceed by the methods of Mīmāṃsā argument.

These questions may be put more simply. Is there a point at which one can take sides, and agree with Bādarāyaṇa's and Rāmānuja's, or Śaṅkara's, version of the *adhikaraṇa*? If so, is it possible to take sides strictly on the basis of philological arguments? I am inclined to think that it is much more difficult to take sides than it might first appear, since the texts are not going to decide matters for us by providing an absolutely clear, decisive meaning. We have to get involved in order to make the necessary decision. To determine which side we are on, we have to be willing to go beyond setting out textual grounds, by also uncovering the presuppositions we have brought to the reading of the text as contemporary scholars. Even if these grounds are not identical with those of (any of) the Vedāntins, the mix of presuppositions and the results of reading may place one clearly on the side of one or another Vedāntin, and thus in a position where, if one is to say anything, one is obliged to argue for that position.

If we assume that the contemporary reader who is not a Vedāntin does not share the "Vedānta faith," and does not bring to the *Taittirīya* text the set of doctrinal positions enunciated in Vedānta, is it the case that the modern reader's set of other commitments, other doctrines, other presuppositions, inevitably have a similar effect on the project of reading the texts? Let us make several concessions: all scholars have presuppositions; some presuppositions are more fruitful than others; a scholar can legitimately strive for objectivity, though this never includes the total exclusion of presuppositions; no scholar will succeed in making all presuppositions entirely explicit; the explicitation of some does not necessarily mean that those made explicit are the most influential. Granting these points, it is still possible to claim, I suggest, that the defining difference is between scholarship that makes its presuppositions explicit and scholarship that does not, and that once this explicitation is undertaken, contemporary scholarship is not on a qualitatively different ground than Vedānta in its ancient or modern forms.

For the sake of clarification, let us consider an example. The volume on early Advaita in the *Encyclopedia of Indian Philosophies* is a responsible contemporary exposition of the *Taittirīya* text, but one that begins from different presuppositions and serves a different purpose than the Vedānta readings and in which, it seems, the grounds for writing are indeed qualitatively different than those of the Vedāntins. It seeks to summarize Vedānta texts with a minimum of interpretation: "this volume is intended, not as a definitive study of the works summarized, but as an invitation to further philosophical attention to them. The plan has been to make available the substance of the thought contained in these works, so that philosophers unable to read the original Sanskrit and who find difficulty in understanding and finding their way about in the translations (where such exist) can get an idea of the positions taken and the arguments offered."[18] Hoping to be of help to philosophers beginning to look about in Indian thought, the volume does not say what a philosopher should do with this information; if it is interested in the transformation of the reader, this goal is advanced by giving the reader information.

The volume summarizes the Advaita consideration of *Taittirīya* 2 in three paragraphs, as this occurs in UMS1.1.12–19. After a concise summation of Śaṅkara's first reading of the *adhikaraṇa*, the second interpretation is introduced:

> According to this alternative interpretation *sūtra*s 12 through 19 are addressed to *Taittirīya Upaniṣad* II.5.1 ["Brahman the tail,

> that on which it rests''], which mentions Brahman as the ''tail'' and ''support'' of the Self of bliss. The problem is: how can Brahman be a mere member of the Self—isn't it the principal, not the appendate? The *sūtras* answer yes, because scripture says so. The suffix ''*-maya*'' is analyzed as involving *prācurya*, which the previous interpretation took as meaning ''being full of'' but on this second interpretation is a technical term meaning a stylistic device. The point of the *sūtra* in which it is mentioned is to explain why II.5.1 speaks of Brahman as ''tail'': the answer is that it's merely a manner of speaking, a device, and not to be taken seriously. Since Brahman is spoken of as the cause (the *sūtras* go on) it cannot be a mere appendage. And so forth.[19]

Studiously uncommitted, the summation more or less clearly captures the major points in Śaṅkara's comment. However, his motives for setting forth a second exposition are not explored. Given the stated chronological limits of the volume—Śaṅkara and his immediate disciples—the later commentaries are not introduced.

By its nature, the *Encyclopedia* project, which is committed to making summaries of works available to scholars—has admittedly excised the *Taittirīya* text from its Sanskrit medium, in the Upaniṣad and in the UMS. More significant, it has also removed the Upaniṣad from its commentarial location. The project, then, may seem to be true exercise in detached scholarship.

But the *Encyclopedia*'s summation may itself be taken as yet another act of commentary. It has also abstracted from the *Taittirīya* and the Vedānta argument regarding it their ''philosophical'' content, though the original text, and its version in the *adhikaraṇa*, invests a great deal of energy in resistance to the separation of philosophical content from theological content. Were a reader actually to read the *adhikaraṇa* and then the Upaniṣad after this summary, this excision would be seen to be at least as significant as those effected by Bādarāyaṇa in his reuse of the *Taittirīya* text. The reader may also find it justified, because the *Taittirīya* and the Vedānta argumentation are being made available to a different community of readers, with different commitments and areas of competence, different canons, and different modes of authority and enforcement.

These points can and need to be argued in detail and at length, and it would serve no purpose merely to announce that all reading is either explicitly or implicitly committed reading, or that there are no qualitative boundaries between philology, philosophy, and theology. Vedānta invests enormous energy in the construction of proper distinctions, and we do it no service by unnuanced generalizations. Nevertheless, there seems to be no sure basis on which to say that Karl Potter, who ably composed the summation, or a philosopher who might responsibly use it, stands in a position more neutral than that of the Vedānta commentators, and this is so even if the point of the *Encyclopedia* is in part to be neutral, simply to provide information. Providing information about the text in a volume of an encyclopedia, or abstracting from it its philosophical content, is as active a transformation of its possibilities as is the Vedānta doctrinalization of the meditational project that the original Upaniṣad, qua text, seems to be.

A possible point of difference appears when one asks what one can do with the Vedānta and modern expositions of the *adhikaraṇa*: what are the conditions under which a reader of the *Taittirīya* text, either in or outside its UMS location, can debate its meaning with the goal of determining its right meaning? At issue here is not merely whether argument is possible, though that is a pertinent issue today, but what the text itself has to do with the argument regarding things the text says. One might, for instance, develop a psychology of the deepest self, based on contemporary scientific research, and ask whether it is meaningful to call this self the ''self consisting of bliss,'' or to use psychological data in support of the *Taittirīya* position. One might ask whether there is a divinity of the sort that can be accessible by an inward, self-analytic journey such as the Upaniṣad describes. In either case, the text could be used as a starting point, referent, or example. But the Vedānta argument is characterized by the claim that the text itself is the privileged location of the argument; its words and phrases signal the points that can be made, and measure the qualities of arguments that are put forward. As the reader reads, she or he must be vulnerable to that reading, and liable to transformation in the course of reading.

The possibility of argument and the identity of the reader are therefore inextricably intertwined considerations, and it is only in a temporary fashion that the reader can separate the two considerations. Can we become the kind of readers who take the Upaniṣads so seriously that we will be ready to read and argue them as carefully and intensively as the Vedāntins? I began this chapter by describing the student, who is likely to move from an initial enthusiasm for the texts to a required scholarly distance from their views and demands: what is lost if one never recovers that initial enthusiasm and urgency? The issue of the identity of the person who argues and reads must now become central, and to this I turn in the concluding section of this reflection.

TRANSFORMATION THROUGH READING

We may now recapitulate this tension between the doctrinal location and careful reading by attention to the implication of reading for its reader:

what are the conditions under which investment in both doctrinal location and continued careful reading is desirable and possible? If argument and careful reading are to remain in a vital relationship, in which one is not merely a self-serving fabrication of the other, our third factor must be taken into account. The availability of a person who argues, who reads, who is educated in arguing and reading, and who is transformed by both, is the decisive factor. The persuasiveness of argument and the rightness of reading depend on the ability of persons to choose correctly, to decide which arguments are more convincing, which parts of texts are more urgent and persuasive than others, and the urgency of the argument and the reading is animated by that person, who is liberated by a right understanding of the rightly identified texts. In other words, the commitment to read texts invested with authority within a determined canon has among its consequences the correction and legitimation of the reader who makes that commitment.

This set of problems we may group under the title of the "ethics of reading," if we understand this to mean both the necessity of a proper reading, as we have examined this thus far, and the persistent liability of the reader to be personally "recomposed" by the reading undertaken. Let us begin by recollecting the Vedānta position.[20] The necessity is easy to explain. The Vedāntins believed that salvation was at stake in the argument over the right meaning of the Upaniṣads, and could be achieved through a gradually, temporally attained understanding of the text; this belief is the practical version of their doctrine on the authority of the Upaniṣads as revelation, *śruti*. Not only are texts invested with internal and external meanings; when understood, they transform their hearers or readers, changing their context. If one dared, one might proffer a slogan: "no information without transformation."

At the heart of Śaṅkara's complex and roundabout reading of *Taittirīya* 2 is a consistent theme in his works: information is not identical with effective knowledge, and one must construct knowledge in such a way that it is allowed to effect dramatic change in the life of the knower. His reading of *Taittirīya* 2 presumes that if we end up with nothing more than the knowledge that *brahman* consists of bliss, we are not necessarily better off than we were in the first place. The Upaniṣad, including its presentation by Śaṅkara, upsets readers' expectations by leading them toward an understanding of *brahman* (2.1–6a), and by criticizing the limits of words and concepts (2.4). It may upset them even more by thereafter insisting, through the statement of the self of bliss (2.5) and the consequent notice that *brahman* is the bliss-maker (2.7) and the knower of texts the one who is blissful (2.8), that the intelligent reading of this text may have a profound effect on the reader's life. The Upaniṣad does not tell the reader what *brahman* is, but if one appropriates the text correctly and is thus guided into the stages of self-knowledge that are mapped out by the Upaniṣad, one reaches an inner edge beyond which one's relation to *brahman* is dramatically, radically transformed.[21]

What is at stake for the Vedānta may be summarized in terms of the tension inherent in it. On the one hand, there is a basic, original desire to know (*jijñāsā*) and the (theoretically) immediately possible realization of *brahman*. On the other, there is the (realistically) narrow path to realization, by way of the cumulatively achieved, arduously practiced, and socially mediated education of the kind of person who can be a proper knower of *brahman*. The entire Vedānta project, as a truly Sanskrit enterprise, seeks to produce, in reliance on innate aptitude, caste, educational connections, and a consequent series of practices, persons who are ripe for knowledge of *brahman*, precisely because they have been affected by what they read and by the arguments they have engaged in regarding the proper methods of reading and conclusions to be drawn from it. This, of course, is the point of introduction for the traditional discussions of *adhikāra*.

The application of these concerns is clear. The texts, inscribed within their commentaries, are both difficult and off-putting, and yet they are the immediately available point of contact with the Vedānta traditions through an encounter with which the contemporary reader can be "admitted" to the Vedānta. There is no way around the necessity of becoming the kind of person who is willing to be changed by what one reads, and therefore to submit to the expectations of proper learning, in all its traditional complexity. Although one will surely continue to read according to contemporary standards, these standards must remain open to modification and in explicit juxtaposition with those of the tradition.

If one is to become a proper, skilled reader of such texts, it is necessary too to define a community of readers—like-minded people who are vulnerable to the demands of this canon of texts, people with whom one cares to read, and to whom one cares to communicate the results of reading. If so, the standards of worthy academic colleagueship may have to be adjusted. Plowing through large bodies of commentarial material requires not merely a respect for all the refinements of the commentarial debates, but also a willingness to measure one's interpretations specifically against those offered by ancient and modern representatives of the traditions involved. At first, this may involve the initial and modest step of simply committing oneself actually to a reading of available contemporary Sanskrit commentaries—not as mere research data, but as the contribution of colleagues. In the long term, it may require yet another revision of the framework within which India is studied in contemporary Indology and religious studies.

Let us turn to the practical side of the issue. As noted early on in this chapter, the *Taittirīya* text as such seems to demand performance; the reader must engage in it, meditating one's way through it, bird by bird. In its Vedānta use, the *Taittirīya* text likewise demands a reasoned attention to its implications for oneself. The commitment to careful reading bears with it a practicar investment in the transformative power of the text, and investment in the text is inseparable from the use of the text. We must therefore ask repeatedly: what ought the reader do in order to read properly, and what happens to the reader who reads properly?

The practice of this transformative reading is exemplified in the *Vivekacūḍāmaṇi*—a text which, though attributed to Śaṅkara, may be from a later period.[22] The *Vivekacūḍāmaṇi* is both an introduction to the major tenets of Vedānta and a narrative of the application of those tenets in teaching and the process of realization. In it the guru's teaching, which takes up the bulk of the work, is divided into two sections, on the nonself and the self. The first of these sections climaxes in an exegesis of *Taittirīya* 2.1–6a and a serial consideration of the five selves, in which the teacher leads the student through an analysis of the "not-self," including a review of the three constituent strands (*guṇa*) of material reality. In the second major section, the analysis moves from this now completed consideration of the nonself to a twofold inquiry into the real self, according to the famous "You Are That" (*tat tvam asi*) of *Chāndogya* 6, a theoretical description of how the true self is uncovered to the *Chāndogya* text, and a practical instruction on the affective appropriate of its truth.

The practical Vedānta claim, which builds on the practice demanded by the *Taittirīya* and *Chāndogya*, is that these texts, when properly understood, contribute to the production of an identifiable result, the liberation of the student. The teacher who has learned and appropriated the *Taittirīya* text leads the student through it in such a way that his existential anxiety begins to dissipate. Texts about bliss contribute to bliss. The final test of careful reading lies there, in that effect on the reader. Whatever one has to say about the text, it is read properly only if one is transformed by that reading: if you have not been liberated, read it again.

Does the practice of contemporary scholarship allow for the possibility that one can be transformed by the texts one studies, and that this is worth talking about in an academic context? Let us leave aside entirely the explicit issues of spirituality, the uses to which these texts may be put by a contemporary scholar who wishes to use them, aside from his or her research, for religious reasons, and let us focus on the effects of sustained careful reading in the context of forthright argument.

The burden of proof lies with those who would argue that the study of the Upaniṣads need not have an effect on the student who reads these texts, and that this need not be a topic in academic circles. They would have to show why one would think that the practice of careful reading—excellent philology, for example—performed in the context of an explicit and argued set of presuppositions that are continually corrective of one's reading, and corrected by it, would not change the practitioner's attitude toward self and world. The ascertainment of right meaning and the skillful negotiation of the space between the practice of reading and theory is not separable from some form of application of the text to the reader. This need not compromise the standards of professional argument or an adherence to rules of exegesis; nor will conflicts about right readings and right meanings be resolved by appeals to the merits of personal transformation. Nevertheless, Vedānta's steadfast insistence on the transformation of the reader suggests most plausibly that the legitimate academic argument will progress only within the larger context of the ongoing transformation of those who read and write, argue and draw conclusions.

An interpretation that takes the Vedānta tradition seriously in its presuppositions and practices as well as in its conclusions will inevitably be a comparative practice, in the sense that when properly understood it sheds light on and makes liable to critique the reader's own theories of how texts mean, how one gets to know those meanings, and what one does after/when meanings are grasped. At every level, this fuller comparison of text, contexts, and practice compels the reader to consider anew her or his examined presuppositions and habits—and to decide on that basis what to do next. Though the kind of transformative moment described in the *Vivekacūḍāmaṇi* is assuredly rare in any context, it will remain always the (perhaps unmentioned) exception in the scholarly world. But smaller transformations will occur more regularly: changes in research goals, revisions of the paradigms by which one organizes one's knowledge, the emergence of new questions, and the abandonment of previously determinative ones.

FROM ANXIETY TO BLISS

We have come to the end of our inquiry. Our main goal has been to show that neither readers in the Vedānta tradition nor those outside it may disassociate their comprehension of a text like *Taittirīya* 2.1–6a from the complex range of practices and negotiations connected with careful reading, the uncovering and straightforward presentation of doctrinal concerns, and an awareness of the possibility that one may be transformed by the texts one reads. The inevitable and entirely proper loss of a naive appreciation of the texts one studies, and the rejection of immediate, transparent applications to oneself, are not the end of the story. Such losses and rejections are only steps on the way to the threefold reappropriation of the texts, the presuppositions one brings to the texts and, finally, the self-identity one had created as part of one's scholarly work.

Three possibilities that are legitimately unacceptable to the scholar remain so: mere reading as mere pedantry; merely declared and barely, if at all, textually defended opinions that precede and eventually render careful reading unnecessary; the confusion and dilution of scholarship by a rhetoric of personal transformation and spiritual gain. Each is a disaster for the scholar. But argument, reading, and education profit from their cooperation; if understood as mutually qualifying and contesting projects, the three fruitfully modify, discipline, and enrich one another. To put it another way: the defense of prior and posterior doctrines, the location of doctrines in texts, and the determined liability to transformation by argument and reading are mutually corrective practices, expected by texts like the Upaniṣads, finely developed in the Vedānta schools, and incumbent upon the modern reader as well.

I began this chapter with attention to a *Taittirīya* verse that read in part as follows: "Different from the self consisting of knowledge is an inner self consisting of bliss. With it this one is filled." I examined our likely use and possible loss of it as we move from a simple, referential naivete to an engagement in the texts that surround, complicate, and yet ultimately make accessible the words we read. Are we any closer to discovering whether there is bliss within the human self, and whether any such interior bliss might be oneself or what some call "*brahman*"? Are we closer even to deciding whether Śaṅkara or Rāmānuja is correct in his reading of the text? Perhaps not, primarily because we still have not read sufficiently: neither this reflection nor its glimpse into Vedānta reading and arguing has been sufficient to construct the basis for an answer to these questions. But if we recognize the triple commitment to reading, argument, and their implications for the person who argues and reads, we are ready to participate in an argument that will make us the kind of readers who can decide what, if anything, is beyond words and concepts, and ultimately interior to knowledge itself.

If so, it is perhaps appropriate to conclude with the verse that ends *Taittirīya* 2. After the meditative analysis of the five selves, after the articulation of a corresponding cosmology, and after the insistent reduction of the mythology of bliss to the rigors of detached reading, at the end (2.9) we read that once one has gained that knowledge of *brahman* which is filled with bliss, "these questions torment him no more: 'Which good thing have I omitted doing?' 'which base or evil thing have I committed?' " Like the student in the *Vivekacūḍāmaṇi* who is tormented by the apparent miseries of life, the contemporary scholar may learn, may acquire the ability, to be bothered by the separation of scholarly discourse from the ability to seek truth and to be open to the possibility of altered commitments because of what one reads. Vedānta, as teacher, instructs its readers to integrate these practices and values, to return to the

Upaniṣad—and, once there, to reach beyond the anxieties of the scholar and find a measure of bliss during the practice of a newly simple reading.

NOTES

1. We will begin our analysis with "arguing" the text, though one might just as well begin with the practices of careful reading, and thereafter examine the presuppositions of that reading.

2. I have differently developed my analysis of the Advaita use of *Taittirīya* 2 in Clooney, *Theology after Vedānta*, chap. 2. There, as here I restrict my examination primarily to the first part of *Taittirīya* 2, vv. 1–6a, as do the Vedāntins. I have used the editions of Sanskrit texts listed in the bibliography, as well as Gambhirananda's translation of Śaṅkara (1983) and Thibaut's translation of Rāmānuja (1976). References are generally given to *sūtras*, and to pages only in the case of particularly long comments. It is important to note that Rāmānuja's numbering of the *sūtras*, 1.1.13–20, differs from Śaṅkara's, 1.1.12–19.

3. The "verses," signaled by quotation marks, comprise the mantra portion of the text; the rest is the Brāhmaṇa portion.

4. 1.1.12–19 in the Advaita reading, 1.1.13–20 according to the Viśiṣṭādvaita.

5. E.G., *Taittirīya* 2.7.1, 2.8, 2.9, 3.6, 3.9.

6. For the majority tradition represented by Bādarāyaṇa, and (as we shall see) later by Rāmānuja, it means also that *brahman* is indeed that self which consists of bliss; for Śaṅkara's important though minority viewpoint, which we shall examine below, *brahman* is not that self which consists of bliss, but lies beyond it, and is the sole significant object of knowledge.

7. See Clooney, "Binding the Text," on *samanvaya* and the systematization of Vedānta.

8. Except indirectly: in his first exposition of the *adhikaraṇa*, he argues that we know from the entirety of the Upaniṣads that *brahman* and the human self really are one, and that it is only for the purpose of argument that Bādarāyaṇa observes here that the self functions as if it were not *brahman*: "In the case of ordinary people, it is seen that, though the Self ever retains its true nature of being the Self, there is a false identification with the body, etc., which are non-Self. . . . [This *sūtra* is spoken] taking for granted such a difference between the supreme self and the self identified with the intellect" [UMS 1.1.17]. Accordingly, the Upaniṣad can for the time being be read as presuming duality, and in that context, one must argue the distinction between *brahman* and the self consisting of bliss. Later, the more advanced reader will reread it with a direct awareness of the nonduality of self and *brahman*.

9. Tr. 73.

10. Tr. 75.

11. See the beginning of Śaṅkara's second version of the *adhikaraṇa*, after the conclusion of the first explanation of UMS 1.1.19; tr. 71–2.

12. By way of illustration I offer one example of this refinement. In his comments explaining the second version of the conclusion, Vācaspati shows that it is impossible to preserve the primary meaning of all the key words in the *Taittirīya* text—"*brahman*," "consisting of bliss" (*ānandamaya*), and "tail" (*puccha*). As the text stands, it is impossible for all three words to keep their primary meanings: 1. "*brahman*" cannot indicate the *brahman* if "*brahman*" here really means "tail"; 2. "*-maya*" cannot maintain a single primary meaning, if in the text it first means "consisting of" and then means "abundant in"; 3. "tail" cannot mean both "appendage," a minor portion, and "base," "support" (*pratiṣṭhā*). A decision has to be made about which of the words are to retain their primary meanings. Why then, Vācaspati asks, is Śaṅkara right in arguing that *brahman* is bliss, but not consisting of bliss, and that *puccha* here means "support," and not "tail," "minor part"? He calculates as follows. There are three ways to resolve the problem. 1. We can take *puccha* as indicating "tail" (meaning "part") and in the sentence "*brahman* is the *puccha*," take "*brahman*" figuratively as indicating a mere part of the configuration, not that, *brahman* which is the object of Advaitic knowledge. 2. Or, we can take the "*-maya*" in "*ānandamaya*" as meaning "abundance," and then we will be able to construe *ānandamaya* ("abundant in bliss") as indicative *brahman*, even if this connection is not stated directly. 3. Or we can consistently interpret "*-maya*" as "consisting of"—in a quantitative sense—and allow "*brahman*" to keep its proper meaning, and attribute only to "*puccha*" a secondary significance, so that it means "base" instead of "tail." Vācaspati argues that 3. is the best option, because it preserves two primary meanings: *-maya* and *brahman* maintain proper meanings, and only one word, *puccha*, loses its primary meaning by coming to mean "base" and not merely "minor part." In alternatives 1. and 2. either "*brahman*" or "*-maya*" would have lost its meaning: in 1., "*brahman*" would lose its primary meaning, and in 2. "*-maya*" would shift from one meaning ("consisting of") to another ("abundant in") after the fourth self. But in all three cases *puccha* would lose its primary meaning, "tail", since no one claims that *brahman* is an actual tail; so 3. is best since two of the three primary meanings are maintained and minimal reinterpretation occurs. Hence, by economy of interpretation—without the direct introduction of philosophical claims about what *brahman* ought to be—Vācaspati can conclude that *brahman* is figuratively referred to as the *puccha*, base, while the "self consisting of bliss" indicates a lower, finite reality, not *brahman*.

13. In the Sanskrit edition I have been using, the *Śrībhāṣya* "aside," with commentaries, runs twenty-four large Sanskrit pages.

14. At the same time the Advaita position is portrayed as arguing also that the self consisting of bliss, which is not *brahman*, is really *brahman*, though at a deeper level: the Advaita is thus presented as arguing an exegetical and metaphysical position at the same time.

15. As mentioned above, Rāmānuja's numbering of the *sūtras*, 1.1.13–20, differs from Śaṅkara's, 1.1.12–19.

16. As in the Advaita, the refinement of correct reading does not end with the master's achievement of the right conclusion. The perfect synthesis of what the text should mean and what it actually says continues to be worked out. For instance, Sudarśana Sūri, author of the *Śrutaprakāśikā* on Rāmānuja's commentary, argues at length that "tail" (*puccha*) cannot refer to *brahman* since "tail" is a neuter noun, whereas in the latter part of 2.6 a masculine pronoun is used to describe the creator, who must be *brahman*. (See the *Śrutaprakāśikā* on UMS 1.1.13; 222 in the Sanskrit.) Or, in the more recent *Gūḍhārthasaṃgraha*, Abhinava Ranganatha describes in detail a number of positions regarding the meaning of *puccha*, in the context of arguing for a definition wherein *brahman* is always possessed of qualities (is *saguṇa*). He focuses on the five repetitions of "tail" and *brahman* together in *Taittirīya* 2.1–6a, and asks whether it is valid for one of the pair to change meaning, while the other remains stable in meaning. His conclusion is that since *brahman* is clearly the primary referent of the passage, and the tail only accessory to the communication of a meaning about *brahman*, it is legitimate to read "*brahman* the tail, that on which it rests" in the first four cases as indicative of the fact that *brahman* is not that self but its tail, support, while in the fifth case readjusting the meaning of tail to support the notion that *brahman* is both the tail and the whole of the self. (See the *Gūḍhārthasaṃgraha* on UMS 1.1.13; 223–26 in the Sanskrit.) That the discussion continues even today may be demonstrated by reference to the modern Advaitin Anantakrisna Sastri. In his *Advaita Tattva Sudhā* he reviews the entire *adhikaraṇa* in eighty-seven paragraphs, as he defends the Advaita interpretation and refutes the Rāmānuja or "dualist" (*dvaita*) position. The former he dubs the "*brahman* is the tail" position (*pucchabrahmavāda*) and the latter, the "*brahman* is all five sheaths" position (*pañcabrahmantavāda*). He devotes about fifteen paragraphs to the nuances of the argument over *puccha*. Each numbered section is a highly distilled, concentrated summation of an aspect of the Vedānta argument; the Advaita position is expounded, not by generalizations as to why *brahman* bliss, or not, but by ever more clearly articulated rules about how to read *Taittirīya* 2.1.–6a and UMS 1.1.12–19.

17. See for instance, Modi's critique of Śaṅkara throughout his two volumes.

18. Potter, *Advaita Vedānta*, ix.

19. Ibid., 132.

20. Throughout this chapter, but in the following section in particular, I have been helped by Scholes, *Protocol of Reading*.

21. On the transformation of the Vedāntin that occurs in the study of Vedānta, see Taber, *Transformative Philosophy*; and Clooney, *Theology after Vedānta*, chap. 4.

22. Potter, (*Advaita Vedānta*, 335) notes the extensive argument among scholars on this point.

REFERENCES

Primary Texts and Translations

Eighteen Principal Upaniṣads

1958 Vol. 1. Ed. V. P. Limaye and R. D. Vadekar. Poona: Vaidika Saṃśodhana Maṇḍala.

Sixty Upaniṣads of the Veda

1987 Trans. V. M. Bedekar and G. B. Palsule from the German translation of Paul Deussen [1897]. 2 vols. Delhi: Motilal Banarsidass.

Rāmānuja

1959, 1970 *Śrībhāṣya with the Śrutaprakāsikā of Sudarśanasūri and the Gūdhārthasaṃgraha of Abhinavaranganātha*. Vols. 1, 2. Mysore: Sri Brahmatantra Parakala Mutt.

1976 *The Vedānta-Sūtras with the commentary of Rāmānuja*. Trans. George Thibault. Delhi: Motilal Banarsidass.

Saccidanandendra

1989 *The Method of the Vedānta*. Trans. A. J. Alston. London: Kegan Paul International.

Śaṅkara

1981 *Brahmasūtra Śaṅkara Bhāṣya with the commentaries Bhāmatī, Kalpataru and Parimala*. 2 vols. Parimala Sanskrit Series, no. 1. Ahmedabad: Parimal Publications.

1983 *Brahma-Sūtra Bhāṣya*. Trans. Swami Gambhirānanda. Calcutta: Advaita Ashrama.

1962 *The Vedānta Sūtras of Bādarāyaṇa with the Commentary of Śaṅkara*. Trans. George Thibaut. 2 vols. New York: Dover.

1982 *Vivekacūḍāmaṇi*. Trans. Swami Madahavananda. Calcutta: Advaita Ashrama.

Sastri, M.S. Anantakrisna
1986 *Advaita Tattva Sudhā*. 3 vols. Delhi: Nag.

Secondary Sources

Clooney, Francis X.
1991 "Binding the Text: Vedānta as Philosophy and Commentary." In *Texts in Context: Traditional Hermeneutics in South Asia* ed. Jeffrey R. Timm. Albany: State University of New York Press.
1993 *Theology after Vedānta: An Experiment in Comparative Theology*. Albany: State University of New York Press.

Modi, P. M.
1956 *A Critique of the Brahmasūtra (III.2.11–IV) with Reference to Śaṅkarācārya's Commentary*. 2 vols. Baroda: private publication.

Potter, Karl H.
1981 *Advaita Vedānta up to Śaṅkara and his Disciples*. Princeton: Princeton University Press.

Scholes, Robert
1989 *Protocols of Reading*. New Haven: Yale University Press.

Taber, John
1983 *Transformative Philosophy: A Study in Śaṅkara, Fichte, and Heidegger*. Honolulu: University of Hawaii Press.

6

"Whither the Thick Sweetness of Their Passion?"

The Search for Vedic Origins of Sanskrit Drama

DAVID L. GITOMER

THE PROBLEM: THE NATURE OF VEDISM IN DRAMATIC SOURCES

KĀLIDĀSA'S SANSKRIT PLAY entitled *Vikramorvaśīya* ("Urvaśī Won by Valor")[1] is the only well known Sanskrit play based on an ancient tale (a "myth") found in a *Ṛg-Veda* hymn, as well as in other Vedic texts. Yet for a variety of reasons both the native dramaturgical texts and European Indologists have continued to develop an intriguing Vedic thesis on the origins of Sanskrit drama. Actually, this is not a unitary thesis, but a cluster of distinct arguments, some relating to the ritual nature of sacrifice and theater, some relating to the "ancient Āryan verbal contest,"[2] others relating to the dialogue hymns in the *Ṛg-Veda* itself. The evidences marshaled for dramatic Vedism are equally various. On the one hand, the primary form of Sanskrit drama, the *nāṭaka*, presents an Arcadian archaism (or whatever the Sanskrit equivalent of "Arcadian" is), a place apart from the political and sexual intrigues of the court, idyllic *āśrama*s where rishis sacrifice and chant mantras. On the other hand, the drama itself is surrounded by a Vedic or quasi-Vedic cluster of rituals, notably the preliminary rites called the *pūrvaraṅga*. Finally there is the complex and vexing question about the deepest project of the drama—whether it in any way extends or replicates the dynamisms and concerns of either Vedic ritual and myth-making, or of Vedic poetic technique.[3]

As a student of Sanskrit drama, it initially seemed to me that none of the materials or motifs proposed as sources bore any more than the most general thematic connection to any of the extant Sanskrit plays I knew, so I wondered how and why it was both within the tradition and outside of it that there is a consistent attempt to ascribe Vedic origins to the drama. While pondering this issue, I came upon the wondrous phrase *sāndramukharāgamanojñamanobhava* in Arjunavarmadeva's commentary to the *Amaruśataka*. The expression may be translated as "the thick sweetness of their passion," though it literally means "sexual love which is beautiful because of intensely varied visible passion."[4] The phrase arises in an extraordinary discussion in which the commentator explains why a group of verses known in the Amaru corpus is not worthy of inclusion. He says that genuine verses—genuine in this case because of their superior poetic virtue, not necessarily because of externally proven authorial originality—are like gorgeous, accomplished actresses who are skillful in their art, complex in their expression, subtle and intricate in their beauty, while the interpolations, on the other hand, are like *aṭṭaceṭakā*s, rude slave giris. Most important, however, these actresses possess an intense and complex visible sexual passion (*manobhava*) which is pleasingly beautiful (*manojña*). In the language of the classical aesthetic theory, what makes them authentic is their *rasa*. They live and breathe their passion, whereas the slave girls are not only unskilled and unsophisticated, they are flat, uninvolved, uncommitted, as a contemporary actor might say. "The thick sweetness of their passion": this phrase from the heart of the Sanskrit aesthetic tradition can help clarify problems with the Vedic theses. On the one hand, the Vedic arguments account for very little in the Sanskrit dramas we know. On the other hand, these arguments, enmired in the older view of the Vedas as ritual and mythology, do not account for many of the most characteristic qualities of the Sanskrit drama, chief among them its passion for beauty and palpable experience, which shows its clear ties to the lyric, perhaps even to Vedic poetry. In any event, traditional views of the relationship between Veda and drama do not acknowledge how deeply the prestigious Vedic canon has been appropriated by dramatic artists for new purposes.

The present chapter cannot rehearse the history of older Indological scholarship on the Vedism of Sanskrit drama.[5] But a broad description of the kinds of evidence and arguments that have been put forth can adumbrate more fully the collusion (perhaps unwitting) of native and Western Vedisms, and help show where the theories may have their limitations. I will move from the text archaeologies, the hypothesizing from ritual shards, of the serious religionists, to the quasi-Vedism of the plays themselves, a self-conscious archaizing, a quasi-Vedism that turns out actually to be epic in its concerns. Then I offer what I see as a more comprehensive, and more evidentiary, theory of "origins," from which vantage point may be seen the intractable interplay of the Vedic and the classical, and the inevitable thematization and appropriation of the Vedic motifs by the classical aesthetic.

MYTH AND RITUAL IN THE *NĀṬYAŚĀSTRA*

The first kind of dramatic Vedism revolves around an analysis not of the plays but of a complex of myth and ritual found in the early chapters of the *Nāṭyaśāstra*. The myth, perhaps better called a "legend," is the so-called *nāṭyotpatti*, "the origin of the drama." The ritual, called the *pūrvaraṅga*, involves mimetic play that precedes not only the drama, but the drama's own opening rites. Since the text of the *Nāṭyaśāstra* employs a frame in which Bharatamuni, the sage of drama, answers questions about the dramatic art, the *nāṭyotpatti* story and the description of the *pūrvaraṅga* become joined in the same narrative. At the same time, the legendary account is so heavily interlarded with *practique* from the dramatic *śāstra* (body of technical instructions) that one wonders if an earlier form of the text simply began, not with a legend, but with instructions for the conduct of a play's preliminary procedures.[6]

The outline of the *Nāṭyaśāstra*'s account of its archaic origin is this: sages ask Bharatamuni about the origin of what they call the *Nāṭyaveda*, "similar to the Vedas" (1.4).[7] Bharata says that the sages should purify themselves in order to hear about how Brahmā created the *nāṭyaveda*. Brahmā, observing the decline of virtue in the peoples of the world in the *Treta Yuga*, says he will create an entertainment for instruction in dharma, knowledge, and all other arts and crafts. It will be a fifth Veda, created from the other four, accessible to all *varṇa*s (the four classical "castes"); it will be created from *itihāsa*, by which he seems to mean something more inclusive than the *Mahābhārata*, but things like the epic stories.[8] Brahmā enjoins Indra to have the gods perform his *nāṭyaveda*, but Indra says that "the gods are neither able to receive it and to maintain it, nor are they fit to understand it and make use of it; they are unfit to do anything with the drama." However, "the sages who know the mystery of the Vedas and have fulfilled their vows, are capable of maintaining the *nāṭyaveda* and putting it into practice." Apsarases, celestial nymphs, are created, and various other celestials are recruited to assist in the various *vṛtti*s, stylistic modes, of the drama, which are described.

Brahmā decides that Indra's banner festival the *dhvajamaha*, would be the perfect time to inaugurate the dramatic performance. Since this festival commemorates Indra's victory over the Dānavas and the Asuras, Brahmā's first play will be an imitation (*anukaraṇa*) of that fight, complete with violence—the mutual cutting off and piercing of limbs and bodies. The gods are delighted with the play, but the demons, incited by the Vighnas (personified obstacles), begin to disrupt the performance, confounding the actors' speech, movement, and memory.[9] First Indra smashes them with his *jarjara* staff, but when they return, Brahmā orders the first playhouse built for protection. The deities and demigods are installed in its various corners and rooms for protection; most significant, Destiny (*niyati*) and Death (*mṛtyu*) are made the doorkeepers, with Indra himself stationed by the side of the stage.

Brahmā tries to conciliate the demons, inquiring why they are intent on disrupting the performance. It turns out that this new *nāṭyaveda* has shamed the Daityas by representing their defeat. Brahmā explains that they really should not be upset, for the drama is intended to represent the good fortune *and* the ill fortune of *both* gods and demons. There follows a rhapsodic passage describing the comprehensive reach of drama: it depicts all orders of being and all classes; it shows all endeavors and all emotions; it provides instruction and counsel for every situation. Apparently the demons are satisfied with the answer, for the text has no reply from them, nor does Bharata mention them again. The first chapter ends with Brahmā's admonition that no dramatic spectacle (*prekṣā*) should be performed without first offering *pūjā* to the gods of the stage.[10]

Chapter 2 of the *Nāṭyaśāstra* is a technical description of the construction of the playhouse, with attendant rites. In terms of the inclusivist thrust of the foregoing myth, perhaps the most interesting element is that each of its four pillars is dedicated to one of the four *varṇa*s, and each is to be worshiped with objects of a symbolic color—white for Brahmins, red for Kṣatriya, yellow for Vaiśyas, and dark (*kṛṣṇa*) for Śūdras. This chapter on the playhouse is obviously the beginning of yet another, separate technical manual, for which the myth of the first chapter—and it seems that its elements are so self-conscious we should begin calling it an "allegory"—was a frame. For the next chapter (Chapter 3) describes in detail the manner of installation, mentioned in the opening story, of the gods in the theater and on the stage. The term used for their worship is exclusively *pūjā*. Next follows an interesting sequence of rites. There is a *homa*, ghee poured into a sacrificial fire, then a jar (the *homa* jar?), is broken for good fortune. Then the *nāṭyācārya* (preceptor of the drama) runs about the stage with a lighted torch, screaming wildly. Following this there is a real fight with real wounds inflicted. Near the very end of the chapter the text proclaims that "offering worship to the gods of the stage is as meritorious as a [Vedic] sacrifice (*yajña*)."

The fourth chapter is primarily a catalogue of dance positions and sequences of dance positions with rules for their use, but the narrative continues from before with the important information that the first play Brahmā requests to be performed is "*Amṛtamanthana*," the story of the churning of the ocean. It is said to be of the dramatic subgenre *samavakāra*, known from other dramaturgical texts. The next and final chapter of this legend-cum-ritual section of the *Nāṭyaśāstra* begins with the sages saying to Bharatamuni, "We have heard from you about the origin of drama and the *jarjara* as well as the means for stopping obstacles, and the worship of the gods. Having grasped the meaning we would like to know in detail about the *pūrvaraṅga* (the ritual preliminary to the stage)." Nothing is said about a production of "The Churning of the Ocean" or the dance postures; this clearly shows the original outlines of the text's components.

The *pūrvaraṅga* chapter is perhaps the most patchwork section in the *Nāṭyaśāstra*, though its seams are quite apparent. It appears to have been constructed from various programs. The first seems quite practical; it provides the performers with an opportunity to warm up their instruments and limber up their bodies. Then at verse 23 a different program group begins, clearly of ritual significance, but dimly explained: we have a "raising up" (*Utthāpana*) ceremony in which, puzzlingly, nothing is raised up; we must infer a ritual antecedent. Then the *sūtradhāra*, or director, performs a "walking around" (*parivartana*) in which he praises the deities installed in the stage. Benedictions follow, then the *raṅgadvāra* ("the gateway to the play"), so-called because, though a preliminary rite, it is the first section in which words and gestures are employed in the manner of the play proper. After some dance steps (*cāris*) depicting *śṛṅgāra* and *raudra rasas*, there is a three-way dialogue between the *sūtradhāra*, his assistant (the *pāripārśvaka*), and the *vidūṣaka*, the stock Brahmin buffoon of many of the dramas. Lastly before the play itself there is a *prarocanā*, which serves to whet the audience's appetite by praising the author and hinting at the action to come.

In true *sūtra* style these topics are introduced in brief, then expatiated. The more detailed treatment begins with a story about how the different kinds of singing and dancing—those I characterized as warm-up sessions—satisfy the different orders of nonhumans. Most peculiar is something called the *Āśrāvaṇā*, which forms the main element of a musical section called the *Bahirgīta*, "outside music." A story is told to explain why this is also called the *Nirgīta*, "devoid of music," (which could ambiguously mean "vehement music," or even "music apart," that is, "outside music"). We are once more involved in a dispute between demons and gods. Apparently when Nārada begins the music, Daityas and Rākṣasas like it so much they don't want to hear anything else. This insults the gods, who ask Nārada to intervene. The sage explains that it indeed can be called *nirgīta*, for it is a collection of sounds that make no sense. Since the demons like it, it will keep them pacified so they will not cause obstruction to the performance. But to please the gods it will be called *bahirgīta*, "outside music." The remainder of the chapter explains in order the other preliminaries. From this point on (beginning with the sixth chapter), although the original frame is maintained—each chapter begins with the Brahmins asking Bharata to explain some aspect of the drama—there is nothing more about Brahmā and Indra, about the promulgation of

Nāṭyaveda by a clan of human sages, about first performances and the role of gods and demons. The many technical and aesthetic discussions that have been fitted into the frame apparently do not require further mythicization.

INDOLOGICAL VISIONS OF VEDIC ORIGINS IN THE *NĀṬYAŚĀSTRA*

The origins of genres intrigue us, perhaps because we think that knowing how things got started will help us understand why things are the way they are now.[11] This is how many scholars understand the operation of the kind of narrative called "myth," following the assertions of the myth-makers themselves. This kind of thinking is very appealing, but it lacks a dynamic, historical dimension. Understanding origin stories may blind us to the process of paradigm replacement, which regularly occurs in the realm of drama. Origin stories that originally thematized a struggle in terms of a particular conflict may contain the seeds of an allegorical interpretation that later comes to replace the original conceptualization. In the work of the two scholars who have done significant work on the origins of Sanskrit drama, Kuiper in *Varuṇa and Vidūṣaka: On the Origin* [note singular!] *of Sanskrit Drama* and Byrski in *Concept of Ancient Indian Theater*, I see a tendency to "religify" the drama, that is, to see cosmogonic, ritual, and transcendental meanings in it,[12] and to be blind to the literature's own socio-political and aesthetic agendas. (I will return to the problem of separating these two realms below.) Ignoring the aesthetic agenda seems to be a widespread problem in the treatment of Sanskrit literature, but I will confine my observations to just a few ways such neglect impacts on Sanskrit drama, which is really the only (Sanskrit) literary form that scholars have tried to make "Vedic" in a comprehensive fashion. This brings us to the broader problem of Vedism itself. Both of the categories identified by Brian Smith[13] come into play here: *yajña* and Veda function not so much as ritual and text, but as "categories that act to provide explanatory power, traditional legitimacy, and canonical authority." Though their approaches are completely different, both Kuiper and Byrski operate under the assumption that access to these old materials in the *Nāṭyaśāstra* will help unlock the mysteries of the dramatic genre.

Writing in the careful tradition of Dutch Indology, Kuiper shows, in the first part of his book, that the Vedic god Varuṇa is *phasically* an Asura, and in that aspect he competes with Indra in the cosmogonic battle which forms part of the contest that renews life at the end of the year. In the second part he analyzes, brilliantly and painstakingly, the *Nāṭyaśāstra*'s first five chapters (summarized above). Recognizing that the text contains elements of different historical and conceptual orders, some of it much less archaic than others, he shows that the rites and terminology that remain unexplained or imperfectly integrated in the central allegory are surviving pieces of an older, preclassical complex that is, again, sacrificial and cosmogonic. By so doing, he has in fact solved many mysteries. He shows, for example, that both the *jarjara* of the preliminary rites, and Indra's *dhvaja* or banner pole, the erection of which is the occasion for the performance of plays, embody the weapon used in the fight against the Asuras;[14] that the breaking of the earthen jar "repeats Indra's cosmogonic act";[15] that, following the discoveries of the first part of his analysis, the Brahmin buffoon of the drama, the *vidūṣaka*, impersonates Varuṇa who, having become an Asura for the year-end contest, is too inauspicious to "protect" (i.e., sponsor) a dramatic character, the way Indra "protects" the *nāyaka*, or hero; that the *vidūṣaka* participates in the three-way dialogue (*trigata* as a recreation of the cosmogonical strife between the Devas and the Asuras;[16] that the *vidūṣaka* further resembles the deformed Brahmin scapegoat who is sacrificed at the end of the *aśvamedha* to alleviate the king of his impurity;[17] and that, finally, the *nāyikā* (heroine) has her origins in Śrī who is churned from the ocean by both Deva and Asuras, as recounted in the first (or perhaps second) drama.

This summary of findings does not even begin to hint at either the soundness or intricacy of Kuiper's investigations in the Brāhmaṇas and other Vedic texts. Still, he is forced repeatedly to acknowledge the gap between his certainty of the religious nature of this material and the evidence of the dramatic literature itself. To account for this gap, he sees not only cultural change, but a "forgetting," a "loss of memory" of the original meaning of the material:

> Whenever a cult act evolves into a piece of literary art, such as tragedy and comedy in Greece, there is always the possibility of secularization if in the context of the culture concerned the religious origin and character of the ritual is forgotten. In Greece Euripedes dropped the chorus in his tragedies as an element that had become cumbersome and had lost its meaning. In India the *pūrvaraṅga*, the religious *drōmenon* par excellence, was shortened and stripped of those elements which had at one time been of the highest importance, and new themes of a non-religious nature, as found in the "bourgeois" drama (*prakaraṇa*), arose at an early date—so early, indeed, that it cannot even be proved on the basis of the dramas that have come down to us, that the *prakaraṇa* was the result of a later development of dramatic art. Its origin is still obscure, and probably will remain so as long as no fresh evidence comes to light.[18]

> The details of the ceremony of the consecration leave no doubt that the stage *raṅgapīṭha* was considered a sacred space, which symbolically represented the cosmos. It is impossible to ascertain how much of these ceremonies survived up to the time of Kālidāsa and the classical drama, but it is clear that the consecration was based on old traditions.[19]

> It is one of the indications of the archaic character of the first chapter [of the *Nāṭyaśāstra*] that here the Indra festival is still represented as a celebration of the god's victory over the Asuras, although the cosmogonical nature of this victory seems no longer to have been recognized.[20]

> It is obvious that the older meaning of a ritual can easily be obliterated or re-interpreted in later times.[21]

> The ritual character of the context in which [the *trigata*) appears leads to the conclusion that this quasi-comical intermezzo must originally have been completely different from the clownish act which it is generally taken to be.[22]

> In the light of these facts [Śrī's emerging from the primal ocean, churned by the Devas and the Asuras], it may not be surprising that the tradition preserved in *Nāṭyaśāstra* 1.96 [Indra protects the hero, Sarasvatī the heroine, Oṃkārah the *vidūṣaka*, and Śiva the rest of the cast], which . . . is probably the last reminiscence of the oldest form of the Sanskrit drama, classes the *nāyikā* among the three principal parts. It must be admitted, however, that of the old pattern that has been reconstructed here no trace can be found in the classical drama.[23]

What Kuiper has done is to show that features of the preliminary ritual can be explained with reference to the sacrificial, cosmogonic mythology of the Brāhmaṇas. The problem is that they do not account for the Sanskrit drama as it is known from actual plays. While it is true that in the text of the *Nāṭyaśāstra* the peculiar rituals of the *pūrvaraṅga* are unexplained, seemingly pasted into the structure of what I am describing as the allegorical myth of Brahmā's creation of the drama, there is reason to believe that their original function has not been so much forgotten as appropriated into another system of meaning, a process far more complex and self-conscious than "secularization." The fact is that the narration is about the struggle of creation, but not the creation of the world; rather it is about the creation of drama. In other words, the theatric universe has reworked the archaic cosmogonic motifs, rituals, and stories and placed them at the service of its own myth.

Compared to Kuiper, the slightly earlier work of Byrski relies less on detailed digging in Vedic texts. But Byrski is even more convinced that the motifs of the allegorical myth and ritual account represent the fundamental (indeed, universal) operations of the drama. Kuiper is uncomfortable conflating the meaning of the myth and the rituals, since the myth of the creation of the "fifth Veda" is obviously later and much more self-conscious than the rituals which recapitulate cosmogonical strife (though these themselves do not represent the earliest Vedic ritual strata). By so doing, he reserves for the rituals a quality of naive survivorship, and a greater authenticity that stands out from the smooth and self-justifying myth. Byrski, on the other hand, sees that the two fit together. This is a talented perception, but not necessarily because structuralist analysis permits a myth's elements to be analyzed as an ensemble:[24] there is a more comprehensive allegorical discourse that has deliberately fitted the *nāṭyotpatti* legend and the *pūrvaraṅga* ritual together.

For Byrski, *nāṭya* is *yajña* (sacrificial ritual) because these protodramas were performed at sacrificial sessions as part of the cosmogonic effort. Further, because these two performances have the same genesis, they partake of the same theory of action, a "standard action," as Byrski calls it.[25] Byrski devotes a great portion of his study to an analysis of the three fivefold structural schemes found in the *Nāṭyaśāstra* and replicated in all later dramaturgical texts. Five elements of the plot (*artha-prakṛtis*) are embodied in five stages of action (*avasthās*). These stages are in turn distilled and given precise boundaries in the five junctures (*saṃdhis*). Roughly, the plot (*itivṛtta*) gets underway with the formation of a desire for some goal. The goal is pursued by the hero through obstacles. Finally the fruit (*phala*) is obtained, bringing the action to its conclusion. Byrski sees resemblance to the "plot" of sacrificial endeavors, thereby understanding that the prescribed architecture of the drama replicates the Sanskrit sacrificial impulse and the sacrificial work. Having accounted for the primal quality of the plot of Sanskrit drama, he needs to develop an archaic source for the other known feature of the drama, *rasa* or "aesthetic mood," something the less speculative Kuiper does not even attempt to deal with. Here he relies on two notions, both influenced by Abhinavagupta's reading of the *Nāṭyaśāstra*: *rasa* as generalized responses to the various stages of the "standard action," and *rasa* as a delicious, intense transcendence, congruent with the delicious intensity of erotic love. This is orthogenetically derived from texts such as the *Bṛhadāraṇyaka*'s 4.3.21,[26] "As a man in the close embrace of a beloved woman knows (*veda*) nothing within or without, so this person in the embrace of the knowing self (*prājñenātmanā*) knows nothing within or without."

How would the *Nāṭyaśāstra*'s textual evidence support the identity of *nāṭya* and *yajña*? There are a few statements evoking the sacrifice. Most of these are like the usual kinds of statements asserting the equality of *pūjā* to *yajña*, suggesting that while they may be "Vedic" in the most chronologically expansive use of the term, they are not especially early. For example, *pūjā* to the presiding deity of stage is said to be "like" a Vedic sacrifice (*yajña*) (1.126). Again, offering *pūjā* to the gods of the stage brings as much *puṇya* as a *yajña* (3.96). "He who with an agitated mind places his offering in a wrong place, is liable to expiation like one who pours ghee into the sacrificial fire without proper mantras" (3.100). But one of the key statements of sacrificial comparison identifies the success as theatrical:

> Let the playwright attain fame,
> and let dharma increase
> and by having performed such a sacrifice (*ijyayā*)
> may the gods always love him. (5.111–12)[27]

A SEPARATE AESTHETIC REALM: NOT THE SAME OLD MAGIC

The Sanskrit poets and aestheticians who looked to the *Nāṭyaśāstra* as their foundational work self-consciously conceived of their task as cosmogonical, but not at all in the sense that they were re-creating the mundane, phenomenal world. The aesthetic ideology generated out of the practice of literature an alternate cosmic perspective, one that seems at once very close in spirit to the Vedic poet's proud assertions about the power of speech yet devoid of personification or apotheosis. In the *Kāvyaprakāśa*, the standard, most widely read, scholastic compendium of literary theory, Mammaṭa in fact dedicates his treatise not to any of the major sectarian gods or goddesses, but simply to his own *bhāratī*, speech.[28] Interleaving his own commentary, he informs the reader that the benedictory verse is for the standard purpose, to keep obstacles at bay:

> The speech of the poet is triumphant!
> It brings forth a creation bereft
> of the strictures imposed by destiny,
> composed solely of gladness,
> dependent on nothing else,
> and sweet with nine aesthetic moods (*rasa*s).

The verse seems not to be addressing the goddess of speech. Mammaṭa's autocommentary explicates the distinctiveness and superiority of the aesthetic creation:

> The creation of Brahmā has been fixed in its shape of force of destiny; its nature is pleasure, pain and delusion; it is dependent on material causes such as atoms, auxiliary causes such as karma,

has but six flavors (*rasas*) and even with these it is not thoroughly enjoyable. But the creation of the poet's Speech is entirely different from this. It is thus triumphant [over the Creator's world]. And from this triumphant quality follows the suggestion of the poet's obeisance: "I bow to her" [as to a deity one normally invokes at the beginning of a work].

Since according to Mammaṭa, the world created by the poet's Speech is superior in its perfection to that of the naturally constituted world of the Creator, we could say that the world of the gods with their human friends and enemies becomes a foil for the world of literature. The verse and its commentary help explain some of the distinctive qualities of Sanskrit literature. It is not a literature of naturalistic description, nor is it utter fantasy. It is like the world, but improved, controlled, perfected. This is, incidentally, precisely the relationship the Sanskrit language has to a natural language after Pāṇini.

Kālidāsa's well-known verse in the *Mālavikāgnimitra* seems at first more directly related to *Nāṭyaśāstra*'s Vedic imagery, and less aggressive in its proclamation of superiority:

> Sages call it a sacrifice to the gods,
> [but] a lovely one and visible;
> it has two modes [violent and gentle],
> since Rudra's own body
> is shared with Umā;
> born of the three strands,
> it shows the ways of the world
> and the range of *rasas*:
> Drama is one, but it pleases
> people of different taste
> in many ways. (1.4)[29]

However, the *Nāṭyaśāstra* nevers calls drama "the visible sacrifice" or "the lovely sacrifice"; it merely says that drama is "like" a sacrifice. These expressions are Kālidāsa's way not only of drawing in Vedic and *śāstric* prestige, but also of suggesting the superiority of drama, as the commentary confirms.[30] Note also the characteristic movement in literary appropriation of Vedic imagery: the verse starts with the Vedic imagery and ends by asserting art as human pleasure.

The Vedic thesis is unworkable, I believe I can show, because such a totalistic thesis ignores the diverse character of the genre, whose diverse features are more directly and sensibly explained by several other sources I will discuss below. In the consideration of other phenomena in post-Vedic India, the Vedic thesis has always had its adherents, both among those in the native tradition, as well as some Western scholars (best represented by the Hindu-Vedist Madeleine Biardeau) of an orthogenetic bent. There are, however, political implications in some assertions of orthogenesis: while orthogenetic arguments allow us to trace certain lines of development, as nationalist and fundamentalist movements have shown time and time again, orthogenesis and cultural fascism can serve each other very well. But there are scholarly, intellectual problems as well. The antiquity assumption involves a species of the *post hoc ergo propter hoc* fallacy. If it can be shown that there is a "Vedic" component in a phenomenon, then one can say that the phenomenon has its source or origin in "the sacrifice" or in "Vedic knowledge." If I point to Tamil sangam poetry, and its descendants in Prakrit lyric, to the narration of kingly potency and childlessness in the *Mahābhārata*, as sources for the actual Sanskrit dramas that we have, those who argue the Vedic thesis will say that since the Vedic ritual setting is the oldest, it will form the basis of the genre, even if they have to admit (like Kuiper) that there is little or nothing of what they hypothesize in any known drama.

But this does not mean that we cannot, with an open mind or in a romantic vein, look again at the various motifs that scholars have seen in the Vedic hymns and rituals and in the classical drama. Could there not be resemblances, continuities, at least in a modal way? After all, we have just cited Mammaṭa to show that the realm of literature is a controlled, improved, perfected version of the world. If the sacrifice, *yajña*, serves to overcome the chaos in the world through its mastery in the sacrificial arena and thereby maintain the business of creation, would it not be unimaginative to deny that *nāṭya* does something similar with human experience and emotions? Byrski maintains that since the Asuras may not overrun the sacrifice if it is to come to its true conclusion, the drama must have its successful ("nontragic") conclusion if it is to be true to *yajña*,[31] which for him it ought to be, since the *yajña* is archetypal "standard action." This "standard action" is not description, but magic, changing the world. Yet the two are radically different in that *yajña* is re-creation; it is always the same but for its mistakes, which are to be quickly corrected. *Nāṭya* may have a similar structure; on its simplest level, it does recompose our emotional world. But *definitionally* it is always different, new. A playwright does not sit down and precisely copy a drama. In fact, the prologues to many of the plays entice the audience with the promise that the work is "new," "novel," "fresh." The playwright, unlike the ritual specialist, does not re-create by repeating, he creates by innovating.

One hears the voice of Heesterman in the background, saddling all who wrestle with the meaning of *yajña* as an activity or a category with a reminder of the anxiety inherent in sacrifice. It would be interesting to consider, in a Heestermanic moment, that the repeated, perfected *yajña* has become entirely self-referential, and that the *nāṭya*, through its constant search for new expression, has recovered the original vigor of the sacrificial magic. But this is not the case. Brian Smith[32] successfully attempts to rescue the discussion of sacrifice from the Heestermanic dilemma of a "preclassical" (which in this case means "preritualized" rather than anterior to the modes Sanskritists refer to as "classical"), phasically violent activity versus the desperately perfected ritual whose meaning was (is) entirely self-referential. Smith shows that, on the contrary, "ritual action was presented in Vedic texts not as symbolic or dramatic playacting, magical hocus-pocus, or 'pure,' transcendent, or meaningless activity."[33] "Rather the sacrifice was displayed as a *constructive* activity, creating the human being (ontology), the afterlife (soteriology), and the cosmos as a whole (cosmology)." Of course, he is entirely correct and consonant with the tradition in his assertion of the meaning-making synthesis of the sacrificial ritual, the work of *resemblance*, as he describes it. Nonetheless, in terms of *performance*, the ritual is a creative act only in the sense that it is a *re*-creative act. I do not mean to attach any sense of dreariness to the ritual performance, nor any sense of emptiness. Rituals may, in fact, be *more* exciting for their predictable expectations. But they are repeated, in the same way that a play, once written, can be repeatedly performed.

Of course, audiences and readers may want to duplicate a previous aesthetic experience by watching again a play that they know. And so strong is the brahmanical tendency of the scholastic *alaṃkāraśāstra* that new rules were constantly being manufactured, only to be ignored, broken, rationalized, or occasionally followed, to the detriment of the literature. And on the other side, ritual specialists create variations on the tried and true, justifying the new by asserting its likeness to the old.[34] Although there is overlap between the two kinds of performance, *nāṭya* and *yajña*, it seems that, by and large, the ritual does its work precisely by *not* being new, drama by being *new*.[35]

LOOKING AWAY FROM THE VEDAS: EPIC ISSUES, PERFORMANCE AGENDAS IN THE *NĀṬYAŚĀSTRA*

The *Nāṭyaśāstra* is distinguished from all later dramaturgical manuals by its relative lack of theoretical discussions. Its only section that is neither injunctive nor descriptive, the opening narration, is intended to formulate a legitimated self-understanding for those concerned with the drama—playwrights, producer-directors, performers. It is unlikely that the proclamation of a "fifth Veda" is contemporaneous with *Ṛg-Veda* (though the expression is known in the Upaniṣads),[36] for even the thematization of "Veda" must be post-Vedic. It is, however, known in the *Mahābhārata*, which also calls itself a fifth Veda, and for much the same reasons as the *Nāṭyaśāstra* (a comprehensive representation of human knowledge in a form fit for all human communities—the four *varṇas*).[37] Since this opening narration maintains the frame of the entire text, we assume that the materials brought within it are appropriated to its system of discourse; their former (rather than "original") meanings are understood, not forgotten, but they have lost their punch in their new context. Archaic rituals and mythic motifs are refocused, pulled up into this new framework. The new framework is performance, and a nascent aesthetic is being generated out of the community of performers. This community of performers has always been not exclusively twice-born; it has, in fact, been denigrated in many kinds of literature.[38] Once the protodrama is separated from its sacrificial setting it must seek its own legitimacy. While the *nāṭyotpatti* myth pursues a characteristically Brahmanical strategy for prestige, setting its story in a past disconnected from history, what the story does with this setting seems more to bolster groups that would be part of a performance community than those who were ritual specialists: the exclusion of the lowest group from the knowledge of the Vedas occasions Brahmā's creation of a fifth Veda, one that is not only accessible to Śūdras, but, like the Vedas, presents the exploits of Asuras and acknowledges their contribution. The process of religification thus involves shifting and overlapping agendas; the social meaning of a ritual myth has been detached and grafted on to a new situation with its "Vedic" resonance intact.

This fifth Veda is to be constructed out of *itihāsa*, a term found in the *Arthaśāstra* (1.5.14) as referring to a vaguely broad spectrum of text types, and in the Upaniṣads (BAU 4.5.11, CU 7.1.2) simply to mean "stories of the past." Since the collocation of "fifth Veda" and "*itihāsa*" is specific in the *Mahābhārata*, we might want to look both in the *Nāṭyaśāstra* as well as in the plays themselves for evidence of epic concerns. Where epic and drama are congruent is in the issue of anxiety over kingly succession. The problems of maintaining a familial dynasty are foregrounded in both epics; they exist in the drama as well, intimately connected to the search for erotic passion. Though in later chapters of the *Nāṭyaśāstra* the depiction of the king is given detailed treatment, in the opening myth and ritual account he is merely mentioned as the beneficiary of the old rituals, possibly because of the author's avoidance of anachronism, since the text achieved its basic form during a period between the protodrama's association with sacrificial sessions (or, perhaps better, sacrifical festivals) and the time when the pattern of royal patronage was so established that dramatic myth-making addressed itself wholly to the predicaments of the king; in these scenarios Indra becomes a foil for the royal type. At any rate, he hardly seems to be located in the center of a ritual/theatric universe.[39]

Moreover, the patron is not specified to be a king, but simply an *arthapati*, "lord of wealth" (1.126). Generally speaking, rather than pursuing a specifically "sacrificial" agenda (Byrski), early dramaturgy would be better characterized as acknowledging a ritual component. In the *pūjā* to the *jarjara*, the various arenas of "success"—cosmogonic, sociopolitical ("dharmic"), royal—are capped with success on the stage. Early dramaturgy declares itself strongly universal (elements from and for all *varṇas*), and possibly transmoral—the interests of both gods and demons are accommodated. Further, it looks to the epic, presumably both epic narration and problems, for its subject matter.

THE VEDIC SCREEN OF THE DRAMAS

A good many of the classical Sanskrit dramas cloak their aestheticized epic substrate with a gauze of Vedic imagery. The plays acknowledged to be the best by the tradition, which are those (with a few notable exceptions) most widely appreciated by non-native readers, are the plays of Kālidāsa and Bhavabhūti. The *Abhijñānaśākuntala* and *Vikramorvaśīya* of Kālidāsa and the two Rāma plays of Bhavabhūti possess a flavor of nostalgic archaism. This is due to the pattern of Gupta and Gupta-style Hindu revivalism, as well as to the overall antihistorical transcendentalizing tendency in classical Sanskrit literature, the latter an infection from the Mīmāṃsā strategy of protecting the Vedas from worldly discourse.[40] Playwrights and poets created an image of "Vedic" life under "Vedic" royal society that still fuels the popular imagination in India today. In the mythological films, for example, we see a never-never land where dharmic kings head their courts, their primary duty that of protecting rishis engaged in the *incessant* performance of sacrifice to the *incessant* chanting of mantras. The Vedism of the dramas consists, in fact, of the rendering of such sylvan "Vedic" tableaux (the epic-classical Arcadian fantasy), the calculated use of Vedic language (as in other belletristic works like the *Bhāgavata Purāṇa*), and the likening of the king to Indra, especially in a consecratory mode.

In the remarkable synthesis of the Kālidāsa plays, the king is engaged in pursuing his passion for a semidivine woman, while in the background (we are not allowed to forget) he is also troubled by the lack of an heir—a transformation and appropriation of the epic's anxiety concerning succession. The neglect of his duties through lovesickness is congruent with a sense of the kingdom's being awry. The play's two problems are resolved by making the rectification of the kingdom dependent on the winning of the woman. (Actually, she is barely more than a girl.) To work out the meaning of the king's role, a mythology of Indra has been developed from the epic king-of-the-gods type, but it has been shaped in such a way as to dharmicize Indra's activities. More to the point, Indra's role has been reduced to, as the aestheticians would say, a *pratyupamāna*, "countercomparison."

The *Vikramorvaśīya* has a heavier-than-usual amount of Vedism owing to its source in RV 10.95, a dialogue hymn,[41] as well in the Brāhmaṇas. At the play's opening King Purūravas rescues the Apsaras Urvaśī who has been captured by Asuras while returning from serving Indra. Her nymph companions know he will succeed, for "Doesn't great Indra [*mahendra*—Indra in his heavily royalized persona] when he's threatened with battle bring Purūravas from earth with all honor, and place him in command of the army of victory?" (1.4 +). When Urvaśī recovers from her swoon she inquires if she has been rescued "by great Indra who sees all things with his supernatural power?" and is told, "Not by great Indra. By a royal sage (*rājarṣi*) whose splendor is as thrilling as great Indra's" (1.7 +).

Here the characteristic trope is not only that the king does the work of Indra, but that he replicates the life of Indra as a friend and equal. This is expressed in a flood of Indra imagery at the end of the play. On meeting the son Urvaśī has secretly borne him:

> Today I become the best of fathers
> through this worthy son of yours,
> like Indra, smasher of citadels,
> father of Jayanta born of Paulomī. (5.14)

Sage Nārada arrives to consecrate this son Āyus as *yuvarāja*, the epic-style "young king" or "king-in-youth" who will provide assurance of familial, dynastic succession. He explains the relationship between the king and Indra:

> Indra, lord of Vasus, should see to your affairs
> and you should undertake what he desires,
> as the sun strengthens fire, and daily the fire
> rekindles the sun with its flames. (5.20)
>
> *He looks up to the sky.*
> Rambhā, bring the materials which Indra himself has supplied for the consecration of Crown Prince Āyus as heir to the kingdom.[42]

and finally Nirada says,

> The royal splendor of crown prince Āyus
> calls to mind the war god Kumāra, Śiva's son,
> when Indra, lord of storms, installed him
> commander-in-chief of heaven's armies. (5.23)

This last verse helps us understand why Kālidāsa can transform Indra from a god into a monumental trope, an eternally offstage figure who is more the mirror for the dramatic king than his model. Kālidāsa is a devotee of Śiva, the lord of the drama and the patron of its practitioners. Indra is in Kālidāsa and everywhere in classical Sanskrit after the rise of the sectarian gods of Hindu mythology a mere symbol, perhaps somewhat in the same way that the Greek gods were for poets and artists of the Renaissance. Actually we can see from the earlier Buddhist uses of Indra that he probably never was much of a candidate for transcendence in the Hindu sense. Other Sanskrit dramas, such as the *Śākuntala*, use Indra the same way, frequently in their closing moments, which depict "royal consecration" or some less ceremonial form of reassurance or rectification of kingship.

Indra is not the only figure in whom the Indologists see ties to Vedic motifs. There is the *vidūṣaka*, who perhaps started out as the stand-in for Varuṇa in a cosmogonic agon against Indra; in the dramas, however, he is the hero's friend. He never *opposes* the hero, though his blunders certainly create obstacles for the *nāyaka*.[43] He does undermine the hero's sentimentality, but he is no consistent critic.[44] Since the *vidūṣaka* has no adversarial function in the drama, and since the *trigata* (three-way conversation) of the *pūrvaraṅga* ritual is so loosely specified to make a normal comic realization seem natural, is this not a case in which a discovery of origins, however well-founded, leads to a misapprehension of the actual phenomenon? In other words, if the original "paradigms" of the dramatic constellation have been replaced, understanding them in their contexts and seeing them behind their classical manifestations will stimulate a misreading of the classical drama as it is. If the classical drama expresses and resolves the predicaments of the royal figures who are patron and audience, it seems likely that the *vidūṣaka*, in his mild parody of the ever-present Brahmin adviser, serves to alleviate some of the tension in the Brahmin-Kṣatriya alliance. Thus the "source" for this feature of the Sanskrit drama is the sociological pattern of differentiated but interlocking realms of power that begins in the historical era known as the late Vedic period,[45] not the cosmological motif of the archaic *daivāsuram* strife between gods and antigods found in Vedic literature. That ancient combat has been thematized as an allegory about performance, as we saw in the *nāṭyotpatti* story.

A parallel situation exists with regard to the *nāyikā*, the heroine of the drama. It works very neatly to form a lineage from Vāc to Sarasvatī to Śrī to Rājaśrī. It is true that, like those other elusive goddesses, she must be won. But in the dramas she is never won by contest, as she is in the primal Vedic scenario.[46] Accompanied by her friend (the *sakhi*) she does not stand aloof from the *nāyaka*; rather, some external situation prevents her union with him. She is ably assisted by her friend who acts as *dūtī* (messenger, go-between), just as the hero-king is comically assisted by his pal, the *vidūṣaka*. If protagonist (*nāyaka*)-antagonist (*vidūṣaka*)-divine female prize was an original triad, it left nothing but the shells of personae in the drama. The functioning triad, on the other hand, is hero (*nāyaka*)-heroine (*nāyikā*)-girlfriend (*dūtī*). Even if the George Hart thesis is not accepted in all of its specifics, we have to admit that this very important feature of Sanskrit drama (and all of Sanskrit poetry) descends to the genre from the early Tamil poems through the Prakrit lyrics.[47] Thus this is a legitimate "source" of Sanskrit drama. Again the *nāṭyotpatti* myth tells us that the archaic source, the cosmogonic contest for Speech, is no longer available; it has been turned back into an allegory for poetic creation and the comprehensive, inclusive nature of theater. This is an allegory so pervasive as to seem archaic.

At least with the characters of the hero, the heroine and the *vidūṣaka*, there are corresponding figures in the myth and ritual of the *Nāṭyaśāstra*'s opening, even if the material does nothing to explain the characteristic political and erotic concerns of the plays. But the dominant aesthetic of *rasa*, being mentioned only in passing in the *nāṭyotpatti*, can be safely ignored by the textual archaeologists; it must be later than these "origins." This is basically what Kuiper does. We saw that Byrski relied on Abhinavagupta to connect the *rasa* of the dramas with the transcendent intensity (*ānanda*) of the Upaniṣadic *brahmajñāna*. There are several problems here. From the very beginning the dramaturgical tradition is concerned with *rasa*s, the eight or more distinctly differentiated and intensely realized aesthetic moods. Though many of us today understand the nature of *rasa* as a quasi-contemplative aesthetic experience, this is an understanding promoted by the interpretation of Abhinavagupta. It is Abhinava who in his transcendental Śaivism insists that *rasa* is not achieved through indentification, but through detachment, and that the distinctive qualities of the various *rasa*s are less fundamental than the *ānanda* that is the essential nature of each.

Abhinavagupta's became the mainstream interpretation in the academic study of poetics (*alaṃkāraśāstra*), largely through its dissemination in compendia like the *Kāvyaprakāśa*, and largely because of its congruence with other Brahmanical knowledges and emotional attitudes. It made the theatrical experience esoteric and safe. But recent work[48] suggests that a view of the *rasa*s as distinct and intensely participatory was an original understanding of the dramaturges, and survived in the religious aesthetic of the Bengal-Bṛndāvan Vaiṣṇava axis. For this community, as for most of the nonscholastic world in India, *rasa* was an intensification of *bhāva*, not an otherworldly transformation of it. The *Nāṭyaśātra* itself has indications of this: it makes a distinction between *lokadharmī* (natural representation) and *nāṭyadharmī* (representation through the conventions of the theater).[49] Only later was this distinction interpreted as *laukika* (mundane) and *alaukika* (transmundane, supernatural). My point here is that we have another crucial element of the Sanskrit drama for which the Vedist can with seeming ease supply a "source," but to characterize the source of *rasa* as a unitary transcendence discovered by late Vedic sages is a distortion of the text.

One can only conclude that the notion of the *rasa*s is a distinct contribution of the theatrical community itself. In the present text of the *Nāṭyaśāstra*, the *nāṭyotpatti* appears at the beginning. As we saw, this loose allegorical myth is designed, on the one hand, to impart quasi-Brahmanical prestige to a profession and cultural form that was regarded as inferior by the emergent orthodoxy, and on the other hand, to provide a paradigmatic context for the appropriation of the ritual setting of which it once was part. Immediately after the *nāṭyotpatti* establishes this ritual paradigm the text launches into an extensive, detailed discussion of *rasa* and the like. Thus there is good reason to believe that one of the dramaturgical manuals from which the *Nāṭyaśāstra* was fashioned began with the *rasa* as its first topic.

CONCLUSION: THE REFERENCE IS PERFORMANCE

If we read the stories of the gods and the antigods in the two myths of the *nāṭyotpatti* as the transformation of struggle into aesthetically perfected performances, there would seem to be a parallel with Heesterman's taming of the sacrificial agon into domesticated ritual bespeaking transcendent order.[50] But we have to remember that these are stories about the *performance* of these myths, not versions of the myths themselves. There is, for example, the question of the first drama. Though some students of the myth have failed to notice it, that honor does not go to "Indra's Victory over the Demons." That drama was never played to its conclusion, since the Asuras violently objected to the shame it brought them. Instead, the "*Amṛtamanthana*," or "Churning of the Immortal Nectar" is the first play to be actually performed in its entirety. It is performed in the playhouse, not out in the open, and it is a story in which both gods and demons have an equal hand.[51] What this means is that Brahmā has indeed respected the Daityas' wishes not to perform a play that portrays them in a bad light. (We have to assume that Brahmā's version ends with the churning itself, and not with the struggle for the ambrosia that followed it.) This makes the story even more sophisticated, and certainly much less like a recapitualation of the cosmogonic conflict. It is in fact a highly self-conscious allegory about the very *lack* of conflict in Sanskrit drama[52]—or at least that is how it is used in the overall structure of the five-chapter section.[53]

Another section of the *nāṭyotpatti* story has to do, as we saw, with the dispute between gods and demons over the music in the preliminaries. Yet the *bahirgītā/nirgīta* controversy may be the mythologizing of a conflict about whether the musical warm-up ("sounds that don't make sense") should be an obvious part of the stage business, or be conducted out back behind the theater. The decision seems to be that it ought to be done right on stage, for, as we all know, hearing the musicians warm up provides a thrill of anticipation. But if we read this recurrence of a Deva-Asura mythology with the material in the first chapter, I believe we can also read it as a strong, intentional allegory about aesthetic practice. For what are, in fact, demons or obstacles to performance, but mistakes and flubs—loss of memory, freezing up, (the text specifically mentions these two), missed cues, technical inadequacy in performance, lack of inspiration? The disordered sounds of warming up resemble the demonic *vighnas* about to break in, but in fact they are not. Let the performance demons have an opportunity to create a little controlled chaos before the actual performance starts. Thus Nārada says, "Don't stop this *nirgīta* of the string instruments, but combine it with the *upohana* and give it seven forms. The Daityas and Rākṣasas will be *ni-badh* 'bound down' or 'composed'—the term is ambiguous—by this *nirgīta* and will create no obstacles." Certainly both parts of the story—the earlier one about the demons attacking the performance of the first play about their defeat at the hands of Indra and this one about Nārada's attempt to resolve a conflict about the place of disordered music—both build upon the original myth celebrated in Indra's banner festival, harkening back to cosmogonic elements in an agonistic sacrifice. But our *Nāṭyaśāstra* authors already recognize that the re-creation of this battle cannot succeed, that the first play better not shame the demons, and that, most important, this mythology is best appropriated as an allegory for their own situation, the arena of producer-directors, playwrights, actors, and musicians. In other words, it is no longer primarily a cosmogonic story, but an aesthetic allegory that uses the cosmogonic story.

Finally, returning to the very beginning of the *nāṭyotpatti* story, we may ponder again what Brahmā really meant when he told the sages he had created a *nāṭyaveda*, a fifth Veda similar to the Vedas. Abhinavagupta, predictably abstracting from the texture, concreteness, and plurality of human life that the drama is able to intensify, comments (after some discussion), "Therefore it is established that *nāṭya* is different from those *śāstras* whose substance is commanding (*śāsana*, which consists of the application of an enforced action [*ākramyayojanā*] or an injunction [*niyoga*], for the *nāṭya* is a manifest expression of the self-arisen knowledge, so it alone has the form of the '*prāṇaveda*,' the living Veda."[54] In the same passage he says that the *nāṭyaveda* is the *nāṭyaśāstra*, not a "Veda" per se. The assertion is complex but indicative of what has happened through Vedism since early times. On the one hand, the notion of "Veda" is broadened, metaphorized, so that it now means some kind of autonomous knowledge that is expressed in a concrete form, like the texts of the four Vedas, or, as Abhinava would have it, like the drama. Here, Abhinava seems to be thinking consonantly with the Mīmāṃsakas—transcendent knowledge known through texts, which must themselves be transcendent—but notice that he has no use for injunction. I don't think it would be unfair to say that his entire commentary is uninterested in dramatic practice. But then he further removes the notion of Veda from its actual texts with the explanation that the term simply means a body of knowledge about a particular field, a peculiar point since many of these "Vedas" (such as "Dhanurveda," the science of archery) are identified as discrete practical manuals. These latter, however, are called *upaveda*s; the *Nāṭyaśāstra* says the *nāṭyaveda* is connected both to the *upaveda* and the scriptural Vedas as well. If the Vedas don't tell us to do anything, and this Veda is not actually a Veda, one wonders why it is that Abhinava is writing a commentary on a text ninety-five percent of whose content is instructional; if this is not really a fifth Veda related to the other four, one wonders why it is that the text tells us which parts of the *nāṭyaveda* come from which of the four Vedas? (1.17) In the familiar strategy for Vedicization, Abhinava has removed from consideration the literal meanings of both the (scriptural) Vedas and the text being compared to the Vedas, in this case the *Nāṭyaśāstra*, and placed them in the realm of transcendent, or at least inaccessible knowledge. And like his successors, his lack of interest in practice shows the vigor of his Vedic totalization.

As with the *nāṭyotpatti* legend, almost every Sanskrit drama has an aesthetic or performance subtext; characters discuss poetry, dance, painting in emotional, aesthetic, and technical terms. Just as these elements refocus audience attention past the predicaments of the heroes and heroines to the world of the playwrights and performers, so, too, the exhaustive account of the building of the playhouse and the twenty-page catalogue of gestures and dance postures within the very chapters containing the *nāṭyotpatti* legend can refocus our attention beyond Bharatamuni and the circle of Brahmins, beyond the legend's nostalgic nod to an archaic past, to the skilled, intelligent dancers who draw us into neither cosmogony nor transcendence but the thick sweetness of their passion.

The dramaturges and the community they served knew about religification. In the midst of the posture catalogue the sages interrupt to enquire why dance (*nṛtra*) exists, referring specifically to the performance given by the female dancer to accompany the *āsārita*, a secular song. After all, the discursive gesture (*abhinaya*) came into existence to explicate discursive song (*gītā*)? The answer, given by no one in particular, is that the dance is occasioned by no specific need; it has come into use simply because it creates beauty. It is because dance is naturally loved by almost all people that it is eulogized as being, the text says, in that most loaded religious term *auspicious*. Feuerbach claimed that people alienate what they can't understand, call "holy" the wishes they project.[55] The Sanskrit dramaturges tell us we call holy what we love spontaneously—how much sweeter, clearer, and more generous an explanation for the gesture that creates the human value of holiness!

NOTES

The first version of this chapter was delivered at the American Academy of Religion Conference in New Orleans, November 1990, as part of a panel entitled "Arguing the Vedas." My thanks to the panel organizer, Laurie Patton, and the discussant, Brian Smith for their valuable comments. Translations are mine except where noted.

1. General references to works are found at the end of the chapter.

2. See Kuiper, "The Ancient Āryan Verbal Contest."

3. Mainkar deals with this question in his *Rigvedic Foundations of Classical Poetics*. The present chapter is concerned not with the general question of poetry but with the drama in specific.

4. *Amaruśataka*, 46. Thanks to Rahul Bonner, in whose University of Chicago dissertation the commentarial reference occurred. Further resonances of these terms: *sāndra*—thick, intense, strong, dense, compact, crowded with different things; *mukharāga*—coloring of the face, visible passion; *manojña*—beautiful; *manobhava*—sexual love. This section of commentary is also important because it is one of the clearest examples of a commentator's doing what we would call "literary criticism," as opposed to "literary interpretatton."

5. The chief investigators of the past fifteen years have done this. The subject has engaged the greats of all the national Indological traditions—Lévi, Renou, Caland, Pischel, Hillebrandt, Thieme, Keith, Luders, Gonda, Kuiper, Byrski, Raghavan—to name just a few. Kuiper's masterful study, *Varuṇa and Vidūṣaka: On the Origin of Sanskrit Drama*, gives an excellent review and bibliography.

6. Another speculation is that the dramatic manual began immediately following the *nāṭyotpatti* with the *rasa* chapter.

7. *Vedasammitaḥ*, lit. "of the same measure as the Veda," "resembling the Veda." See the end of this chapter for a discussion the term *nāṭyaveda*.

8. Cf. Sieg's philological background to this question in his introduction.

9. The Vighnas are led by one Virūpākṣa, sometimes a name of Śiva, giving the legend a Vaiṣṇava cast in the manner of *Mahābhārata* redaction, and sometimes a name for a *rākṣasa*, the ogres who typically disrupt ritual procedures.

10. The ceremony (*yajana*, a general term for sacrificing and worshiping) should include offerings, *homa*, mantras, *japa*, etc.

11. Looking at Vedism in Sanskrit drama as exemplary of the "evolutionary" approach in the study of religion would move this chapter away from its dramaturgical, performance orientation. Nonetheless, such tropes have exerted a powerful influence in the formation of many disciplines. See Detienne, *L'invention de la mythologie*, introduction and chap. 1; Smith, *Imagining Religion*, the chapter "In Comparison Magic Dwells"; Inden, *Imagining India*, introduction.

12. Actually, the notion of "religification" implies two parallel and related processes: the first, for an orthodoxy to appropriate various (usually earlier) cultural phenomena into its historical systematic, and second, for professional scholars of religion to make a cultural phenomenon the object of religious discourse, often by mistaking the traditional, mythic content of a text or performance for an ultimate concern with ritual magic or transcendence.

13. Smith, *Refections on Resemblance, Ritual and Religion*, 202.

14. Kuiper, *Varuṇa and Vidūṣaka*, 158, 159.

15. Ibid., 164.

16. Ibid., 192.

17. Ibid., 217ff.

18. Ibid., 115.

19. Ibid., 157.

20. Ibid., 158.

21. Ibid., 159.

22. Ibid., 179.

23. Ibid., 239.

24. Byrski's structuralism yields optimistic parallels that may or may not have been intended by the redactors. For example, he uncritically blends together the allegorical meaning of the "fifth Veda" trope: the availability of a comprehensive "text" to all human communities with the perception that the involvement of both Devas and Asuras in the Churning points to its capacity to represent both divine and demonic forces—another kind of universality. Of course this is only one possible reading of the Churning story; see n. 53 for further thoughts on the Churning.

25. Byrski, *Concept of Ancient Indian Theatre*, chap. 8 and 9.

26. Incorrectly cited as 1.4.6 in ibid.

27. Since the phrase *ijyayā cānayā* refers to to the *pūrvaraṅga*, not to the drama itself, it would tend not to support Byrski's identity of *nāṭya* and *yajña*. See also the discussion of the *Mālavikāgnimitra* 1.4 below.

28. Mammaṭa, *Kāvyaprakāśa*, 1.1.

29. devānāmidamāmananti munayaḥ kāntaṃ cākṣuṣam
rudreṇedamumākṛtavyatikare svāṅge vibhaktaṃ dvidhā
traiguṇyodbhavamatra lokacaritaṃ nānārasaṃ dṛśyate
nāṭyam bhinnarucerjanasya bahudhāpyekaṃ
samārādhanam.

Note that the reference to the two modes suggests that *nāṭya* at first refers to dance (as the verse's context in the play demands), but by the end of the verse the meaning is clearly drama.

30. *Mālavikāgnimitra, prasiddhakratoḥ vyatirekaṃ kāntaṃ cākṣuṣamiti ca viśeṣaṇe.*

31. Byrski, *Concept of Ancient Indian Theatre*, 137.

32. Smith, *Reflections on Resemblance, Ritual and Religion*, 38–46.

33. Ibid., 46

34. Here and at the discussion of the drama's being "novel" above, cf. Staal, "Ritual Syntax," 119–43, on the "embeddedness" of "old" ritual patterns in the transfer and transformation of elements from one ritual to another.

35. There are, of course, dramas that have a primarily ritual purpose. In the vernacular theater, festival plays that recreate the lives of beloved gods will aim for consistency from year to year so as to produce the known devotional result. Variation and innovation are inevitable, but usually not aesthetic goals.

36. *Chāndogya Upaniṣad* 7.1.2,4.

37. See *Mahābhārata* 1.1.19, 204–10; 1.2.235ff. As far as I can see, the *Mahābhārata* does not explicitly proclaim itself a "fifth Veda," but speaks of itself as complementary, even superior to the other four. Sieg, *Die Sagenstoffe*, 22, *passim*, has other references to passages not in the Critical Text.

38. E.g. *Manusmṛti* 4.215, 8.65, 8.362; *Mahābhāṣya* 6.1.13; *Viṣṇusmṛti* 16.8; *Kuṭṭanīmatta* v. 855; the *Arthaśāstra* routinely lumps them with prostitutes; the *sūtradhāra* and actress in the prologue to the *Mṛcchakaṭika* make a point of their social inferiority.

39. The *Nāṭyaśāstra* understands the drama as beneficial to many sectors of society:

> [Drama gives] diversion to kings, firmness to persons afflicted with sorrow, methods of acquiring wealth to those seeking it, and composure to those agitated in mind. (1.110)

> A grandest playhouse is for the gods [remember the framing story] a medium one is for kings, and the lowest kind is for the rest of the people. (2.11)
>
> Mantras recited at the raising of the pillars dedicated to the four *varṇas* will bring victory to the king. (2.62)
>
> When offering *pūjā* to the *jarjara*, it should be addressed: "You are Indra's weapon killing all the demons; you have been fashioned by all the gods, and you are capable of destroying all the obstacles; bring victory to the king and defeat his enemies, welfare to cows and Brahmins, and progress to dramatic undertakings."

40. Cf. Pollock, "Mīimāṃsā and the Problem of History in Traditional India."

41. There is no reason to imagine that that dialogue hymns are any more likely a source for classical Sanskrit drama than any other type of literature containing dialogues (Upaniṣads, epics, etc.). Here is another example of a wish for Vedic origins.

42. *kumārasyāyuṣo yauvarājyābhiśekhaḥ*

43. Kuiper, *Varuṇa and Vidūṣaka*, 193, 207–9, admits the connection between adversary and blunderer is not strong.

44. Jefferds, "Vidūṣaka versus Fool."

45. I am thinking of the issue as formulated by Heesterman in *Inner Conflict of Tradition*, and as modified by critique of others, such as Inden, "Tradition Against Itself."

46. As described by Kuiper, *Varuṇa and Vidūṣaka*, 236ff.

47. Hart, *Poems of Ancient Tamil*; cf. also "Relation between Tamil and Classical Sanskrit Literature."

48. Delmonico, "Sacred Rapture," which builds, in part, upon Raghavan, *Bhoja's Śṛṅgāraprakāśa*.

49. *Nāṭyaśāstra* 14.62–65.

50. I am thinking here especially of "Vedic Sacrifice and Transcendence," chap. 6 in *Inner Confict of Tradition.*

51. Both Byrski and Kuiper do notice this equality.

52. Perhaps Heesterman's thesis works better for drama than it does for sacrifice.

53. The Churning is a highly ambiguous myth, for it describes a paradoxically cooperative agon, admitting of various emphases in its readings: the gods and demons are engaged in a struggle that creates the world. (This reading assimilates the story to the primordial, programmatic struggle between gods, led by Indra, and demons—a struggle that must be repeated, but one in which ultimately Indra wins.) Or, alternatively,

as here in Brahmā's drama, the demons and gods cooperate, combining their phasic forces—out of greed?

54. Byrski interprets this passage to mean that *nāṭya* brings about "self-existent manifest wisdom." Abhinava is not quite that transcendent in speaking of *rasa*.

55. Feuerbach, *Das Wesen des Christentums.*

REFERENCES

Amaruśataka

1954 With commentary *Rasikasaṃjīvinī* of Arjunavarmadeva. Bombay: Nirnaya Sagara.

Byrski, M. Christopher.

1974 *Concept of Ancient Indian Theatre.* Delhi: Munshiram Manoharlal.

Dāmodaragupta.

1944 *Kuṭṭanīmatta*. Ed. Madhusudan Kaul. Calcuta: Royal Asiatic Society.

Delmonico, Neal

1990 "Sacred Rapture: A Study of the Religious Aesthetic of Rūpa Gosvāmin." Ph.D. diss., University of Chicago.

Detienne, Marcel

1981 *L'invention de la mythologie.* Paris: Gallimard.

1986 Translated by Margaret Cook as *The Creation of Mythology.* Chicago: University of Chicago Press.

Feuerbach, Ludwig

1841 *Das Wesen des Christentums.* Leipzig: O. Wigand.

1957 Translated by George Eliot as *The Essence of Christianity.* New York: Harper.

Hart, George

1975 *The Poems of Ancient Tamil.* Berkeley: University of California Press.

1976 "The Relation Between Tamil and Classical Sanskrit Literature." *A History of Indian Literature,* ed. J. Gonda, 10:317–52. Wiesbaden: Otto Harrassowitz.

Heesterman, J. C.

1985 *The Inner Confict of Tradition: Essays in Indian Ritual, Kingship and Society.* Chicago: University of Chicago Press.

Inden, Ronald

1990 *Imagining India.* London: Blackwell.

1986 "Tradition Against Itself." *American Ethnologist* 13(4): 762–74.

Jefferds, Keith N.

1981 "Vidūṣaka versus Fool: A Functional Analysis." *Journal of South Asian Literature* 16(1):61–74.

Kālidāsa

1961 *Vikramorvaśīya*. Ed. H. D. Velankar. Delhi: Sahitya Akademi.

1889 With the commentaries of Kāṭayavema and Raṅganātha. Ed. S. P. Pandit. Bombay Sanskrit Series, no. 16. Bombay: Central Book Depot.

1984 Translated by David L. Gitomer in *Theater of Memory: The Plays of Kālidāsa*. Ed. Barbara Stoler Miller. New York: Columbia University Press.

1929 *The Mālavikāgnimitra of Kālidāsa*. With the commentary Sārārthadīpikā by Sahṛdaya Rāma Pisharody. Ed. C. Sankara Rama Sastri. Madras: Sri Balamanorama.

1984 Translated by Edwin Gerow in *Theater of Memory: The Play of Kālidāsa*. Ed. Barbara Stoler Miller. New York: Columbia University Press.

Kauṭilya

1965–72 *Arthaśāstra of Kauṭilya*. Ed. and trans. R. Kangle. 3 vols. Delhi: Motilal Banarsidass.

Kuiper, F. B. J.

1960 "The Ancient Āryan Verbal Contest." *Indo-Iranian Journal* 4:217–81.

1979 *Varuṇa and Vidūṣaka: On the Origin of Sanskrit Drama*. Verhandelingen der Koninklijke Nederlandse Akademie van Wetenschappen, Afd. Letterkunde, Nieuwe Reeks, deel 100. Amsterdam: North-Holland.

Mainkar, T. S.

1977 *The Rigvedic Foundations of Classical Poetics*. Delhi: Ajanta.

Mammaṭa

1985 *Kāvyaprakāśa*. With the commentary *Bālabodhinī* of V R. Jhalkikar. Ed. R. D Karmarkar. 7th ed. Poona: Bhandarkar Oriental Research Institute.

Mānavadharmaśāstra

1887 Ed. Julius Jolly. London.

1991 Translated by Wendy Doniger with Brian K. Smith as *The Laws of Manu*. London and New York: Penguin.

Nāṭyaśāstra of Bharata

1956–67 Ed. and trans. by M. Ghosh. 2 vols. Translation, vol. 1. Calcutta: Manisha Granthalaya, 1956, 1967. Translation, vol. 2. Calcutta: Asiastic Society, 1961.

1934–64 With *Abhinavabhāratī* commentary of Abhinavagupta. Ed. M. R. Kavi. Gaekwads Oriental Series, 4 vols., nos. 36, 68, 124, 145. Baroda.

1971–75 Text with Hindi and Sanskrit commentaries. Ed. A. Madhusudan Shastri. 2 vols. Banaras: Banaras Hindu University.

Patañjali

1883–92 *Mahābhāṣya*. Ed. Kielhorn. 3 vols. Bombay Sanskrit Series, nos. 18, 21, 28. Bombay.

Pollock, Sheldon

1989 "Mīmāṃsā and the Problem of History in Traditional India." *Journal of the American Oriental Society* 109(4):603–10.

Raghavan, V.

1978 *Bhoja's Śṛṅgāraprakāśa*. Madras: Punarvasu.

Sieg, Emil

1902 *Die Sagenstoffe des Rig Veda und die indische itihāsa tradition.* Stuttgart: W. Kohlhammer.

Smith, Brian

1989 *Reflections on Resemblance, Ritual and Religion*. London: Oxford University Press.

Smith, J. Z.

1982 *Imagining Religion: From Babylon to Jonestown*. Chicago: University of Chicago Press.

Staal, F.

1980 "Ritual Syntax." In *Sanskrit and Indian Studies: Essays in Honor of Daniel H. H. Ingalls*, ed. M. Nagatomi et al. Dordrecht, Netherlands, and Boston: D. Riedel.

Śūdraka

1950 *Mṛcchakaṭika*. Ed. K. P. Parab, rev. N. R. Acarya. 8th ed. Bombay: Nirnaya Sagara.

1968 Translated by J. B. van Buitenen as *The Little Clay Cart*, in *Two Plays of Ancient India*. New York: Columbia University Press.

Viṣṇusmṛti

1962 Ed. Julius Jolly. Chowkhamba Sanskrit Series, no. 95. Varanasi: Chowkhamba Sanskrit Series Office.

PART THREE

The Vedas in Modernity and Beyond

7

The Authority of an Absent Text

The Veda, Upangas, Upavedas, and Upnekhata in European Thought

DOROTHY M. FIGUEIRA

INTRODUCTION

ALTHOUGH FRIEDRICH AUGUST ROSEN published a partial Latin translation of the *Ṛg-Veda* in 1838,[1] manuscripts could be found in Europe almost a century earlier. As early as 1739 the catalogue of Fourmont attests to the existence of the Veda in the Bibliothèque Imperiale in Paris. In 1789 Antoine-Louis-Henri Polier presented another copy to the British Museum. However, and most important, the Veda existed in the European imagination and in speculative thought well before its appearance in translation. In the form of spurious fragments, misattributions, and forgeries, it stimulated critical discussion. As Brian Smith has shown, the Veda poses interesting problems from a hermeneutical point of view. Louis Renou has noted that while the Vedas are revered and recognized as omniscient, the texts themselves are weakened, altered, or even lost.[2] Other chapters in this volume address issues concerning the destiny of the Veda in India. In the following pages, we will examine the role of the Veda as an alienated object or symbol in European consciousness.

We must begin, however, by qualifying the hermeneutic parameters of the Veda's reception in Europe. The Veda entered European discourse as a fraudulent, lost, absent, misnomered, or "fantasy Veda." Therefore, when we speak of the European reception of the Veda, we are referring to either an absent or a falsely present text. In literary critical terms, the Veda functioned as an aporia. The following discussion will also address the issue of canonicity. Was the Veda used in the West to legitimize assertions of faith or law? Was there an accepted procedure for interpreting the Veda as a canonical text or an accepted interpreter whose exegesis was seen as binding (even before it was given)? Or, rather, did we have a situation in which "the Devil can quote Scripture to his need"? A canonical literature arises through the consensus of a group (elite) and normally serves to stabilize that group. It lends value to the interests and products of that group. Was the fictive Veda or the fiction of the Veda used in Europe to this effect?

I will begin with an examination of the Veda, as it was understood in the Enlightenment and Sturm und Drang periods. Here, the focus will fall on the discourse engendered by the false Veda (*Ezour Veidam*) introduced to Europe by Voltaire. The belief that the first Veda was lost developed from the controversy surrounding the authenticity of the *Ezour Veidam*. If the *Ṛg-Veda* was lost, and had been so for a long time, then, according to Herder, Indian religion was cut off from primitive revelation and reduced to the status of speculative thought. Thus, although the Veda was interesting in itself, it was ultimately insignificant since it was unable to establish the authenticity of Judaism and Christianity. Both Herder's and, to a much greater extent Friedrich Schlegel's reception of Indian philosophy were based upon this premise of insignificance. The Veda's function as a necessary aporia set the groundwork for the subsequent treatment that the Veda would receive at the hands of romantic mythologists and Max Müller. The Veda began its career in the West as a fraud and was subsequently transformed into the alternative philosophy par excellence. We shall trace this evolution and conclude with a discussion of its final avatar, the Aryan gospel.

VOLTAIRE AND THE FALSE VEDA

For Voltaire (1694–1778), Asia was the ideal. In fact, in the eighteenth century Voltaire was a principal panegyrist and official defender of Asia's moral rectitude. Voltaire presented the Orient as having revealed the origin of the European past. It also held the key to understanding future events. India had, like China, his unreserved sympathies. Voltaire believed that Indian philosophers had discovered a new universe "en morale et en physique."[3] The Indians were the inventors of art. The original inhabitants of India lived in a state of paradise: naked vegetarians who lived off fruit rather than cadavers and without luxury. They were sober, chaste, temperate, and law-abiding. Unlike the Saracens, Tartars, Arabs, and Jews who lived by piracy, Indians subsisted through their religion.[4]

As elsewhere in his oeuvre, even in his most virulent critiques of the church, Voltaire was never truly distant from his Jesuit masters. The Jesuitical documentation on India supplied Voltaire with a theme he was to exploit with verve. In the *Lettres edifiantes et curieuses*, the reverend fathers expressed their horror of idolatrous superstition. Tempered by Christian restraint, they admitted that the Hindus were not unredeemable; their beliefs were "not absolutely terrible." In fact, they were eminently capable and worthy of conversion. After all, one could find in their "ridiculous" religion belief in a single God, suggesting a kind of proto-Christianity.[5] Voltaire took from the Jesuits what suited his polemic: he asserted that Vedism comprised the oldest religion known to man dedicated to a pure form of worship. Its lofty metaphysics formed the basis of Christianity. Voltaire found no difficulty in reconciling the sublimity of Indian religion with its modern superstitions: the Vedic Indian had simply been made soft by the climate.[6] Thus, Voltaire disengaged the *Urform* of Hinduism from all superstition and fanaticism. In fact, the initial Brahmins had established a government and religion based upon universal reason.

One can almost forgive Voltaire his subjective portrayal of India, given the amount and quality of the information culled from voyage accounts, missionary letters, scholarly works, and translations. Having literally read everything available concerning India, edited and unedited, Voltaire realized only too well the necessity of basing any future discussion of India upon an authentic Sanskrit text. He, therefore, set out to discover one. In the *Ezour Veidam*, Voltaire initially believed that he had unearthed an original source as well as the lost Veda.[7]

Voltaire received the manuscript of the *Ezour Veidam* from the Comte de Maudave, whom he believed to be a close friend of a francophone Brahmin[8] who had tried to translate the manuscript from Sanskrit into French.[9] Voltaire made a copy of the manuscript[10] and deposited the original in the Bibliothèque du Roi.[11] In *La defense de mon Oncle*, Voltaire characterized the *Ezour Veidam* as the true *veidam*, the *veidam* explained, the pure *veidam*. Voltaire initially thought the *Ezour Veidam* was "a copy of the four vedams."[12] However, by 1761 he described it as merely a commentary of the *Veidam*.

In fact, it did not matter to Voltaire that this text was not really the Veda; what mattered was that it satisfied the idea of a Veda which, for Voltaire, represented an exemplum of sublimity, the scripture of the world's oldest religion. This "Veda" announced a pure cult, disengaged from all superstition and all fanaticism.[13] The initial Brahmins, who also served as kings and pontiffs, had established a religion based upon universal reason.

However, these Vedic Brahmins had degenerated, along with their cult. The religion existing in modern India had obscured sage Vedic theology, marketed superstition, and profited modern Brahmins.[14] Whether through suppression or loss, the *Ezour Veidam* had been virtually lost to India until its retrieval and circulation by a Frenchman. By citing lengthy excerpts, Voltaire sought to show how the *Ezour Veidam* combats the very superstition that destroyed "Vedic" religion. By basing its polemic on citations from the lost Veda,[15] the *Ezour Veidam* combats the growth of idolatry. For his part, Voltaire hoped to prove how all the principles of Christian theology could be found in the *Veidam*.[16]

Raymond Schwab characterized the *Ezour Veidam* as an insidious piece of propaganda consisting of certain "Vedic" materials translated by Jesuits with the intention of isolating elements most in harmony with Christianity.[17] With this fraud, Schwab maintained, the Jesuits sought to refute idolatry and polytheism in the name of the purer doctrine of the "Vedas," and, ultimately, convert Indians. As the Indologist Willem Caland noted, the fraud was clever: the *Ezour Veidam* did not reject all Hinduism, but granted those tenets not in contradiction with Christian doctrine. Its author tried to make his readers believe that the *Veidam* differed entirely from what they believed it to be.[18] The *Ezour Veidam* defined the Veda as a "*corps de science*" divided in four parts (the *Rik, Chama, Zozur* and *Adorbo, adarvan* or *obartah-Bah*), each with a supplement (*oupa bédam*) and summary (*sanitah-védam*). While the text of the *Ezour Veidam* refers to itself as "the Veda,"[19] it makes no attempt to rank itself among the Vedas. Moreover, the text clearly presents itself as a commentary; its original title (*Zozur Bedo*) was not included as one of the original Vedas identified by Ellis.[20]

The editor of the *Ezour Veidam*, the Baron de Sainte Croix, did not present it as one of the four Vedas,[21] but offered it as the first original Sanskrit text published on religious and philosophical dogma. He did believe, however, that the *Ezour Veidam*'s scriptural citations were authentic. Sainte Croix also believed that Vedic fragments were extant in the form of the Purāṇas, which communicated the substance of the Veda without its tiring and nauseating extravagances.[22] Sainte Croix also maintained that the four Vedas were lost.[23] Given the large fees offered by the West for their retrieval and the mendacity of Brahmins, Sainte Croix felt that they would have long since fallen into missionary hands had they still existed.[24]

It was upon its arrival in Europe that the confusion concerning the *Ezour Veidam*'s identity occurred. Rocher suggested that error arose due to the work's title. The *Ezour Veidam*'s reference to itself as a "Veda" should have been understood in a generic sense, as the term "Veda" is used in India by both missionaries and Indians alike. In fact, Rocher suggested that the *Ezour Veidam* did not pretend to be one of the four Vedas, but rather a Veda in the general sense of the term, a holy book. By resolving the *saṃdhi* of the *Ezour Veidam*'s original title (*Zozur Bedo*), Rocher translated the title as the "Gospel of Jesus."[25]

What the *Ezour Veidam* actually was is less significant than the use to which it was put during the Enlightenment. The Veda (in the form of the *Ezour Veidam*) allowed Voltaire and Sainte Croix to draw a distinction between what was Vedic and post-Vedic, the latter being a degenerate form of the former. Just as scripture had degenerated, so had its interpreters. A considerable portion of this early discourse surrounding the "Veda" consisted in diatribes directed against the Brahmin elite who did not instruct their people, did not themselves desire instruction,[26] were mendacious and generally corrupt. Even Diderot (under the rubric *vedam*) joined in such Brahmin-bashing when he asserted that the fourth Veda had been lost for a long time, to the regret of Brahmins who would have gained tremendous power had it still existed. Diderot further noted that the Vedas were held in such great respect by Brahmins that they did not wish to share copies of them with anyone, especially the Jesuits who had made great efforts to obtain them,

The polemic directed against the Brahmin clergy, engendered by the quest for the lost Veda, was inscribed within the narrative structure of the *Ezour Veidam* itself. That the degenerated Brahmins possessed neither their fathers' virtues nor their knowledge is clearly articulated in the character of Biache who preaches superstition. The philosopher Chumontou rejects popular theology imparted to him by Biache. The philosopher then imparts pure wisdom and supports his teaching with Vedic citations concerning the unity of God, creation, the nature of the soul, the doctrine of suffering and reward, and the proper forms of worship.[27] The text of the *Ezour Veidam*, we are told by its editor, thus emphasizes how the original theism of the Veda had degenerated into polytheism.[28]

With time, Voltaire concluded that original Vedic revelation was not to be found in the *Ezour Veidam*. His failure to discover the true Veda in the *Ezour Veidam*, however, did not deter him in his quest. Voltaire subsequently believed that the *Shastabad of Brahma* possessed real wisdom and the pure, original expression of Indian religion. This small "theological" treatise of recent date had been transmitted to Holwell who included it in his *Interesting historical events relative to the Provinces of Bengal and the Empire of Indostan*. The *Shastabad* came to supersede the *Veidam* in Voltaire's estimation.[29]

Another "source" of documentation for Voltaire was Dow's *Shaster Bedang*, a four thousand-year-old exposition of the doctrine of the "Bedas" written by the philosopher Beass Muni. Finally, Voltaire discovered a manuscript entitled the *Cormo Veidam*. He did not believe the *Cormo Veidam* was a Veda, but its opposite, a ritual manual replete with superstitious ceremonies. Voltaire deemed the *Cormo Veidam* to be a text worthy of the modern Brahmins—a ludicrous ritual "pile" of superstitions.[30] Voltaire cited the *Cormo Veidam* to show how the Veda and Brahmins had degenerated.

The Veda was never a more symbolic text than for Voltaire who, in constant search for the Sanskrit *Urtext* imbued its simulacra with characteristics tailor-made for his polemic against the pretensions and alleged crimes of the Catholic Church. His view of India, however, continued to be framed by Jesuitical ideology. While, on the one hand, India supported the contention that barbarians were more Christian than Catholics, on the other hand, they were so mired in superstition and so prey to priestly machination, they were sorely in need of salvation, of which the first step entailed conversion to the true faith. The former argument idealized all things Indian. The Indians invented art, were paragons of morality and physical perfection. They lived in a state of paradisaical innocence and sobriety. Their gentleness, respect for animal life, and deep religiosity incarnated the virtues of "Christianity" far more than anything found in the civilized West. Inversely, India mirrored the human condition in its fall from grace: untainted proto-Christianity had degenerated into superstition and abominable cultic practices. The prime actors in Vedic India's demise were the Brahmin priests. They offered Voltaire a most pregnant symbol: where in the world could he have directed his anticlerical polemics so successfully? The Brahmin priests allowed him to "*écraser l'infâme*" and, for once, the objects of his critique were not Catholic, Jesuits, or Frenchmen.

The *Ezour Veidam* supplied Voltaire with the tools to launch his attack. Its editor supported the contention that theism had degenerated into polytheism. The *Ezour Veidam*'s speculation concerning the origin of world civilization concluded with the judgment that the Indian Aryans taught the Hebrews their religion. The aim of this argument, given the *Ezour Veidam*'s role as a work of Catholic propaganda, is clear. In arguing the anteriority of the Indians, Voltaire questioned the authority of the Bible and in doing so contributed to the growth of historiography. Hidden behind Voltaire's ponderous polemic lie the seeds of the modern study of comparative mythology and history of religions. Voltaire tried not to depend on secondary sources and sought his documentation in a genuine text. In each case, he was deceived. He sought European accounts he felt were exempt from prejudice, only to fall prey to glaring discrimination.[31] He read those Europeans who purported to know Sanskrit but actually knew none, or had spent sufficient time in India yet were woefully ignorant of the culture.[32] With such source material, Voltaire initiated the comparative study of religion by seeking to show how we owe our rituals to the Indians.[33]

Voltaire's hostility toward the Jews was manifested in his sarcastic invective against the Old Testament and stemmed from his inability to pardon them for being the source out of which Christianity issued. However, Voltaire's discourse on the Veda was not solely directed at displacing the Jewish people. He attacked the Jews in order to attack Christianity. He stressed the wisdom of the first Brahmins in order to emphasize the ignorance of Catholic priests. He reproached Europeans for their attitude of superiority vis-à-vis India and sought to prove how Indian religion was founded upon rationality and a high standard of ethics.[34]

HERDER: THE VEDA AS ABSENT TEXT

Voltaire placed the origin of humankind in the East on the banks of the Ganges, as opposed to the account found in Genesis. Johann Gottfried Herder (1744–1803) followed Voltaire to the extent that he too sought the childhood of humanity in the East (*Auch eine Philosophie der Geschichte zur Bildung der Menschheit*, 1774). However, Herder did not, as did Voltaire, attack Christian claims to truth; only its place of origin (i.e. with the Jews) gave him pause. Thus, for Herder the Oriental origin for humanity was called into question rather than Christian revelation itself.

Herder ceded to India the locus of the cradle of humanity[35] as well as the birthplace of all languages, European as well as monosyllabic, the alphabet, sciences, and art.[36] In an early work, the *Ideen*, Herder described the Hindus as the gentlest race of man. The Indian has respect for all that is endowed with life. His nourishment is sound and his demeanor is as graceful as his spirit; he is endowed with supernatural qualities of spirit, body, and mind.[37] However, Herder did not give India the least importance in the comparative history of primitive revelation. It was as though Indian religion, since the supposed loss of the *Ṛg-Veda*, was estranged from primitive revelation and functioned only as a system of empty speculation. Herder treated Indian religion (to cite Gérard) as a *metaphysique à part*, with a certain intrinsic value but unable to stand as a system of religious thought next to Christianity or Judaism, which, after all, were the objects of his exegesis. Given the respect Herder had for India, and his recognition of the authority wielded by the absent Veda, it was not illogical for him to seek elsewhere in Indian literature the locus of revelation. And, indeed, the text he chose as emblematic of Indian thought highlighted everything that he presumed the absent Veda did not. Kālidāsa's *Śākuntala* was more valuable than all "the Vedas, Upavedas and Upangas" put together. Its poetry, undistorted by tendentious religious speculation, provided greater beauty and truth than was thought possible in Indian literature. The absent Vedas, Upavedas, and Upangas are interminable, less useful and far less agreeable than the poetry of Kālidāsa. The absent Veda blunts the spirit and character of the Indian people. Compared to Indian poetry, all those Upeknats and Bagavedams present faint notions of the Indian mentality.[38]

In Herder's mind, the Orient and the primitive world, the primitive world and nature, nature and poetry become synonymous and interchangeable. He joined the eighteenth-century belief in the anteriority of poetry to his own variation of the *bon sauvage* theme and posited an equivalence of the Orient and poetry.[39] The compiler of the *Stimmen der Völker in Liedern* also encouraged Germans to seek new inspirational models and question the absolute value of Greek classical norms. The *philosophes* and their German disciples believed that reality and, by extension, the arts were ordered in terms of universal, timeless, objective, and unalterable laws that rational investigation could discover. Their detractors believed that logic was incompatible with the force of inspiration necessary for poetic creation. Herder sought a middle ground between these diametrically opposed alternatives. He rejected the particular concept of reason propounded by Enlightenment rationalism and endeavored, rather, to interpret rationality in such a way that it was not inimical to spontaneity and vitality.

The *Fragmente, Über die neuere deutsche Literatur*, and *Abhandlung über den Ursprung der Sprache* reveal Herder's struggle with problems of the possibility of discovering a native German literature. The movement of German authors to found a German national literature developed along two distinct lines: the first consisting of a need to establish a clear criterion for assessing a work's national characteristics; the second, to create a literature unique in itself. As a corollary, this movement stimulated speculation on the nature of artistic inspiration in general. To assert that language developed from poetry and to name the Orient as the wellspring of the poetic, to raise popular songs to the level of the Classics and to declare poetic inspiration an aspect of the divine effected the Creation of a *Weltliteratur*. Moreover, it placed the Vedas on the same exalted aesthetic plane as *Parzival* and *Tristan*.

Contrary to the polygenous theory, Herder believed that all men descended from one and the same race;[40] environmental forces were responsible for different cultures[41] and languages. Language, the purest expression of the spiritual character of a national group,[42] like man himself, developed from a unique source.[43] By positioning the childhood of humanity in the Orient, Herder referred not only to the ancestors of Europeans, but also to a common origin of all humankind. With man's origin in India, it followed that Sanskrit poetry provided the source from which all poetry descended. Sanskrit poetry thus played a pivotal role in Herder's thought. Its beauty and sublimity provided an excellent argument in favor of Herder's humanistic aesthetic. The study of songs, fables, and myths of nationalities such as India[44] contributed to the development of one's national culture which, in turn, contributed to the development of humanity.[45]

Due to the West's necessarily incomplete knowledge of Sanskrit literature, Herder could cut it to measure out of the poetic presuppositions of an unpoetic age. As a result of Herder's theories and instigations, Sanskrit poetry became required reading for anyone who desired to experience "real" poetry. In Herder's thought, the *Śākuntala* possessed everything the absent Veda lacked. In fact, for Herder, Kālidāsa's *nāṭaka* assumed an importance that subsequent writers attributed to the Veda in their depiction of an "Aryan humanity." Herder chose to emphasize the *Śākuntala* for two reasons. Kālidāsa's masterpiece existed and could be read in support of romantic claims that found their germ in Herder's writings. The Veda did not exist. But, even as an absent text, Herder rejected it due to its degeneracy and superstitious beliefs.

According to Herder, the first sect, that of Brahmā, was destroyed long ago by Vaiṣṇavite and Śaivite sectarians. Its legends have come down to us only in the form of more recent interpretations. While some residue of primitive religion remain in these legends, they have been grossly distorted by superstitious belief (i.e., the aquatic origin of earth and life, the belief in a primitive egg). While quasi-biblical and quasi-Christian, Indian spirituality and morality are nevertheless afflicted with an occult malady, metempsychosis. Herder suspected what modern Indologists can prove from *Ṛg-Veda*: that the Vedic Aryans did not believe in metempsychosis. Such a belief betokened the regression of Aryan spirituality from contact with aboriginal tribes given to totemism.[46] For Herder, metempsychosis signified the illusion of sensual men who envied the fate of animals. Populations that are more evolved and happier invent a locus where their terrestrial life can be prolonged in idealized form. Not so the Indians who had degenerated since Vedic times. Their belief in metempsychosis resulted in quietism and indifference, and was disastrous on the social plane: it encouraged compassion for plants and animals rather than for people.[47]

Herder distinguished therefore two Indias: the primitive source of poetry and religion provided by the presence of the *Śākuntala* and the metaphysical thought represented by what he believed to be the contents of the absent Veda. For subjective reasons, the first alone was authentic; he rejected the second as an abberation. Nevertheless, his depiction of India as the locus of true poetry would have repercussions with the romantics. It was the task of the romantic mythologists to incorporate India within an interpretation of the Semitic-Christian religious cycle. India, at Herder's time, was still too distant and too new. However, once the Veda appeared on the literary scene, many of Herder's notions concerning language and poetry would be applied to it.

With Herder, many of the romantic theses begin to coalesce with respect to India. Already in Voltaire, we saw India as the site of a Golden Age; its religion offered a tradition older than the Bible. In India, primitive revelation had with time and under the influence of a corrupt priesthood degenerated. Monotheism had been reduced to polytheism. Upon these conceptions the romantics projected their own aesthetic concern: the desire to discover true national poetry wherever it existed. Herder proposed Sanskrit drama as the natural and national folk poetry of the ancient Aryans. Although the Veda was rarely mentioned in his lengthy discussions on Indian poetry, it was never absent as a counterpoint to Sanskrit poetry and a negative authority in his discourse.

THE ROMANTIC VEDA

Friedrich Schlegel and the Foundations of Romantic Indology

In offering a vision of India in which myth triumphed over reason, chaos stood in place of olympian calm, and the primitive impulse left system and structure scattered in its wake, Herder (at least in his Sturm und Drang period) instigated the cult of the primitive and the symbolic and, as such, was a precursor of romantic mythology. Since Herder's time, the source material on India had changed. Many more Sanskrit texts had been translated and the Asiatic Society of Bengal had published a number of groundbreaking articles. Friedrich Schlegel, a pioneer in the study of the Sanskrit language and author of the first direct translation from Sanskrit into German, maintained that mythology had been revitalized[48] and was now generally recognized as a largely untapped reservoir of poetic inspiration.[49] Since the modern Occident had no mythology he noted that "one would have to be invented."[50] The inspiration for this new mythology and, hence the new, romantic poetry was to be found in the Orient.[51] By Orient, Schlegel meant India.[52]

What the West recognized as religion, mythology, and poetry originated in the Orient. Classical Indian culture exhibited in a pure, undiluted form what, in the West, was a mere vestige of the union of philosophy and poetry. Just as one would go to Italy to learn about art, one should now go to India to learn about beginnings,[53] God, and poetry.[54] Schlegel clearly saw himself as the guide for this aesthetic and religious pilgrimage. The unique fruit of his metaphorical journey, *Über die Sprache und Weisheit der Indier* (1808), comprised, as it were, the romantic manifesto on India. However, *Über die Sprache* also discloses the difficulties that made Schlegel's dream of a philosophical and aesthetic revolution via India[55] an impossibility.[56]

This volume charts the degeneration of the land of primitive revelation into the atomistic and materialistic India that Schlegel came to discover. Although traces of divine truth could still be found in Indian philosophical systems, Schlegel came to the conclusion that they had been inextricably mixed with error. Schlegel's devaluation of Indian speculative thought prompted him to emphasize in the remaining chapters of the book the divine nature of the Sanskrit language. In fact, Schlegel maintained that the only valid inquiry into the Aryan past consisted in the science of language.[57]

Schlegel met with problems when he tried to resolve the question of the origin of language by basing his arguments on "*historische Forschung*." He erred in his insistence on linguistic polygenesis ("Von Ursprung der Sprache"), which entailed breaking languages into inflected and agglutinative groupings. The former had divine origin; the latter, animal. Using the then popular analogy of botany, Schlegel saw inflected languages as linguistic vegetation. Just as a stem, branches, and leaves develop from a plant's root, so nominal and verbal forms come from the linguistic root.[58] Schlegel postulated that German and other languages developed from Sanskrit because they possessed inflection.[59] He believed that other languages, such as Chinese and Hebrew, lack this inflection and were agglutinative by means of affixes joined to the roots.[60] Because of inflection, Sanskrit and its derivative languages were seen as living organisms, capable of penetrating intelligence.[61] Agglutinative languages were labeled mere agglomerations of atoms.[62]

This erroneous linguistic theorizing served Schlegel as a metaphorical edifice constructed to isolate Sanskrit from other languages and thereby support his belief in its perfection and divine origin. The larger plan was to salvage palatable aspects of the Divine from his abortive Indic studies. He projected onto Sanskrit what he could not find in Indian philosophy and religion. Unfortunately, the divine status he accorded to inflected Sanskrit necessitated a less than divine origin for what he perceived as the agglutinative languages. This was clearly a negative by-product rather than a motivating factor. While in the philosophical, religious, and translation sections of *Über die Sprache*, Schlegel presented India as a problematic locus of the Divine, in the linguistic chapters, India emerges as the cradle of humanity and Sanskrit the mother tongue of Indo-European languages. Language itself provides source material for the comprehension of history.[63] Through the study of the language of the ancient Indians, the most talented and wisest *Volk* of antiquity, we find the "Spuren der göttlichen Wahrheit."[64]

Original revelation, however, had long since been lost to the Indians with the loss of the Veda and the subsequent degeneration of its theological message.[65] It had been Schlegel's intention to show that as in language, so with mythology, there exists an inner structure, a fundamental texture whose similarity signifies a related origin. However, the absence of the

Veda prevented Schlegel from completing the comparative analysis of mythology, as he had done with language. Given this lacuna, his judgments had to be preliminary.[66] Nevertheless, had the Veda been available, Schlegel judged its value as limited. Of necessity, the Veda would have long since been falsified.[67]

What results from its distortion and loss? On the verge of truth, Indians fell prey to wild fiction and coarse error (''System der Seelenwanderung und Emanation''). The Veda in its imagined pure form implicitly represented this lost truth and thus had authority as an irretrievable artifact. With the absence of this source of revelation, myth, and poetry, Schlegel suggested the possibility of using a comparison of languages as an auxiliary science for historical research (''Von den ältesten Wanderung der Volker''). In the final book of the volume (''Von den indischen Kolonien und der indischen Verfassung''), he connected the seemingly disparate strands of his argument to maintain that history, religion, and mythology can be understood by their relationship to speech. Thus, Schlegel sought to use philological research rather than the mythology lost with the Veda to prove the thesis that Asia and Europe ''ein unzertrennbares Ganzes bilden.''

In *Über die Sprache*, Schlegel placed language in the foreground and developed a ''scientific'' method to be able to promote comparative linguistics and *Urgeschichte*. Having approached India in search of unity and revelation, Schlegel came away only with a faulty theory that allowed him to transform Herder's depiction of India as the cradle of humanity into the *Urheimat* of his own language and *Volk* family. Although Herder rejected the authority of an absent text and Schlegel disregarded the Veda, both thinkers developed a hermeneutic structure for viewing India and Indian texts that resonated in subsequent discussions of the Veda.

Romantic Mvthologists and the Upnekhata

Up to this point, the European discourse concerning the Veda has centered upon the authority of an absent text and its significance as an essential aporia in the emplotment of India. Voltaire, Herder, and Schlegel established this interpretive model and it was the task of romantic mythologists to incorporate a ''Veda'' into the previously established ideological edifice. With the romantic mythologists, we are still talking about an absent text. They differed from their predecessors only in the increased availability of possible ''Vedas.'' The idea of the Veda had been so clearly delineated that it was merely an issue of grafting it onto texts as they appeared.

The Heibelberg philologist Friedrich Creuzer identified the essence of the Veda[68] with Anquetil Duperron's Latin translation from a Persian rendition of the Upaniṣads, the *Oupnek 'hat* or *Upnekhata*.[69] Creuzer remarked in his autobiography that one of the reasons he delved into the history of religion was Anquetil's seeming proof of the thesis that polytheism developed from primitive monotheism.[70] In his magisterial opus, *Symbolik und Mythologie der alten Völker, besonders der Griechen*, Creuzer sought arguments in favor of Anquetil's thesis and, toward this end, India proved more fruitful than the yet undeciphered Egypt. India revealed a marvelous humanity, different in all respects from other nations.[71] Anquetil's "translation" of the "Veda" taught the most ancient religious system of the world[72] as well as an instance of authentic monotheism.[73]

At several reprises, Creuzer emphasized the issue of primitive monotheism in India.[74] The "Veda" posited Brahmā as God the Father. Its religion was older than those of Greece and Egypt. Indeed, it presented the oldest religion known to man and its language, the most organic and alive.[75] The view that the initial wisdom of the Vedas had subsequently degenerated, while a common romantic tenet, can be traced back to deism and Sturm und Drang responses to Indian speculative thought. Creuzer also held to the view that "Vedic" religion had degenerated into polytheism. The "Veda," once pure and simple, had been destroyed by the orgiastic cults to Śiva, themselves reformed by Vaiṣṇavism.[76]

The real innovation that Creuzer effected upon previous emplotments of the Veda in the West consisted in the role he ascribed to "Vedic" religion. While others touted the sublimity, purity, and antiquity of Indian speculative thought relative to the Judeo-Christian perspective, Creuzer specifically assigned it an equal position to that of the Hebrews. "Brahmaism," the primitive worship of Brahmā as articulated in the "Veda," may well have formed the basis of the Hebrews' religion. The purest cult of Jehovah, as practiced by Abraham, represented an isolated branch of old "Brahmaism."[77] With such assertions, Creuzer went further than other polemicists in deemphasizing the role of Judiasm in the history of religions. The Jews were not the only recipients of the true doctrine.[78] Schlegel's ultimate consideration of the Old Testament was called into question. For Creuzer, Israel became an equal partner with "Vedic" India.[79]

In his search for primitive religion, Creuzer departed from the Judeo-Christian tradition only to rediscover it in the *Oupnek'hat*. A decade earlier, Joseph Görres had also found primitive religion inscribed in the *Oupnek'hat*. For Görres, Christianity constituted the penultimate stage in religious evolution. The fifth and final stage consisted in a return to primitive monism.[80] Görres concluded from a wide spectrum of study that there existed in primitive times one god, religion, cult, law, and bible.[81] All prophets spoke the same language in different dialects. However, the *Urform* was to be found in India. Görres placed the cradle of humanity in Kashmir.[82] The oldest prophet, law, and cult on earth was that of Brahmā in India ("der uralte gesunkene Brahmadienst in Indien"). Subsequent objects of worship ranked as imitations of it.[83] The closer the diverse religions were to India, the more they retained a rich, pure, and living form.[84]

As others of his generation, Görres identified the "Veda" with the *Oupnek'hat*, which he took to be the oldest document known to man[85] and its religion, ***Brahmaismus***, the oldest religion.[86] Dated at 2240 B.C.E., Görres identified his "Veda" as the source from which all other myths derived.[87] The hermetic books of Egypt, a land once colonized by the Hindus, agreed with the "Veda." Görres also reduced the religion of Judea to primitive "Brahmaism" imparted by Brahmā-Abraham.[88] Once again, the center of gravity has shifted from Judea to India,[89] and the Hebrews have become a subgroup of the elected people.

Görres characterized "Vedic" ***Brahmaismus***, the religion of the Golden Age, by its innocence. It entailed simple, pure, bloodless sacrifices of fruit offerings. Such a religion could not endure on this evil earth; it weakened and became extinct; its adherents suffered persecution. Eventually, a wild orgiastic phallic worship and teaching were imposed on Vedic *Brahmaismus*.[90] The *Urreligion* thus degenerated and its pure and simple faith was reduced to the "Glauben der Menge." The naive nature myths of the "Veda" finally developed into their present lamentable form in the *Oupnek'hat*.[91] However, ***Brahmaismus*** did not disappear before it formed the basis for the Jewish faith. Not only do the Jews owe their religion to the Vedic Indians, but vestiges of what was positive in Greek thought are attributable to India. Moreover, Christians worship the Vedic Brahmā as Christ.[92]

While Herder tried to incorporate India within his exegesis of the Old Testament, Creuzer posited the equivalence of India and Judea, and Görres elevated Indian religion above Judaism. He associated other prophets (Toth, Zoroaster, Fohi, Theut, and Othin) with Brahmā (Abraham) only to the degree that their doctrines reflected those of the *Oupnek'hat*, viewed as the first, oldest, and most faithful repository of primitive revelation. Creuzer and Görres (as well as other romantic mythologists, such as Majer and Kanne) attributed the universality of myth to divine revelation. They all situated this revelation in India. But, the idea of the existence of a purely Indo-European religious community did not enter their formulations. It was Karl Ritter who developed the first features of an Indo-European primitive religion.

Ritter characterized India as the vestibule (*Vorhalle*) of Western history; it represented a *Völkerbühne*.[93] He derived a religious and cultural community from the linguistic community of European peoples grouped around ancient India.[94] Within this community, Ritter made important distinctions. The ancient Indians represented a breed apart from their successors. The European stands certainly far closer to the ancient Aryan than the modern Oriental. Most important, however, Germans are closer to the ancient Indians than to their modern neighbors.[95] Ritter, although ascribing an Indian origin to religion, did not consequently attribute Indian religious and civilizing ideas to India, but rather saw them as intrinsic to his own culture. The oldest and most important documents of humanity came to us from India. We have far more affinity with them than Greek or Christian church teaching has led us to believe.[96] There existed a direct lineage between the Aryans and the Teutons.

All myths, rituals, and *Völkergruppen* originated in India. Ritter identified the "*Buddhakult*," his term for Vedic religion with the cults to Apollo, Odin, Woden, and the like. Priestly teachings concerning metempsychosis and salvation had eroded the primitive belief in a single god of freedom and resulted in polytheism.

While religion had originated in India, it was merely individualized and localized elsewhere. Ritter reconstituted the Indian religious message of our ancestors from Persian, Hebrew, and Sanskrit documents, of which the Veda constituted the earliest document known to man.[97] Ritter discovered exactly what Schlegel had found: emanatist monotheism and metempsychosis. Whereas this discovery led Schlegel to reject Indian philosophical thought, for Ritter these dogmas formed the bridge between Old German and Sanskrit.[98]

The Veda provided the first seed and parallels to the Veda could be found in other *Volksglauben*. Ritter grounded the religious, linguistic, and racial community of Indo-Europeans in a vision of monotheistic religion originating in India. Having left Judea and traveled to India and Persia searching for arguments in favor of the Old and New Testaments, Ritter discovered a civilization, religion, and language irreducible to that of the Hebrews. Judeo-Christianity became the intruder in his as well as other romantic mythologists' schemata. Indeed, it appeared to have turned Europe from its historic path, subverting its true mission.

The historical school emphasized the national aspect of myth as popular phenomenon. This conception of myth developed throughout the nineteenth century. When the *Vedas* finally permitted one to compare diverse national mythologies, the romantic thesis, especially that of Ritter, enjoyed renewed favor. The translation of the *Ṛg-Veda* substantiated the eminence of India, proved the existence of primitive monotheism, and gave credence to the belief in the fallacy of the Greek miracle.[99] The irony was great: the fulfillment of the romantic quest eastward in the discovery of the Veda thus negated the very aesthetic and religious aspirations that animated this quest.

Nevertheless, certain mystico-linguistic speculations developed by the romantics would continue to resonate even after the appearance of the Veda and, in fact, found their legitimization in the scientific research of its editor, F. Max Müller. Müller effectively kept alive an important Romantic thesis that by the mid-nineteenth century was far from moribund—the idea of an Indo-European religious community inferred from the concept of the Indo-European linguistic community. With his edition of the *Ṛg-Veda*, one had finally discovered the source of sources.[100]

THE VEDA AS AN EDITED TEXT

> The Veda, by its language and its thoughts, supplies that distant background in its history of all the religions of the Aryan race, which was missed indeed by every careful observer, but which formerly could be supplied by guesswork only.[101]

As we have seen, the early European reception of the Veda exhibits a cultural attempt to restore one's own tradition. In a similar manner, early European Vedic scholarship also consisted of an internal conversation. The scientific era of the Veda began in 1798 with the publication of Sir William Jones' translations of extracts from the Vedas. Jones portrayed a Vedic Golden Age devoid of despotism, sati, Kali worship, and tantricism. He characterized the Vedic Indians as outgoing, nonmystical, robust beef-eaters who were socially egalitarian.[102] Skilled in arts and arms, they were happy in government, wise in legislation, and eminent in various forms of knowledge. This idealized vision introduced by Jones gained further support in the work of Colebrooke.

In the *Asiatick Researches* of 1805, Colebrooke offered an approximate idea of the contents of the Veda.[103] Brought by Governor-General Wellesley to teach Sanskrit at the College of Fort William in 1800, Colebrooke found an ideal opportunity to collate Vedic fragments residing in the college library that had been collected by Jones, Halhed, Martin, and Chambers. From this material, he concluded that Indian civilization was now in decline.[104] Western duty consisted in coming to India's aid: by interpreting India's history, Europe could help India help itself.[105] At first Colebrooke doubted whether the Vedas were extant or whether anyone was capable of reading them.[106] Polier's discovery of a purportedly complete copy dispelled Colebrooke's doubts. The Veda did, in fact, exist. Revealed by Brahmā and compiled by Vyāsa, it was divided in four parts (Rich, Yajush, Saman, Atharvan), with the Purāṇas comprising the fifth Veda. Colebrooke felt he could attest to the authenticity of the Veda, given that references in other works corresponded to its text. Moreover, Colebrooke verified many of these references himself and found sufficient grounds to argue that no forger's skill was equal to the task of fabricating large works in all branches of Sanskrit literature to agree with Vedic citations. The manner in which the Veda was read, its explanatory table of contents, and the existence of commentary would assure its survival in an unadulterated form.[107] Corroborating Jones' assertions, Colebrooke held that the worst abuses of Hinduism were absent from Vedic religion. The rituals of Vedic India as well as its social practices[108] dramatically differed from those of modem India.[109]

Colebrooke's thesis, while evidently more expert than the nonspecialist commentary, was remarkably similar to that of the Enlightenment and Romantic discourse on the Veda in its emphasis on an ideal Vedic age whose religion had degenerated through superstition and clerical abuse. Colebrooke's specific conclusions were, however, scant and uninspiring. He limited his discussion to offering his readers merely a notion of the Vedas; they were too voluminous for a complete translation, their language was obscure and they presented too little reward to the reader and the translator. They deserved to be consulted occasionally by the Oriental scholar for those few remarkable and important things found in them, however difficult to extract. Until Colebrooke's essay, European Indology focused primarily on the Classical period. While Colebrooke's essay was instrumental in introducing the Veda to Europe, it took another quarter-century to reverse this trend of European Indology.[110]

We have seen the discourse surrounding the absent Veda. How did its presence alter this emplotment? What difference did its presence make in the authority the text had in the West? How did this presence relate to the earlier reception of the absent text?

Friedrich Max Müller's *editio princeps* of the *Ṛg-Veda* codified and spread to a worldwide audience the Romantic ideology concerning the Veda. While very few Westerners would be capable of reading Müller's Sanskrit text, many came into contact with Müller's vision of Vedic India through his numerous public lectures and books on India directed toward a popular audience. Müller's edition (1849–74) is noteworthy for many reasons, not the least of which was his inclusion of Sāyaṇa's commentary. The inclusion of this medieval commentary generated a debate concerning the feasibility and accessibility of reading and interpreting the Veda. Could the Veda be read? And, ideally, by whom? Specifically, it raised the issue of the European's relation to the Veda as a text. Rudolph von Roth, who produced the first important work after Colebrooke's essay ("*Zur Literatur und Geschichte des Weda*," 1846), disparaged the need for the use of native commentaries. He noted that a "conscientious European interpreter" of the Veda may understand the Veda far better, "being in a position to search out the sense which the poets themselves have put into their hymns and utterances." Such a statement suggests just to what extent the use or rejection of Sāyaṇa's commentary reflected not only issues of translation technique, but, more interesting, ideological concerns. As we have seen, throughout the reception of the Veda in the West, even when it was not an issue of translation convention, the Veda always engendered discussions on race and ethnicity and exhibited a European attempt both to appropriate and distanciate it from anything Indian. The claim, championed particularly by Roth, that the conscientious Anglo-Saxon understood the Veda better than Sāyaṇa presupposed a common cultural heritage with the Vedic people.[111] We have charted how such a belief had been expressed at several reprises in the German reception of the Veda. The tradition was lost to the Indians in the post-Vedic period but not to the Anglo-Saxon who, no matter how far removed from the tradition, was never far removed from its vision. The German Romantics set the stage for European readers to believe that, *Sprachwissenschaft* would open doors to knowledge that would remain closed to Indians.

The *Ṛg-Veda* supplied Müller with the material by which he could discover the true nature of the Aryan *Volk*. The Veda offered "solutions to some of the greatest problems of life, and the needed corrective for the inner life of Europe."[112] While many of the hymns sound "childish and absurd,"[113] "vulgar and obscure,"[114] or "utterly unmeaning and insipid,"[115] the Veda still remains the most important document of "Aryan humanity"[116] and the first book of the "Aryan nations."[117] In fact, it was precisely what was "childish," what harkened back to the childhood of humanity, which made the Veda particularly instructive.[118]

Who comprised this "Aryan humanity" and what their characteristics were were questions which, although articulated before Müller, gained legitimacy when asked and answered by the self-proclaimed authority on the Veda. Müller identified the Aryans as "our nearest intellectual relatives,"[119] understanding these ancestors (his term *Arier*) to be the northern branch of the *Indogermanen*[120] who became the Celts, Greeks, Persians, Hindus, and Romans. At one time, they lived "together under the same roof, separate from the ancestors of the Semitic and Turanian races."[121]

Until Müller's translation, "our own" history was only gleaned through guesswork and endless, baseless speculations. Now it was available through Vedic references.[122] Whitney, not one to ignore Müller's flights of poetic fancy, mocked such passages in which Müller seemed to depict the Aryans "perched for a couple of thousand years upon some exalted post of observation, watching thence the successive departure from their ancient home of the various European tribes."[123]

> . . . the fathers of the Aryan race, the fathers of our own race, gathered together in the great temple of nature, like brothers of the same house, and looking up in adoration to the sky as the emblem of what they yearned for, a father and a god.[124]

Whitney then questioned whether Müller wrote these descriptions under the influence of paintings such as the Kaulbach in Berlin, depicting people at the foot of the ruined tower of Babel. While not a kind assessment, Whitney touched upon our very argument: Müller's entire discussion of the Veda elaborated Romantic ideological concerns.

It is to be remembered that the Romantics held that the simplicity of religious dogmas defined the original state of man and its corollaries that monotheism was anterior to polytheism and primitive revelation had progressively degenerated. Once a people has unfolded its spirit to its fullest expression—from the Romantic point of view—it has fulfilled its role in history and only "repetition" (revivals), stagnation, and decay could follow. Müller's conclusions concerning the Veda recapitulated this Romantic thesis.

Müller's unique task, as he envisioned it, was to discover the first germs of the language, religion, and mythology of "our" forefathers.[125] The Veda presented the "sharp edges of primitive thought, the delicate features of a young language, the fresh hue of unconscious poetry." These have been "washed away by the successive waves of what we call tradition, whether we look upon it as a principle of growth or decay."[126] The Veda, through its "simplicity and naturalness"[127] brings us closer to our oririns in religious thought and language.[128]

What we see still growing in the Veda, we have only encountered full grown or fast-decaying elsewhere, where mythology has become a "disease" because "its poetical intention has been forgotten."[129] The Veda is strong, original, pure, and natural; the later creations are modern and artificial.[130]

By the term "Veda," Müller always meant the *Ṛg-Veda* and he was careful to distinguish the *Ṛg* from the other Vedas, which he viewed as solely liturgical and belonging to an entirely different sphere.[131] The other Vedas, like the subsequent literature, epitomized what Müller found absent from the *Ṛg*, namely, that unfortunate religious and cultic apparatus. Consistently, Müller confirmed the Romantics' idealization of the Veda[132] as well as their contempt for the priestly caste[133] under whose influence the spontaneous and truthful revelation of the Veda became misunderstood, perverted, and absurd.[134] Müller noted that the Veda itself bore witness to this long process of decay in religious thought,[135] the ruins of faded grandeur, and the memories of noble aspirations.[136]

Müller's constant concern was to distinguish between the Vedic Aryan and the degenerate Hindu who is ineffectual as a historical being.[137] Moreover, Müller was intent to show how one could not confuse Aryans with really barbarian races, such as Africans or American Indians.[138] No matter how corrupted, the *Ṛg-Veda* was still a monument without equal.[139] The hymns of the ancient rishis were spontaneous expressions of a pure race;[140] the Veda, spontaneous poetry[141] created by simple hearts.[142] The oral composition of the Veda testifies to its natural spontaneity.[143]

Müller maintained that the study of language (comparative philology) gives us reliable results in the study of comparative mythology. Mythology would be forever unintelligible without a knowledge of languages, especially grammar and the phonetic law of languages.[144] Similarly, without the study of language and without comparative philology, Müller asserted that there can be no adequate study of religion. In fact, Müller used the same system of classification for the study of language as he used for mythology and religion. From the discovery of linguistic relationships between Indo-European nations, he sought an etymological interpretation of mythology.[145] Just as language began as monosyllabic and developed agglutination and inflection, so did monotheism precede polytheism.[146]

One can see a pattern to Müller's classifications. The process always moves from the material to the immaterial, the concrete to the abstract, simple to complex, single to general in language, gods, and mythology. By placing mythology and polytheism at the door of language, Müller continued a tradition begun by Schlegel. Just as Müller's reception of the Veda mirrors the Romantic view of India as the seat of true poetry, primitive revelation, and the site of its degeneration, so too does one find vestiges of Romantic linguistics in his science of language.

Until the deciphering of the Veda, there had been "but one oasis in that vast desert of ancient Asiatic history, the history of the Jews." The Veda now offers another such oasis[147] as well as another instance, of revelation,[148] the wisdom of Him who is not the God of the Jews alone.[149] It was only with the passage of time that Müller distanced himself from the misuse of such formulations by racial theorists,[150] most notably in his *Antrittsrede* at the University of Strassburg in 1872. Here, Müller articulated the distinction between linguistic and racial classification. He noted that there were only Aryan and Semitic linguistic families, but no Aryan race, blood, or skulls. In other words, he firmly stated that you cannot base ethnological classification on linguistic and anthropological terms.[151] Müller eventually became defensive. He ultimately did not speak of races and *Völkern*, rather "the Aryan family " "Aryan humanity," and "the civilization of the Aryan race, that race to which we and all the greatest nations of the world . . . belong."[152]

However, Müller's myth of the Aryan throughout the thirty odd years of editing the *Ṛg-Veda* entailed the very type of categorical mixing that he condemned in the Strassburg lecture. How do we explain this paradox? I have tried to show how it was far less an issue of Müller's blindness toward his methodology than his adherence to a Romantic emplotment of India. His need to construct the Vedic Aryan from the text and identify with this Aryan stemmed from religious and aesthetic concerns far more akin to the aims of Romanticism than nineteenth-century race theory. As a worthy heir to his father, the German Romantic poet Wilhelm Müller, Max Müller represented the final avatar of Romanticism in service of linguistics. He popularized previously articulated concepts concerning the Aryan that would have serious repercussions.

CONCLUDING REMARKS

Let us remember the date of Müller's *Ṛg-Veda*. Rather than have it begin our examination of the reception of the Veda in the West, we have allowed it to mark the conclusion of our inquiry. The Veda as a "real" text was unknown to the authors we have discussed. Nevertheless, we have shown how prominent a role the Veda played in pre-Romantic and Romantic literary and philosophical speculation. As an absent text, it wielded great authority. Although neither discovered nor fully translated, the Veda served as an important tool in formulating European discourse concerning literature and religion. The possibility of the existence of the Veda effected a renewed interest in the Romantic theses of a revealed and primitive monotheism and the degenerescence of Greek culture. What the Romantics sought in India was not Indo-European religion, but an argument in favor of Judeo-Christianity. The development of the concept of an Aryan religion proved to be a consequence, rather than the goal of the Romantic metaphorical journey to the East.

The Romantics, whose origins can be traced to pre-Romanticism and Herder, sought in the Veda a religious and national poetry. By "national," they meant indigenous and popular and the Veda, in particular, permitted comparison with an ultimately diverse national mythology. As the publication of the Veda marks the birth of Indology, the philological, historical, and religious studies of ancient India, its appearance in print should have announced the death of Romantic Indomania. However, one is surprised by the similarity between Müller's exegesis and the critical discussion of the Veda that preceded his work. When juxtaposed to the Enlightenment, Sturm und Drang, and Romantic emplotment of the Veda, Müller's commentary of the Sanskrit text and its medieval native commentary revivifies (with the aid of "science") those very Romantic yearnings believed dormant.

The Romantic concepts of the degeneration of primitive monotheism into polytheism and the view of history as an unfolding expression of the spirit of a people followed by degeneration and stagnation influenced the European intellectual climate late into the nineteenth century. Stagnation would become a keyword in characterizing Indian civilization and would eventually find its way into the general writings of philosophers like Hegel, Marx, and Spengler.[153] The *Ṛg-Veda*'s ''appearance'' in Müller's abundant commentary merely confirmed these Romantic hypotheses.

The discovery that there existed in India a tradition older than or, at least, as old as the biblical tradition was regarded as an event of the first magnitude, only to be compared in its consequences to the rediscovery of classical antiquity in the Renaissance. Through the study of India's past, it was hoped that scholars could reconstruct the history of humankind's past and origin, the development of religions and philosophies. By giving Vedic Aryans a place in universal history, a covert (and overt) displacement of the Jews was effected. Much of the discourse concerning the Veda effectively resulted in assigning the Jews a subaltern role in history. In Voltaire's case, valorizing the Vedic Indians who had been ignored by the Bible and universal histories justified his reordering of the Catholic Church's role in contemporary society, which was Voltaire's primary agenda. For others, the motivations for this displacement were less clear.

Testimony from Vedic India also allowed Europe to refute and/or denounce the Greek miracle. In India, one could discover an old civilization whose cultural riches were, in many ways, passed down to Greece. Indian religious thought could be cited to prove that ancient Greece represented a real catastrophe, a mutilation that turned man away from his true mission by replacing the cult of god with the cult of man.

Finally, the Veda provided essential information concerning the European past. Thought to be the oldest available literature of an ''Indo-Germanic'' language, the *Ṛg-Veda* promised to reveal the state of civilization closest to the supposed common ancestors of all Indo-German peoples. Specifically, certain Germans believed that the study of the old Aryans could elucidate the history and fate of the *Indo-Germanen* as a whole. One can distinguish, therefore, two motives for the beginnings of Vedic scholarship. First, there entailed the search for the oldest forms of man's religion and language. Second, it set the stage for the inquiry into the origin and past of the German people through information drawn from old Indian sources. In hindsight, it is difficult to keep in focus the historical reality of the Romantic reception of the Veda. We must acknowledge, however, that the European discourse on the absent Veda created a portrait of pure and cultivated Aryan ancestors that wielded such authority that the appearance of the text itself could not alter the welter of assumptions and fantasies that formed the canonical interpretation. This ideology of the Veda participated in the formation of a new mythology of the past. This mythology, most intensely in Germany, was fueled by irrational impulses growing out of anxiety regarding questions of national identity and mission. Themes that recur in the works of the authors we investigated found their way into the new mythology: the displacement of the Jews from a central position on the stage of history; theories regarding the degeneration of peoples and religions from unity and purity to multiplicity and polytheism; and the idealization of imaginary ancestors and their fictitious descendants.

NOTES

1. Begun in 1830 and stopped by his death at the age of thiry-two, Rosen completed the translation of the first *aṣṭaka* (one eighth). A. H. L. Heeren (*Quarterly Review*, 14:6) cited in Adelung, *Historical Sketch of Sanskrit Literature*, 73: "his specimen is but of limited extent" yet sufficient to give insight into the language, poetry, and contents of the Vedas.

2. Renou, "Le Destin du Véda dans l'Inde," 1.

3. Voltaire, *Essai*, 2:318.

4. Ibid., 1:229, 231; 1:60; 1:234.

5. This discussion can be found in the two letters of P. Bouchet to Huet.

6. Voltaire, *Essai*, 1:235–37.

7. Sir Alexander Johnston (1775–1849) found a copy of the *Ezour Veidam* in Pondicherry along with other manuscripts similar in format. Guided by Johnston's discovery, Francis Whyte Ellis wrote an important analysis of this trove in *Asiatick Researches* (1822:1–59). Ellis identified these manuscripts as imitations (written in Sanskrit with Roman characters and in French) of the three other "Vedas" and concluded that the *Ezour Veidam* was authored by the Italian Jesuit Roberto De Nobili. Ellis did not charge De Nobili as the perpetrator of the forgery; he attributed that act to another who must have edited, transcribed, and translated the Sanskrit text into French. Ellis agreed with Sonnerat's contention that the *Ezour Veidam* was written for converting idolators.

Ellis had made several significant comments concerning the style of the *Ezour Veidam*. He noted that the French was loose, defective, and not at all stylistically consistent with what he learned about the Vedas from Colebrooke's article on the style and contents of the Vedas, which appeared in the *Asiatick Researches* (1805:369–476). Ellis judged its style to be rather purāṇic or similar to the dialogue of the *Bhagavad Gītā*, texts with which the Jesuits were familiar. Most important, Ellis noted the existence of marginal notes, which did not correspond to the text in the original or in translation. This seemingly minor point, disregarded in all subsequent discussions on the *Ezour Veidam*, proves pivotal to Ludo Rocher's recent monograph which, to my mind, lays to rest the mystery surrounding the *Ezour Veidam* fraud.

Rocher examines the manner in which the manuscript came to Europe, possibilities as to its authorship, and the reason for which it was composed. Rocher rejects De Nobili as author of the work (*Ezourvedam*, 30–42). Since the *Ezour Veidam* was written entirely in French without the facing Sanskrit translation found in other Pondicherry manuscripts, Rocher concludes that the French text constitutes the original. Due to certain idiomatic French expressions, concepts totally European in nature, the consistent lack of orthographic unity, and transliterations typical to the French language, Rocher speculates that its author was a Frenchman who had learned Sanskrit from various people in different regions of India.

8. Letter of Oct. 21, 1769, to Michel Ange André Le Roux Deshauterayes, in *Voltaire's Correspondence*, 44:254.

9. Letters of Feb. 22, 1761, to François Achard Joumard Tison, Marquis d'Argence, and July 13, 1761, to Jean Capperonnier, in *Voltaire's Correspondence*, 45:170; 46:117.

10. Letter of Oct. 1, 1761 to Jacob Vernes, in *Voltaire's Correspondence*, 47:72.

11. Letter of March 3, 1761, to the *Journal encyclopédique*, in *Voltaire's Correspondence*, 45:195; see also July 13, 1761.

12. See *Voltaire's Correspondence*, Oct. 21, 1760.

13. Voltaire, *Essai*, 1:236 This revised interpretation of Indian speculative thought, documented by the *Ezour Veidam*, appeared in the 1761 edition of the *Essai*.

14. Ibid., 2:405–6.

15. *Ezour Veidam*, 1:156. See also Voltaire, *Essai*, "Des Brachmanes, du Veidam et de L'Ezour-Veidam," 1:237–45.

16. Voltaire, *Essai*, 1:240–42.

17. Schwab, *La renaissance orientale*, 166–68.

18. See Rocher, *Ezourvedam*, 24.

19. *Ezour Veidam*, 203.

20. Ibid., 200. Ellis identified the third manuscript of the Pondicherry corpus as the *Yajur-Veda*, debunking the theory that the title *Ezour Veidam* was a misnomer for the *Yajur-Veda*.

21. Ibid., 116. Sonnerat (*Vovage aux Indes orientales*, 1:7) and Paulinus, a Sancto Bartholomaeo, had attacked its authenticity (*Systema Brahmanicum*, 315–7).

22. *Ezour Veidam*, 126. He noted that Europe possessed an exemplary Purāṇa in the *Bagavadam*.

23. Moreover, the Shasters are not to be confused with the Vedas; they are commentaries of the Veda (*Ezour Veidam*, 130).

24. *Ezour Veidam*, 109–10.

25. As further proof of his theory, Rocher relied on the curious manner in which the *Ezour Veidam* concluded:

Fin de l'Ezour Veidam

Jesus Maria Joseph

26. Voltaire, *Essai*, 1:243–44.

27. *Ezour Veidam*, 150.

28. Ibid., 13.

29. Voltaire dated it as exactly 4,666 years old.

30. Voltaire, *Essai*, 1:242–43.

31. By avoiding the prejudice perpetrated by the Jesuits, he fell prey to documentation slanted by Protestant anti-Catholic rhetoric, as in the case of La Croze and Niecamp.

32. Dow and Howell knew no Sanskrit and Anquetil Duperron was surprisingly duped by the *Ezour Veidam*.

33. The *Ezour Veidam* speaks of baptism, the immortality of the soul, metempsychosis, the identity of Abraham with Brahm (*sic*), and of Adam and Eve with Adimo and Procriti. The description of the creation of angels found in Holwell's *Shasta* prefigures the biblical account of Lucifer.

34. Voltaire, *Essai*, 1:55ff.

35. Herder, *Sämtliche Werke*, 13:38, 399 403, 406–13. For India as the site of Eden, see 13:432–3.

36. Ibid., 13:407–8, 411.

37. Ibid., 14.32, 73–74, 222, 225–6.

38. Herder, *Zerstreute Blätter*, 91: ''Werden Sie nicht vielmehr mit mir wünschen, dass statt ihrer unendlichen Religionsbücher der Weda's Upaweda's, Upanga's u.s.f. man uns mit nützlichern und angenehmern Schriften der Indier, vor allen ihren besten Poesien in jeder Art beschenke? Diese machen uns den Geist und Charakter des Volks am meisten lebendig, wie ich denn gern bekenne, aus der einzigen Sakontala mehr wahre und lebendige Begriffe von der Denkart der Indier erlangt zu haben, als aus allen ihren Upeknats und Bagawedams.''

39. Herder, *Sämtliche Werke*, 5:50; 1:32.

40. Ibid., 13:252, 405; 5:447.

41. Ibid., 5:539.

42. Ibid., 17:58–9.

43. Ibid., 30:8.

44. Ibid., 16:13; 4:357, 425; 5:214; 8:208; 11:247.

45. Herder defined *Humanität* as the sum of the virtues and talents peculiar to man, that is to say it was the divine in man. See ibid., 13:350; 14:230.

46. Ibid., 16:78.

47. Metempsychosis led to caste rules and the inhumanity directed to pariahs and suttees (ibid., 14:31).

48. Schlegel, *Seine prosaische Jugendschriften*, 1:136.

49. Schlegel, *Sämtliche Werke*, 4:174.

50. Ibid., 4:197.

51. Schlegel, *Seine prosaischen Jugendschriften*, 2:362.
52. Ibid., 2:357ff.
53. Schlegel, *Kritische-Friedrich-Schlegel-Ausgabe*, 7:261, 263.
54. Ibid., 7:74.
55. Schlegel, *Sämtliche Werke*, 7:39,40.
56. Figueira, ''Politics of Exoticism,'' 427–29.
57. Traditional methods sought to demonstrate the superiority of one language over another, that is, to distinguish languages from each other by superficial differences, and to view such differences as manifestations of the diverse national genius of individual populations. Not relying upon superficial similarities among Greek, Latin, German, Persian, and Sanskrit roots that the standard methodology would have emphasized, Schlegel sought, by analyzing grammatical structures, conjugations, and declensions, a criterion for the relationship between languages in morphological comparison.
58. Schlegel, *Über die Sprache*, 41–59, 65–70.
59. Ibid., 3, 35–36, 71, 62, 66.
60. Ibid., 33, 44ff., 48, 50ff.
61. Ibid., 68–69.
62. Ibid., 51. Timpararo sees the problem of monogenesis and polygenesis of languages as having consequences for the debate on monogenesis and polygenesis of the human race and its racist beliefs.
63. Schlegel, *Kritische-Friedrich-Schlegel-Ausgabe*, 257.
64. Ibid., 209.
65. Ibid., 207.
66. Ibid., 172–73, 199, 235.
67. Ibid., 251.
68. As he understood it from Colebrooke, ''On the VEDAS.''
69. Creuzer, *Symbolik*, 1:551, 554: ''Es ist nämlich dieses Werk (die Upnekhata) eine offenbare Übersetzung des Veda's. . .Vergleichen wir aber das, was diese Upnekhata, wo durch uns also die ältesten indischen Quellen vermittelt worden sind, enthält, mit dem, was uns die englischen Forscher bis jezt aus den Vedas gegeben haben, so können wir wohl sagen: es ist in dem Veda's das älteste Religionssystem auf Erden enthalten, und es möchte nicht leicht ein Volk seyn, das ältere Religionsurkunden augzuweisen hätte, als die Indischen sind.''
70. Creuzer, *Aus dem Leben eines alten Professors*, 65.
71. Creuzer, *Symbolik*, 1:539.
72. Creuzer dates the Veda from 4900 B.C.E.
73. Creuzer, *Symbolik*, 1:546–47.
74. Ibid., 1:569, 586, 642.
75. Ibid., 1:569, 544, 570, 548.
76. Ibid., 1:576.

77. Ibid., 1:570.

78. Ibid., 2:375–76.

79. Ibid., 1:375. "dass man nämlich nicht zu einsichtig das Volk Israels als alleinigen Inhaber jener wahreren Gotteslehre denken müsse."

80. Görres, *Mythengeschichte*, 1:xxxvi–324.

81. Ibid., 1:13–14; 2:649.

82. Ibid., 1:37–40.

83. Ibid., 2:611. Among these, Görres cites Kneph in Thebes, Bal in Chaldea, Ormuz in Persia, Changti in China, Ouranos in the West, and Odin in the North.

84. Ibid., 1:54.

85. Ibid., 1:117–19: "Das erste die Darstellung dieser alten Lehre, wie sie das Oupnekhat enthält, wenn wir sie verglichen mit dem was uns aus andern indischen Büchern und den Fragmenten der Reisebeschreibern über die Lehre der Vedams Kund geworden ist, dann wird uns kein Zweifel an die Indentität beider übrig bleiben." See also 1:129–41.

86. Ibid., 1:569. See also 1:xi: "Von jenem Grundsatz bin ich ausgegangen, mit dieser Kritik habe ich die Urkunden jener Zeit angesehen, und gleich anfangs hat sich mir die Ueberzeugung aufgedrungen, und während der ganzen Arbeit sich behauptet, dass von allen keine in Rücksicht auf Alterthümlichkeit und die treue des Natursinns an die Vedas der Indier reicht. Auf das Upnekhata, und die im Verlaufe der Untersuchung bewähre Voraussetzung, dass in ihm ein treuer Auszug der Vedas gegeben sei."

87. Ibid., 1:xiii.

88. Ibid., 2:329, 435–6, 556.

89. Ibid., 1:xxxiv–xxxvi, see Gérard, *L'Orient*, 184–5.

90. Ibid., 1:570–1, 576.

91. Ibid., 1:590, 593.

92. Ibid., 1.571.

93. Ibid., 1:33.

94. Ritter, *Die Vorhalle*, i–xix; 1–479, see Gérard, *L'Orient,* 192.

95. Ibid., 23.

96. Ibid., 33–34.

97. Ibid., 24–25, 27, 30, 32–33.

98. Ibid., 23–24, 26.

99. Creuzer, *Symbolik*, 2:376.

100. In this regard, see Burnouf, *Commentaire sur le Yasna* (1833); Kuhn, *Image of Aryan Civilization before the Separation of Peoples* (1845); Coulanges, *Cité antique* (1864).

101. Müller, *Chips from a German Workshop*, 1:25.

102. Kopf, *British Orientalism and the Bengal Renaissance*, 41.

103. Colebrooke, "On the VEDAS," 377–497.

104. Müller, *Miscellaneous Essays*, 1:3.

105. Ibid., 1:2.

106. Colebrooke, "On the VEDAS," 377.

107. Ibid., 480.

108. Colebrooke, "Enumeration of the Indian Classes," 33–67.

109. Colebrooke, "On the Duties of a Faithful Hindu Widow," 209–19.

110. In addition to Rosen's *Rig-Vedae Specimen* (1830) and translation of the first *aṣṭaka* of the text with a Latin translation and notes, other translations and excerpts of the Vedas appeared roughly simultaneously with Müller's edition: the Stevenson edition of the *Sāma-Veda* was brought to press by Wilson in 1843, Roth's *Contributions to the History and Literature of the Veda* (1846); Weber's *Vājasaneyi-Sanhitae Specimen* (1845), followed by the beginning of an edition of the White Yajus text (1852), its Brāhmaṇas (1855) and Sūtras (1859); Benfey's *Sāma-Veda* text with translation and glossary (1848); Whitney's and Roth's text with translation and glossary (1848); Whitney's and Roth's *Atharva-Veda* (1856). When W. D. Whitney noted the various translations and editions of the various Vedas, he relegates his notation of the *Ṛg-Veda* to a footnote and omits Müller's name from the textual citation. See Whitney, *Oriental and Linguistic Studies*, 1:3.

111. See H. Tull, "F. Max Müller and A.B. Keith," 40. The American Whitney voiced similar sentiments when he noted that "The conditions and manners depicted in (the *Ṛg-Veda*) are. . .of a character which seems almost more Indo-European than Indian." He maintained that European Indologists command the Sanskrit idiom more thoroughly than brahmins who have been trained in it since boyhood. See Whitney, *Oriental and Linguistic Stadies*, 1:112.

112. Müller, *India, What Can It Teach Us?* 6.

113. Müller, *Auld Lang Syne*, 282.

114. Müller, *Rig Veda Saṃhitā*, 3:xliii.

115. Müller, *Chips from a German Workshop*, 1:37.

116. Müller, *India, What Can It Teach Us?* 97.

117. Müller, *Chips from a German Workshop*, 1:67.

118. Müller, *India, What Can It Teach Us?* 97.

119. Ibid., 15. See also *Chips from a German Workshop*, 1:63.

120. For the history of the concept *Arier*, see Römer, *Sprachwissenschaft und Rassenideologie in Deutschland*, 65–66.

121. Müller, *Chips from a German Workshop*, 1:63–64, 66.

122. Ibid., 1:4, 62.

123. Whitney, *Oriental and Linguistic Studies*, 1:95–96.

124. Müller, *Chips from a German Workshop*, 4:210.

125. Müller, *History of Ancient Sanskrit Literature*, 3.

126. Müller, *Ṛg Veda Saṃhitā*, 3:xiii.

127. Müller, *Auld Lang Syne*, 188.

128. Ibid., 212.

129. Müller, *Chips from a German Workshop*, 2:12; 5:90.

130. The Brāhmaṇas consist of "twaddle, and what is worse, theological twaddle" (*Chips from a German Workshop*, 1:113). They deserve to be studied as a physician studies the twaddle of idiots and the ravings of mad men (*History of Ancient Sanskrit Literature*, 389). See also *Chips from a German Workshop*, 1:88–89, 67.

131. Müller, *Chips from a German Workshop*, 1:72.

132. Müller, *History of Ancient Sanskrit Literature*, 12–15.

133. Müller, *Chips from a German Workshop*, 2:19.

134. Müller, *Auld Lang Syne*, 282.

135. Müller, *Auld Lang Syne*, 281; *Chips from a German Workshop*, 1:54; see also *History of Ancient Sanskrit Literature*, 456, where Müller notes that the signs of degeneration could be seen as early as the mantra period of the late hymns, when "a spirit was at work in the literature of India, no longer creative, free and original, but living only on the heritage of a former age, collecting, classifying and imitating."

136. Müller, *History of Ancient Sanskrit Literature*, 389.

137. Müller, *Chips from a German Workshop*, 1:65.

138. Müller, *History of Ancient Sanskrit Literature*, 558.

139. Müller, *Auld Lang Syne*, 281–82.

140. Müller, *History of Ancient Sanskrit Literature*, 526.

141. Müller, *Chips from a German Workshop*, 1:16.

142. Ibid., 1:71.

143. Müller, *History of Ancient Sanskrit Literature*, 498.

144. Müller, *Contributions to the Science of Mythology*, 1:3–12, 18–19.

145. Ibid., 1:178–80. Whitney correctly pointed out the flaw in deriving from changes of meaning of two words conclusions respecting races. He noted that this method did not entail a very good form of science (Whitney, *Oriental and Linguistic Studies*, 1:258). Comparative mythology could not be viewed as a branch of linguistics (ibid., 1:261).

146. Müller, *History of Ancient Sanskrit Literature*, 510–12, 528, 559; see also *India, What Can It Teach Us?* 143, 146. This thesis was refuted by Whitney, *Oriental and Linguistic Studies*, 1:91, 92, 94; 2:132.

147. Müller, *Chips from a German Workshop*, 1:5.

148. Ibid., 1:17.

149. Müller, *History of Ancient Sanskrit Literature*, 3.

150. Müller, *Essays*, 4:103–27.

151. Müller, *Über die Resultate der Sprachwissenschaft*, 17.

152. Müller, *India, What Can It Teach Us?* 116.

153. This notion of stagnation of Indian civilizations might explain the absence of the study of Indian history outside of ancient India; specifically in Germany, it has been postulated as the rationale behind the Western institutional disregard for Indian philosophy. See Halbfass, *India and Europe.*

REFERENCES

Adelung, J. C.

1832 *An Historical Sketch of Sanskrit Literature*. Oxford: D. A. Talboys.

Colebrooke, H. T.

1798 "Enumeration of the Indian Classes." *Asiatick Researches* 5:33–67.

1795 "On the Duties of a Faithful Hindu Widow." *Asiatick Researches* 4:209–19.

1805 "On the VEDAS or SACRED WRITINGS of the Hindus." *Asiatick Researches* 8:377–497.

Creuzer, Georg Frederick

1840 *Aus dem Leben eines alten Professors*. Heidelberg, Leipzig and Darmstadt: C. W. Leske.

1819–23 *Symbolik und Mythologie der alten Völker.* 6 vols. Leipzig and Darmstadt: Heyer und Leske.

Dow, Alexander

1772 *The History of Hindostan from the earliest account of time to the death of Akbar (. . .) with a dissertation concerning the Religion and Philosophy of the Brahmins*. London: Printed for Vernor and Hood.

Ellis, Francis Whyte

1822 "An Account of a Discovery of a Modern Imitation of the Vedas with Remarks on the Genuine Works." *Asiatick Researches* 14:1–59.

Figueira, Dorothy

1989 "The Politics of Exoticism: Friedrich Schlegel's Metaphorical Journey to India." *Monatshefte* 81(4):425–33.

Gérard, René

1963 *L'Orient et la pensée romantique allemande.* Paris: Didier.

Görres, Joseph

1810 *Mythengeschichte der asiatischen Welt*. Heidelberg: Mohr und Zimmer.

Halbfass, Wilhelm
1988 *India and Europe.* Albany: State University of New York Press.

Herder, J. G.
1877–1913 *Sämtliche Werke,* ed. B. Suphan. 33 vols. Berlin: Weidmannsche Buchhandlung.
1786–92 *Zerstreute Blätter.* Gotha: C. W. Ettinger.

Holwell, John Zephaniah
1766 *Interesting historical events relative to the Provinces of Bengal and the Empire of Indostan...As also the Mythology and Cosmogony, Fasts and Festivals of the Gentoos, followers of the Shastah, and a Dissertation on the Metamorphosis, commonly though erroneously called the Pythagorean doctrine.* London: n.p.

Kopf, David
1969 *British Orientalism and the Bengal Renaissance.* Berkeley: University of California Press.

Müller, F. Max
1909 *Auld Lang Syne.* New York: Charles Scribner's Sons.
1895 *Chips from a German Workshop.* 5 vols. New York: Charles Scribner's Sons.
1897 *Contributions to the Science of Mythology.* 2 vols. New York: Longmans, Green.
1837 "Discourse at the Royal Asiatick Society of Great Britain and Ireland." *Miscellaneous Essays.* 2 vols. London: William H. Allen.
1869–76 *Essays.* 4 vols. Leipzig: W. Englemann.
1978 *History of Ancient Sanskrit Literature so far as it illustrates the primitive religion of the Brahmans.* New York: AMS Press.
1892 *India, What Can It Teach Us?* London: Longmans, Green.
1891 "Lectures on the Origin and Growth of Religion as Illustrated by the Religions of India." *The Hibbert Lectures.* London: Longmans, Green.
1849–74 *Ṛg-Veda Saṃhitā: The Sacred Hymns of the Brahmins.* 6 vols. Preface to the 3d vol. of the 1st ed. London: William H. Allen.
1978 *The Science of Language: Founded on Lectures Delivered at the Royal Institution in 1861 and 1863.* New York: AMS Press.
1872 *Über die Resultate der Sprachwissenschaft. Vorlesungen gehalten in der kaislerlichen Universität zu Strassburg am xxiii. ami MDCCCLXXII.* Strassburg: K. J. Trübner.

Paulinus, a Sancto Bartholomaeo
1791 *Systema Brahmanicum, Liturgicum, Mythologicum, civile ex monumentis Indicis, Musei Borgiani Velitris dissertationibus historico-criticis illustravit.* Rome: Antonio Fulgoni.

Renou, Louis
1960 "Le Destin du Véda dans L'Inde." *Etudes védiques et paninéennes.* Vol. 6. Paris: De Boccard.

Ritter, Carl
1820 *Die Vorhalle der europäischen Völkergeschichte vor Herodots, um den Kaukasus und an den Gestaden des Pontus. Eine Abhandlung zur Alterthumskunde.* Berlin: G. Reimer.

Rocher, Ludo
1984 *Ezourvedam: A French Veda of the 18th Century.* Amsterdam and Philadelphia: John Benjamins.
1978 "Max Müller and the Veda." *Mélanges Armand Abel*, ed. A. Destrée, vol. 3. Leiden: Brill.

Römer, Ruth
1985 *Sprachwissenschaft und Rassenideologie in Deutschland.* Munich: Wilhelm Fink.

Sainte-Croix, Guillaume Emmanuel Joseph Guilhem de Clermont Lodève, Baron de, ed.
1778 *L'Ezour Veidam ou ancien commentaire du Veidam contenant l'exposition des opinions religieuses & philosophiques des Indiens. Traduit du Samscretan par un Brame. Revu et publié avec des observations préliminaires, des notes & des èclaircisssemens.* 2 vols. Yverdon: De Felice.

Schlegel, Friedrich
1966 Kritische-Friedrich-Schlegel-Ausgabe, ed. Ernst Behler. 24 vols. Munich: Ferdinand Schöningh.
1846 *Sämtliche Werke.* 15 vols. Vienna: I. Klang.
1906 *Seine prosaische Jugendschriften, 1792–1802*, ed. Jakob Minor. 2 vols. Vienna: C. Konegan.
1977 *Über die Sprache und Weisheit der Indier*, ed. S. Timpararo. Amsterdam: John Benjamins.

Schwab, Raymond
1950 *La renaissance orientale.* Paris: Payot.

Smith, Brian
1989 *Reflections on Resemblance, Ritual and Religion.* New York: Oxford University Press.

Sonnerat, Pierre

1782 *Voyage aux Indies orientales et à la Chine.* 2 vols. Paris: the Author.

Tull, Herman W.

1991 "F. Max Müller and A. B. Keith—Orientalism versus Indology—Twaddle, the Stupid Myth, and the Disease of Indology." *Numen: International Review for the History of Religions* 38(1):27–58.

Voltaire, François-Marie Arouet de

1963 *Essai sur les moeurs et l'esprit des nations.* 2 vols. Paris: Garnier Frères.

1953–65 *Voltaire's Correspondence,* ed. Theodore Besterman. Geneva: Institut et Musée Voltaire.

Whitney, W. D.

1987 *Oriental and Linguistic Studies.* 2 vols. Delhi: Sri Satguru.

8

From Interpretation to Reform

Dayānand's Reading of the Vedas

JOHN E. LLEWELLYN

DEBATE OVER THE INTERPRETATION of the Vedic canon did not die out in the classical period, but continues to the present. Among modern interpreters of the Vedas one of the most important was Swami Dayānand Sarasvatī (1824–83). As is well known, Dayānand was the founder of the Ārya Samāj, a Hindu revivalist organization that advocates religious and social reform on the basis of an appeal to the Vedas. Dayānand developed a new understanding of the Vedas, making those books the foundation of the living religion of millions of Hindus. This chapter is dedicated to analyzing Dayānand's reinterpretation of the Vedic canon.[1]

We will be particularly concerned with the strategies that Swami Dayānand used to universalize the canon. The most obvious way in which Dayānand did this was by making the Vedas available to a large audience of people who did not have access to them previously. Along with this transformation in the canon's readership, Dayānand also developed original ideas about what the canon is and what it means. Dayānand argued that the term "Veda" should only be applied to the most ancient strata of canonical literature, the Saṃhitās, and not to the Brāhmaṇas, Āraṇyakas, and Upaniṣads.[2] In this way Dayānand dramatically reduced the corpus of texts that one must know to be a master of the canon. Dayānand also simplified the interpretation of the Vedas in a number of ways. One of his most important and innovative ideas concerned Vedic theology. Dayānand was a monotheist, and he argued that the many divine names in the Vedas refer to various aspects of the one God, not to many different gods and goddesses (which is how the Vedas have been generally understood).[3] By this argument Swami Dayānand eliminated the complicated pantheon that usually accompanies Vedic commentary, thus, in his mind, making the canon more accessible.

There are several works that the reader can consult for information about Swami Dayānand. For the early Ārya Samāj, including the historical context in which the movement developed, Kenneth Jones' *Arya Dharm* is helpful. Yet Jones is a social historian of British India, not a Vedicist. In the chapter-long discussion of Dayānand's life and work there are only a few pages on his reinterpretation of the Vedas. J. T. F. Jordens gives more serious attention to the development of Dayānand's religious thought in *Dayānand Sarasvatī: His Life and Ideas*. Those interested in Dayānand's understanding of the Vedic canon must do some work to put things together, however, since the biography is organized chronologically. Still, Jordens' book is important for any scholar trying to probe Swami Dayānand's reading of the Vedas. Most students of the religions of South Asia probably identify Dayānand with the notion that the Vedas are the sole source of absolute religious truth, unaware that this is a position that he came to only relatively late in his life. A study of Dayānand's intellectual odyssey reveals a much more complex figure than his later detractors or defenders would be willing to admit.

While Swami Dayānand has attracted the attention of some students of the modern South Asia religious scene, he has received much less kind treatment from scholars whose research has concentrated on the Vedas. The comments of the great French Vedicist Louis Renou are typical in this regard. In his book *The Destiny of the Veda in India*, which is supposed to be about the place of the Vedas in later Hinduism, Renou devotes all of one sentence to the Ārya Samāj, dismissing Dayānand's reading of the Vedas as "a vigorous (and from our point of view, extremely aberrant) interpretation."[4] This chapter is based on the assumption that Dayānand's influential interpretation of the Vedas is deserving of serious consideration, Renou's criticism notwithstanding. The focus here will not be on Dayānand's mature theories about the Vedas, with which the Indologist will be well acquainted, but on the development of those theories. Before that work is undertaken, something more general must be said about the role of the Vedic canon in Hinduism.

THE CANON AND J. Z. SMITH

In "Sacred Persistence: Toward a Redescription of Canon" Jonathan Z. Smith invites historians of religion to return to the issue of canon. He proposes that the formulation and use of canons in religion are marked by limitation and ingenuity. First, a religious community chooses one body of texts (or other material) that will have a special status. Then it goes on to overcome this seemingly arbitrary self-limitation by constantly reinterpreting the canon. Smith suggests an analogy with cuisine. Out of the universe of things that can be eaten, each culture selects some items and rules out others. But then considerable ingenuity is invested in developing a number of different ways to prepare the chosen food in order to avoid the monotony that follows from a limited canon of edible things.

Smith's model of limitation and ingenuity is a useful heuristic for thinking about the history of the canon in the religions of South Asia. Since the classical period orthodox Hindus have accepted the authority of the Vedic canon. In fact, assent to that authority has defined orthodoxy. The boundary of Hinduism has not been charted theologically; indeed the tradition has included a diversity of opinions about theology. Rather, in Hinduism the measure of orthodoxy has been acceptance of the authority of the Vedas, of the rituals in which they are used, and of the priests whose vocation it was to teach those texts and perform those rituals. The Vedas are the shibboleth that has been used to distinguish "true" Hindus from others.

It is because of this eternal return to the Vedas that Brian Smith has defined Hinduism as "the religion of those humans who create, perpetuate, and transform traditions with legitimizing reference to the authority of the Veda."[5] At first this definition seems outrageous, since it is true today and probably has always been true that most Hindus do not actually know much about what the Vedas say. Yet Smith demonstrates that many different Hindu religious works take pains to express that they are consistent with the Vedas. Then again the acknowledgment of the authority of the Vedas is often a part of a strategy by which the Vedas are practically superseded. The *Bhāgavata Purāṇa*, for example, claims to contain the essence of the Vedas, as Frederick Smith's chapter in this volume points out. The text implies that one need not study the Vedas, since the truth they express is more readily available in the *Bhāgavata Purāṇa*.

Yet the Hindu tradition has remained innovative, despite the apparently limiting choice of one corpus of texts as a canon.[6] There have been occasions when a Hindu scholar has written a commentary on a Vedic work to demonstrate that new religious ideas are grounded in the Vedas. But more often than not original Hindu thinkers have limited their ingenuity to developing the means to appropriate the authority of the Vedas without laboriously working through them. Hindus have been at least as creative in finding ways to co-opt the Vedas as they have been in hammering out new readings of them. J. Z. Smith does not deal explicitly with this type of ingenuity in "Sacred Persistence," though it does not seem inconsistent with his basic argument.

There is, however, an important element in the Hindu treatment of the Vedas that could be further emphasized in J. Z. Smith's discussion of canon in the history of religions. In debates about the canon one of the factors that is at play is a struggle for power. When people argue about what should go into the canon, about what the canon means, and about who has the right to decide these things, they often do so for reasons that are often quite worldly. Hindus believe that the Vedas contain transcendent truths that may not be available to humans in any other way. On a more mundane level, command over these texts has always had very powerful social consequences in South Asia. The accepted interpreters of the Vedas gain access to power, prestige, and partonage that they would not otherwise enjoy. In general, J. Z. Smith's scholarship is marked by an acute sensitivity to the frequent practical, secular consequences of sacred belief and practice. This is a theme that is not expressed in "Sacred Persistence," but it is appropriate to a discussion of the role of canon in the history of religions.[7]

The Vedic canon in South Asia has always been the center of a struggle for power. From the Hindu perspective the quintessential heretics were the Buddhists. Arising in the late Vedic period around the sixth century B.C.E., the Buddhist movement rejected the authority of the Vedas, of the rituals in which the Vedas were used, and of the priests who were the masters of those texts and rituals. This attack forced Hindus to begin to define the boundaries of the Vedic canon. That canon has been a measuring rod for determining Hindu orthodoxy ever since. This is indicated indirectly by the common argument that various Hindu works make that they are in line with the Vedas. There must have been opponents who argued that the religion of each of these works was not Vedic and, therefore, not valid.

Swami Dayānand sought to reform the Hindu tradition consistent with the religion of the Vedas, thereby continuing the long tradition of basing religious innovation in the authority of the canon. Dayānand's project was fraught with powerful consequences for the society in which he lived. There were many who argued with Dayānand, trying to forestall the religious change that he advocated. In the end Dayānand was driven by these debates to a new understanding of what the Vedas are, what they mean, and who may read them. It is to these arguments that we now turn.

DEBATING ABOUT THE CANON

By his own account, Swami Dayānand Sarasvatī became skeptical about traditional Hinduism at a tender age. In an autobiographical essay Dayānand described how he went to a temple with his father as a young boy and was shocked to see that the image of Śiva, which was supposed to embody a powerful divinity, could not protect itself even from the rats that scurried up to nibble at the offerings at the foot of the statue. Dayānand's father attempted to explain the theology of image worship to the young boy, but he was unsuccessful. "Upon hearing this a doubt was born in my mind, 'Surely there is some confusion here.' "[8]

Even after becoming a renouncer, Dayānand remained skeptical about image worship, criticizing this practice publicly in his sermons. His unbelief naturally spread to the Purāṇas, those great repositories of Hindu mythology that sometimes commend the worship of images. From 1860 to 1863 Dayānand studied with a blind grammarian named Virjānand, who reinforced Dayānand's critical bent. Dayānand's guru maintained that only the most ancient Sanskrit works should be accorded any authority. The Purāṇas and other late texts were not even worthy of study, according to Virjānand. Dayānand accepted this doctrine and continued to speak out against aspects of popular Hinduism. His criticism was met by other scholars, who tried to defend their tradition.

An important debate took place in Benares on November 16, 1869, between Dayānand and some of the leading pandits of the city. The issue to be resolved was whether or not the Vedas sanction the worship of images of gods and goddesses. Dayānand argued that there is no image worship in the Vedas, while the other pandits took the contrary position. By all accounts the debate was a grand affair. More than a score of eminent traditional scholars were present on the stage to defend the worship of images. The maharaja of Benares presided over the disputation, and thousands came to witness it.

Why was there such great public interest in such a seemingly arcane argument? It was because this was a struggle over the very essence of Hinduism. The worship of images was prevalent in the Hinduism of the nineteenth century as it is today. Most Hindus probably assumed that it has always been an ingredient of the religion, but Swami Dayānand claimed that this is not true. He believed that image worship was not a part of the religion of the ancient Vedas, but that it had only developed in the medieval period. Dayānand proposed that the Hindu religion should be reformed by going back to its Vedic roots, which would involve excising practices that he condemned as idolatrous. Dayānand's interlocutors accepted the authority of the Vedas, but they believed in image worship, too. Now they were challenged to demonstrate that this was consistent.

Unfortunately, exactly what happened in the debate is unclear. There are two conflicting accounts of this event, one by supporters of Dayānand and the other by his opponents, which disagree particularly about the outcome of the argument. Not surprisingly, traditional Hindus maintain that the pandits got the better of Dayānand and that image worship was successfully defended. Reformers, on the other hand, insist that the pandits were discomfited in their attempt to find Vedic precedent for idol worship, and so Dayānand was the victor. As is so often the case in disputes of this kind, apparently those who observed the debate came away with their prejudices confirmed.[9]

Descriptions of the substance of the debate are also unsatisfying. The discussion lurched from topic to topic as the participants frequently changed the subject rather than admit an impasse. For example, in the first few minutes of the debate the subject moved from a discussion of the authority of the Vedas, to a discussion of the authority of *The Laws of Manu*, to the interpretation of an aphorism from the *Vedānta Sūtras*. The most substantial exchange involved not the Vedas, but the Purāṇas. The pandits defended the Purāṇas, maintaining that they were an expression of the same religion as the Vedas and were binding. In fact, in this debate the pandits argued that the Vedas themselves uphold the authority of the Purāṇas.

It was in the midst of the discussion of what the Vedas say about the Purāṇas that the debate in Benares came to its dramatic conclusion. One of the pandits, Mādhvācārya, produced several sheets with verses containing the word *purāṇa*, which he maintained were Vedic, and he demanded that Dayānand explain them.[10] Dayānand took a few minutes to peruse the verses and to formulate a response. Before he could speak up, the pandits declared that he was defeated. The crowd then began to pelt Dayānand with stones, and he was whisked away by the police. Ārya Samājists understand these events to have been the outcome of a conspiracy against their guru. As Harbilas Sarda has written, "The pandits and the goondas of Benares determined to secure victory by force or fraud, if it was not possible to do so in regular debate."[11]

Despite the ambiguous outcome of this contest Swami Dayānand continued to publicly demand the reform of Hindu society. Over time Dayānand came to view the Vedas as the texts that express the ideal religion, concluding that they are, in fact, totally free of error. They are the source of truth such that all valid knowledge has its seeds in the Vedas. When Dayānand founded the Ārya Samāj, he charged it with the mission of reviving Vedic religion. One of the ten principles of that organization drawn up in 1877 is, "The Veda is the book of true knowledge. To study the Veda and to teach it, to hear and expound it is the highest dharma of all Ārya Samājists."[12]

The Vedas continued to be a central concern of Swami Dayānand up to the time of his death. In 1877 he began to publish a commentary on the *Ṛg-* and *Yajur-Veda Saṃhitās*. He intended to comment on the entirety of the *Ṛg-, Yajur-, Sāma-,* and *Atharva-Vedas*, but he was only able to complete the work on the *Yajur-Veda*. A long but only partial commentary on the *Ṛg-Veda* by Dayānand is also available. In these books Dayānand provides an explanation of each Vedic verse in Sanskrit. This is followed by a Hindi translation of that explanation. Swami Dayānand was determined to make the Vedas available to an audience that was not limited to the pandits who knew the Sanskrit language. Over the course of his public career Dayānand focused ever more narrowly on the Vedas. In the later years of his life Dayānand turned more and more to writing to disseminate his religious vision. These two transformations are not unrelated.

FROM ORAL TO WRITTEN REINTERPRETATION OF THE CANON

Although he eventually became the founder of an important Hindu revivalist organization and a prolific author, Dayānand's public work began with debates. There are reliable records of these disputes and other biographical information that we can use to gain insight into these conflicts. While Dayānand was trying to change Hinduism in these controversies, it is clear that the polemics were also changing Dayānand. It is the latter process that we will concentrate on in this section and the next. First we will look at the importance of canonical books in Dayānand's work; then we will turn our attention to the social context of reinterpreting the Vedic canon.

As the chapters in this volume by David Carpenter, Barbara Holdrege, and Brian Smith indicate, the Vedas have often been understood as sacred speech. Yet when contemporary Ārya Samājists think of the Vedas they tend to think of books. Almost all of the portraits of Dayānand in popular calendar art, for example, include four books. They are conveniently placed so that the viewer can read "*Ṛg-Veda*," "*Yajur-Veda*," "*Sāma-Veda*," and "*Atharva-Veda*" along the spine. As a master of the Vedas Dayānand was for his disciples a reader and a writer of books. This is not just a question of form, but it has substantial consequences. In understanding the Vedas as written works and writing about them, Dayānand made them accessible to groups that were not a part of the elite community of oral recitation.

Swami Dayānand was reared in a Brahman household, and he learned parts of the Vedas by rote as a child. So he knew of the Vedas as an oral text. Dayānand also believed that the Vedas are the eternally true knowledge of God, as such transcending any human word, whether oral or written. Yet Dayānand also studied the Vedas in books and published books of commentaries on them. Perhaps the Vedas were not just books for Dayānand, but they were books. An exchange at the very beginning of the Benares debate illustrates this point nicely:

> Then Swami Dayānand asked the Maharaja [who accompanied the pandits to the debate], "Have the Vedic books been brought or not?"
>
> Then the Maharaja said, "What use are books when these pandits have memorized the Vedas?"

> Then Swami Dayānand said, "Without books there cannot be accurate reflection on the context [of passages discussed in the debate]. Let it be. The books have not been brought."[13]

Swami Dayānand Sarasvatī's work revolved around books. In his own writings Dayānand identified the Vedas as the source of all religious authority. He was explicit not only about the works that were Vedic, but also about the ones that were not. At several points in his oeuvre Dayānand gave detailed lists of authoritative and unauthoritative Hindu texts.[14] The Purāṇas are prominent among unauthoritative books, but Dayānand also identified other works that advocate practices that he rejected such as tantra and astrology.

Dayānand's bookishness is even more salient in his writings about other religions. ***Satyārth Prakāś***, Dayānand's most important work, is divided into two parts. The first ten chapters are dedicated to describing the true religion, supported by copious quotes from Hindu literature. In the last four chapters Dayānand exposes the errors of religions that deviate from his ideal. Specifically, Dayānand attacks Hindu groups, non-Hindu religions that originated in South Asia (notably Buddhism and Jainism), Christianity, and Islam in successive chapters. In each of the final critical chapters the method is the same. Dayānand quotes passage after passage from works with which he does not agree, and then he gives arguments for why each passage is absurd. The chapters on Christianity and Islam are limited exclusively to commentary on the Bible and the Qur'an. This fact is especially striking given that South Asia had been dominated by Muslim and then Christian rulers for centuries at the time that Dayānand was writing. Dayānand did not criticize those rulers and their vices in ***Satyārth Prakāś***. His argument was with the Bible and the Qur'an.

The case of Jainism is particularly instructive on this score. In the introduction to ***Satyārth Prakāś*** Dayānand complains about the Jains: "it is their nature that whenever one of their books falls into the hands of a follower of another religion or is published, then someone or other calls it unauthoritative."[15] Apparently the Jains were a kind of a moving target. Whenever the swami would say something in public critical of one of their religious books, a Jain would respond that it was really not a part of their scripture anyway. The notion that a religion could have an open-ended corpus of beliefs and practices and books apparently did not appeal to Dayānand. For the purpose of engaging in interreligious dialogue everybody had to put a book on the table, and Dayānand seemed to resent the fact that the Jains did not play by the rules.

This model of religious discussion must have been based at least in part on Swami Dayānand's experience in formal debates. Over the course of a public career that spanned almost two decades Dayānand participated in at least thirty-nine disputations.[16] The peripatetic swami took part in debates in what are now Bengal, Bihar, Uttar Pradesh, Punjab, Rajasthan, Gujarat, and Maharashtra. The opposing parties were sometimes defenders of traditional Hinduism, but Dayānand also tussled with Christian and Muslim preachers. Increasingly over the course of Dayānand's career these controversies were about books.

The term that is used to describe these debates, *śāstrāth*, gives some indication of their book-bound character. *Śāstrāth* is a compound that could be literally translated "the meaning of the scriptures [the *śāstrās*]." Traditionally pandits who met for these debates agreed that the *śāstras* are authoritative, but then tried to iron out their disagreement on what the *śāstras* dictate. Thus, Dayānand's disputations started out as arguments over books, and if anything they became more text-centered over time. In his biography Jordens notes that Dayānand became dissatisfied with the free wheeling but inconclusive fracases of his early public life and began to demand a more formal structure before he would participate in a contest.[17] In order to prevent the promulgation of competing versions of what transpired in these debates (as had happened in Benares), Dayānand insisted on an official transcript of the discussion that all parties had to sign before publication. And the combatants had to commit themselves to a list of authoritative books before hostilities commenced. This rule did not mean that everyone had to agree on the same books. That would have made interreligious dialogue impossible. Rather, each party had to admit to some book or list of books. This provision was designed to forestall the Jain strategy that so frustrated Dayānand. No apologist could escape from a fusillade of criticism by saying, "We don't really believe in that book anyway."

It is not surprising that Swami Dayānand regarded religious truth as a thing to be found in books, when he spent a good deal of his life arguing about them. Jordens presents evidence that the canon of books that Dayānand was prepared to defend in debate became progressively more narrow over time.[18] This process may hold the key to understanding the origins of Dayānand's antipathy to much Hindu literature. The fact that Dayānand regarded the Vedas as authoritative hardly distinguishes him, since this has been such a central tenet in Hinduism. His rejection of a good deal of popular Hindu literature in favor of the Vedas is more distinctive. Early in his career Dayānand was more liberal in the range of books that he was willing to try to defend. Later, perhaps partially because he found some of these texts indefensible, his list of authoritative works became much more limited.

AGAINST TRADITIONAL INTERPRETERS OF THE CANON

In order to establish the authority of his new definition of the canon, and his new understanding of its meaning, Swami Dayānand Sarasvatī had to wrest control of the text from others. Dayānand argued with traditionally trained scholars about the Vedas, attempting to prove that his knowledge was superior to theirs. He also criticized a new elite of Vedic pandits, Western scholars. In this section we will look at the contemporary pandits who owned the canon. In the next section we will turn to the colonialists.

In general Swami Dayānand was sharply critical of the priests of his day. He believed that many of them were ignorant and indolent, relying simply on their high social and religious status to make a living. In Dayānand's opinion only those deserved to be called "Brahmins" who earned the title by their learning and virtuous conduct. And Dayānand's meritocracy was not limited to the priestly class. He argued that each individual's caste status should be determined by her or his own qualities and not by birth. In other words, Swami Dayānand accepted that it is logical to divide people into castes, but insisted that the assignment of each person in this system should depend upon deeds and not birth. If the son of a Brahmin was stupid and lazy, then he should be treated as a servant, and, what was perhaps even more shocking to the sensibilities of traditional Hindus, if the son of a servant was smart and hard working, then he should be treated as a Brahmin.[19]

To realize this utopian program there is one practical and very radical measure that Swami Dayānand embraced: he taught the Vedas to groups that ordinarily would not have had access to them. It is well known that traditionally only Brahmins may be Vedic teachers. The other twice-born castes, the warriors and merchants, could study the Vedas, but they could not teach them. Members of the lowest caste groups, including servants, were not permitted any purchase on these works, as students or teachers. Consistent with its patriarchal bent, classical Indian culture also debarred women from these powerful books. Dayānand rejected these restrictions, believing that anyone with the interest and ability should be allowed to study the Vedas. In his introduction to his Vedic commentaries Dayānand wrote:

> Does everyone have the right to study the Vedas and other scriptures (*Vedādisāstra-*) or not?
>
> Everyone does, because the Vedas were spoken by God, because they are intended for the benefit of all men, and because they disseminate true knowledge. We know that whatever thing God has made is intended for all.[20]

To claim that God intended the Vedas only for some groups, but not others, would be tantamount to accusing God of playing favorites, and this Dayānand rejected.

Swami Dayānand lectured in public about the Vedas to audiences that included low caste people as well as high, women as well as men. Early in his career he gave his discourses in Sanskrit, but he was convinced by the great Bengali reformer Keshub Chandra Sen discussed by Rambachan elsewhere in this volume, to begin to speak in Hindi instead.[21] In his commentaries on the Vedas Dayānand provided an explanation of each verse in Sanskrit and then a translation of his gloss in Hindi. In that way those who were literate could study the Vedas even if they had not had an opportunity to learn the Sanskrit language. Dayānand was one of the earliest authors to make the Vedas available in Hindi. Of course, Dayānand's books could be purchased by any interested party regardless of caste or gender. Dayānand has sometimes been called "the Luther of India."[22] He is identified as such because he, like Luther, took the scripture from the priests and gave it to the common people. However, given the record of public debate that we have already discussed, it might be more accurate to say that Dayānand wrested the Vedas from the hands of the priests, and then hit them over the head with them, before passing them along to the general public.

AGAINST THE COLONIAL INTERPRETERS OF THE CANON

Swami Dayānand had to liberate the Vedas from the control of the traditional elite of pandits, but he also had to deal with another emerging elite of Vedicists, the community of Western scholars. Though the criticism of Western Vedic commentators is not as salient in Dayānand's work as it was to become in the rhetoric of later Ārya Samājists, he did deal with them.[23] The general thrust of his argument was that these students of the Vedas derived their own ideas from the commentaries of the classical scholiasts such as Sāyaṇa, whose interpretation of the Vedas Dayānand rejected. The modern academic reading of the Vedas is, therefore, marred by the same errors as the traditional one. Dayānand was not above using ridicule in his criticism of this new class of pandits. About Max Müller, the German-British scholar who was one of the giants of nineteenth-century Vedic study, Dayānand wrote:

> When people say that there has been a great deal of study of Sanskrit learning in Germany, and that no one has read as much Sanskrit as Max Müller, this is all just talk. For "a castor oil plant is thought of as a big tree in a country where there are no trees." In just the same way, because there has been no study of Sanskrit learning in Europe, and Max Müller has read a little, for that area it is sufficient. But if you give attention to India, then it must be accounted very little.[24]

Müller might have been acclaimed as a giant in the West, but in Dayānand's judgment he was a midget. Swami Dayānand is often considered a forerunner of Indian nationalism, since he developed a vision of ancient Vedic culture that inspired self-respect in his followers. He was not about to allow that vision to be undermined by India's imperial overlords.

Despite the explicit criticism of Western Vedicists, there may be a deeper level on which Swami Dayānand was indebted to Christians and to Muslims, too. It is tempting to speculate that Dayānand's canon became more circumspect especially because of contact with Christians and Muslims, though it is impossible to prove this. It is not hard to imagine that missionaries and maulvis might have objected when Dayānand threw a whole library of Hindu literature onto the scales to counterbalance their Bible or Qur'an. In the case of Christianity it is important to point out that most of Dayānand's debates were with Protestant preachers, not Catholics, who might have been more content with a discussion of the Christian religion oriented toward scripture rather than tradition.

There is one minor but very interesting indication that Dayānand's understanding was substantially influenced by his encounter with Protestant Christians. In the eleventh chapter of *Satyārth Prakāś* Dayānand exposed the errors of Hindu groups who did not share his understanding of what true religion is. The villians of the piece are priests who have according to Dayānand manufactured all kinds of superstitious practices in order to relieve the gullible of some of their wealth. The label that Dayānand consistently uses for these hypocrites is "pope." The pope, Dayānand explains, is someone who offers others a salvation that he does not have the power to confer in exchange for contributions.[25] It need hardly be pointed out that this understanding of the papal office was probably not derived from Roman Catholic sources.

Swami Dayānand's emphasis on the Vedas as his scriptural authority may have been influenced by his contact with Europeans. The main reason that Dayānand chose the Vedas was because they enjoy almost universal acceptance among Hindus. Dayānand condemned sectarianism in the Hindu community. Again the Purāṇas come in for criticism here because of their mutually conflicting theological claims. He identified his own project as an attempt to develop a universal religion based on principles that everyone could accept.[26] When Dayānand searched for texts in the Hindu tradition that predated the rise of the sects, texts that all revered, he came upon the Vedas. So the main reasons that Dayānand chose the Vedas were derived from the Hindu tradition. But it is perhaps significant that Dayānand lived at a time of burgeoning Western interest in the Vedas. Indians were not the only ones who found in the Vedas a "pristine" faith above the alleged grotesqueries of contemporary Hinduism. Some Orientalists had the same opinion.[27]

REINTERPRETING THE CANON: A SUMMARY

Swami Dayānand's belief in the unique authority of the Vedic Saṃhitās is well known. The process by which he came to that position may be more unfamiliar even to the Indological reader. Dayānand's career of critical reflection began with an early rejection of the worship of images. Eventually he was led to condemn those priests who make their living at least in part on the basis of image worship. Along the way he became skeptical about those Hindu religious works that extol the benefits of making offerings to statues of gods and goddesses, most notably the Purāṇas. Having discarded these books, Dayānand was driven to search for other texts, texts that do not promote the worship of images. He finally came rather late in life to the conclusion that it is the Vedas that express the true religion. From the nibbling of rats Dayānand was led after many years to a reinterpretation of the Vedic canon.

Public debates were an important part of this intellectual odyssey. Through them Swami Dayānand was forced to define ever more specifically and narrowly the Hindu religious works that he took to be authorative. Over the course of his career Dayānand came to see religious truth as something that resides in books, which was to be expected given that the debates that he took part in were generally about books. For Dayānand the Vedas were a part of living oral tradition, but they had also been bound in books. This understanding of the canon was central to Dayānand's general reform effort. While only high caste Hindu males were granted membership in the club of oral transmitters of the Vedas, anyone with a modest amount of money could buy a printed copy of the Vedic Saṃhitās, if they were made readily available, and anyone who is literate could read them. To further this end Dayānand published the Vedic Saṃhitās, with a commentary explaining his understanding of those texts.

When Dayānand disseminated the Vedas to a general audience without regard to social status of gender, he was attacking the power of the priests at its very heart, because their privileges depended upon a monopoly in teaching the canon. Swami Dayānand did not shrink from a thoroughgoing rethinking of caste, rejecting birth in favor of merit as the determiner of caste identity. Thus, along with a reinterpretation of the canon, Dayānand advocated fundamental social change. While Dayānand was determined to liberate the Vedas from the control of the priests, he was not prepared to surrender them to those Western scholars who were then emerging as a new community of interpreters. It is difficult to determine precisely what Swami Dayānand may have learned from his encounters with Westerners, since his own biases and those of his disciples make acknowledgment of indebtedness difficult. But whatever the sources may have been, it is clear that Dayānand was committed not only to a rereading of the canon but also to a reconstruction of society.

Swami Dayānand was a revolutionary with an original and in some ways quite modern vision of an ideal Hinduism. Yet Dayānand maintained that this vision was grounded in the Vedas, the most ancient and revered Hindu scripture. While some aspects of Dayānand's reinterpretation of the canon were innovative, the strategy of returning to the Vedas was in fact traditional. For millennia Hindus have gone back to those texts to establish the legitimacy of their work. In this the Hindu tradition has displayed remarkable ingenuity, the kind of ingenuity that J. Z. Smith has described in "Sacred Persistence." Even as we marvel at this ingenuity, we cannot allow ourselves to lose sight of the practical struggle for power it involved. Swami Dayānand's reinterpretation of the Vedas was a violent assault on the prerogatives of the privileged. It should come as no surprise that Dayānand and his followers had to face verbal abuse and social ostracism from the traditional elite. If the Ārya Samāj version is correct, the pandits of Benares did not stop short of hiring goons to drive Dayānand from the debating stage with a hail of stones. Some even believe that Swami Dayānand suffered attempts on his life because of his outspoken call for change. There are times when it takes physical courage to reinterpret the canon.

NOTES

1. This chapter is based in part on research that I conducted in India in 1985–86 as Junior Fellow of the American Institute of Indian Studies. I am grateful to the institute for its support.

2. Dayānand, *Ṛgvedādibhāṣyabhūmikā*, 94–105.

3. Idem, *Satyārth Prakāś*, 14–51.

4. Renou, *Destiny of the Veda in India*, 4.

5. Smith, *Reflections on Resemblance, Ritual, and Religion*, 13–14.

6. It must be acknowledged that the sheer size and diversity of the Vedic corpus makes this choice less limiting than it might seem.

7. It is significant that Smith in his article quotes Sigmund Freud's essay "Obsessive Acts and Religious Practices." Smith (38–39) finds Freud's discussion of the "obsessiveness common to both neurosis and religion" suggestive. In the two cases there is an inordinate concern over things that appear "little," "petty," and "trivial" to the outside observer. Given the substantial consequences that follow from the interpretation of the canon in South Asia, the proper analogy to this continuing concern with the canon may not be the behavior of obsessives, those neurotically worried about things that do not matter, but the behavior of constitutional lawyers, those whose struggles over the reading of the legal canon matter a great deal.

8. Dayānand, *Ātma-Kathā*, 8. All translations from Hindi and Sanskrit in this chapter are my own.

9. I must confess that I have not had the opportunity to read an account of this debate that takes the side of the pandits, but I gather that such documents have been published. Dayānand, *Ṛṣi Dayānand Sarasvatī ke Śāstrārth aur Pravacan*, 15. For the Ārya Samāj version of the text of the debate, the reader may consult ibid., 23–44. This has been translated into English in a pamphlet entitled *Kashi Shastrarth*.

10. Ārya Samāj sources indicate that these verses were actually not from the Vedas but from the Gṛhyasūtras, but unfortunately they do not provide more detail about the specific texts. Dayānand, *Ṛṣi Dayānand Sarasvatī ke Śāstrārth aur Pravacan*, 38, n. 3.

11. Sarda, *Life of Dayanand Saraswati*, 69.

12. Lekh Rām, *Jīvancaritra*, 329–30. In many versions of the principles, including the one quoted here, the word "all" (*sab*, in Hindi) is inserted before "true knowledge." "The Veda is the book of *all* true knowledge." Bhārtīy has established that the word *sab* is not to be found in the oldest versions of the principles (Bhārtīy, *Navjāgaraṇ ke Purodhā*, 326–27). Still, it should be noted that "knowledge" is plural, so that more than just one type of knowledge is intended here.

13. Dayānand, *Ṛṣi Dayānand Sarasvatī ke Śāstrārth aur Pravacan*, 24–25.

14. I have analyzed these lists in *Ārya Samaj as a Fundamentalist Movement*, chap. 3.

15. Dayānand, *Satyārth Prakās*, 11.

16. Sarda provides a detailed list of them: *Life of Dayanand Saraswati*, 345–46.

17. Jordens, *Dayānand Sarasvatī*, 186.

18. Ibid., 54–56.

19. Dayānand, *Ṛgvedādibhāṣyabhūmikā*, 360.

20. Ibid., 358.

21. Jordens, *Dayānanda Sarasvatī*, 224.

22. See, for example, Farquhar, *Modern Religious Movements in India*, 111.

23. When I studied with Ārya Samājists from 1985 to 1987 I was frequently treated to denunciations of the Western understanding of the Vedas. It was interesting that the authors mentioned were often scholars of the nineteenth century, such as Max Müller, contemporaries of Dayānand. Later Vedicists such as Louis Renou were rarely mentioned.

24. Dayānand, *Satyārth Prakāś*, 432.

25. Ibid., 436–38.

26. Ibid., 7.

27. In this context it is interesting that a Christian missionary claimed to have been the first person to show Dayānand a copy of the *Ṛg-Veda* (Jordens, *Dayānand Sarasvatī*, 40).

REFERENCES

Bhārtīy, Bhavānīlāl

1983 *Navjāgaraṇ ke Purodhā: Dayānand Sarasvatī*. Ajmer: Paropkarini Sabha.

Dayānand Sarasvatī

1973 *Ṛgvedādibhāṣyabhūmikā* [Introduction to the commentaries on the *Ṛg*- and other Vedas]. Vol. 1, 1–430 in *Ṛgveda-Bhāṣyam* [Commentary on the *Ṛg-Veda*], ed. Yudhṣṭhir Mīmāṃsak. Āryasamāja-Śatābdi-Saṃskaraṇam. Bahalgarh (Sonipat): Ram Lal Kapoor Trust. First published from 1877 to 1878.

1974 *Kashi Shastrarth*. Trans. Ratan Lal. Ajmir: Paropkarini Sabha. This is an account of the Benares debate of 1869.

1975 *Satyārtha-Prakāśaḥ* [Light for truth]. Ed. Yudhiṣṭhir Mīmāṃsak. 2d ed. Āryasamāj-Śatābdi-Saṃskaraṇ. Bahalgarh (Sonipat): Ram Lal Kapoor Trust. First published in 1884.

1983 *Ātma-Kathā* [Autobiography]. Maharṣi Dayānand-Nirvāṇ-Śatābdī-Saṃskaraṇ. Ajmer: Vaidik Pustakālay. This is the Hindi original of autobiographical essays that were first published in English in *The Theosophist* in 1879 and 1880.

1988 *Ṛṣi Dayānand Sarasvatī ke Śāstrārth aur Pravacan* [Rishi Dayānand Sarasvatī's Debates and Speeches]. Ed. Bhavānīlāl Bhārtīy and Yudhiṣṭhir Mīmāṃsak. Bahalgarh (Sonipat): Ram Lal Kapoor Trust.

Farquhar, J. N.

1977 *Modern Religious Movements in India*. Delhi: Munshiram Manoharlal. First published in 1914.

Freud, Sigmund

1963 "Obsessive Acts and Religious Practices." Trans. R. C. McWatters. In *Character and Culture*. New York: Collier. First published in 1907.

Jones, Kenneth W.

1976 *Arya Dharm: Hindu Consciousness in 19th-Century Punjab*. Berkeley: University of California Press.

Jordens, J. T. F.

1978 *Dayānanda Sarasvatī: His Life and Ideas*. Delhi: Oxford University Press.

Lekh Rām
1984–85 *Jīvancaritra: Maharṣi Swāmī Dayānand Sarasvatī*. Ed. Bhavānīlāl Bhārtīy, trans. Raghunandansiṃh, 2d printing. Delhi: Ārṣ Sāhitya Pracār Trust.

Llewellyn, J. E.
Forthcoming. *The Arya Samaj as a Fundamentalist Movement: A Study in Comparative Fundamentalism*. Delhi: Manohar.

Renou, Louis
1965 *The Destiny of the Veda in India*. Ed. Dev Raj Chanana. Delhi: Motilal Banarsidass.

Sarda, Harbilas
1968 *Life of Dayanand Saraswati: World Teacher*. 2d ed. Ajmer: Paropkarini Sabha.

Smith, Brian K.
1989 *Reflections on Resemblance, Ritual, and Religion*. New York: Oxford University Press.

Smith, Jonathan Z.
1982 "Sacred Persistence: Toward a Redescription of Canon." In *Imagining Religion: From Babylon to Jonestown*, 36–52. Chicago: University of Chicago Press.

9

REDEFINING THE AUTHORITY OF SCRIPTURE

The Rejection of Vedic Infallibility by the Brahmo Samaj

ANANTANAND RAMBACHAN

THE VEDAS IN THE INDIAN RENAISSANCE

IN HIS WELL-KNOWN WORK, *Imagining Religion.*, J. Z. Smith argues for the centrality of canon in the study of religion. The significance of canon may be illustrated quite easily by the study of those exegetes within a tradition who defend and justify its authority and for whom its study and interpretation have salvific value. In a different way, however, the significance of canon is also affirmed by those interpreters of a tradition who modify and redefine its authority, enlarge its contents, or create new authoritative canons. None of the seminal figures examined in this study understood or affirmed the authority of the Vedas in a manner comparable to the Mīmāṁsā exegete, Śabara, or to Vedānta commentators like Śaṅkara or Rāmānuja. Two of them, Debendranath Tagore and Keshub Chandra Sen, were explicit in their rejection of the infallibility of the Vedic canon. All of them, however, were clearly cognizant of the status and functions of the Vedas within the Hindu tradition to see the necessity for attempting to clarify their positions vis-à-vis the authority of these texts. While our subjects did not adopt a common stand with reference to the Vedic canon, they were united in having to grapple with its authority. All of them, in their different ways, were engaged in lively debate about the authority of the Vedas and, in this way, were affirming its significance.

The leaders of the Brahmo Samaj were interpreting their tradition in a historically unique hermeneutical context. As Wilhelm Halbfass points out, this was a hermeneutic situation "which had no real precedent on either the Indian or the European side, a situation in which India and Europe, the traditional and the contemporary, self-understanding and awareness of the other were linked to one another in new and peculiar ways."[1] The Western impact significantly altered and influenced the Hindu self-understanding and, in particular, attitudes toward the authority of the Vedas. The reinterpretation of the authority of scripture is a legacy of the Brahmo Samaj which, through various Neo-Vedānta movements, has considerably influenced the contemporary articulation of Hinduism. In the case of the Brahmo Samaj, the acceptance or rejection of Vedic infallibility was such a central issue that it defined one's membership within the tradition.

The Western challenge, in contrast to Hinduism's earlier encounters with other civilizations and cultures, was total. The main challenge of the West was in respect of the religion of the Hindus. The missionaries questioned the validity of Hinduism and denounced it as a mass of superstitions; many of its practices were condemned as idolatrous and polytheistic. Social customs for which religious legitimation was claimed invoked the severest disapproval. These included such practices as the burning of widows on the funeral pyres of their husbands, infant marriages, compulsory widowhood, and the institution of caste with the acceptance of untouchability. The structure of Hinduism was challenged by the concept of equality, which became part of the legal system. Economically, India's handicraft industry was subjected to the pressures of industrialization, and politically the divisions and fragmentations of Indian society were challenged by the British sense of community and nationalistic pride. The British, in other words, offered an observable, functioning, and successful alternative to India's own system. The West presented economic, social, religious, and intellectual alternatives.

The Western impact on India, which resulted in what is now quite commonly referred to as the Indian Renaissance, transmitted itself to the Indians through English education, the preaching of Christian missionaries, and the research work of Orientalists. The first great impetus to English education was the establishment in Calcutta of the Hindu College in 1817. A large number of schools and colleges were founded during the next forty years in Bengal and in other parts of India, creating a small but influential English-educated class. The spread of English as an all-India language, along with improved transport, facilitated communication and the spread of ideas from one part of the country to another.

Among the writers most influential in shaping Indian thinking around this time were J. St. Mill, A. Comte, and H. Spencer. Mill's political writings, in which he argued that social tyranny might be more oppressive than political subjugation, and his arguments in favor of female equality were well known. Comte, on the other hand, made an effort to discover "laws of progress." He argued that the key to progress was moral development leading to altruism; moral development depended on religion. Comte also insisted on the necessity for female equality. Indians were also inspired by Spencer's ideas of evolution as applied to human society, showing that social change was a natural process that could be guided, that violent breaks with the past were unnecessary, and that ultimate progress was certain. Spencer's writings were translated into the major Indian languages, reaching a wide audience.[2] The significance of these philosophies was the emphasis on reason rather than tradition and authority as the factor in determining the norms and values of society. The objective assessment of tradition was encouraged. The Christian missionaries were among the leading vehicles of Western ideas and concepts. Their scathing criticisms of Hindu doctrine and practice were a major impetus to religious reform and revaluation. They were influential also in a positive manner through their example in education, welfare work, uplift of the backward classes, and female emancipation.

The contribution of the Orientalists is also well documented and accepted.[3] In the history of Indology, the names of W. Jones, H. H. Wilson, and H. T. Colebrooke are legendary. Jones related Hindu civilization to that of Europe by linking Sanskrit to the European language family, and reanimated the idea of a Golden Age in the past. The Golden Age concept was given further shape by the work of Colebrooke. He argued that the West owed a debt of gratitude to the East for their contributions in the arts and sciences. Civilization, which had its origin in Asia, was now in a state of decline there whereas the West was steadily progressing. He concentrated his research upon the Vedic Age of India, characterizing it as an age of gold and comparing it with present decline. He demonstrated from textual sources that the practice of sati was a departure from the authentic tradition and discovered many other discrepancies between ancient texts and actual practices. Colebrooke romanticized the virtues of the Aryan inhabitants of North India, describing their worship as a nonidolatrous monotheistic faith, free from the fertility goddesses, rites, and rituals of contemporary Hinduism. Wilson, unlike Jones and Colebrooke, concentrated his efforts on translating, describing, and analyzing the Purāṇas. In contrast to Colebrooke, who was harsh in his judgment and evaluation of all post-Vedic developments in Hinduism, Wilson argued, "that it was neither necessary nor desirable, and was perhaps even absurd, to eliminate traits that through the ages had become deeply ingrained in Hindu culture."[4] His work, as Kopf suggests, linked contemporary traditions with their "historically authenticated pristine forms." The Orientalist conception of the Golden Age directly influenced the reformist arguments of men like Rammohun Roy and was perhaps their greatest contribution. "Knowledge of this golden age would become the cohesive ideology underlying a new sense of community. It is doubtful that the rise of nationalism would have been possible without the sense of community, the sense of community without a collective feeling of self-respect, and self-respect without the stimulus of a rediscovered golden age."[5]

The Indian Renaissance had effects of the most far-reaching kind, touching almost every aspect of Indian life. It set up a high standard of rational thinking, leading to religious and social reform, and developed the political ideas and institutions that led eventually to the freedom of India. Its chief effect, relevant to the authority and status of the Vedas, was the growth of the spirit of criticism. R. C. Majumdar argues that this spirit of inquiry and criticism is the most important result of the impact of Western culture on India.[6] The claim of the Vedas to be an infallible revelation was questioned and its authoritativeness and role eventually redefined. This change had serious consequences for the understanding of the specific role of these texts and of Hinduism in general.[7] The reinterpretation of their meaning which the texts underwent in this period eventually came to be accepted, among many Neo-Vedānta movements, as the true and original role they had always been assigned.

A study centered on any aspect of this fervent period in the history of Hinduism must inevitably concern itself, in a large measure, with the Brahmo Samaj. This study is no exception. From the days of Rammohun Roy until the death of Keshub Chandra Sen in 1884, the Brahmo Samaj, although numerically small, was the center of all progressive religious, social, and political movements and exerted considerable influence. The movement produced a series of charismatic leaders who determined its doctrine and direction.[8]

RAMMOHUN ROY: REDEFINING THE UNIQUENESS OF THE VEDAS

The question of the significance of canon is important in respect to Rammohun Roy because his work on religion consists largely of attempting to interpret the scriptures to people who considered the texts to be of divine origin and infallible. The complexity of Rammohun Roy's hermeneutical situation, however, is underlined by the fact that his audience not only consisted of fellow Hindus whom he wanted to awaken from error, but also of Europeans to whom he wished to demonstrate that the original and true Hinduism must not be confused with present degenerate beliefs and practices. He was drawn into debate, therefore, with both Hindu traditionalists who defended the status quo and Christian missionaries who denounced his Unitarian interpretations of Christianity. The result, as we will see, was a considerably modified attitude to Vedic authority.[9]

Rammohun Roy (1774–1833) is the acknowledged pioneer of the Indian Renaissance. He was born in an orthodox Hindu Brahmin family and his early education in Persian and Arabic was intended to prepare him for a career in the Muslim administration. He also learned Sanskrit and had a working knowledge of Greek and Hebrew. He settled in Calcutta in 1815 and involved himself in the campaign for religious and social reform, establishing the Brahmo Sabha in 1828.[10] Roy died on September 27, 1833, at Bristol, while on a visit to England.

Opinions are divided among modern scholars on Roy's real attitude to scriptural authority. S. K. Das is doubtful whether Roy really believed in the inspiration of the Vedas.[11] On the other hand, B. G. Ray sees Roy as a champion of Vedic infallibility.[12] Ray's opinion is shared by S. Mitra. He sees the Vedas as the authoritative basis of Hindu theism for Rammohun Roy.[13] According to S. Mitra, the Vedas were for Roy, "extremely luminous works, affirmed to be co-eval with the creation and containing the whole body of Hindu Theology, Law and Literature."[14]

The difficulty of ascertaining Roy's true position on the scripture arises from his tendency to use texts he himself did not necessarily uphold but his opponents did. He preferred to avoid questioning the authoritativeness of the scripture in his controversies with Hindu opponents.[15] Rammohun Roy, like most other Brahmo Samaj leaders, was not a theologian, and his purpose was not to provide a rounded, consistent theology. Unlike Dayānand's more theologically inspired championing of Vedic infallibility, discussed elsewhere by Llewellyn in this volume, Roy was not so definite on either theology or infallibility. He had an abiding interest in social reform. It is difficult, however, to agree with Mitra and Ray that Roy upheld, without reservations, the traditional authority of the Vedas and their absolute infallibility. There is a strong case for modifying this view.[16]

Rammohun Roy saw the Vedas as directing our attention to the regular and orderly operation of the natural world, enabling us to form a concept of the creator:

> The Vedas (or properly speaking the spiritual parts of them) . . . recommend mankind to direct all researches towards the surrounding objects, viewed either collectively or individually, bearing in mind their regular, wise and wonderful combinations and arrangements, since such researches cannot fail, they affirm, to lead an unbiased mind to the notion of a Supreme Existence, who so sublimely designs and disposes of them, as is everywhere traced through the universe.[17]

It is very significant that in this view the Vedas do not themselves give certain knowledge of God, but point to the means by which such knowledge may be gained. There is already a shift here in the nature of traditional scriptural authority. It is interesting to note that Roy expresses an idea that becomes very important in later Brahmo doctrine. This is the notion that nature provides the basis for a particular type of revelation. This idea features prominently in the thought of Keshub Chandra Sen and will be explored more fully when his work is treated.

For Rammohun Roy, the criterion by which the authoritativeness of any text may be evaluated is whether or not it teaches the "true" religion. This view enabled him to accept as authoritative texts of the Hindu tradition other than the Vedas. In this the Vedas were not, for him, a unique and incomparable source of knowledge:

> If the spiritual part of the Vedas can enable men to acquire salvation by teaching them the true and eternal existence of God, and the false and perishable being of the universe, and inducing them to hear and constantly reflect on these doctrines, it is consistent with reason to admit, that the *smṛti,* and *āgama,* and other works inculcating the same doctrines, afford means of attaining final beautitude.[18]

One may add that it is also consistent with reason and the logic of his thought, that the texts of other traditions inculcating the "true" religion, would also be accepted as authoritative. There is no reason to suppose that this view would have been disagreeable to him. His wide sympathies with Christian and Islamic thought are well known. This, of course, further erodes the uniqueness of the Vedas. The view that a text is authoritative only if it teaches the "true" religion implies that Roy has an extrascriptural concept of right doctrine that he brings to bear in his evaluation of any text. In his earliest known work, a Persian tract entitled *Tuhfatu'l al-Muwāhhidīn* (*A Gift to the Deists,* 1803–4), Rammohun Roy outlines a minimal theology common to all religions.[19] Its tenets include the existence of God, derivable from the design of the universe and the human being's innate capacity to infer God from it, and a morally accountable soul existing after death—a belief necessary for the maintenance of social order. The minimal moral principle was a concern for the welfare of humankind. These basic beliefs were contrasted with the doctrinal diversity of historical religions and they were seen as the converging points of all traditions. Here is the germ of the idea of the unity of all religions, which, in various forms, became a prominent feature of Hindu thought in the modern period.

A very important clue to Roy's attitude to the Vedas emerges in his contrast with Śaṅkara on the question of *adhikāra* (entitlement). Roy differs from Śaṅkara in upholding the view that householders and not only *saṅnyāsin*s are entitled to the knowledge of *brahman.* The question of whether Śūdras are able to know *brahman* is related to the question of the indispensability of the Vedas for a knowledge of *brahman.* Śaṅkara, who argues for the indispensability of the Vedas as a source of knowledge of *brahman,* sees the Śūdras, who are debarred from Vedic study, as not being entitled to this knowledge. Rammohun Roy, however, in a dispute with one Subrahmanya Sastri, argues that the knowledge of the Vedas is not necessary for a knowledge of God, wrongly citing Śaṅkara's support for this view.[20] As far as Roy was concerned. the entitlement of people to true or inferior forms of religion was not determined by formal qualifications of birth or ritual status, but by inclination and ability.

It is clear, then, that although Rammohun Roy did not unambiguously reject Vedic authority and infallibility, he had a considerably modified attitude to it. He never worked out a cohesive theology, but if he had, it is difficult to see how he could have consistently maintained a position on the authority of the Vedas similar to that of Mīmāṁsā exegetes or Śaṅkara. His view of nature as revelation, his extrascriptural concept of a type of minimal theology, his idea that religious truth is not confined to the texts of the Vedas, and his argument that knowledge of the latter is not necessary for a knowledge of God, all mollify the traditional attitudes toward the Vedas. It is also relevant to note that Roy adopted an extremely critical view of Biblical texts, expunging matters he felt to be irrational. He sometimes argued, in fact, that the Vedic texts themselves and not only the interpretations of them must be subjected to rational analysis.[21] Rammohun Roy did not lay down a detailed set of doctrines for the Brahmo Samaj, but his general approach certainly influenced the theological evolution of the movement and its formulation of a definite stance toward the Vedas.

DEBENDRANATH TAGORE: THE AUTHORITY OF INTUITION

While Rammohun Roy's position on the authority of the Vedas was ambiguous and left room for some doubt, Debendranath Tagore (1817–1905) openly questioned the authority of the Vedic canon and eventually rejected its claim to infallibility. This was a turning point in the status of these texts in the ensuing history of modern Hinduism.[22] Unlike Rammohun Roy, Debendranath Tagore was less concerned to address himself to a European audience or to engage this community in debate. He had little interest in social reform or in making connections between Hinduism and other religions.

Debendranath Tagore was born in Calcutta in 1817. He received his early education in a school founded by Rammohun Roy. In 1834 he obtained admission to the Hindu College where he spent about four years before joining his father, Dwarkanath Tagore, a close associate of Rammohun Roy, in the family business.[23]

In 1839 Debendranath Tagore founded the Tattvabodhini Sabha (Knowledge of Truth Society) for propagating the ideas of the Upaniṣads.

To carry out the objective of the Sabha, the Tattvabodhini Pathsala, a school for the training of the young, was established in 1840, and a monthly journal, the *Tattvabodhini Patrika,* started in 1843. Akshaykumar Datta, who proved to be an important influence on Debendranath Tagore and indeed on the whole movement, was a teacher at this school and editor of the journal. The relations between the vigorous Sabha and the Brahmo Samaj, which was in a state of decline after Roy's departure for England, were extremely close. The Tattvabodhini Sabha served as the organizational wing of the Brahmo Samaj, finally merging with the latter in 1859.[24] The assumption of leadership by Debendranath Tagore initiated a new phase in the growth of the Samaj. There was a rapid increase in the power and influence of the Brahmo movement. New rituals and ceremonies were added, the most important being a special form of initiation for membership.

Debendranath Tagore followed Rammohun Roy in his belief that original Hinduism was a spiritual theism and that the Upaniṣads were its source. The spark that led to a change of this view was ignited, strangely enough, as a result of controversy over missionary proselytization. In 1845 the Hindus of Calcutta were aroused and incensed by the conversion to Christianity of Umesh Chandra Sarkar and his young wife. A movement in opposition to Dr. Alexander Duff's school, where Sarkar was a student, was launched. Duff's work, *India and Indian Missions,* which appeared at that time, was assailed in the pages of the *Tattvabodhini Patrika.* Duff responded by denouncing the doctrines of the Samaj in the *Calcutta Review,* fixing his fury on the idea of the infallibility of the Vedas.[25] The initial response of the Samaj was to defend the concept:

> We will not deny that the reviewer is correct in remarking that we consider the Vedas and the Vedas alone, as the authorized rule of Hindu theology. They are the sole foundation of all our beliefs and the truths of all other Śāstras must be judged according to their agreement with them. What we consider as revelation is contained in the Vedas alone; and the last part of our holy Scriptures treating of the final dispensation of Hinduism forms what is called *Vedānta.*[26]

This categorical public declaration of adherence to Vedic infallibility soon provoked dissent and unease within the Samaj and also found expression in its columns. Akshaykumar Datta, the editor of the *Tattvabodhini Patrika,* was the leading dissident, and it is generally accepted that it was under his influence that Debendranath Tagore and the Samaj discarded the notion of infallibility.

It is important to briefly consider Datta's religious views, because his linking of religion and science became a constantly reiterated theme throughout the period. His notion of natural religion was also prominent.[27] Datta (1820–86) posited a deistic concept of God as the supreme maker, who created a purposeful universe. God's plan for the universe is apprehended through the discovery of natural laws, which reveal the unity and interrelatedness of all phenomena. The approach to God was not through worship or monism but through the study of the natural sciences. A complete understanding of these natural laws or "God's scripture" reveals the harmony of all things. The logic of this thinking led him to reject Vedānta as the revealed source of the Brahmo Samaj. Because of his belief in natural laws, he felt that the emphasis in the Brahmo Samaj should be less on national character and more on the religious impulses common to all men. In this way it could offer itself to the world as a scientifically constructed natural religion. In his own way, Datta was developing the embryonic theme of Rammohun Roy, which was further enlarged by Keshub Chandra Sen. Sastri is of the opinion that Datta's arguments against Vedic infallibility had wide support in the Samaj.[28]

As part of his effort to ascertain the truth of the issue, Debendranath Tagore sent four Brahmin youths to Benares to study the Vedas. His own visit to that city in 1847 was partly in pursuit of the same inquiry.[29] In 1850 the doctrine of infallibility was finally abolished.[30] In order, however, to keep the movement along the lines of Upaniṣadic monotheism, Debendranath Tagore published in 1850 a compilation of carefully selected passages from the Upaniṣads entitled *Brahmo Dharma*. Perhaps the main cause that led Tagore to the final rejection of the authority of the Upaniṣads was his refusal to accept those passages proclaiming the identity of *ātman* and *brahman*. Earlier, Rammohun Roy had also refused to accept this identification. He preferred to treat *brahman* as the lord and regulator of the cosmos, related to the soul as its superintendent. Both the soul and the universe depend on God for existence.[31] In a revealing passage of his autobiography, worthy of being quoted in full, Tagore writes,

> How strange. Formerly I did not know of the existence of this thorny tangle of Upaniṣads: only eleven Upaniṣads were known to me, with the help of which I started the propagation of Brahma Dharma, making its foundation. But now I saw that even this foundation was shaky and built upon sand; even here I did not touch firm ground. First I went back to the Vedas, but could not lay the foundation of the Brahma Dharma there, then I came back to the eleven authentic Upaniṣads, but how unfortunate, even there I could not lay the foundation.[32] Our relation with god is that of worshipper and worshipped—this is the very essence of Brahmoism. When we found the opposite conclusion to this

> arrived at in Śaṅkarāchārya's *Śarīraka Mīmāṁsā* of the *Vedānta Darśana* we could no longer place any confidence in it; nor could we accept it as a support of our religion. I had thought that if I renounced the *Vedānta Darśana* and accepted the eleven Upaniṣads only, I would find support for Brahmanism, hence I had relied entirely upon these, leaving aside all else. But when in the Upaniṣads I came across, 'I am He' and 'Thou art That', then I became disappointed in them also.[33]

Here might be the real clue to his rejection of scriptural infallibility. The identity posited in the Upaniṣads between the *ātman* and *brahman* undermined, in Tagore's view, the necessary worshiper-worshiped relationship between the individual and God. This was, for him, unacceptable. Unlike the Upaniṣadic exegetes, Bādarāyaṇa, Śaṅkara, and Rāmānuja, discussed in Francis X. Clooney's chapter, Tagore's practice of carefully reading the texts of the Upaniṣads led not to salvific knowledge, but to disappointment and the rejection of their infallibility.

Henceforth, the nonauthoritative status of any text became enshrined in the creed of the Brahmo Samaj. This was a tenet adamantly and inflexibly upheld through all the fragmentations of the movement in later years.[34] In the absence of any authoritative standard of doctrine, nature and intuition became the twin sources of knowledge.[35] The basis of Brahmoism became "the pure heart filled with the light of intuitive knowledge."[36] Debendranath Tagore became increasingly reliant upon personal intuition as his authority and the concept of divine command (*ādeśa*) played an important part in his life. Divine command was also to become an unquestionable source of authority to Keshub Chandra Sen. The idea of intuitive experience as an immediate source of spiritual knowledge, which rose to prominence at this time, became a leading idea of the period.

The decision to reject scriptural authority was not entirely accepted without protest. Rajnarian Bose, for example, an early associate of Tagore, was not pleased with the decision and left the employ of Debendranath Tagore.[37] The strongest voice of protest, however, came from Sitanath Tattvabhusan, who joined the movement under Keshub Chandra Sen in 1871, and later broke with him to become a member of the Sadharan Brahmo Samaj. Tattvabhusan saw the weakness of the movement in its lack of any systematic theology. It is extremely interesting also that all efforts of the Brahmo Samaj to establish and maintain a regular theological school ended in failure.[38] Tattvabhusan felt that the appeals to natural religion and intuition were tenuous, and he saw the difficulties of arriving at any philosophical consensus through these.[39] The rejection of the Vedas by Debendranath Tagore, he felt, had led to a neglect of the scriptures and positively discouraged scholarship. He wanted a movement back to the Upaniṣadic-based Vedānta. Unfortunately, voices like Tattvabhusan appealing for systematization, refinement, and clarity of doctrine were solitary ones. Within the movement itself Tattvabhusan was decried as an advocate of barren intellectualism and scholasticism. He was branded as a reactionary who wanted to abolish the spontaneity of the religious life and suspend the right to private judgment.[40] The opposition to any systematic and methodical approach to doctrine went hand in hand with the accentuation of the importance of the intuitive experience. Such an emphasis on intuition is another legacy to modern Hinduism, where the emphasis is very often upon the lack of a necessity for any belief in doctrine or dogma.

Debendranath Tagore adopted a very conservative attitude on questions of social reform. In fact, he saw the mission of the Brahmo Samaj as a narrowly defined religious one. and felt that in matters of social reform, individual tastes and inclinations should prevail. This approach conflicted with the demands of the younger and radically minded members of the Samaj and led to the first split in 1866. This group wanted the movement to promote actively such practices as intercaste marriage and widow remarriage. They were opposed to the wearing of the sacred thread. There was also a division of opinion over the quality and extent of female education, many of the younger members advocating the ideal of complete social equality. In the vanguard of this progressive party was Keshub Chandra Sen (1838–84).

KESHUB CHANDRA SEN: THE TRIUMPH OF INTUITION

While Debendranath Tagore went much further than Rammohun Roy in his rejection of the infallibility of the Vedas and in his assertion of the supremacy of religious experience, Keshub Chandra Sen was the most articulate in the precedence he gave to intuition over all other forms of revelation, including the Vedas. He was the most distant from the Hindu tradition and the closest to Christianity among all those discussed in this chapter. Yet, as Halbfass points out, Sen did indeed see himself as the fulfiller of Hinduism. As Sen advanced in years, his audience not only dwindled but also became more difficult to define. While trying, more than any other, to harmonize Hinduism and Christianity, his ties with both communities were so frail that one is not surprised by his eventual claim to be the proponent of a new revelation.

Sen was born in a Vaiśnava family of Calcutta and educated at the Hindu College. Sen's Western education had eroded his childhood religious beliefs and created a void that left him restless and searching. He sought solace in Unitarian philosophy and the writings of Theodore Parker and established the Goodwill Fraternity in 1857. It was at a gathering of this society in the same year that he first met Debendranath Tagore. There was a mutual attraction and Sen was soon active in the Brahmo Samaj. He was an enthusiastic worker and largely responsible for the reinvigoration of the movement and its attraction to the young. His tour in 1864 to the Presidencies of Madras and Bombay facilitated the expansion of the Samaj as an all-India movement. After the schism in 1866 he became the leader of the Brahmo Samaj of India. The section under Debendranath Tagore called itself the "Adi (Original) Brahmo Samaj."

In Sen's eyes, the rejection of the Vedas as inspired texts was a grand step in the evolution of the Samaj. Before this, it was simply revivalist in intention. In a sermon delivered during his English visit at the Mill-Hill Chapel in Leeds on August 28, 1870, Keshub contrasted the two stages of the Brahmo Samaj:

> For twenty years the movement was carried on in that spirit, based all the time upon the national Scriptures of the Hindoos. The same god that lifted this noble band of Hindoos out of the darkness of superstition and idolatry, the same God, led them further onward and heavenward, until they gave up completely and thoroughly the doctrine of the inspiration of the Vedas. They took a broader and more unexceptionable base; they went into their own hearts in order to hear the voice of God, and they went forth throughout the amplitudes of nature in order to study in silence the direct revelation of God's spirit. Thus the Hindoo Pantheists became Hindoo Theists. They embraced pure monotheism, such as was not confined to Hindoo books, to the Scriptures of their own countrymen, but was to be found in human nature in all the races and tribes and nations in the world.[41]

Sen wanted to sever all links between the Brahmo Samaj of India and Hinduism. The Hindu image of the movement under Debendranath Tagore was a point of contention. When in 1872 the Brahmo Samaj of India proposed a Marriage Reform Bill, the Adi Samaj argued that the bill would lead to the separation of the Brahmos from the general body of Hindus. Sen interestingly countered this by rejoining that Brahmos had already ceased to be Hindus, using nonbelief in the Vedas as the dividing line.[42]

Of all the leaders of the Brahmo Samaj, Sen has left the largest legacy of speeches and writings, some of which contain very clear pronouncements on the nature of revelation and sources of religious knowledge. The problem with Sen, as with other Brahmo leaders, is the unsystematic and often contradictory quality of his thought, a reflection perhaps of the paradoxical times in which they lived.[43]

In a lecture delivered at the Town Hall in Calcutta on September 28, 1866, Sen propounds what amounts to be a general theory of revelation.[44] According to Keshub, the primary and ordinary revelation of God, accessible and intelligible to all, is God's self-evident manifestation in nature: "The universe exhibits on all sides innumerable marks of design and beauty, of adaptation and method, which we cannot explain except by referring them to an Intelligent First Cause, the Creator of this vast universe. Each object in nature reminds us of its Maker, and draws the heart in spontaneous reverence to His infinite majesty."[45] Nature, however, does not only reveal God as her creator, comparable to a watchmaker who has invested his object with independent powers of functioning. Nature also reveals God's immanent function of sustaining and preserving, in addition to God's goodness in supplying daily needs.

In two lectures delivered the following year at the Calcutta Brahmo School, Sen repeats this argument. Here, however, he distinguishes between the importance of external nature and internal nature as sources of theological knowledge; as an example of the inconsistency of his thinking, external nature is here undervalued as a type of revelation: "There is nothing in matter itself, not even all the power and wisdom it manifests, which can lead us to the True God, whose spiritual nature, intelligence, personality, and holiness can only be deducted from the facts of our consciousness."[46] Here, as the quotation suggests, the mind is eulogized as the instrument of revelation. Theology, Sen claims here, is essentially dependent on psychology, and the doctrines and arguments of religion are derived primarily from the constitution of the human mind: "The value and importance of the mind as an object of speculation through which we obtain a knowledge of the fundamental principles and main arguments of religion cannot be over-estimated. To what source are we to refer but to the human mind for our ideas of God, immortality and duty, and where do we seek for their proof but in the mind?"[47]

It is obvious that Sen was not consistent in the significance he attributed to the different forms of revelation. After the revelation of God in nature, the next in Sen's typology is what he calls "God in history." History, he contends, is not the mere chronicle of past events, but, if read properly is full of religious significance displaying the workings of Providence. The manner in which God reveals Himself in history is through "Great Men."[48]

> For what is history but the record of the achievements of those extraordinary personages who appear from time to time and lead mankind? and what is it that we read therein but the biography of such men? . . . It is through these great men, these leaders of mankind, that God reveals Himself to us in history: in short, they constitute what we mean by "God in history."[49]

Sen sees "Great Men" as the apostles and missionaries of God, owing their talents and success not to personal exertions, but to an inherently superior constitution endowed by God. Sen is scrupulous, however, in distinguishing his "Great Men" theory from the Hindu notion of the *avatāra* and the Christian concept of incarnation.[50] To him, it is not a case of the perfection of divinity embodied in a mortal frame, the God of the universe in a human body. It is God manifest in man; "not God made man but God in man." These extraordinary men, who are representative of their country and age and also embody specific ideals, are born as a result of a moral necessity in times of crisis and turmoil. They are characterized by originality of wisdom, sincerity, invincible power, and selflessness.[51] Christ commands a special regard from Sen, but he pleads for reverence and honor to all dispensations.

In comparison with the final and highest category of revelation, the first two types, according to Sen, are merely external. Inspiration is the loftiest; it is direct communion with the spirit of God, vouchsafed only through God's mercy, and its effects on the human person are total. In Sen's own words, inspiration is "the direct breathing-in of God's spirit—which infuses an altogether new life into the soul, and exalts it above all that is earthly and impure. It is more powerful, being God's direct and immediate action on the human soul, while the revelation made through physical nature and biography is indirect and mediate."[52] It is very significant that in this lecture, where we are provided with Sen's most detailed statements pertaining to revelation, no mention is made of any text and scripture as revelation, as these have no place in his scheme.

There are three tendencies in Sen's writings and lectures that have very important implications for our study of the changing status of scriptural authority and for our understanding of salient orientations in modern Hinduism. The first of these is his powerful invective against the importance of dogma and doctrine. These were seen to relate to intellectual cognition, reasoning, and logical thought, all of which were cold and lifeless, in contrast to the "fire of inspiration" and "direct communion with God." The processes of the intellect had nothing to do with the attainment of salvation. The following quotation will suffice, as it is typical of his outbursts on this point: "Do not preach to me dogmas and traditions; talk not of saving my soul by mere theological arguments and inferences. These I do not want; I want the living God, that I may dwell in Him, away from the battle of the world."[53]

The second tendency, a direct consequence of the first, is his repudiation of all forms of authority, a type of spiritual anarchism. The claim was made that the Samaj was free from teachers, priests, books, ceremonies, and rites.[54]

The third and most important tendency in his thought is his stress on direct perception as the means for gaining spiritual knowledge, foreshadowing an argument that rose to prestigious significance. Sen sees the direct perception approach as a most familiar topic of the Upaniṣads:

> No expression is more frequently used in the Upaniṣads than the "perception" of God (*darśan*). It appears that Hindu sages, not content with intellectual conceptions of the Almighty or abstract contemplation of certain Divine attributes, sought earnestly and indeed successfully, to behold the Supreme Spirit directly and to apprehend Him as a distinct and vivid Reality in their inner consciousness.[55]

This certainty, Sen contends, which arises from the direct perception or realization of reality, is comparable to the assuredness arising from the sensual apprehension of objects around us. It is a self-evident truth, the only satisfactory kind of proof: "The Real God is seen as plainly as we see ourselves and the world. We must place our belief in God upon direct evidence or eyesight. I will apply the same demonstration in reference to God as we do to material objects. All arguments a priori or a posteriori are feeble."[56]

In 1878 the Brahmo Samaj underwent its second schism. This time the rebellion was against Sen and the causes were many.[57] It is interesting that many of the issues that provoked the first rift were still very much alive, and on this occasion Sen was the accused. Sen's ideas on female education and emancipation were seen as being retrograde. He was opposed to university education for women and their exposure to subjects like mathematics, philosophy, and science. He feared that they would lose their sexual identity. He refused the demand of some members that their wives should be at their sides during Samaj services. There was opposition also to Sen's authoritarian management of affairs and a demand for constitutional government and public control of the Samaj property. There was a deep suspicion about Sen's own perception of his role in the movement and the attitude of hero worship that was growing around him. Sen was giving increasing prominence to the idea of having received a special dispensation from God and the fact that his decisions with regard to the movement were above question, being motivated by *ādeśa* (divine command).[58]

From 1875 on Sen began to emphasize the importance of asceticism in the religious life, giving prominence to meditation and withdrawal from the world. The social reform and welfare-oriented activities of the movement fell into neglect. The issue, however, which finally precipitated the split was Sen's consent to the marriage between his eldest daughter and the young maharaja of Cooch Behar, in violation of the principles of the Marriage Act of 1872, and in spite of considerable protest within the Samaj. Both had not attained the marriageable age stipulated by the act, and the rites were non-Brahmo. The schism led to the formation on May 15, 1878, of the Sadharan Brahmo Samaj. One year later Keshub inaugurated the Nava Vidhan or New Dispensation.

The launching of the New Dispensation was motivated by Sen's conviction that he was inspired by a new revelation from God, the special feature of which was to harmonize and unify all conflicting creeds. It was not, he claimed, his intention to form a new sect;

> It is the harmony of all scriptures, and prophets and dispensations. (Nava-Vidhan) is not an isolated creed, but the science which binds and explains and harmonizes all religions. It gives to history a meaning, to the action of Providence a consistency, to quarrelling churches a common bond and to successive dispensations a continuity. . . . It is the wonderful solvent, which fuses all dispensations into a new chemical compound. It is the mighty absorbent, which absorbs all that is good and true and beautiful in the objective world.[59]

The Nava-Vidhan did not alter Sen's attitude to the scriptures even though his views on the necessity of authority in religious matters were dramatically reversed. For example, he strongly refuted deism because of its disavowal of authority in religion.[60] In one of the most revealing pieces of writing belonging to this period, Sen expounds what the New Dispensation understands by the concept of revelation.[61] His illustrations here, as in most of his speeches and writings. are drawn from the Christian tradition, but it is fair to assume that his views are applicable to the scriptures of other traditions as well. He draws a distinction between the New Dispensation and deism, claiming that the former, unlike the latter, does not deny revelation, but reserves the right to interpret it in its own way. This interpretation is based on a contrast between the inspiration of words and the inspiration of events. The former is categorically denied.

Events alone, according to Sen, are inspired and revealed. In this sense, both the Old and New Testaments and the leading figures of its drama are inspired. By revelation, he means,

> the living history not the dead narrative; the fresh events as they occurred, not the lifeless traditions recorded on paper. The letter killeth. Convert a saint into a beautiful picture on canvas, convert living apostles into antiquated doctrines, transform living events into lifeless ceremonies, and burning enthusiasm into the cold dogmatism of books and creeds, and you kill inspiration. What you read in the Bible *was inspired.* It would be incorrect to say

> that the Bible *is* inspired. Inspiration dwells in the fact-Bible not in the book-Bible, in the living Gospel, not in the letter of the book.[62]

The effect of this kind of view was to further reduce the significance of the scriptural text. The unique claim of any scripture was dissolved in the unbounded eclecticism of Sen's thought. In fact, the scriptures of Nava-Vidhan included "the whole of science, physical, meta-physical and moral and also the science of religion."[63] Sen continued the trend noted earlier, especially with A. K. Datta in the time of Debendranath Tagore, of attempting to justify his religious experiments in the name of science. The special mission of the New Dispensation to unite all creeds was proclaimed as scientific, for "science and salvation" were identical, and its enemies were not atheists but "unscientific men." Its truths, Sen argued, were demonstrable for they were based upon observation and experiment and the movement was ready to expunge any tenet falsified by scientific discoveries.[64] Strange also, but perhaps not surprising, was his attempt to justify the Nava-Vidhan on the authority of Śaṅkara. The latter was seen as foreshadowing the Nava-Vidhan, which Sen described as a "New Śaṅkarāchārya, loftier and grander far than the Old Śaṅkara."[65]

THE INFLUENCE OF THE UNITARIANS

The debates about the authority of scripture that were taking place within the Brahmo Samaj were not limited to Indian circles. Here also the influence of the West is significant. Throughout this period, Unitarian influences were most significant in prompting the questioning of scriptural authority and also in the formulation of the new attitudes that eventually emerged. The Unitarian association with the Brahmo Samaj existed from its early beginnings in the time of Rammohun Roy, continued through all the vicissitudes of its history, and was strong in the Sadharan Brahmo Samaj at the close of the nineteenth century. Roy died at the Bristol estate of Reverend Lant Carpenter, the well-known English Unitarian with whom he maintained a friendship. He also corresponded with famous American Unitarians like William Ellery Channing and Joseph Tuckerman, and had planned to visit America in the hope of meeting Channing.[66] He often referred to himself as a Hindu Unitarian.[67] In the time of Keshub Chandra Sen, the American missionary C. H. A. Dall was active in the circles of the Samaj, even though both men later parted ways as Sen became less interested in social reform.[68] As late as 1896 the Sadharan Brahmo Samaj was visited by R. J. T. Sunderland, a representative of the British and Foreign Unitarian Association. The Brahmo Samaj Committee was organized by Sunderland for the annual selection of a suitable candidate interested in the propagation of Brahmoism, for theological training at the Manchester New College of Oxford. Funds for the scholarship were provided by an English Unitarian gentleman, and many were trained under the scheme.[69] There were further visits by representatives of the same organization in 1897 and 1899.

The attraction of Unitarianism for Rammohun Roy was perhaps the critique of Trinitarian Christianity it provided, which he used in his disputation with the missionaries. The entire critique was adopted by the Brahmo Samaj. Following the Unitarians, the Samaj objected to the doctrine of the Trinity, arguing that it subverted the unity of God. They felt that Christ ought to be regarded as distinct from and inferior to God and discussed the problems of representing him as both human and divine. He was an emissary of God to effect a spiritual regeneration of humankind, and his agony and suffering were real. Unitarians rejected the idea that Christ's death made God more placable and merciful. They also opposed the doctrines about the natural depravity of man and the predestination of a select few for salvation.[70]

The Unitarian thinkers who exercised the greatest influence on the formation of Brahmo theology were Channing and Theodore Parker. The works of both men were widely circulated among Brahmos and Parker's writings were translated into Bengali. The strength and extent of the influence become very clear when the writings of both men are compared particularly with those of the prolific Keshub Chandra Sen. Channing, for example, does not question the existence of a valid scriptural revelation, but argues for a wider concept of revelation:

> But we shall err greatly, if we imagine that his Gospel is the only light, that every ray comes to us from a single Book, that no splendours issue from God's Works and Providence, that we have no teacher in religion but the few pages bound up in our Bibles. Jesus Christ came, not only to give us his peculiar teaching, but to introduce us to the imperishable lesson which God for ever furnishes in our own and all Human Experience, and in the laws and movements of the Universe.[71]

Channing does not appear to question the significance and status of the Bible as revelation, but argues for the thorough exercise of reason in its interpretation, for it is a book "written for men, in the language of men, and its meaning is to be sought in the same manner as that of other books."[72]

Channing's concern is with enunciating the principles of its right interpretation. Rammohun Roy appears more akin to Channing in his attitude to the scriptures, whereas Sen seems to have imbibed his views mainly from Parker, who radically rejected any idea of scriptural infallibility and argued for the human origin and character of all scriptures.[73] Keshub's arguments for the human origin of the Vedas foreshadow the twentieth-century interpreters treated by Patton elsewhere in this volume. What these interpreters do, however, is to create an 'ideal' human origin in the person of the inspired, poetic, but democratically oriented rishi.

The alternative forms of revelation suggested by Sen are culled from the writings of Channing and Parker. Sen's views on internal and external nature as revelation were earlier affirmed by Channing and his ideas on inspiration are a close restatement of Parker's own. Channing understood internal human nature to be a revelation in the sense that our primary emotions urge a relationship with a perfect being. In human nature is wrapped up the idea of God, and God's image is carried in our moral and intellectual powers:

> Thus we see that human nature is impelled by affections of gratitude, esteem, veneration, joy, not to mention various others, which prepare us to be touched and penetrated by the infinite goodness of God, and which when directed to Him, constitute piety. That these emotions are designed to be devoted particularly to the Creator, we learn from the fact that they are boundless in their range and demand an Unbounded Object. They cannot satisfy themselves with the degrees of love, intelligence, and power which are found in human beings. . . .They delight in the infinite, and never can find repose but in an Infinite Being, who combines all good.[74]

Parker argues here that inspiration is superior to the revelation of God in nature, and is a regular mode of God's operation on the human spirit. It is universal, varying in degree not in kind, and its revelation is modified by the peculiar circumstances of the individual who receives it. "It is the direct and intuitive perception of some truth, either of thought or of sentiment. There can be but one mode of Inspiration: it is the action of the Highest within the soul, the divine presence imparting light."[75] Inspiration, according to Parker, is the only means by which we gain knowledge of what is not seen and felt, and it is not confined to any single religious tradition, nation, or age. The variation in the degree of inspiration, however, is dependent on the natural intellectual, moral, and religious endowment of the individual, as well as upon the use each individual makes of this inheritance.

J. Z. Smith has argued that "the radical and arbitrary reduction represented by the notion of canon and the ingenuity represented by the rule-governed exegetical enterprise of applying the canon to every dimension of human life is that most characteristic, persistent and obsessive religious activity."[76] If Smith is indeed correct about the centrality of canon, one would expect that the rejection of Vedic infallibility by a prestigious group like the Brahmo Samaj in the nineteenth century would be consequential. The rejection of the Vedas as the authoritative basis of Hinduism profoundly influenced the character of many Neo-Hindu movements and though a detailed treatment of these effects is beyond the scope and length of this study, I can conclude by briefly identifying aspects of this legacy.

I have argued that in order to be consistent, Rammohun Roy's position compelled him to adopt a considerably modified view of Vedic authority even though he did not unambiguously reject the doctrine of infallibility. Many of Roy's concerns, however, continue to be a focus of contemporary Hindu concern. A prominent example of this is his belief in the essential unity of all religions based on what he considered to be a minimal doctrinal and ethical consensus. This led naturally to claims for a universal religion and, in persons like Swami Vivekananda, to the assertion that this universal religion is best embodied in Hinduism. Of all the Brahmo Samaj leaders, however, Roy strove most assiduously to justify his views by resort to scriptural authority, through interpretation and commentary.

With the formal rejection of Vedic infallibility under the leadership of Debendranath Tagore, appeals to scriptural authority were no longer indispensable, for intuition emerged as the valid source of knowledge. For Keshub Chandra Sen, the rejection of the Vedas as the authoritative source of Hinduism went to the very heart of Hindu identity, confirming Smith's view of the significance of canon. The denial of the Vedas as revelation, in the view of Sen, placed Hinduism in the universal stream of monotheism. Identifying with this stream, however, meant that he no longer considered himself to be a Hindu. In a more recent context, the Ramakrishna Mission has argued that it is not Hindu by reason of its universality. Brian Smith has correctly remarked that "the very element that many think defines Hinduism (its tolerance and universality) is the one that others claim to distinguish themselves from Hinduism."[77]

The triumph of individual intuitive experience over all forms of religious authority attained its climax with Keshub Chandra Sen; the triumph was consequential in many ways. Dogma and doctrine were accorded little importance, and were seen to have no connection with the attainment of liberation. Hindus today often find it difficult to understand the significance of doctrinal claims and differences in other religions. The popular claim that all religions lead to the same goal is often affirmed only at the cost of ignoring differences in doctrine.[78]

Keshub Chandra Sen connected the emphasis on doctrine with intellectual cognition, reason, and logic, all of which were continuously devalued. When scripture was upheld as an authoritative source of knowledge, reason had a valued and integral function in clarifying, interpreting, and applying the claims of the canon. When individual intuition is upheld as sacrosant, reasoning and intellectual processes become more obstructive in character and scholarship is divorced from spirituality. Exegesis becomes an indulgence.[79] None of the interpreters treated here understood the Vedas as a source of valid knowledge (*pramāṇa*) in the same orthodox sense as Śaṅkara. For Śaṅkara, knowledge gained through right understanding of the Upaniṣads, which constituted the knowledge section (*jñāna-kāṇḍa*) of the Vedas, led directly to liberation.[80] The right reading of Vedic texts therefore, as Francis X. Clooney emphasizes, was salvific. With the triumph of intuition, the Vedas were no longer seen as an immediate source of liberating knowledge; the poverty of exegesis in modern Hinduism is a direct consequence.

Paradoxically, the upholding of personal experience as sacrosant was also part of the attempt to argue for the harmony of science and Hindu claims. Keshub, as we have seen, in continuity with persons like A. K. Datta, contended that religious truths were as demonstrable as scientific ones. In modern Hindu apologetic writing, the superiority of Hinduism is often argued on the basis of its scientific character.[81]

The rejection of Vedic infallibility by the Brahmo Samaj was a pivotal moment in the history of Hinduism, and the legacy of this decision continues to influence the self-understanding of its adherents. The Samaj itself completed a full paradoxical circle. Founded in the name of rationalism, it ended up with a denial of the role of reason and the intellect in the religious quest and the upholding of individual experience as supreme.

NOTES

1. Halbfass, *India and Europe,* 203.
2. For Spencer's influence, see Heimsath, *Indian Nationalism and Hindu Social Reform,* 49–50.
3. Kopf's excellent study, *British Orientalism and the Bengal Renaissance,* is still authoritative.
4. Wilson, quoted in ibid., 176.
5. Ibid., 284.
6. See Majumdar, *History of the Freedom Movement in India,* 3:259–60.
7. I am not aware of any study that has examined the effects of this period of change on the authority of these texts.
8. For a critical study of the growth and development of the Brahmo Samaj, see Kopf, *Brahmo Samaj.* For a specific discussion of the legacy and wide influence of the movement, see chap. 2.

9. For an excellent discussion on Roy, see Halbfass, *India and Europe,* chap. 12. Halbfass, however, is less concerned with Roy's attitude to scriptural authority and more with the complexity of Roy's context and hermeneutics.

10. In 1943 Debendranath Tagore changed the name of the Brahmo Sabha to Brahmo Samaj.

11. See Das, *Shadow of the Cross,* 64. Das is of the opinion that Roy mixed up the issues of religion and nationalism, the inevitable result of the colonial context in which he operated. According to him, the use of the texts as a medium of instruction was primarily the result of nationalistic sentiment.

12. See Ray, *Religious Movements in Modern Bengal,* 13. It is important to note that, for Roy, the Upaniṣads were an integral part of the Vedas and not outside their scope.

13. Mitra, *Resurgent India,* 65.

14. Ibid., 66.

15. See, Killingley, "Rammohun Roy's Interpretation of the Vedānta," 342–44. As an example of this tendency, Killingley cites Roy's explanation that those parts of the Vedas that teach the worship of figured gods represent an inferior view for the benefit of worshipers incapable of grasping the higher truths. Rammohun Roy justified this interpretation as the only way of preserving the consistency of the text.

16. This attempt to suggest a different view relies a great deal upon Killingley's study. His work is concerned primarily with contrasting the interpretations of Śaṅkara and Rammohun Roy, but it also provides significant clues for ascertaining Roy's attitude to the authority of the Vedas.

17. Rammohun Roy, quoted in ibid., 341. Roy's significant writings appeared in both Bengali and English. For a view on the hermeneutical significance of his use of English, see Halbfass, *India and Europe,* 203–4.

18. Rammohun Roy, quoted in Killingley, "Rammohun Roy's Interpretation of the Vedānta," 341.

19. Ibid., 328–36.

20. Ibid., 349–51.

21. Ibid., 343.

22. It is strange that such a consequential decision has not received any detailed treatment in recent works discussing the movement under Debendranath Tagore. Kopf, *Brahmo Samaj,* makes only brief mention of it. See 51. Kopf's concern is more with the sociological dimensions of the movement.

23. See Mitra, *Resurgent India,* 79–82.

24. Biswas, "Maharshi Debendranath Tagore and the Tattvabodhini Sabha," in Gupta, ed., *Studies in the Bengal Renaissance.* See 33–46.

25. See Sastri, *History of the Brahmo Samaj,* 63.

26. Quoted in ibid., 63–64. Sastri is of the opinion that this article was penned by Rajnarain Bose, who had then recently joined the Brahmo Samaj. Mitra, *Resurgent India,* attributes this piece of writing to Debendranath Tagore.

27. For a good summary of Datta's views, see Kopf, *Brahmo Samaj,* 49–54.

28. Sastri, *History of the Brahmo Samaj,* 65.

29. Ibid., 65. See also Ray, *Religious Movements in Modern Bengal,* 13–14.

30. It is unfortunate that there are no records of the details of argument on both sides of the question, or of the nature of the studies and inquiries undertaken by Debendranath Tagore and his emissaries at Benares. These would have thrown great light on the nature of the debate and the propositions that led Debendranath Tagore to concede to Datta.

31. See Killingley, "Rammohun Roy's Interpretation of the Vedānta," 349.

32. The eleven authentic Upaniṣads mentioned here are probably those of the same number commented upon by Śaṅkara.

33. Debendranath Tagore, quoted in Das, *Shadow of the Cross,* 70–71.

34. See Farquhar, *Modern Religious Movements in India,* 71–73. See also 41.

35. Debendranath Tagore's *Brahmo Dharma* does not offer a detailed discussion on the source of knowledge of God. Tagore speaks of an innate knowledge of God hidden in the hearts of all human beings. This innate knowledge is kindled by the study of the universe, in which is revealed the wisdom, beneficience, glory, and majesty of God.

The few discussions in the *Brahmo Dharma* on the nature of intuition are not very lucid. At one point the innate knowledge of God is presented as the presupposition of our sense of dependence and imperfection. There is no basis for considering ourselves to be dependent and imperfect, says Tagore, unless there is a perfect and independent being. This intuitive knowledge of God is described as being natural to every soul. These views of Debendranath Tagore closely parallel the Unitarian ideas of Channing and Parker discussed below, and are suggestive of the influence of the Unitarians.

36. Debendranath Tagore, quoted in Mitra, *Resurgent India,* 85. Halbfass points to the influence of various European sources on Debendranath Tagore's search for personal experience. See *India and Europe,* 396.

37. Kopf, *Brahmo Samaj,* 175.

38. Ibid., 79.

39. Ibid., 81.

40. Ibid., 82–83.

41. Sen, "The Living God in England and India," a sermon delivered at Mill-Hill Chapel, Leeds, August 28, 1870, in Sen, *Discourses and Writings,* 5.

42. Sastri, *History of the Brahmo Samaj,* 149.

43. I am not aware of any work that specifically studies and analyzes Sen's thought. There are a few texts containing surveys of a very general kind only.

44. Sen, "Great Men," a lecture delivered at the Town Hall, Calcutta, September 28, 1866, in Collet, ed., *Lectures and Tracts,* 49–93.

45. Ibid., 53. One is reminded of the same argument in Rammohun Roy. In Sen, the arguments are worked out in more detail.

46. Sen, "The Religious Importance of Mental Philosophy," two lectures delivered to the students of the Calcutta Brahmo School, May 5 and 12, 1867, in Collet, ed., *Lectures and Tracts,* 184.

47. Ibid.

48. Sen, "Great Men," in Collet, ed., *Lectures and Tracts,* 57.

49. Ibid., 57–58.

50. The Brahmo Samaj has consistently rejected the orthodox theory of the *avatāra.*

51. Collet, ed., *Lectures and Tracts,* 71–74.

52. Ibid., 88.

53. Sen, "Regenerating Faith," a sermon preached on the occasion of the thirty-eighth anniversary of the Brahmo Samaj, January 24, 1868, in Collet, ed., *Lectures and Tracts,* 110.

54. Sen, "Living God in England and India," 9–11.

55. Sen, "Primitive Faith and Modern Speculations," substance of an anniversary lecture at the Town Hall, Calcutta, January 23, 1872, in Sen, *Discourses and Writings,* 46.

56. Sen, "The Existence of God," substance of an unpublished lecture at Albert Hall, Calcutta, January 29, 1879, in Sen, *Discourses and Writings,* 58.

57. See Kopf, *Brahmo Samaj,* chap. 9. See also Sastri, *History of the Brahmo Samaj,* 163–86.

58. The idea of *ādeśa* was noted in connection with Debendranath Tagore.

59. Sen. "Apostles of the New Dispensation," a lecture delivered at the Town Hall, Calcutta, January 22, 1881, and quoted in Sastri, *History of the Brahmo Samaj,* 230.

60. Sen, *New Dispensation or Religion of Harmony,* 259–59. This particular work is a compilation of his writings of May–December 1881.

61. See ibid., 33–35.

62. Ibid., 34–35.
63. Ibid., 257.
64. Ibid., 250.
65. Ibid., 86.
66. Kopf, *Brahmo Samaj,* 4.
67. Ganguly, *Raja Ram Mohun Roy,* 141.
68. Kopf, *Brahmo Samaj,* 15–26.
69. Sastri, *History of the Brahmo Samaj,* 336.
70. For a full discussion of the basic doctrines and arguments of Unitarian Christianity, see Channing, *Complete Works,* 292–306.
71. Ibid., xvii.
72. Ibid., 293.
73. Parker, *Collected Works,* 1:216.
74. Ibid., xii.
75. Ibid., 140. For full discussion, see 138–50.
76. Smith, "Sacred Persistence," 43.
77. Comments made on papers presented at the "Arguing the Vedas" panel, American Academy of Religion, Annual Meeting, New Orleans, 1990.
78. For a Neo-Vedānta view on the limits of scripture and doctrine, see Rambachan, "Where Words Fail," 361–71.
79. For a detailed treatment of the implications of the authority of intuition on the status of scripture, reason, and exegesis, see Anantanand Rambachan, *The Limits of Scripture* (Honolulu: University of Hawaii Press, forthcoming).
80. For a discussion of the way in which the Vedas function as a valid source of knowledge for Śaṅkara and a contrast with Neo-Vedānta interpretations, see Rambachan, *Accomplishing the Accomplished.*
81. For an attempt to develop an argument along these lines, see Rambachan, "Swami Vivekananda's Use of Science," 331–42.

REFERENCES

Channing, W. E.
1880 *The Complete Works.* London: Williams and Norgate.

Das, S. K.
1974 *The Shadow of the Cross: Christianity and Hinduism in a Colonial Context.* Delhi: Munshiram Manoharlal.

Farquhar, J. N.
1977 *Modern Religious Movements in India.* Delhi: Munshiram Manoharlal.

Ganguly, N. C.
1934 *Raja Ram Mohun Roy.* Calcutta: YMCA Publishing House.

Gupta, M.
1977 *The Gospel Ramakrishna.* Trans. Swami Nikhilananda. New York: Ramakrishna Vivekananda Center.

Halbfass, W.
1988 *India and Europe.* Albany: State University of New York Press.

Heimsath, C. H.
1964 *Indian Nationalism and Hindu Social Reform.* Princeton: Princeton University Press.

Isherwood, C.
1974 *Ramakrishna and His Disciples.* 3d ed. Calcutta: Advaita Ashrama.

Jones, K. W.
1976 *Arya Dharm: Hindu Consciousness in Nineteenth Century Punjab.* Berkeley: University of California Press.

Killingley, D.
1977 "Rammohun Roy's Interpretation of the Vedānta." Ph.D. diss., London, School of African and Asian Studies.

Kopf, D.
1969 *British Orientalism and the Bengal Renaissance.* Berkeley: University of California Press.
1979 *The Brahmo Samaj and the Shaping of the Modern Indian Mind.* Princeton: Princeton University Press.

Majumdar, R. C.
1962–63 *History of the Freedom Movement in India.* Calcutta: Firma K. L. Mukhopadhyay.

Mitra, S.
1963 *Resurgent India.* Delhi: Allied.

Panikkar, K. M.
1963 *The Foundations of New India.* London: Allen and Unwin.
1964 *Hinduism and the West.* Chandigarh: Panjab University.

Parker, T.
1863–65 *The Collected Works.* Ed. Frances Power Cobbe. 12 vols. London: Trubner.

Rai, L.
1967 *A History of the Arya Samaj.* Bombay: Orient Longmans.

Rambachan, A.

1991 *Accomplishing the Accomplished: The Vedas as a Source of Valid Knowledge in Śaṅkara.* Honolulu: University of Hawaii Press.

1990 "Swami Vivekananda's Use of Science as an Analogy for the Attainment of *Mokṣa.*" *Philosophy East and West* 40 (July): 331–42.

1987 "Where Words Fail: The Limits of Scriptural Authority in the Hermeneutics of a Contemporary Advaitin." *Philosophy East and West* 37 (October): 361–71.

Ray, B. G.

1965 *Religious Movements in Modern Bengal.* Santiniketan: Visva-Bharati.

Sastri, S.

1974 *History of the Brahmo Samaj.* 2d ed. Calcutta: Sadharan Brahmo Samaj.

Sen, K. C.

1870 *Lectures and Tracts.* Ed. S. D Collet. London: Strahan.

1904 *Discourses and Writings.* Calcutta: Brahmo Tract Society.

1903 *The New Dispensation or Religion of Harmony.* Calcutta: Bidhan Press.

Smith, Brian

1990 Comments at "Arguing the Vedas" panel, American Academy of Religion, Annual Meeting, New Orleans.

Smith, Jonathan

1982 *Imagining Religion.* Chicago: University of Chicago Press.

Tagore, D.

1928 *Brahmo Dharma.* Trans. H. C. Sarkar. Calcutta: H. C. Sarkar.

10

Poets and Fishes

Modern Indian Interpretations of the Vedic Rishi

LAURIE L. PATTON

THE PROBLEM OF THE RISHI

THE STORIES VARY ABOUT the composers of the *Ṛg-Veda* (RV) 8.67. According to two Vedic commentaries, the *Nirukta* (fifth century B.C.E.)[1] and the *Bṛhaddevatā* (first century C.E.),[2] some fishes caught in a net are the rishis of the hymn. The commentary tells the tale in the following way:

> Fishermen, having unexpectedly caught sight of some fish in the water of the [river] Sarasvatī, cast a net, caught them and threw them out of the water onto the ground. And they, quite frightened by the flight of their bodies, praised the sons of Aditi. And [the Ādityas] released them, and kindly spoke with the fishermen. (BD 6.88–89)[3]

A related commentary from the fourth century C.E., Kātyāyana's *Sarvānukramaṇī*, states that the rishi of the hymn could be either a person, Matsya Sāmmada, also mentioned in the *Śatapatha Brāhmaṇa*; or another person, Mānya Maitrāvaruṇi; or simply, "many fishes caught in a net." A twentieth-century interpreter, Ram Gopal, suggests that king Matsya might well have been the real rishi, but due to confusion in tradition he was later mistaken for a fish.[4]

The above example is one among many such puzzles of authorship of the Ṛg-Vedic hymns, or *sūktas*.[5] Most interpretive approaches to the canon have had to grapple with such a long-standing tradition of obscurity—perhaps only another version of the *parokṣa,* or hiddenness, which many Vedic texts declare the gods to love so dearly. It has become a commonplace to observe that the Vedas, their meaning, and their authors have been "constructed" by both Western and Indian interpreters for centuries. In this sense, the history of Vedic interpretation can take its place as an intriguing, but rather straightforward, lesson of canon formation. J. Z. Smith[6] has provided a compelling definition of the construction of canon, one that involves a process of taxonomical thought. Canon creation involves the collection of data into a list, the discovery of a pattern, and the determination of some common principle that underlies the pattern. Canonical interpretation involves the use of this principle for prediction (omen), interdiction (taboo), or retrospection (history).[7] If one is to take Smith's suggestions seriously in the study of Indian religions, the point is not simply to admit that some construction is inevitable in the study of Vedism. As the other chapters in this volume attest, the point is to examine strategies involved in that construction.

One aspect of canon construction involves the question of authorship. Leaving aside for the moment the question of whether one should attribute the origins of the Indian heritage to a man or a fish, this chapter will attempt to discuss the problem of authorship from another angle: how have the creators of canon, in this case the Vedic rishis, been interpreted? Sheldon Pollock has tackled one aspect of the problem in his article, "Mīmāṃsā and the Problem of History in Traditional India." Pollock discusses the suppression of historical consciousness in India via the claims of the religio-philosophical school of Mīmāṃsā about the transcendental nature of the Vedas. According to the *Pūrva Mīmāṃsā Sūtra*s (PMS), the Vedas' status as *apauruṣeyatva* texts—texts "existing beyond the human"—is proven by the strategy of removing authorship from the *Ṛg-Veda* entirely. According to Mīmāṃsā, the Vedas are transcendent because they have no beginning in time and no author; those men whose names are associated with particular hymns or particular recensions (such as Paippalādaka) are simply scholars specializing in the transmission of the Vedas (PMS 1.1.29–30).[8]

Yet despite Mīmāṃsā's influence in many areas of Vedic interpretation, the question of authorship has not been erased. As the above commentaries indicate, despite Mīmāṃsā's strategies, the rishis are nonetheless discussed in a variety of Vedic texts. And, even if the rishis are not viewed as authors in the Western sense, they remain powerful agents of canon, and their lineage (*gotra*) and narrative traditions are used in a number of different ways throughout the history of Vedic interpretation.[9]

This chapter will address the twentieth-century interpretation of the Vedic rishis. More specifically, it will focus on the points of interaction between India and the West, where the discussion of authorship of the Vedas arises most clearly. The nineteenth- and twentieth-century Orientalist portrayal of the rishis of the *Ṛg-Veda* is well known, at least as such a portrayal is part of the larger Indological project of discovering origins. Whether such scholarship characterizes the rishis as childlike, following Max Müller;[10] as intuitively metaphorical, following Abel Bergaigne;[11] or barbarian, following Hermann Oldenberg,[12] the colonialist ring is unfamiliar and unmistakable.

Moreover, recent Western discourse exposing the biases of such Orientalist constructions as that of Edward Said,[13] Ronald Inden,[14] Romila Thapar,[15] and many others is also well known. These scholars have outlined the ways in which conventional Western writing about India is essentialist—reducing the multifaceted complexity of geographically defined religious beliefs and practices to a series of essences that fall under the false rubric, "Hinduism."[16] On the one hand, argue the post-Orientalists, Orientalist scholars have pedestalized these beliefs and practices by seeing them as mystical, magical, dreamlike, and feminine. On the other hand, the post-Orientalists go on, Orientalists have denigrated these beliefs and practices by characterizing them as, to use Max Müller's description of the Brāhmaṇas, "theological twiddle-twaddle," childlike in their simplicity and wonder, and primitive in their "savage" worship of "idols." In either case, the underlying point of the post-Orientalist critique is that such practices are always portrayed as essentially "other" than the West.

While in this chapter I intend to applaud and welcome much of the post-Orientalist critique, I also want to suggest that it, too, contains seeds of bias. Although much of the post-Orientalist perspective has fueled the present Subalternist school of thought, which includes many Indian writers trained in Indian universities, a great deal of post-Orientalist theory is a critique of the West by the West. More specifically, the Indian response to such Orientalist constructions, written long before the post-Orientalist critique gained full momentum either in India or in the West, has been ignored.

To address this situation, I will discuss the work of three different Ṛg-Vedic interpreters of the mid-twentieth century,[17] all of whom possess a startling breadth and depth of response to the Western portrayal of the Vedic rishi—C. Kunhan Raja, T. G. Mainkar, and Ram Gopal. Some intellectual and historical background of these three authors might be helpful.

In the 1930s, C. Kunhan Raja edited Skandasvāmin's *Ṛgvedabhāṣya* and Mādhavabhaṭṭa's *Ṛgvedānukramaṇī*. Raja's earlier work also includes numerous historical articles on the chronology and identity of various Vedic interpreters, such as Mādhavabhaṭṭa, Skandasvāmin, and others.[18] In his later years, Raja wrote more philosophical works, such as *The Quintessence of the Rig Veda,* and the work to be discussed below, *Poet-Philosophers of the Ṛgveda* (1963).

In contrast, T. G. Mainkar has concerned himself with classical poetics for much of his career, but even his earlier works show a keen interest in the *Ṛg-Veda*.[19] He combined these interests by attempting to establish

Ṛg-Vedic antecedents for Sanskrit aesthetic theory. His work, *The Ṛg Vedic Foundations of Classical Poetics* (1977), is the result. Both Kunhan Raja and Mainkar wrote analyses on the Sanskrit classics, such as the works of Kālidāsa and the *Bhagavad Gītā,* and edited a number of other, less well-known Sanskrit texts.

Ram Gopal's earlier work addresses the textual history of Vedic and post-Vedic India.[20] His more recent work branches out into a critique of Western scholarship, resulting in his *History and Principles of Vedic Interpretation* (1983). This work undertakes a critical history of Western interpretation from an Indian perspective quite similar to previous Western operations on the Indians.

Yet a brief review of these authors' publications does not fully convey their role in the development of Sanskrit education in India, much of it taking place in the decades before and after the events leading to Indian independence from British colonial rule. As a member of the Thalapilli royal family in Malabar, C. Kunhan Raja's childhood education was traditional—comprising *kāvya, alaṃkara, ayurveda,* and *jyotiṣa*. After completing this education at the turn of the century C. Kunhan Raja then went on to a government high school, and finally to the University of Madras in 1915. He earned a doctorate under the British Sanskritist A. A. Macdonell in 1920, and had the chance to meet and exchange ideas with a number of Orientalists in Europe: Moriz Winternitz in Poland, Rudolph von Roth in Germany, and so on. His work pioneered a number of Sanskrit projects, including the Sanskrit Series of Madras University, the *Annals of Oriental Research,* and the *New Catalogus Catalogorum,* revising Theodor Aufrecht's earlier work. He is also responsible for organizing a number of manuscript libraries, most notably the Adyar Library, where he served as director in the 1930s. His various popular writings in the editorial columns of *Brahmavidya,* the bulletin of the Adyar Library, attempt to fuse a relationship between Sanskrit learning and the regeneration of Indian culture.[21] His *Survey of Sanskrit Literature* (1962) is a somewhat more scholarly attempt to achieve the same end. Kunhan Raja advocated a higher position for Indian literatures in the educational schemes of India, and the establishment of Sanskrit universities as a means of regenerating the post-Independence educational system.

T. G. Mainkar, on the other hand, hailed from a slightly later generation of Sanskrit scholars.[22] He completed his B.A., M.A., and Ph.D. (1943) at Bombay University. In the 1940s and 1950s Mainkar went on to teach at Willingdon College, Sangli, and Fergusson College in Pune. He served as head of the Department of Sanskrit at Delhi University from 1967 to 1969, and at the University of Bombay from 1969 to 1978, before returning to Pune as head of the Bhandarkar Oriental Research Institute. Apart from these prominent positions, however, Mainkar was also known as an educator and teacher, serving as secretary of the Deccan Education Society, and principal of Fergusson College. He also delighted in delivering lectures to the wider public, speaking at such institutions as Max Müller Bhavan in Pune, and University Extension in Aurangabad, Ujjain, Bombay, and Kurukshetra. Like Kunhan Raja, Mainkar had much occasion to work with and teach students from the West, and was particularly fond of introducing Western literary figures such as Keats and Coleridge into his theories on Kālidāsa, Naṭyaśāstra, and the Veda. Mainkar even introduced into Sanskrit writing a new form of expression—the sonnet. Yet Mainkar's emphasis also worked in the opposite direction. In his informal talks he stressed the need of applying Sanskrit theory to modern literature and other topics of contemporary interest. The role of Sanskrit in rejuvenating modern Indian cultural life, while less programmatic than Raja, remains a vivid theme throughout Mainkar's writings.

Ram Gopal, the youngest of the three scholars, received his doctoral degree in 1953 from Delhi University—in fact the first Ph.D. degree in Sanskrit awarded by that university.[23] Ram Gopal taught at Hans Raj College in Delhi in the late 1950s, and later taught as the Kālidāsa Professor of Sanskrit and head of the Department of Sanskrit at Punjab University, Chandigarh. Distinct from Kunhan Raja and Mainkar, Ram Gopal's work is most vehemently critical of Western scholarship. His remarkable book, *India of the Vedic Kalpasūtras*, begins this critique by advertising itself as the completion of the rather incomplete *Vedic Index* compiled by A. A. Macdonell and A. B. Keith, which neglects the Kalpa Sūtras entirely.

While Raja, Mainkar, and Ram Gopal each possess a distinct style and authority of their own, they do share three things: a belief that Sanskrit education can revivify Indian culture, a common critique of the West, and an attempt to rectify Western distortions. In their efforts to counteract the Orientalist dismantling of the rishi into a series of etymologies, verb forms, and tale types, they in turn portray a Ṛg-Vedic rishi who is intentional, spiritual, and insightful. This notion of the rishi is then inserted back into history, to create a national prototype of the Indian Renaissance Man.

DĪRGHATAMAS IN RECENT IMAGINATION

In order to illustrate the attitudes of Kunhan Raja, Mainkar, and Ram Gopal, a leap back into the world of the Vedic rishi is called for. In order to be as specific and persuasive as possible, I will compare these authors' respective treatments of a single Vedic theme. All of them share an interest in the life of one Ṛg-Vedic rishi, Dīrghatamas, and his hymns of praise found in the first maṇḍala of the *Ṛg-Veda*. Thus, he provides an excellent frame for an analysis of these twentieth-century authors.

What one can piece together of this rishi from Vedic texts is fairly straightforward. Dīrghatamas ("Long Darkness") Māmateya (son of Mamata) Aucathya (son of Ucatha) is mentioned as a singer in *Ṛg-Veda* 1.158.1; in several other hymns, he is mentioned by his matronymic, Māmateya.[24] Tradition attributes *Ṛg-Veda* 1.140–1.164 to him—1.164 being the much-analyzed "*Asya Vāmasya*," the *sūkta* of the riddle of the sacrifice.[25] Composed of fifty-two stanzas, this hymn incorporates a great deal of traditional Vedic imagery to weave a labyrinthine set of explicit and implicit riddles. In a series of grammatically simple but semantically obscure verses, meanings are piled upon meanings to create an elaborate vision. For example, cows are assimilated to the Dawn and to the goddess of Speech; birds symbolize both the sun and the mortal; yet Dawn may also appear in the guise of a woman and the sun in the guise of a horse. In addition to the long-standing exegetical challenge of making sense of the hymn as a whole, the further puzzle is establishing how the poem could have possibly been composed.

While the hymn is not accompanied in the commentaries by an elaborate explanatory narrative, as are other Vedic hymns, the later Vedic texts and commentaries do tell us something of the life and times of Dīrghatamas himself. In both the Ṛg-Vedic hymn and the *Śaṅkhāyana Āraṇyaka* (2.17), he is said to have reached the tenth decade of life, thus reaping the benefits of his eloquence in true Vedic style. In the *Aitareya Brāhmaṇa* (8.23), he is the priest who consecrates the great Vedic king Bhārata Dauḥṣanti, who then traveled around the earth conquering, offering sacrifice, and singing verses.

The *Bṛhaddevatā* contains two legends about him: in one, there is a rivalry between two sons of a rishi, Ucathya and Bṛhaspati. While Ucathya's wife, Mammatā, is pregnant, Bṛhaspati approaches her for sex. The embryo cries out to him not to cause a "mixing up of seed." Bṛhaspati, unwilling to tolerate such obstruction, curses him with the words, "Let a long darkness be yours." As a result of this curse by his uncle while still in the womb, Dīrghatamas is born blind, but recovers his sight from the gods. In the second story, as a blind old man, Dīrghatamas is thrown into a river by his servants, one of whom, Traitana, attacks him, but cuts off his own torso instead. As Dīrghatamas floats downstream he is cast up in the country of the Āṅgas, where he marries Usij, a servant, and his son Kakṣīvant is born. (The two stories are in fact inconsistent, since the second ignores the fact that the rishi recovered his sight after being born.)

Versions of these same two stories are told in the *Mahābhārata* (1.7.98) as a legitimation for the dynasty of Bhārata. In the epic, the tale of the birth of Dīrghatamas provides an example of an occasion in which a Brahmin of virtue, Utathya, fathers a child, and the woman Mamatā, showing herself a lover of dharma, protests at Bṛhaspati's violation of her already implanted seed. Moreover, the *Mahābhārata* tale of Dīrghatamas shows how the sources of dharma themselves, the Vedas, can be endangered; because they have already been "learned in the womb" by Dīrghatamas, the new seed threatens interference with their birth in the form of the great rishi.[26] Similarly, in the story of Dīrghatmas' drowning, the adharmic sons, unwilling to support their father in his old age, are the villains who wish to drown the rishi, and not the servants. Moreover, when Dīrghatamas washes up on the banks, he is hired by an infertile king to beget sons upon his wife. When his wife rejects the seer in disgust, he begets sons on a servant woman instead. Finally, when the queen does accept him, he sires a great rishi, Aṅga. So too, in the main plot of the *Mahābhārata,* Satyavatī's daughter-in-law Kausalyā proves herself to be a lover of dharma, since she lies with the seer Vyāsa at her mother's command, thus giving birth to Dhṛtarāṣṭra, the Kaurava king and a principal character in the *Mahābhārata.*

Thus, both Vedic and Epic texts portray a poet with remarkable tenacity, who has strength, virility, and an ability to overcome adversity. However, it is clear that there is no single, unified tradition of the famous rishi Dīrghatamas. In fact, each version manipulates the progress of the narrative according to its particular perspectives. While the *Bṛhaddevatā* story is faithful to its Vedic ends, granting Dīrghatamas a pedigree, the *Mahābhārata* tale is told to illustrate dharmic behavior. As will be evident below, the same kinds of orchestrations and inferences are operative in twentieth-century interpreters.

RAJA

Modern Indian interpreters, too, engage in such interpretive construction of the Vedic rishi, only this time with interlocutors—Western scholars. C. Kunhan Raja begins his study of poetic voice in the *Ṛg-Veda* by criticizing the Western "metanarrative" about the march of objectivity and rationality. For Raja, modern Western histories deny that sense of rationality to the Indians. From the Western view, he writes, India is simply a series of entanglements and battles between matter and spirit, ritual and intellectualism, priests and warriors. He comments, "Thus Indian history [according to Western Indology] became an analysis of conflicting elements, with nothing that can be called a unifying genius."[27] Western Indology for Raja can best be characterized as a study of primitive contrasts, even of primitive conflicts. In the present intellectual climate, such discourse about the primitive has been well analyzed. The critique could almost be conceived of mathematically; if Indians are seen as contemporaries, they are equal to (=) "primitives"; if they have a history and we are studying their past, then their past must not be greater than (>) the Greeks.

Writing a good fifteen years earlier than even the earliest of post-Orientalist critics, Raja remarks that Greek literature alone marks the beginning of human civilization for the West. Western scholars have coped with the problem of Indian civilization by "wedging it between creation and historical times," allowing it to mark only some beginnings of civilization. The effect of this arrangement was to give a place to Indian civilization close to the beginning, but at the same time to dub it as primitive. Raja goes on:

> The *Ṛg Veda,* which forms the earliest record of the Indians, was taken as the starting point in the development of civilization in India, and as such it was supposed to form the record of only a primitive culture. Only thus could Greek civilization be taken as continuing the real civilization of man and making further contribution to human civilization.[28]

Because the similarities are remarkable, I will succumb to the temptation of comparing Raja's statements about this classic Western procedure with those of postmodern classicist Detienne:

> At the dawn of the nineteenth century, the Greek no longer has a legal right to error or foolish things: born in the land where arises consciousness of the self, where is formed the spiritual universe which is still ours. . . .The Greek is the bearer of Reason. . . .everything in the mythology of civilized peoples that can shock us is in fact only the remains of a state of mind assumed not long ago by all of mankind and of which the contemporary primitives show us the paramount influence as well as the cohesion.[29]

Raja's strategy of reconstructing Dīrghatamas is motivated by an attempt to construct a Vedic "spirit" that parallels the Greek in depth and brilliance. In a kind of modified Vedāntan position, he views the Ṛg-Vedic system of thought as a series of changes being rung on the power of the Absolute—the ultimate unity. Moreover, the Vedas express a unity of ritual, art (in the form of poetry and song), and philosophy regarding the origin of the world and man's relation to the world.[30] All of these Vedic formulations express an Indian continuity of thought. Raja emphasizes Dīrghatamas' genius as part of this overall project. Dīrghatamas' master-work, RV 1.164, is the ultimate expression of this seamless Vedic wisdom and artistic unity, whereby a hymn "full of nature and mysticism and symbolism" pulls together and unifies combinations and contrasts. Raja writes of 1.164,

> The way in which the common people gather in street corners or in city squares or in the open fields to roast a bull in cow dung. . .cannot but attract our admiration, with the common people and their simple ways of life, brought into a situation of the grand religious ritual; this is another remarkable combination of contrasts which only a real poet can reconcile.[31]

In Raja's analysis of this and earlier *sūktas*, Dīrghatamas proves to be the philosopher sage who possesses his own distinctive poetic voice. Dīrghatamas' credibility is strengthened by the fact that ancient indices mention his father, Utathya ("Worthy of poetry"), and his son, Kakṣīvan. And since this lineage is known to other poets, and said to have been patronized by the Aśvins, then scholars have reason to assume that Dīrghatamas' lineage was a famous and ancient one.[32]

Raja treats Vedic poets other than Dīrghatamas with the same degree of admiration. "Authors" such as Śunaḥśepa, Yama, Manu, and others are analyzed as individual geniuses supported by lineages. Kavaṣa Ailūṣa is a remorseful Gambler thirsting in the desert, and Yama is lauded as an innovator, the discoverer of the Path. Their "oeuvres" consist of the poems attributed to them by Vedic tradition.[33] In short, Raja appeals to the ancient *gotra* system and the stories that support it. While John Brough[34] and others[35] have shown the *gotra* system to have been an amalgam of "myth" and "history," manipulated in the Sūtra literature to establish the predominance of particular families of priests, Raja usses it to create a history of personal experience and poetic inspiration.

Raja's treatment of Śunaḥśepa's poems is worth citing as an example of his perspective. In a long discussion of *Ṛg-Veda* 1.24 and 1.25, Raja agrees with other scholars that the Śunaḥśepa story in the *Aitareya Brāhmaṇa,* in which the poet Śunaḥśepa is sold to the king and offered at the stake to Varuṇa, is a later creation about the Vedic Śunaḥśepa. Yet Raja assumes that the earlier Śunaḥśepa, the rishi, was an actual person who must have suffered tremendously in his life, otherwise he would not have been able to create such profound poetry. As Raja puts it,

> It was suffering that roused up his philosophical genius. Why should there he suffering in this life? Why should there be this sense of bondage, this loss of freedom in man? Suffering is the root of philosophy. A philosopher has his own suffering and philosophy shows him the way out of that suffering. It is this philosophy of suffering that is found in this poem.[36]

All Vedic poets—Dīrghatamas, Yama, Manu, Bṛhaspati, and others—have their own individual creative genius, which in turn contributes to the continuity of the Indian voice as a whole.

MAINKAR

Like Raja, T. G. Mainkar has his own disagreements with Western interpretation from a literary point of view. Mainkar insists that the Ṛg-Vedic imagination is not, as Oldenberg suggests, in love with the "gross and the brilliant." He shows how Western interpreters restrict similes that could be applied in various ways, even within a single hymn, a precursor to *alaṃkaraṇa* in later Indian poetics.[37] For him, the similes are proof of the delicate sensibilities and sensitivities of the Vedic seers. In another attempt to reverse the idea of the primitive, he claims that the Ṛg-Vedic poets, even at "this early hour in man's civilization," touched the archetypal pattern of the Muse, the lady who embodies inspiration.[38] He finds this Muse in the female figures of Sūryā, Sūryasya Duhitā, Uṣas, and others.

Moreover, Mainkar disagrees with the Western idea that no literary criticism exists in the *Ṛg-Veda.* Far from being an "unreflective" work, for him the *Ṛg-Veda* possesses a form of theory in the similes themselves. As often as the rishis compare their work to that of a carpenter or a weaver, they are putting forward what he terms the "craft theory" of poetry. Yet "craft theory" should not be opposed to more sophisticated theory, for it does not dispense with other equally valuable aspects of poetry, such as spontaneity, profundity, and originality. He then makes the inevitably favorable comparison with the Greeks; Plato and Aristotle, too, had a craft theory of poetry.

Mainkar's reconstruction of the rishi Dīrghatamas follows these literary lines. Mainkar discusses the Vedic seer at the end of his section on the dialogue *sūkta*s—Purūravas and Urvaśī (RV 10.95), Yama and Yamī (RV 10.10), Saramā and the Paṇis (RV 10.108), among others. Each of these dialogue *sūkta*s contain the "seeds" of dramatic form; the characters of the Vṛṣākapi *sūkta,* RV 10.86, for instance, Indra, Indrāṇī, and Vṛṣākapi, can be seen the King, Queen, and Viduṣaka of the classical drama. Like the other rishis, Mainkar views the specific genius of Dīrghatamas as a "pure, literary urge," where mythological themes are dealt with in a riddling dialogue with the gods, neatly composed and with calculated effect. Dīrghatamas' song of riddles, RV 1.164 is credited as one of the origins of metaphor and symbolism. In its paradoxical questions about the gods, the hymn is the link between the Indo-European heritage of mythological poetry and the later tradition of the Prahelikās and the Samasyapurtis.

In an additional rather bold attempt to make the Vedic poets accessible to modern readers, Mainkar writes that the rishis were referring in plain words to the natural, human inspiration all people are familiar with. Coleridge's writing of Kubla Khan is no different than Śunaḥśepa's momentary flash of insight at the hour of his death, detailed in a similar manner by Raja, above. Mainkar's notion of "artistic unity" is summed up in these human, almost romantic terms: "Poetry is born in the midst of nature, on the lap of a mountain and by the side of a confluence of rivers; from the chambers of truth and from the mind and heart of man. . . .When [the rishis] speak of *viśvapeśas* or *sucipeśas dhī* they have caught the true essence of really great poetry."[39]

Like Raja, Mainkar also emphasizes ancient family tradition, or *gotra,* pointing out that the Ṛg-Vedic seers themselves quite often speak of their three generations—the ancients, those of the middle period, and the moderns, or the *pratnas*, the *madhyamas*, and the *nūtanas*. To him, the poets must have been anxious to preserve the paternal pattern of teaching the art of composing pieces by passing it on from father to son. The rishis' "pride and joy" in the act of creation as well as their satisfaction at their loyalty to the set pattern are both prominently to be seen in any Vedic hymn. However, Mainkar, too, stresses the unity of Vedic vision; larger, profession-wide patterns as well as family patterns of composition were formative influences for the Vedic seers.[40] Mainkar further conjectures that they must have freely drawn upon a *common* property of vocabulary and idiom.[41] Only a long period of sustained, communal poetical activity could give rise to such an intricate system of rules and regulations.

RAM GOPAL

Like Mainkar and Raja, Ram Gopal launches a thorough critique of Western Vedic scholarship—only he adds an intriguing twist. In his *History and Principles of Vedic Interpretation,* Ram Gopal assumes that the dilemma of interpretation is everybody's problem, intrinsic to the difficulty of the *Ṛg-Veda* itself. Ram Gopal reminds his readers that early texts such as the *Nirukta* and the *Bṛhaddevatā* are already unclear as to the meanings of Vedic words, and hold conflicting views as to the meaning of Vedic concepts. Then, in a rather ingenious move, Ram Gopal goes on to place all interpretation, Indian and European alike, under the rubrics of traditional Indian categories: *Aitihāsika* (legendary); *Yajñika* (ritual); *Nairukta* (etymological); and *Parivrājaka* (mystical). Each approach is then subject to criticism. Since Oldenberg and Kātyāyana alike often take the view of the *Yajñikas*, they are both vulnerable to the same charge of arbitrary ritualist readings.[42] Yāska (author of the *Nirukta*), Śaunaka (or pseudo-Śaunaka, as the case may be), Renou, and Dandekar are all subject to criticism as *Aitihāsikas*, who often claim more for mythological tradition than is warranted.[43] Almost all of them—Yāska, Pāniṇi, Patañjali, Hermann Grassmann, Monier Monier-Williams, Max Müller, H. H. Wilson, and many others—are subject to critique as *Nairuktas*, executing their fanciful etymological procedures.[44] And mystics from Ānandatīrtha to Aurobindo are all scrutinized for their mystical readings of Vedic texts. Among other advantages, this ingenious grouping allows Ram Gopal to undertake a systematic comparison of the Vedic commentators (*bhāṣya-kāras*) and the modern interpreters of the Vedas, which he goes on to do in the rest of the volume. Although a discussion of all of Ram Gopal's critiques would far outlast the scope of this chapter, it suffices to say that the structure outlined above allows him to undertake a systematic comparison of the Vedic *bhāṣyakāra*s and the modern interpreters of the Vedas. This move underscores both the lack of originality of much of Western scholarship and reverses its general disdain of Indian interpretation.

Ram Gopal's writing borders on disgust for much of the Western predilection to pass judgment on the Vedas without ever having looked at an original text.[45] Ram Gopal centers much of his comparison on the Western evaluation of *Vedabhāṣya*s such as Sāyaṇa's. Rudolph von Roth and Hermann Oldenberg, among others, were "afraid of admitting publically" that they had ever looked at Sāyaṇa.[46] Ram Gopal claims rightly that Roth's famous utterance, "Los von Sāyaṇa!" (Get rid of Sāyaṇa!) had led or misled scholars for a significant period of time. And although Ram Gopal does allow that scholars such as Karl Geldner and Richard Pischel have stated that due help must always be derived form the *Vedabhāṣya*s,[47] he nonetheless goes to conclude:[48]

> A comparative analysis made by me of the *Vedābhāṣya*s and the modern exegetical studies. . . reveals that most of the modern attempts at Vedic exegesis are little more than a rehash and translation of the meanings already suggested by the *Vedabhāṣyakāra*s, and that the study of the *Vedabhāṣyakāra*s is as important as that of the modern interpretation and lexicons for determining the correct meaning of the Veda.[49]

In one of his pithier criticisms, repeated often throughout the book, Ram Gopal remarks that "The translations of the Vedas attempted by modern scholars do not fully justify their claim of objectivity and leave much to be desired."[50] In a tone resembling much of the more recent scholarship on Orientalism, Ram Gopal writes that what is "absurd" is not Vedic culture, but the quest for rationality and simplification within the Vedas, and the attempt (both Indian and Western) to explain away all of its multileveled meanings and verbal constructions.[51] Indeed, Ram Gopal does not arrange these criticisms along exclusively cultural lines. In fact, he praises Abel Bergaigne for complaining that European exegesis is "under an obsession to remove all bizarre things and to bring the hymns of the rishis in line with our own aesthetic sense."[52]

For all of his acrimony, Ram Gopal also embarks upon a reconstructive project; his attitude toward the work of Dīrghatamas reflects this attitude. For Ram Gopal, all linguistic embellishments, all poetic effects are a deliberate allegorical intention on the part of the rishi. He writes, "It must be admitted without demur that the seers must have intended to express absolutely definite and unequivocal meanings through the words employed in the Vedas which are undoubtedly literary compositions of a very high order."[53]

Although Ram Gopal does not spend time analyzing the poetic personality of Dīrghatamas, the poet's work is no less intentional in his eyes. Ram Gopal explicitly favors the *parivrājaka,* or mystical/allegorical interpretation of Dīrghatmas' hymn 1.164, citing the *Aitareya Āraṇyaka* and the *Jaiminīya Upaniṣad Brāhmaṇa* as credible sources for this method. These sources regard *praṇa* as the referent of RV 1.164.31: "I have seen the tireless cowherd, traveling up and down along the paths. Clothing himself in those [rays], concentric and spreading, he keeps revolving among the worlds." Similarly, *ātman* is rightly the referent of 1.164.38: "The one goes away; one comes back, compelled by its own nature; the immortal comes from the same womb as the mortal. The two constantly travel in opposition; when people perceive the one, they do not perceive the other." As he comments on RV 1.164 and similar *sūkta*s, "It cannot be gainsaid that the spiritual interpretation of certain Vedic hymns reflects the real intentions of the seers, and most of the ancient and modern scholars are inclined to agree on the tenor of such hymns, though they may differ about the minute details."[54]

In contrast, Ram Gopal cites with disapprobation Sāyaṇa's *Vaiyākaraṇa* (grammatical) interpretation of verse 41 of the same *sūkta,* dismissing it as "fanciful, arbitrary, and of little relevance." The verse makes a single allusion to an eight-footed buffalo cow. According to the grammatical interpretation of the verse, the eight-footed buffalo cow is characterized as speech; she is one-footed in crude form only; two-footed in declension and conjugation; four-footed in its division into nouns, verbs, prepositions, and particles; eight-footed through the eight cases; and nine-footed as the eight cases with the addition of the indeclinables.

THE WRITING OF HISTORY

One can gather from these writers' works why the exclusively historical, grammatical, mythological, or ritual interpretations of the Vedas draw such cries of protest from these interpreters. Any understanding of the Vedas must involve a sense that the rishis knew what they were doing. Moreover, in the creation of a Vedic Renaissance Man, Raja, Mainkar, and Ram Gopal all imply that the rishis were bound together by a similar outlook, a singular spirit of the times. In addition, all of these modern exegetes put a good deal of stress on the fact that there must have been a highly developed, sophisticated pre-Vedic society with its own ancient tradition from which the poets could draw for their inspiration.[55]

Mainkar puts the same idea more elaborately:

> [The rishi] was a wise man well conversant in the life around him and he actively participated in the religious and political life of his times. . . his similes cover a wide variety of themes, coming as they do from religion, sacrifice, home and war. The Ṛg Vedic poet therefore was not a mere cobbler of words, but knew much and had first hand experience of the life around him . . . life with all its complexities was known to him and this fact is reflected in his poetical compositions. The Ṛg Vedic poet was not a mere singer but a rishi in this sense. His wisdom was further strengthened by his assiduous study of the compositions of the previous generations. The man of knowledge was a practical man too and it is therefore that the Ṛg Vedic poet, a wise man, a *vipra,* was a man of the world as well.[56]

The wise Vedic *vipra* was also a shrewd politician and a scholar, moving between the various aspects of Vedic life (which bears a striking resemblance to modern life) with ease and aplomb.

Yet occasionally such attempts to establish a larger, unifying "genius," to use Raja's term, do not simply take advantage of obscurity, but blatantly contradict the evidence. Raja, for instance, attempts to overcome the ritualist bias by stressing that rishis do not form a hierarchy of priests. On the contrary, rishis "are citizens of ordinary life, honored and accepted for their innate worth and not as members of any order."[57] However, one does not need to look much farther than the *Puruṣa sūkta* (RV 10.129), or the numerous references to the privilege and eloquence of the sacrificers (RV 10.125; 10.71), to discern that indeed hierarchization of the social order was a primary motif in many Vedic hymns!

Other methods of solving historical puzzles are perhaps not as blatant, but just as problematically wedded to the inviolability of the Vedic rishi. Ram Gopal, usually much more suspicious in his scholarship, solves the dilemma of the identity of the Vedic iconoclast Kautsa in this manner. In Yāska's fifth-century B.C.E. dictionary, the *Nirukta,* Kautsa is named as a poet who decries the Vedas as meaningless and useless.[58] Yet other Vedic literature describes Kautsa as a teacher of dharma, a renowned and respected scholar.[59] Moreover, Kutsa, supposedly Kautsa's ancestor, is also described as a heroic seer in the *Ṛg-Veda.*[60] Thus, a problem arises: how could Kutsa be Kautsa's predecessor? Ram Gopal asks, "Could a descendent of the illustrious seer Kutsa be so disrespectful to and ignorant of the Vedic lore as depicted by Yāska?''[61] How could Kautsa be both the descendant of an esteemed and honored poet and the denigrator of the Vedas at the same time? The idea is intolerable to Ram Gopal, and the conflict inspires him to look to the tradition for other Kutsas and Kautsas—which in fact, there are: the Kautsa mentioned in the Śrauta Sūtras as the despicable soma vendor and the Kutsa mentioned as the adversary of Indra in the *Ṛg-Veda.*[62] Ram Gopal thus conjectures that the soma vendor Kautsa must be descended from the ignorant wrestler Kutsa, Indra's enemy, and that the soma vendor must be the model for Yāska's irreverent figure.[63] Ram Gopal cannot be proved or disproved on this point; what is relevant is that for Ram Gopal, the ''great poet'' principle of writing history must not be violated. Neither the rishi Kutsa nor his descendants could ever have been chosen by Yāska as a figure to criticize the Vedas.

The Kautsa problem demonstrates that, by creating the image of a conscious, inspired, powerful rishi, modern Indian interpreters attempt to respond to charges from another tradition that the Vedas are primitive. Yet Ram Gopal and Raja go even further, referring several times to the Indian nation itself. Ram Gopal writes that when the Indian intellectuals became aware of the keen interest evinced by the Western scholars in the study of the Vedas, such attention aroused a feeling of national pride among the Indian people and created a new awareness about the importance of their ''ancient scriptures.''[64] He speaks approvingly of the few Western scholars who have understood that Indian people in their thoughts and feelings still remain what they were in the past, and so long as they live in history they are Indians and possess an Indian spirit, which we meet in the hymns of Viśvamitra no less than in the Kādambarī of Bāṇa.[65]

Raja, as we have seen, protests the history of India as one of conflict and strife. He asserts that there is no evidence for a conflict between the Brahmin class and the warrior (Kṣatriya) class. On the contrary, he writes, ''These two [classes], along with the people in general, formed a single nation, properly integrated in their emotional and intellectual abilities; they were all proud of the achievements of their forefathers and they were full of hope regarding their present and their future.''[66] The tolerance, the harmonious development of religion, philosophy, the sciences, and art is also the result of this original genius of the nation: ''The foundation for such a state of affairs, unknown to any other nation in the world, was laid firmly in the Vedic period itself. People with different intellectual abilities, people following different professions and avocations, all together formed a united nation.''[67]

Although a case could be made for some cultural unity of the Vedic period, a large-scale, politically organized unit such as a ''nation'' does not appear in Vedic literature.[68] Yet the historical idea of a Vedic Indian nation might well be a useful way to create a history of national identity in the present. Raja, Mainkar, and Ram Gopal are all writing during the generations following independence. Raja, the earliest, is explicitly concerned with a nationalist ideal. As he writes in *The Quintessence of the Ṛg Veda,* "The *Ṛg Veda* must be lifted out of sectarian religion and presented as a national literature with a universal appeal."[69] Ram Gopal's invocation of an Indian spirit, cited above, is not far removed from Raja's sentiments; Mainkar, too, invokes the democratic ideal in his analysis of the Vedic seers. Thus, all are involved in a struggle to determine a cultural and national identity. And, as Ram Gopal himself almost suggests, the Vedas, and the Vedic rishi as the Indian prototype, can serve in this project.

CONCLUSIONS

An examination of these Vedic interpreters teaches certain lessons. It is clear that a certain ethnocentrism exists even in the Western "discovery" of its own Orientalism. To put it in all-too-familiar terminology, the West was not the first to discover its own cultural bias. Even in its self-criticism, the West has turned a deaf ear to the other. The other, meanwhile, has been correcting the West for decades.

Indeed, the above discussion also reveals some of the problems with using the term "other" at all. Raja, Mainkar, and Ram Gopal write in English and explicitly engage European discourse while defending the unity of Indian culture; their status as "other" thus becomes infinitely complex. Such complexity reveals the fact that, even as a self-critical term, the "other" threatens to become a "master-word," with too little meaning and too much power, or as Gayatri Spivak writes, "so institutionalized we should put it on T-shirts."[70]

This exploration also reveals, however, that modern Indian interpreters have their own strategies for exonerating the image of the rishi in this face of others who are dishonoring him. Although Mainkar, Raja, and Ram Gopal correctly attempt to humanize and historicize the rishis, their seers become virtually invincible, and Vedic culture is generalized into a unified, coherent whole. In a recent article Romila Thapar suggests that Hindu communal ideology tends to claim legitimacy from the past.[71] Such ideology asserts that there has always been a well-defined and historically evolved religion that we now call Hinduism and an equally clearly defined Hindu community. One can discern a similar strategy at work in the reconstruction of the Vedic rishi.

As Thapar suggests, these strategies, too, must be subject to critique. However, they must also be distinguished from Western constructions in one important way. While Western scholars might worry about who shall articulate what for whom, and what one might call "them" in the meanwhile, these authors are not so self-absorbed. Raja, Mainkar, and Ram

Gopal are engaged in an explicit attempt to wrest the rishi back from the West, and to make a claim to American and European attention. Yet these early objections of Indian scholars have gone unheard in the West. Thus, as Spivak also notes, the question of "who will speak" is less crucial than the question of "who will listen."

Finally, one might return to the problem of the poet and the fish. The brief exploration above has shown that reconstructive strategies are commonplace in interpretive works of the *Ṛg-Veda*; myth-making is endemic to any retrieval of the Vedic past, whether in Sanskrit, German, English, or Hindi. If this is indeed the case, then the boundaries between India and the West become newly blurred. Relatedly, one might speculate that the author of the *Bṛhaddevatā,* himself well-versed in tradition, might not have ignorantly misclassified the rishi of *Ṛg-Veda* 8.67 at all. He might have known that myth and history, fish and poet, are always interwoven, and known it better than anyone has assumed thus far.

NOTES

I wish to thank Sheldon Pollock, Brian Smith, Wendy Doniger, and Linda Hess, who gave their helpful comments before and during the panel, "Arguing the Veda: Studies in Authority and Anxiety," American Academy of Religion, 1990. I also wish to thank Bruce Chilton, David Pierce, Anthony Guerra, Sanjib Baruah, and other members of the Bard College faculty for their helpful comments on this chapter.

1. Nirukta 7.27. See *The Nighaṇṭu and the Nirukta, The Oldest Indian Treatise on Etymology, Philology, and Semantics,* Critically Edited From Original Manuscripts and Translated by Lakshman Sarup. Also see his *Nirukta: Sanskrit Text, with an Appendix Showing the Relation of the Nirukta with other Sanskrit Works.*

2. *Bṛhaddevatā* 6.88–89. See the *Bṛhaddevatā,* edited and translated by Arthur Anthony Macdonell, 2 vols. For a revised edition and a discussion of the date, see Tokunaga, "On the Recensions of the *Bṛhaddevatā*"; also his earlier work, "Text and Legends of the *Bṛhaddevatā.*"

3. dhīvarāsahasā mīnān dṛṣṭvā sārasvate jale/
jālam prakṣipya tān baddhvodakṣipan salilāt sthalam//
śarirapāt abhītāste tuṣṭuvuś cāditeḥ sutān/
mumucus tāṃs tatas te ca prasannās tān samūdire//

4. Gopal, *Principles,* 191.

5. To name two of the more striking examples, in the *anukramaṇīs*, Kapota, "dove" is named as the rishi of RV 10.165; so too "Hiraṇyagarbha" is declared as the seer of hymn 10.121. As one scholar puts it,

A comparative analysis of the various traditions concerning the rishis shows that none of them is fully reliable. . . .most of the available traditions seem to be based on mere conjectures which are conflicting in some cases. . . .At best, they can only be *aitihāsika,* legendary, in character but not necessarily in keeping with the original meaning in tended by the seer (Gopal, *Principles,* 191)

6. "Sacred Persistence," 36–52.

7. Ibid., 48

8. See Pollock, "Mīmāṃsā and the Problem of History," 608, for a full discussion of these proofs of transcendence in Śabara, Kumārila, and other commentators. Moreover, according to Mīmāṃsā, the Vedas have no historical contents. All those references that are suggestive of historical contents are, via the strategy of word derivation, proven to be merely phonemic resemblances to the names of historical persons (PMS 1.1.31).

9. I have discussed this point at length in "Beyond the Myth of Origins"; also see my "Transparent Text."

10. *Chips From a German Workshop*, 2:27.

11. *La Religion Vedique*, 3:319–21.

12. Oldenberg, *Religion des Veda*, 3.

13. See Said, *Orientalism*.

14. Inden, *Imagining India*.

15. See her "Imagined Religious Communities?"; "Sati in History"; and *Cultural Transaction and Early India*.

16. In the Orientalist view, the essentials of such a Hinduism have constituted recognition of the Vedas, belief in reincarnation, the doctrine of karma, and the hierarchical caste structure. Many post-Orientalist scholars point out that, contrary to what Western scholars have written, there never has been in precolonial times any such thing as a single "Hinduism" for all of India. Von Stietencron argues that given the various sects within India constitute coherent distinct systems, but what the West has called "Hinduism" is a geographically defined group of distinct but related religions. Lumping together these different religions in one religion according to preconceived Western/Christian notions is comparable to the ludicrous project of lumping together all of Judaism, Christianity and Islam, which are also cognate religions united by origin in the same region.

17. Of course, the pitfalls of paternalism have not been altogether transcended by such a move. One still risks paternalism "once removed," articulating "for" the Indian interpreters. Yet Indian writers have already published extensively themselves. Thus, one might still wonder about the reasons for the Western ignorance of such writers; it may well be

due to the West's own ambivalence about taking others' discourses truly seriously. Western scholars have reached the point where they can blame themselves for imposing their categories on others, but actually to bring those others into the realm of interpretive debate might still be too threatening. At any rate, given the fact that Indian interpreters have already placed themselves in the arena of public debate, it is up to Westerners to notice.

18. See his *Ṛg Veda Vyākhyā Mādhavakṛtā*; "Commentaries on *Rigveda* and *Nirukta*"; "Chronology of the *Vedabhāṣyakāras*"; *The ṚgVedabhāṣya of Skandasvāmin*; *In Defense of Mīmāṃsā*.

19. See his *Studies in Sanskrit Dramatic Criticism; Kālidāsa, His Life and Thought; Sanskrit Theory of Drama and Dramaturgy; The Theory of the Saṇdhis and the Saṇdhyaṁgas*. Also see his edition and translation of Iśvarakṛṣṇa's *Sāṃkhyakārikā*, with the commentary of Gauḍapāda; *The Vāsiṣṭha Rāmāyaṇa; The Making of the Vedānta; Mysticism in the Ṛg Veda; Some Poetical Aspects of Ṛg Vedic Repetitions;* and *Ṛgveda-kavi-vimarśaḥ*. Mainkar also collaborated on an edition and translation of the *Dhammapada* with C. Kunhan Raja.

20. See his *Vaidika Vyākaraṇa; India of Vedic Kalpasūtras;* and *Kālidāsa, His Art and Culture*.

21. See *C. Kunhan Raja Presentation Volume*, published by the Adyar Library for a full biography.

22. See *An Homage to Dr. Mainkar*, a memorial volume published shortly after his untimely death, for full biogaphical details. In addition to a foreword by R. N. Dandekar and several scholarly essays, it also includes students' and colleagues' recollections of his scholarly life.

23. Although I was unable to contact Ram Gopal in person, much of the biographical detail presented here I have obtained from personal interviews with Professor Patyal of Deccan College and Professor T. K. Sharma, of S.G.T.B. Khalsa College, Delhi.

24. RV 1.147.3; 1.152.6; 4.4.13.

25. See Raja's *Asya Vāmasya Hymn*; Agrawala, *Thousand Syllabled Speech*; Brown, "Agni, Sun and Sacrifice," for some representative interpretations of this hymn.

26. In addition, the implicit rivalry set up between Dīrghatamas and Bṛhaspati in the *Bṛhaddevatā* tale is expanded in the *Mahābhārata* version. Dīrghatmas becomes Bṛhaspati's "upper in might."

27. Raja, *Poet-Philosophers*, xviii.

28. Ibid., 2.

29. Detienne, *Creation of Mythology*, 8–13. And, for good measure, also compare Ram Gopal: "Most of the Western Orientalists have striven to find in the Vedas such primitive and puerile ideas as could be compared with the practices and beliefs of the most primitive and uncivilized tribes of the world" (*Principles*, 183–84).

30. Raja, *Poet-Philosophers*, xviii.

31. Ibid., 47.

32. Ibid., 47–49.

33. It should be noted here that Raja's constructions are often based upon extrapolation backwards from the later texts. In his discussion of Bṛhaspati, for instance (*Poet-Philosophers*, 50–55), Raja insists on treating "The Lord of Speech" both as a god and a poet. Raja bases his analysis entirely on the fact that Bṛhaspati is named as a poet twice in the "ancient indices", as well as invoked as a god.

34. See his "Early History of the Gotras"; and *Early Brahmanical System of Gotra and Pravara*.

35. See Oldenberg, "Über die Liedverfasser des Ṛigveda," 235.

36. Raja, *Poet-Philosophers*, 95.

37. RV 1.130.6 is one of his more salient examples:

imām te vācam vasūyanta āyavo
rathaṃ na dhīraḥ svapā atakṣiṣuḥ/
sumnāya tvām atakṣiṣuḥ/
śumbhanto jenyam yathā vājeṣu
vipra vojinam//

Here, fashioning a song as a carpenter fashions a chariot is a central image, yet it is followed by the second image of decorating a conquering steed. Mainkar disagrees with Griffith here, who restricts the second simile only to Indra. He believes it could also be applied to the making of a song; the simile is stated in such a manner that it suggests both decorating a song and decorating Indra. This double reference is, in Mainkar's mind, a precursor of *alaṃkārana*. (17)

38. Mainkar, *Foundations*, 15.

39. Ibid., 20.

40. He goes on to appeal to Max Müller's notion of a "*chandas* period" before the "mantra period." Moreover, since the Vedic poets looked to patterns both outside and inside the family, Mainkar conjectures that there must have been a school of poets to which all the seers belonged. Moreover, these set patterns and the poets' adherence to them imply their conscious effort, again emphasizing the agency of the rishi. This view argues against the Mīmāṃsā *apauruseya* view of the rishis, mentioned above. Mainkar agrees that indeed these visions were "seen," but seen in an ordinary, human way.

41. Ibid., 9. In this regard, even the suspicious Ram Gopal admits that the tradition of the family Maṇḍalas (2–7) is reliable to the extent that the hymns in each of these six Maṇḍalas were composed mostly by rishis belonging to the particular family to which the ancient tradition ascribes that Maṇḍala (*Principles*, 192).

42. Ram Gopal, *Principles*, 33.
43. Ibid., 59.
44. Ibid., 79, 180–87.
45. For example, he disparages Sir Leonard Woolley's habit of publishing careless remarks, without ever having looked at the Vedas. One such gem is, "The *Ṛg Veda* is the epic of destruction of one of the great cultures of ancient world." Ram Gopal writes that "It is entirely due to the wrong and misleading translations of the Rg Veda that eminent scholars like Sir Leonard Woolley do not hesitate to pass such derogatory remarks about it" (*Principles*, 19). For an exposition of the "non-Veda" of Western imagination, see Figueira, "Authority of an Absent Text," elsewhere in this volume. Moreover, Ram Gopal has analyzed those who *have* read the Veda with equal thoroughness. He even mentions Griffith's and Winternitz's tendency to compare the *Ṛg-Veda* unfavorably with Biblical poetry of the Hebrews. Even Müller, who usually gets gentler treatment from Ram Gopal, is chastised for his comment, "A large number of Vedic hymns are childish in the extreme, tedious, low and commonplace" (ibid., 184).
46. As Bergaigne states, "I declare in the most formal manner that, if I ever happen to agree with Sāyaṇa (it happens rarely), it is always without meaning it, and in the majority of cases (why should I not confess it) without knowing it. . . . I have studied the commentary of Sāyaṇa, I say this in all humility, only in fragments" (*La Religion Vedique*, 3:282, cited in Ram Gopal, *Principles*, 174).
47. "It is, therefore, a biased and baseless allegation to say that the Vedic interpretation suggested by the *Vedabhāṣyakāras* is all arbitrary and conjectural. . . . Although we do not mean to defend the shortcomings and mistakes found in the *Vedabhāṣyas*, at the same time we do not approve of the campaign of condemnation and calumny let loose against them by some biased modern scholars. . . . Some of the principles of Vedic interpretation enunciated by them are as rational as the systematic approach of modern scholars" (Ram Gopal, *Principles*, 177).
48. Ram Gopal drives the final nail into the coffin by a comparison of three different Western translations of *Ṛg-Veda* 1.1.1, two of which are based on Sāyaṇa and one of which is based on modern exegetical methods alone, with an open rejection of Sāyaṇa. The difference is, of course, minimal. Ram Gopal's experiment is also a bit of a set-up, since the verse itself is fairly straightforward and needs little commentary. Yet for him, the fact that a dependence on Sāyaṇa leads to the same translation as a rejection of Sāyaṇa shows that there is nothing inherently valuable about throwing over all indigenous interpretations:

om agnim īḍe purohitaṃ yajñasya devam ṛtvijam hotāraṃ ratnadhātamam

Wilson (who accepts Sāyaṇa): I glorify Agni, the high priest of the sacrifice, the divine, the ministrant, who present the oblation (to the gods), and is the possessor of great wealth.

Griffith (who accepts Sȳaṇa): I laud Agni, the chosen priest, God, minister of sacrifice, the hotar, the lavishest of wealth.

Oldenberg (who rejects Sāyaṇa): I magnify Agni, the Purohita, the divine ministrant of the sacrifice, the Hotri priest, the greatest bestower of treasures.

49. Ibid., 188.

50. Ibid., 14.

51. The *Nairuktas* of all cultures, of course, are the biggest culprits in this regard. Yet other approaches, both Western and Indian, are not let off the hook. Perhaps the most amusing "absurdity" is T. G. Rele's *The Vedic Gods as Figures of Biology*. Rudriyas are "simplified" into the sensory motor cerebral nerves, Parjaṇya is the reflex activity that excites the sexual organs, and the god Viṣṇu is comparable to the spinal cord! (Cited in Ram Gopal, *Principles*, 174.)

52. Ram Gopal, *Principles*, 182.

53. Ibid., 5. One is tempted here to compare the medieval Christian theologian's attempt to "allegorize" the Song of Solomon. In a sense, the Song of Solomon exegetes are a mirror image of the Vedic exegetes. In the Vedas, we have good reason to suspect that the poets were more sophisticated than a literal translation would allow; thus, we put a positive emphasis on allegorical interpretation. In the Song of Solomon, we suspect that those who allegorize the poem are simply covering up for the fact that it was originally a sensuous love song.

54. Ibid., 85.

55. Raja declares boldly that he has never believed that the available texts of the Veda mark the beginnings of Indian civilization. There must have been a long antecedent stage whose highly polished creations are now lost to us, for the poets themselves speak of their forefathers.

56. Mainkar, *Foundations*, 51.

57. This value consisted of the ability to integrate a number of worlds into their poetic constructions. And yet again, we have the almost rote comparison with the classics. Raja claims that although Greece had art, science, and philosophy, they were never together in the same genius, whereas India has tolerance of emotion and intellect within the same person, that of the rishi (*Poet-Philosophers*, xxvi).

58. In the *Nirukta*, for instance, Yāska censures those persons who have learned the Vedic texts by rote without understanding their meaning—an oft-repeated protest throughout Indian interpretive history

(Ram Gopal, *Principles*, 11; *Nirukta* 1.18; cf. *Ṛg-Veda* 10.71.5, cited in *Nirukta* 10.19).

59. *Śatapatha Brāhmaṇa* 10.6.5.9; *Apaṣṭambha Dharma Sūtra* 1.19.4.

60. RV 4.26.1; 7.19.2; 8.1.11. The hymns 1.94–115 and 9.97, 45–48 are ascribed to the seer Kutsa. See also *Atharva-Veda* 4.29.5; BD 3.11; *Nirukta* 3.25, among other references.

61. Gopal, *Principles*, 8.

62. RV 1.53; 2.14; 5.18; 8.53. According to the *Jaiminīya Brāmaṇa* version of this legend, Kutsa Aurava closely resembles Indra on account of his birth from Indra's thigh, and goes to Indra's wife Saci in the guise of Indra. He is thus dismissed from Indra's service as a charioteer and becomes a wrestler. See O'Flaherty, *Tales of Sex and Violence*, 74–78.

63. Gopal, *Principles*, 7.

64. Ibid., 164.

65. Ibid., 159. It is ironic that, if this had been written by a Western scholar he or she would have been accused of the worst of essentialism, but written by an Indian the statement becomes a concluding rationale for taking Indian interpreters seriously.

66. Raja, *Poet-Philosophers*, xix.

67. Ibid., 256.

68. Certainly, the most analagous unit of social organization was the tribal kingdom (*rāṣṭra*), containing tribes (*jana*), tribal units (*viś*), and villages (*grama*). Even there, however, the kingdom as such was very much derived from tribal identity (see RV 4.42.1; 7.34.11; 10.109.3).

69. Raja, *Quintessence*, vii.

70. Spivak, *Post-Colonial Critic*, 166.

71. Thapar, "Imagined Religious Communities," 210.

REFERENCES

Selected Sanskrit Texts

Aitareya Brāhmaṇa

1920 Trans. A. B. Keith in *Ṛg Veda Brāhmaṇas*. Harvard Oriental Series, no. 25. Cambridge: Harvard University Press.

1931 2 vols. Ānandñandāśrama-saṃskṛta-granthāvaliḥ, granthañkḥa, no. 32. Poona: Ānandāśrama.

Bṛhaddevatā

1904 Ed. and trans. Arthur Anthony Macdonell. 2 vols. Harvard Oriental Series. Cambridge: Harvard University Press.

Katyāyana Śrauta Sūtra
1972 Ed. Albrecht Weber. Chowkhamba Sanskrit Series, no. 104. Reprint: Varanasi: Chowkhamba Sanskrit Series Office. Trans. H. G. Ranade. Poona: Dr. H. G. Ranade and R. H. Ranade, n.d.

The Mahābhārata
1933–60 19 vols. Ed. Visnu S. Sukthankar. Poona: Bhandarkar Oriental Research Institute.
1973–78 3 vols. Ed. and trans. J. A. B. Van Buitenen. Chicago: University of Chicago Press.

The Nighaṇṭu and the Nirukta
1920–27 Ed. Lakshman Sarup. London and New York: Oxford University Press.

Ṛg Veda Saṃhitā, together with the Commentary of Sāyaṇa Āchārya
1966 Ed. F. Max Müller. Varanasi: Chowkhamba Sanskrit Series.

Sarvānukramaṇī, with Commentary of Ṣaḍguruśiṣya
1886 Ed. Arthur Anthony Macdonell. Oxford: Clarendon.

Śatapatha Brāhmaṇa
1940 5 vols. Bombay: Laxmi Venkateswar Steam Press.
1882–1900 Trans. Julius Eggeling. *Sacred Books of the East*. Oxford: Clarendon.

Secondary Sources

Adyar Library
1946 *Dr. C. Kunhan Raja Presentation Volume.* Madras: Vasanta Press.

Agrawala, V. S.
1963 *The Thousand-Syllabled Speech*. Varanasi: Vedāraṇyaka Ashram.

Bergaigne, Abel
1878–83 *La Religion Védique d'Après les Hymnes du* Rig-Veda. 3 vols. Paris: F. Vieweg.

Brough, John
1946 "The Early History of the Gotras." *Journal of the Royal Asiatic Society* (April):32–45.
1953 *The Early Brahmanical System of Gotra and Pravara.* Cambridge: Cambridge University Press.

Brown, W. Norman
1968 "Agni, Sun and Sacrifice." *Journal of the American Oriental Society* 88:199–218.

Chapekar, Nalinee et al., ed.
1982 *An Homage to Dr. Mainkar.* Bombay: Bombay University Press.

Detienne, Marcel
1986 *The Creation of Mythology.* Trans. Margaret Cook. Chicago: University of Chicago Press.

Gonda, Jan
1963 *The Vision of the Vedic Poets.* The Hague: Mouton.

Gopal, Ram
1965–96 *Vaidika Vyākaraṇa.* Delhi: National Publishing House.
1962 "Manu's Indebtedness to Śankhāyana." *Poona Orientalist* 27:39–44.
1963 "Influence of the Brāhmaṇas on the Gṛhyasūtras." *Vishveshvaranand Indological Journal* 1:291–98.
1983 *India of Vedic Kalpasūtras.* Delhi: Motilal Banarsidass.
1983 *The History and Principles of Vedic Interpretation*, New Delhi: Concept.
1984 *Kālidāsa: His Art and Culture.* New Delhi: Concept.

Guha, Ranajit, and Gayatri Spivak, eds.
1988 *Selected Subaltern Studies.* New York: Oxford University Press.

Inden, Ron
1986 "Orientalist Constructions of India," *Modern Asian Studies* 20:401–55.
1990 *Imagining India.* London: Basil Blackwell.

Long, Charles
1986 *Significations.* Philadelphia: Fortress.

Mainkar, T. G.
1961 *Mysticism in the Ṛgveda.* Bombay: Popular Book Depot.
1962 *Kālidāsa: His Art and Thought.* Poona: Deshmukh Prakashan.
1966 *Some Poetical Aspects of Ṛgvedic Repetitions.* Poona: University of Poona.
1969 *A Comparative Study of the Commentaries on the Bhagavadgītā.* Delhi: Motilal Banarsidass.
1971 *Ṛgveda-kavi-vimarśaḥ.* Delhi: Śrilālabahādura Śastrī Kendrīya Saṃskṛta Vidyāpīṭham.
1977 *The Vāsiṣṭha Rāmāyaṇa.* Delhi: Meharchand Lachmandas.
1977 *The Ṛg Vedic Foundations of Classical Poetics.* Delhi: Ajanta.
1980 *The Making of the Vedānta.* Delhi: Ajanta.

Müller, F. Max
1867–76 *Chips from a German Workshop*. New York: Scribner, Armstrong.

O'Flaherty, Wendy
1981 *The Rig Veda*. New York: Penguin, Books.
1985 *Tales of Sex and Violence*. Chicago: University of Chicago Press.

Oldenberg, Hermann
1898 "Über die Liederverfasser des Rigveda." *Zeitschrift der Deutsche Morgenlandischen Gesellschaft* 42.

Patton, Laurie
1991 "Vāc: Myth or Philosophy?" In *Myth and Philosophy*, ed. Frank Reynolds and David Tracy, 183–214. Albany: State University of New York Press.
1993 "Beyond the Myth of Origins: Types of Tale-Telling in Vedic Commentary." In *Myths and Fictions: Their Place in Philosophy and Religion*, ed. Shlomo Biderman. Leiden: E. J. Brill.
1993 "The Transparent Text: Puranic Trends in the *Bṛhaddevatā*." In *Purāṇa Perennis*, ed. Wendy Doniger. Albany: State University of New York Press.

Pollock, Sheldon
1989 "Mīmāṃsā and the Problem of History in Traditional India." *Journal of the American Oriental Society* 109(4):603–10.

Raja, C. Kunhan
1928 "The Commentaries on *Rigveda* and *Nirukta*." *Proceedings and Transactions of the Fifth All-India Oriental Conference* 1:223–73.
1935 Editor, *The Ṛgvedabhāṣya of Skandasvāmin*. Madras: The University of Madras Press.
1936 "The Chronology of the Vedabhāṣyakāras." *Journal of Oriental Research* 10:256–68.
1956 *Asya Vāmasya Hymn*. Madras: Ganesh.
1962 *Survey of Sanskrit Literature*. Bombay: Bharatiya Vidya Bhavan.
1963 *The Poet-Philosophers of the Ṛgveda*. Madras: Ganesh.
1964 *The Quintessence of the Rig Veda*. Bombay: D. B. Taraporevala Sons.

Renou, Louis
1965 *The Destiny of the Veda in India*. Delhi: Motilal Banarsidass.
1955–69 *Etudes Védiques et Paninéènnes*. 17 vols. Paris: Publications de l'Institut de Civilisation Indienne.

Said, Edward
1978 *Orientalism*. New York: Vintage.

Smith, Brian K.
1989 *Reflections on Resemblance, Ritual and Religion*. New York: Oxford University Press.

Sontheimer, Guenther D., and Hermann Kulke, eds.
1989 *Hinduism Reconsidered*. New Delhi: Manohar.

Spivak, Gayatri
1990 *The Post-Colonial Critic: Interviews, Strategies, Dialogues*. New York: Routledge.

Thapar, Romila
1966 *A History of India*. Vol. 1. New York: Penguin.
1977 "Ideology and the Interpretation of Early Indian History." In *Society and Change*. ed. K. S. Krishnaswamy et al., 1–19. Bombay.
1984 *From Lineage to State: Social Formation in the Mid-First Millenium B.C. in the Ganga Valley*. Bombay: Oxford University Press.
1988 "Sati in History." *Seminar* 342 (February).
1989 "Imagined Religious Communities? Ancient History and the Modern Search for a Hindu Identity." *Modern Asian Studies* 23(2):209–31.

Tokunaga, Muneo
1979 "The Text and Legends of the *Bṛhaddevatā*." Ph.D. diss., Harvard University.
1981 "On the Recensions of the *Bṛhaddevatā*." *Journal of the American Oriental Society* 101(3):275–86.

Afterword

WHILE THIS VOLUME RAISES issues of authority, anxiety, and canon in the context of the cultural history of India, some of its early readers have suggested that it may raise relevant questions significant to other, larger inquiries— specifically those of the comparative study of religions, literatures, and histories. These readers' suggestions also challenge the field of Vedic studies (or any specialized field, for that matter) to broaden its scope without losing its rigor. I will briefly take up this challenge, then, in the hope that these small steps might offer other scholars the beginnings of attractive paths to follow in the future.

CULTURE AND CANON

All of the chapters in this volume make the connection between canon and the dominant ideology of a particular culture. Brian Smith puts it most succinctly in the context of Vedic India: "The legitimacy, or even indisputability, of the distinctive social scheme of historical and contemporary India rides piggy back on the unquestionable truth of the Veda, and both are part of the eternal cosmic order of things." In her essay on literature, "Contingencies of Value,"[1] Barbara Herrnstein Smith embarks upon a similar critique of Western canon formation that exposes the ways in which the classical literary texts that survive tend to reinforce and reflect establishment ideologies.

However, the Indian cases of canonical authority and anxiety bring to light one particular assumption that Herrnstein Smith and other literary critics tend to hold: that canonical power is transmitted through the model of the European, Enlightenment encounter with the text. She writes, "To the extent that we develop within and are formed by a culture that is itself in part constituted by canonical texts, it is not surprising that those texts seem, as Hans-Georg Gadamer puts it, to 'speak' to us 'directly' or even 'specially.' "[2] Thus, although we would agree with Herrnstein Smith's general strategy of linking canon and culture, her particular assumptions about the transmission of canonical value tend to privilege the individualized, "special" reception of text and reader.

The chapters of the present volume imply that the Western understanding of what constitutes canonical power and hegemony might be culturally circumscribed, specifically in its construction of the relationship between "text" and "reader." More specifically, the chapters suggest that performed canon (Holdrege, B. Smith, and Carpenter), imagined canon (Gitomer, F. Smith, and Figueira), and read canon (Clooney, Llewellyn, and Patton) are three distinct forms that can be combined in a variety of ways, depending upon the values of the interpretive community that conceives of and transmits canonical power. The Vedic canon assumes a variety of different powers that cannot be fully understood until one has grasped the investments of its community of reception, whether it be Indian dramaturgical discourse, the Sturm und Drang period in Europe, or the flowering of Advaita Vedānta philosophy in medieval India.

A specific critique of canonical power must therefore be cautious; before it assumes a particular model of the cultural reception of canon, it must explore the interaction between interpretive strategies and the cultures or subcultures of interpretation. If culture and canon are to be analyzed as mutually reflective entities, then the particulars of the canonical process cannot be divorced from the particulars of culture. Only if this commitment to specificity is made will the study of the canonical process be deepened. It is no longer enough to say, as numerous scholars and cultural critics already have, that there are many peoples who cannot join the orthodox, educated elite of the West; or that the socio-political realities of these peoples relativize the transcendent claims of Western literary and religious canons. One must also examine the history of interpretive strategies within those communities themselves, in their hegemonic (the linking of Veda to social hierarchy), resistant (the triumph of Keshub Sen's intuitionism over the Veda in any form), or legitimating (the Vedicization of dramatic theory) forms.[3]

Moreover, such culturally specific study also assumes that definitions of cultural boundaries themselves shift in significant ways. Thus, to say that culture and canon are integrally bound up with each other cannot assume a dynamic definition of canon, on the one hand, and a static definition of culture, on the other. One must have a clear sense of the ways in which the definition of cultural identity itself is argued out. For example, the arguments about Vedic canon in the nineteenth and twentieth centuries have been in part influenced by the competing definitions of Indian culture. One must ask whether nineteenth-century culture has been defined by Hindu reformers or British lawmakers, or, in the late twentieth-century version, by Western or Indian scholars and cultural critics. Indeed, the twentieth-century dilemma poses an intriguing case: on the one hand, cross-cultural arguments proceeded on the same scholarly terms of the university, or the same romantic terms of the poet. On the other hand, the participants were speaking in two different voices—that of the former colonizers and that of the formerly colonized. In each case, the terms of the definition of culture have changed, and it is those shifts that have created new forms of argumentation.

PERFORMED CANON

One particularly fruitful comparative issue that these chapters raise is the role of performance in canonical interpretation. As noted in the introduction, all of the chapters consider at some level the persistence of performance in Vedic interpretations. In the Vedic period itself, the Veda was not a book, or even a recitation that was intended for the individual enlightenment of the "hearer." It was a canon of efficacious speech in its own right, reestablishing important cosmogonic and social connections every time it was performed. The Vedas thus articulated a highly public, social vision concerned with establishing hegemony within performance. Thus, on a most basic level, scholars of canon in other fields might learn from the Vedic case to ask questions about the performative value of canon—even when such performative value is not readily apparent in the cultural context in which it is being interpreted.

Yet even after taking into consideration such a performative context, students of canon might benefit from other, even more specific comparative issues that these chapters suggest. One can examine further the particularly status-oriented nature of the Vedas' performative values, articulated as they were from the perspective of the Brahmanical directors of the performance. In this feature, the ritually performed Vedas played a role quite similar to the elaborate visions of the temple mapped out in Ezekiel 40–48. As J. Z. Smith has argued, in this Judaic context the elaborate unification of all ritual elements in a single, systematic vision of the temple tended to be articulated exclusively from the perspective of the rulers, and not from the ruled.[4] Thus, scholars from other disciplines might learn to be suspicious of such elaborate systems presented in ritual and architectural texts. While the system appears to be more inclusive, incorporating and respecting the integrity of each of the subsystems, it is, as Smith goes on to argue, an inclusivity possible only from the perspective of domination of the highest order, with its attendant clarity as to classification of each of the subordinated parts.[5] The perspective of those who are performers, but not directors, of ritual is more fragmented, and their experience of hierarchy more immediate.

Moreover, the chapters suggest that even in situations not focused upon perfomance per se, the residues of performance change the way we understand a canon's value. In the case of the Vedas' initial move from oral canon to written text, their canonical value became ambiguous. As Figueira, Rambachan, and Patton imply, the process of editing the Vedas as texts eclipsed the possibility that Americans and Europeans, as well as some Westernized Hindu reformers, would appreciate their performative value. Moreover, the Vedas' transformation into texts encouraged an understanding of their *textual* value as less than those canons that began *as* texts. The Vedas were necessarily filled with repetitions and obscure allusions that would only make sense in a ritual context—obvious affronts to the "classical" sensibilities of the Western textual scholar.

The Vedic case has parallels in other religious and literary traditions. The Shinto case is particularly instructive in this regard. As Joseph Kitagawa has written of the Japanese classics of *Kojiki* and *Nihongi*,[6] special lenses are needed to gain a full appreciation of the value of a written canon that was once performed. Briefly put, the *Kojiki* texts were compiled in 673 by Emperor Tummu in order to uphold certain religio-political principles, but were themselves oral traditions. In order to establish what Kitagawa calls an "immanental theocracy," whereby the power of the sovereign was communicated through prescripts, the Japanese used Chinese models of writing, as well as a great deal of Japanese oral folklore and mythology. The case is even further complicated by the fact that some scholars would assert that the *Shinto Norito*, or ritual prayers, have attained more canonical status than the *Kojiki* or the *Nihongi* since performance has provided more of a unifying foundation for Shinto than text per se. Thus, in addition to the oral/written patterns of the *Kojiki* and the *Nijongi*, the Japanese case also includes the challenges of a canonical text quite similar to the *Ṛg-Veda*: the *Engi-shiki*, a list of *Shinto Norito* compiled in 927. Given the *Engi-shiki*'s change of status from a collection of oral propitiations to a text of written prayers, it has some of the same traces of performative concerns, and therefore presents some of the same interpretive challenges as do the Ṛg-Vedic hymns.

The complexity of such hermeneutical, text-critical concerns in the analysis of canon should not create a false chronology, however. One must be equally aware of situations in which there exists a struggle between modes of performance, such as the oral and the written. We have seen this in the case of Swami Dayānand, railing against the pandits who refused to refer to texts and rely only on their "performance"-oriented memories. Some have suggested that such competition may be the case in Jewish tradition as well. The heterogeneous and contradictory Book of Jeremiah is a case in point. Without delving too protractedly into the history of Biblical criticism, suffice it to say that many passages in Jeremiah seem to construct an opposition between the written priestly Torah and the prophetic word of Yahweh. Other passages seem to affirm openly the Deuteronomic, priestly perspective even in the context of prophecy. More moderate theorists, such as Brevard Childs,[7] have argued that the Book of Jeremiah as canonical text is a "fusion of prophetic and Deuteronomic horizons." As Childs puts it, the book is not what Jeremiah said in his own historical moment, but the way in which his words were received and understood by those in a radically different, Deuteronomic perspective.[8]

However, scholars such as Gerald L. Bruns[9] (following the more controversial Joseph Blenkinsopp[10]) have argued that canon should be viewed as a category of power as well as literacy. Bruns' less benevolent reading is that Jeremiah represents the priestly appropriation of prophetic authority by means of writing and textuality. Writing was a way of doing away with prophecy. Jeremiah's attack on the pen of scribes is aimed not at the message of the Torah, but at the misplaced priestly confidence in the institution of the "Law written down." Such confidence blinds religious and political leadership to God's action in the world, as perceived and proclaimed by the prophet.

The historical examples of competing modes of canonical interpretation, outlined briefly above, demonstrate that the received distinction between "thought" and "action" is inappropriate. In the case of oral and written modes of canonical transmission, this separation between performance and idea is assumed either because oral and written forms constitute a rigid chronology (whereby the oral belongs to the "performance-oriented" primitive, and the written to the sophisticated exegete), or because, even while they might co-exist, the two modes are assumed to be discrete, unrelated spheres of human activity.

Fields other than history of religions struggle with the same dichotomy. Joseph Kerman, for instance, writes eloquently of the persistence of this dualism in Western classical music. In his article, "A Few Canonic Variations," he characterizes the musical performer's typical attitude: "A canon is an idea; a repertoire [performance] is a program of action."[11] Our concern here is not musicological debate; suffice it to say that Kerman as well as scholars in other disciplines believe that the situation of canonical transmission is far more complex. As many of the chapters in this volume show, it is precisely when these different modes come in contact with each other that arguments about canon become most lively and the most instructive. The intellectual move of assuming that different modes of canonical transmission can and do co-exist and compete would benefit the philological historian, the comparative religionist, and the literary critic alike.

THE ROLE OF THE INTERPRETIVE AGENT

The issue of the modes of canonical transmission leads us to a reevaluation of the various roles of the interpretive agent. If we ask about the various media of transmission, we must also inquire about the agents of transmission: what is the social and political relationship between performers, authors, or redactors of canon, on the one hand, and the interpreters of canon who come after them, on the other?

Certain themes suggest themselves as useful avenues to follow. Scholars in related fields have collapsed the distinctions between performer and interpreter. In his recent book, *Ritual Criticism*,[12] Ronald Grimes discusses the role of the performer as an interpreter, working alongside the ethnographer in evaluating ritual occurrences. Grimes' move joins a massive recent literature that attempts to level the playing field between anthropologists and their objects of study. However, the authors of this volume show us the ways we can take this move one step farther. Some of these authors suggest that, in the Vedic period, the interpreter of canon was quite frequently the performer of canon as well. As discussed in part above, such a combination of roles led to an explicitly hegemonic mode of canonical interpretation, in which brahmin prestige was protected through interpretive strategies themselves. Thus, the leveling works in both ways: not only must the ethnographer admit to limits to his or her objectivity, but the performer must admit to his or her active role in shaping canonical knowledge.

Some of these chapters also show that, in later occasions of Vedic exegesis, such as that of Sanskrit dramaturgy or Purāṇic theology, the interpreter tended to be not a performer, but an appropriator of Vedic authority. Thus, this volume suggests that those who no longer perform canon themselves in ritual situations are likely to be different kinds of interpreters from those who actively perform it. Reading canon as a written text in less ritualized situations, or imagining canon as a background to one's larger devotional theology, are two forms of interpretive agency that differ dramatically from the interpretive agency that derives from actual recitation within a sacrificial context. In the case of a recited Veda, the interpreter manipulates canon from the perspective of an insider who is intimately, even bodily, responsible for its sacrificial efficacy and power. In the cases of "read" or "imagined" Veda, the interpreter manipulates canon to lend Vedic weight to an activity that may not have been intrinsic to sacrificial performance.

These ideas suggest new ways of thinking about outsiders and insiders in the canonical process. Who holds cultural authority for the creation and perpetuation of canon, and, perhaps more appropriate to the post-modern situation, who holds such authority for the dismantling of canon?

In his introduction to *Canons*, a series of essays on canonical knowledge from a variety of disciplines, Robert von Hallberg remarks upon the tensions produced by academic involvement in the canonical process—more specifically, the tension between the canon creator and the canonical critic, or performer and academic. He writes: "Perhaps. . .we should recognize that. . .there is a danger of academic critics overestimating their own importance and autonomy in the process of canon formation and wrongly thinking that they can choose to dispense with canons."[13] Von Hailberg goes on to argue that, even while recent academic writing may be correct in its suspicions that the canonical process may be ideologically motivated, professors and students are not the only commentators in the conversation. In the Western world, at least, artists have been commentators on their own work far longer than academics have been writing on art.

Like the various Vedic controversies and strategies outlined in this volume, the academic debate about canon itself cannot avoid arguments about cultural definition. Even the "ideological" model of canonical formation is itself interested, and must admit to having some stake in the outcome of its analysis of the canonical process. Despite its pretensions to being removed from the sweaty workshops of canonical production, be they artistic, religious, or literary, the academy finds that it too is swept up in the controversies, and that the definitions of insider and outsider become increasingly blurred. Such blurring does not mean that we all must resign ourselves to the depressingly infinite regress of politically interested discourse about canon. Rather, canon-creators and canon-critics might wisely develop a guarded mutual respect. For the rich contingencies of the canonical process suggest that, whichever side we may argue for in one historical moment, we may find ourselves arguing for the other in a matter of time.

Laurie L. Patton
Annandale-on-Hudson, New York

NOTES

1. Barbara Herrnstein Smith, "Contingencies of Value," in *Canons*, ed. Robert von Hallberg (Chicago: University of Chicago Press, 1984), 5–40. For other works of general theoretical relevance, see especially Charles Altieri, *Canons and Consequences* (Evanston, Ill: Northwestern University Press, 1990), and Susan Noakes, *Timely Reading Between Exegesis and Intrepretation* (Ithaca, N.Y.: Cornell University Press, 1988).
2. Ibid., 33.

3. The essays in Paula Richman's recent edited volume, *Many Rāmāyaṇas* (Berkeley: University of California Press, 1992), do an excellent job of exposing these strategies in the now quasi-"canonical" epic of India.

4. J. Z. Smith, *To Take Place: Toward Theory in Ritual* (Chicago: University of Chicago Press, 1987), 56–71.

5. Ibid., 70.

6. Joseph Kitagawa, "Some Remarks on the Study of Sacred Texts," in *The Critical Study of Sacred Texts*, ed. Wendy O'Flaherty, 231–42. (Berkeley: Graduate Theological Union, 1977).

7. See Brevard Childs, *Introduction to the Old Testament as Scripture* (Philadelphia: Fortress, 1979), 346; also J. Phlllip Hyatt, "Torah in the Book of Jeremiah," *Journal of Biblical Literature* 60 (1941): 384.

8. As discussed by Gerald L. Bruns, "Canon and Power," in *Canons*, 77.

9. Ibid., 65–84.

10. See Blenkinsopp's *Prophecy and Canon: A Contribution to the Study of Jewish Origins* (Notre Dame: University of Notre Dame Press, 1977), 38, following Julius Wellhausen, *Prolegomena to the History of Israel*, trans. J. Sutherland Black and Allan Menzies (Edinburgh: Adam and Charles Black, 1885).

11. Joseph Kerman, "A Few Canonic Variatlons," in *Canons*, 177–96.

12. *Ritual Criticism: case studies in its practice, essays on its theory* (Columbia, S.C.: University of South Carolina Press, 1990).

13. Robert von Hallberg, introduction, in *Canons*, 2.

Contributors

David Carpenter is Assistant Professor of Theology at Saint Joseph's University, Philadelphia. His articles have appeared in *Wiener Zeitschrift für die kunde Südasiens*, the *Journal of the American Academy of Religion*, the *Journal for Ecumenical Studies*, and in a number of edited volumes.

Francis X. Clooney, S. J., is an associate professor of comparative theology in the Theology Department of Boston College, where he has taught since 1984, and has been its Director of Graduate Studies since 1991. He has recently completed research in Madras for a book on the Śrivaiṣṇava religious tradition, supported by a grant from the American Institute of Indian studies. He is the author of *Thinking Ritually*, vol. 17 in the De Nobili Research Series (Indological Institute of the University of Vienna, 1990), and *Theology after Vedānta* (Albany: State University of New York Press, 1993). His articles have appeared in *History of Religions, J.E.S.* the *Journal of Religion*, the *Journal of the American Oriental Society*, the *Journal of the American Academy of Religion*, and *Theological Studies*, as well as in such Indian journals as *Prabuddha Bharata*, and the *Journal of Oriental Research*.

Wendy Doniger is Mircea Eliade Professor of the History of Religions at the University of Chicago. She is translator of *The Rig Veda* and the *Laws of Manu* (with Brian K. Smith), and the author of *Śiva: The Erotic Ascetic; Hindu Myths; The Origins of Evils in Hindu Mythology; Women, Androgynes and Other Mythical Beasts; Textual Sources for the Study of Religion; Dreams, Illusion, and Other Realities;* and *Other Peoples' Myths.*

Dorothy M. Figueira teaches literature in the Department of Comparative Literature at the University of Illinois, Champaign-Urbana. She holds a Master of Theological Studies from Harvard and a Doctorate in Comparative Literature from the University of Chicago, and is the author of *Translating the Orient* (Albany: State University of New York Press, 1991). She has recently completed a study of the exotic in the European imagination, *Exoticism: A Decadent Quest* (Albany: State University of New York Press, forthcoming 1994) and has written extensively on French and German literature.

David L. Gitomer is Assistant Professor of Religious Studies at DePaul University. He has translated Kālidāsa's *Vikramorvaśīya* in *Theater of Memory* (Columbia University Press) and the *Veṇīsaṃhāra* of Bhaṭṭa Nārāyaṇa, forthcoming as *The Catastrophe of the Braid*. He will contribute *Bhīṣma* and *Droṇa Parvan* to the University of Chicago's *Mahābhārata* translation project, and is the author of a number of articles on Sanskrit epic, drama and aesthetics.

Barbara A. Holdrege is Associate Professor of the comparative history of religions at the University of California, Santa Barbara. Her research has focused on historical and textual studies of selected topics within Hindu and Jewish traditions, as well as cross-cultural analyses of categories such as scripture, myth, and ritual. She is the author of *Veda and Torah: Transcending the Textuality of Scripture* (Albany: State University of New York Press, 1994); and edited collection, *Ritual and Power, Journal of Ritual Studies* 4, no. 2 (summer 1990); a forthcoming book, *The Mythic Dimensions of Religious Life* (London: Routledge); and numerous articles on representations of scripture in the brahmanical tradition and the rabbinic and kabbalistic traditions.

J. E. Llewellyn ia an assistant professor in the Department of Religious Studies at Southwest Missouri State University. He is the author of *The Arya Samaj as a Fundamentalist Movement: A Study in Comparative Fundamentalism*.

Laurie L. Patton is the author of *Myth as Argument: The Bṛhaddevatā as Canonical Commentary* (Berlin: DeGruyter/Mouton, forthcoming), and numerous articles on Vedic commentary and interpretive theory in the history of religions. She is also co-editor of *Myth and Method: New Perspectives on Sacred Narrative* (Charlottesville: University of Virginia Press, forthcoming). She teaches in the Department of Religion at Bard College, Annandale-on-Hudson, New York.

Anantanand Rambachan is an Associate Professor of Religion and Asian Studies at Saint Olaf in Minnesota. He has been working in recent years on Hindu epistemology and on the interplay between scripture and personal experience as sources of valid knowledge. His publications include *Accomplishing the Accomplished: The Vedas as a Source of Valid Knowledge in Śaṅkara* (Honolulu: University of Hawaii Press, 1991), *The*

Limits of Scripture: A Critical Study of Vivekananda's Reinterpretation of the Authority of the Vedas (Honolulu: University of Hawaii Press, forthcoming), and *The Hindu Vision* (Delhi: Motilal Banarsidass, 1992). His writings also appear in various scholarly journals.

Brian K. Smith is Professor of Religious Studies and History at the University of California, Riverside. He is the author of *Reflections on Resemblance, Ritual, and Religion* (Oxford University Press, 1989) and *Classifying the Universe: The Ancient Indian Varna System and the Origins of Caste* (Oxford University Press, 1994).

Frederick Smith is Assistant Professor of Sanskrit and Classical Indian Religion at the University of Iowa and Head of the South Asia Studies Program at Iowa. He has spent many years in India conducting research on Vedic sacrificial ritual and other topics in Indian religion. His first book, *The Vedic Sacrifice in Transition*, was published by the Bhandarkar Oriental Research Institute in Pune in 1987.

Index

Abhinava, 188, 190, 191
Abraham, association with Brahma, 213–14
adhikāra (entitlement), 258–59
adhikaraṇa ("places" of interpretation), 146, 149, 151, 154, 156, 165n. 8
adhvaryu priest, 71, 73, 84, 90n. 30
Aditi, 102
Āditya(s), 48–50, 71–73, 81, 88n. 16, 281
Advaita school, 151. *See also* Vedānta
  interpretative mode of, 146–47, 153
  Western conception of, 157
Aṅga, 118
Agni, 25, 28, 29, 48, 70, 71, 72, 80–81, 88n. 16
  different aspects of, 107–8, 128n. 56
  Purāṇic geneologies of, 108–10, 128–29n. 63
  Purāṇic reinterpretation of, 97, 106–11
Agnicayana, 114
āgnīdhrīya (sacrificial fire), 71, 73
Agnihotra, 102, 107, 117, 118
Agnitīrtham, 110
Agrawala, 128n. 56
āhavanīya, 71, 73, 110
Aila, 108
Aitareya Āraṇyaka, 69, 71, 72, 77–78, 293
Aitareya Brāhmaṇa, 46–47, 49, 81, 286, 289
Ajāmila, 106
Ākūti, 115
Amalānanda, 153
Amaru corpus, 172
Amaruśataka, 172, 192n. 4
amṛta, 111
Amṛtamanthana (Churning of the Ocean), 174, 189
  as first play, 189
ānandamaya, 147–48, 154, 156
Ānandatīrtha, 292
Antadhāna, 118
anti-Orientalists, vii
Anumati, 102
anuṣṭubh, 91n. 91. *See also* meter
Appaya Dīkṣita, 153
apūrva, 118
Āraṇyaka(s), 36–39, 103, 235
Arjuna, 110
Arjunavarmadeva, 172
Ārya Samāj, 87n. 9, 235, 236, 240. *See also* Dāyanand
Aryan(s). *See also* Brahmin class, caste
  as forefathers of Anglo-Saxon race, 206, 208, 209, 218–19, 220–21
  romanticization of, 255
  social classes, 73
Aryanism, 29–30, 218, 220
aryanization of language, 29
asceticism, 267
Āśrāvaṇā, 175
Āśvalāyana Ṛg-Veda, 21
Aśvamedha, 118
Asya Vāmasya, 286
Atharva-Veda, 86, 88–89, 99, 102, 111
Atharvana, 57n. 24
ātman, 9, 80, 261–62, 293

Atri, 112
Aurobindo, 292
avabhṛtha (ritual bath), 116, 119
avatāra, 114, 266
Ayus, 186

Bādarāyaṇa, 141, 147–49, 152, 154, 158, 262
Bahirgīta, 175, 190
Bali, 118
bandhus (connections), 4, 8, 39, 42, 46, 47–49, 51, 87 n. 11. *See also* Brāhmaṇas
Bāṣkala Ṛg-Veda, 21
Beass Muni, 205
Bell, Catherine, 7
Benares debate (of 1869), 12, 239–40, 241–42
Bergaine, Abel, 283, 292
Bhagavadgītā, 9
Bhagavan, 101, 125
Bhāgavata Pūraṇa, 4, 9, 97–99, 100–6, 107, 110–20, 123, 124, 133, 185, 237
Bhāgavatas, 105
bhakti (devotion), 9 55–56n. 17, 105, 116–18
Bharata, 118, 173-75
Bhārata dynasty, 286–87
Bhavabhūti, 185
Biache, in *Ezour Veda*, 205
Biardeau, Madeleine, 182
Bible, 268–69. *See also* canon, Christianity
  Hindu criticism of, 242
bird, Upanisadic imagery of, 142–45
  Vedic image of, 9
Black Yajur-Veda, 21
Blenkinsopp, Joseph, 313
Bose, Rajnarian, 262
Brahmaṇḍa Purāṇa, 107–9, 112, 128 n. 63
Brahmā, 10, 100, 102, 103, 110, 111–12, 114, 173–76, 178, 184, 190, 216
  association with Abraham, 213–14
  association with Christ, 214
  cult of, as first cult, 209
Brahmaismus, 214
brahman, 4–10, 40, 43, 45, 50–51, 68, 79–80, 142–49, 151, 155, 258–59, 261–262
  and bliss, 147–48, 150, 152–55, 160–1, 164, 165, 166n. 12. *See also* *ātman*
Brāhmaṇa(s), 2, 3–4, 8, 9, 23–25, 36–39, 101, 103, 118, 120, 235. *See also* bandhus, canon
  concept of, 24
  cosmogony of, 39, 41–52, 178
  cosmology of, 39, 41, 46–52
  view of the nature of the Veda, 25
Brahmanical tradition, Veda within, 35, 37–39, 41, 42, 52
Brahmin class, 52, 83. *See also* caste, *varṇa*
  authority of, 68, 84–85
  connection with deities, 73, 80–81
  cosmic associations with, 73–74, 80–81
  culture, establishment of, 29–30
  and *Ṛg-Veda*, 74–75, 83
  and Veda, 68, 84–85
Brahmins
  attacks on the power of, 247
  conflict with Kṣatriyas, 295
  criticism of, 244, 246
  relations with Kṣatriyas, 187
  Western view of, 205–206
Brahmoism, 257–59, 260, 261, 262
Brahmo Samāj, 268, 269
  schisms within, 260–63, 264, 267
Brahmo Samaj, Adi, 264
Bṛhadāraṇyaka Upaniṣad, 22, 43
Bṛhaddevatā, 281, 286–87, 291, 297
Bṛhaspati, 289
Brhaspatisava, 118
bṛhat, 42
Britain, 254
Brough, John, 289
Bruns, Gerald L., 313
Byrski, 176, 179, 182, 185, 188
Buddhism, 238, 242

Caland, Willem, 204
canon, 19, 67, 85–86n. 1, 253, 271–72. *See also* Upaniṣads, Veda, sacred text
  authority of, 236–37
  construction of, 282
  and culture, 309–311
  and exegis, 12–13
  and form, 20, 36
  and ingenuity, 236–37, 238
  and interpretation, 310, 312–313, 314–15
  issues of definition, 2, 6–9, 11, 23, 31–32
  limitation and closure, 8, 35, 235, 236–37, 242
  oral, 3, 7
  and performance/performative, 7–10, 310, 311–13, 314–15
  and power, 237–38, 309–310, 313
  and social order, 84
  and status, 36
  and Vedic Saṃhitās, 20–24
  and Western conception of, 309, 310, 313
  written, 7, 10–11, 241–43
  written vs. practiced, 140–41
canonicity, 155
  limitation and closure, 20, 24, 30–31
Caraṇavyūha Ṛg-Veda, 21
Carpenter, Rev. Lent, 269
Carpenter, David, 2, 3, 7–8, 40, 241
caste system. *See also* Brahmin, Kṣatriya, Vaiśya, Śudra, *varṇa*
  criticism of, 244–45
  as primordial in origin, 68
  and Veda, 68, 84
Catholicism, criticism of, 246
Cāturmāsya, 102
celibacy, 118
Chandogya Upaniṣad, 73, 162
Channing, William Ellery, 269, 270
Childs, Brevard, 313
Christ, 266, 270
  association with Brahma, 214
Christianity, 242, 246
  attempts to harmonize with Hinduism, 263, 265–66
  as deriving from Hinduism, 202, 203, 213–14, 216, 219
  missionaries to India, 255, 260
  Trinitarian, 270
  Unitarian, 269–71
Chumontou, in *Ezour Veda*, 205
Clooney, Francis X., 2, 4, 9, 262, 273
Coburn, Thomas, 120, 125
Colebrooke, H. T., 216–17, 255
Compte, A., 254–55
Cormo Veidam, 205–6
cosmic order
  as corresponding to social order, 69, 73–74, 80–81
  as divine, 101
  hierarchy of, 74–75, 77, 82, 88n. 20
  interdependence of, 101
  tripartite division, 46–51
  tripartite structure, 68–74, 80–82
  and Veda, 68–69, 73–74, 83
cosmogony, 68–70, 81
  Brāhmaṇa, 39, 41–52
  and Sanskrit drama, 176–78, 180, 188, 189–90
creation, role of speech (Vac), 42–50
  stages of, 42–47, 60
Creuzer, Friedrich, 212
culture, and canon, 309–11

Daksa, 110, 112–13, 118
dakṣiṇā (sacrificial fee), 71, 73
Dakṣiṇā (personified), 115
Dall, C. H. A., 269
dance
  in *Nāṭyaśāstra*, 174, 175
  origin of, 191–92
Dandekar, R. N., 291
Darśa (New Moon), 102
Datta, Akshaykumar, 260–61
Death, (*mṛtyu*), in *naṭyotpatti*, 174
Deism, 261, 268
Destiny (*niyati*), in *naṭyotpatti*, 174
Detienne, Marcel, 288

Devas and Asuras
cosmogonic strife between, 177, 187
recreated by trigata, 177
dharma, Purāṇic view of, 102–3, 106, 116, 117–18
Dharma (personified), 112
Dharma-Śāstras, 36
tradition of, 99, 117, 122
Dhātā, 102
dhvajamaha, 173
Diderot, Denis, 205
Dīrghatamas
interpretation of, 288–89, 290, 293
life of, 285–87
Doab, 23, 24, 29
dogma, rejection of, 263, 266. *See also* canon
drama. *See also Nāṭyaśāstra*
and epic, 173, 183–86
and kingly succession, 184–86
Draupadi, 119
Duff, Alexander, 260
Duperron, Anquetil, 212–13
Dutch Indology, 176

Ellis, F. W., 204
Engi-shiki, 312
English language, in India, 254
Enlightenment
interpretation of Veda, 5, 11
understanding of Veda, 202–210
view of canon, 309, 380–81
view of textuality, 11
epic. *See also Mahābhārata, Rāmāyaṇa*
and drama, 173, 183–85
and kingly succession, 184–86
European Indology, 217. *See also* Enlightenment
Ezour Veda (false Veda), 5, 11, 203–5, 206
transmission to West, 203–5
use in Christian conversion, 204, 206

Fifth Veda, claims to be, 37–38, 54n. 10, 55n. 17, 98, 105, 173, 183, 190–91. *See also* canon, *Naṭyaśāstra, Purāṇa*[s]
Figueira, Dorothy, 3, 5, 11
Findly, Ellison B., 24

Gadamer, Hans-Georg, 309
gārhapatya (fire), 71, 73
gāyatrī meter, 75–81, 90nn. 38, 39
Geldner, Karl F., 22–3
geneology, Purāṇic use of, 101–3, 108, 115, 120–21, 126n. 32, 131n. 88
Gandharvas, 27
Garuda, 9, 114, 117
Ghose, Sri Aurobindo, 54–55n. 13
Gitomer, David, 2, 4–5, 9–10
"golden age," and modern decline, 255–56
Gonda, Jan, 23, 55n. 16
Goody, Jack, 14
Gopal, Ram, 6, 281, 284, 285, 291–93, 294–95, 296
Gorres, Joseph, 213–14
Graham, William, 85–86
Grassmann, Hermann, 291
Gṛhya Sūtras, 75
Grimes, Ronald, 314
Gupta period, 185

Halbfass, Wilhelm, 14, 105, 253
von Hallberg, Robert, 315
Hari, 98, 101, 103. *See also* Viṣṇu
havir, 71
Havyavāhana, 108
Heesterman, J. C., 38, 182, 189
Hegel, G. W. F., 222
Hellenism, critique of, 208, 222, 288
Herder, Johann Gottfried, 5, 202, 207–8, 214
Hindi language, translation of Vedas into, 240, 245
Hindu reform movements, 11, 239–40
Hinduism. *See also* bhakti, India, Purāṇa, Veda
attempts to harmonize with Christianity, 263, 265–266
Christian criticism of, 255
Christian view of, 202–3, 207
definition of, 237, 239
importance of Veda within, 237, 238
orthodoxy of, 237
Western impact upon, 254–55

Hirsh, E. D., 12–13
history, religious significance of, 265–66
Holdrege, Barbara, 2, 3, 7–8, 20, 25, 68, 241
Holwell, J. Z., 205
hotṛ priest, 71, 73, 83
Hutāśana, 108

Ilā, 108
image worship, 238–39, 247
  criticisms of, 254, 255
Inden, Ronald, 283
India. *See also* Hinduism
  as "cradle of humanity," 207, 210
  Western impact upon, 254–56
  Western perception of, 283, 287
  Western romanticism of, 202–3, 206, 216
Indian nationalism, 245–46
Indian Renaissance, 253, 254–56. *See also* Arya Samaj, Brahmo Samaj
Indo-European language, 211, 216. *See also* philology
Indo-European religion, 214, 215, 216
Indology, 255–56
Indra, 73, 79–81, 103, 111, 126n. 27, 295
  association with kingship, 184, 185–87
  and Asuras, 178, 186
  imagery of, 185–87
  in Sanskrit drama, 173, 174, 177, 178, 189
inspiration, 266, 268–69, 271
Islam, 242, 246
Iśvara, 54n. 9
Itihāsa(s), 36–38, 102, 105
  and creation of drama, 173
  definition of, 184
  and "fifth Veda," 184
  and school of interpretation, 291

jagatī meter, 75–81, 90n. 70
Jaiminīya Saṃhitā, 22
Jaiminīya Upaniṣad Brāhmaṇa, 48–49, 58n. 27, 76, 293
Jaiminīya Brāhmaṇa, 43, 44, 46, 52, 81
Jainism, 242
Janaka of Videha, 22
Janamejaya, 118
Jeremiah, Book of, 312–13
Jesuit documentation on India, 202–3
Jewish canon, 312–13. *See also* Judaism
Jones, Kenneth, 236
Jones, W., 216, 255
Jordens, J. T. F., 236, 243
Judaism, as deriving from Hinduism, 213–14, 220

Kabir, 1
Kādambarī of Bāṇa, 295
Kālidāsa, 171, 185, 187, 207, 209, 284, 285
Kalpa Sūtras, 285
Kaṃsa, 103
Kāṇva Yajur-Veda, 22
Kapiṣṭhala Saṃhitā, 21, 26
Kashikar, C. G., 22–23
Kashmir Śaivism, 56n. 17
Kaśyapa, 117
Kāṭhaka Saṃhitā, 21, 26
Katyāyana, 281, 291
Kauṣītaki Brāhmaṇa, 71, 76
Kauthuma Saṃhitā, 22
Kautsa, 294–95
Kavaṣa Ailūsa, 289
Kāvyaprakāśa, 180
Kerman, Joseph, 313
kinnara, 126n. 33
Kitagawa, Joseph, 312
Kopf, 255
Kṛṣṇa. *See also* Viṣṇu
  identified with Veda, 104
  identified with Viṣṇu, 101, 114, 123
  in the Purāṇas, 97–98, 102–3, 111, 116, 117, 123
kṣatra, 79–81
Kṣatriya class. *See also* caste, *Varṇa*
  connection with deities, 73, 79–81
  connection with *triṣṭubh* meter, 75–79
  cosmics associations with, 73–74, 80–81
  and *Yajur-Veda*, 74–75, 84

Kṣatriyas, conflicts with Brahmins, 295
  relations with Brahmins, 187
Kuhu, 102
Kuiper, F. B. J., 60, 176–79, 188
Kūrma Purāṇa, 107
Kutsa, 294–95

language, 104. *See also* philology
  English, in India, 254
  Hindi, 240, 245
  Indo-European, 211–12
  origins of, 207, 208, 211
  Sanskrit, 124, 211–12, 284–85
Laws of Manu, 8–9, 240
Lincoln, Bruce, 69, 88
Lingat, Robert, 57n. 12
Llewellyn, J. E., 2–3, 5, 12, 257

Macdonnell, A. A., 285, 297n. 2
Mādhavabhaṭṭa, 283
Mādhyaṃdina Yajur-Veda, 22
Magadhas, 23
Mahābhārata, 97, 100, 102, 113, 116, 117, 123, 173, 182, 183–84, 286–87. *See also* epic
Mainkar, T. G., 6, 283–85
Maitrāyanīya Saṃhitā, 21
Majumdar, R. C., 256
Mammaṭa, 180–81, 182
Māṇḍūkāyana, 21
mantra, 3, 8, 10, 14, 15, 20, 24, 38, 40, 47, 53, 116, 145
  meters of, 45. *See also* speech, Vāc
    rc, 23–24, 36, 39, 42, 46, 50–51, 71, 75
    saman, 23, 36, 39, 42, 46, 47, 50–51, 63n. 103, 71, 75
    yajus, 23, 36, 39, 50–51, 63, 71, 75
  role in Brāhmaṇa cosmogony, 38–39, 40, 43, 46–47
  role in Vedic canon, 35–36
  and *śruti*, 38
  three types of *chandas*, 23–24, 25, 28
Manu, 88n. 16, 89n. 24, 102, 289
Manus, 103, 114
Manusmṛti, 110
Mānya Maitrāvaruṇi, 281
Mārīṣā, 112
Marriage Act of 1872, 264, 267–68
Maruts, 81
Marx, 222
Mātariśvan, 108, 111
Matsya Purāṇa, 98, 100, 107, 110–11, 116, 124, 128n. 56
Matsya Sāmmada, 281
Maudave, Compte de, 203
māyā, 111, 123, 147
Mehta, J. L., 56n. 20
meters, 104, 120
  and cosmic order, 70, 75, 80–83, 90
  hierarchy of, 76
  ritual use of, 75–76, 89n. 24
  and *varṇa*(s), 75–81, 89–90n. 29, 30
Mercury (planet), 112–13
Mill, J. St., 254
Mīmāṃsā, 9, 100, 119, 122–23, 253, 259, 282
mind, and speech, 41–42, 60
Mitra, 119
Monier-Williams, Monier, 291
monotheism
  in Hinduism, 255, 264
  as original state of man, 213, 219, 220
moon, association with Soma, 111–12
Mūjavant, 111
Muller, F. Max, vii, 5, 12, 283, 291, 217, 218–22, 245–46
Muller, Wilhelm, 221
Muse in vedic poetry, 290
myths(s)
  national aspect of, 210, 215, 221
  as *natyotpatti*, "origin of the drama," 173–74, 179, 184, 187, 188, 189
  of origin, 102–4
  and philology, 212, 220–221
  role in Sanskrit drama, 173–76, 178, 189
  and romantics, 212–216
  universality of, 210–12, 214

Nābhi, 118
Nammāḷvār, 55n. 17
Nanda, 119

Narada, 175, 186, 190
Narasiṃha, 114
Nārāyaṇa, 98, 100, 106
nāṭaka, 171
natural religion, 261, 262
nature, as basis for revelation, 257–58, 265
nāṭya
  and *yajña*, 179–80, 182–83
  as *prāṇaveda*, 190–91
Nāṭyaśāstra, 10, 285
  structural schemes of, 179
  Vedic imagery in, 173–76, 176–80
nāṭyaveda, 10, 173
nāṭyotpatti
  and *pūrvaraṅga*, 179
  myth, 4–5, 173–74, 189–192
Nava Vidhan (New Dispensation), 268–69
Neo-Hindu movements, 272
neo-Vedānta movements, 254, 256
Nirgīta, 175, 190
nirukta, 281, 291, 294
Nyāya school of Indian philosophy, 36, 54n. 9

Oldenberg, 22, 283, 290, 291, 292
Om, 49–50, 62, 105, 127, 132n. 100
Orientalists, 255. *See also* Indology
  critique of, 285
  and *Ṛg-Veda*, 282–83
orthodox (Hinduism), 67. *See also* Hinduism
orthodoxy (Vedic), 100, 105
  in Hindu tradition, 237
Oupnek'hat, 213

padapātha, 22–23, 24
Pañcaviṃśa Brāhmaṇa, 26–27, 42, 43–44, 47, 76–77, 81
Pāṇini, 181, 291
Parāśara, 126
Parker, Theodore, 270–71
parokṣa (hiddenness), 281
Paśu, 102
Paśupati, 107
Patañjali, 291
Patton, Laurie, viii, 32, 85, 192, 271
Paurāṇikas, 100
Pāvaka, 107
Pavamāna, 107
performance. *See also* drama, *Nāṭyasāstra*
  and canon, 310, 312, 313
  and interpretation, 311, 314–15
philology. *See also* language
  significance to mythology, 220–21
Polier, Louis-Henri, 216
Pollock, Sheldon, 37, 38–39, 282
polytheism, critique of, 213, 215
post-Orientalists, 283
post-Vedic India
  as decline from "golden age," 255
  as degenerated from Vedic ideal, 203–4, 205, 209, 211, 217
Potter, Karl, 158
Pracetases, 112
Prahelikās, 290
Prajāpati, 39–40, 71, 87, 100, 125. *See also* Brāhmaṇas
  as creator, 3, 70–71, 74
  as creature, 41–49, 51–52
  as identification with Veda, 40–41
  as mind, 41–42
  and sacrifice, 40, 58
  and Vac, 26–27, 40–47
Prakit lyric, 188
prāṇamaya, 154
Pratah, 102
Prātiśākhyas, 22
Pravargya, 118
Pre-vedic society, 294
Prince Āgnīdhra, 114–15
Priyavrata, 114
Protestantism, and Hindu reform, 246
Providence, 268, 270
Pṛśni, 101, 112
Pṛthu, 107, 111
puja (worship), 174
  as *yajña*, 180
Punjab, 23
Purāṇa(s), 4, 10–11, 36–38, 102, 113, 122, 124, 204, 216, 255
  authority of, 239, 240, 242, 246

Purāṇa(s) (*continued*)
canoncity of, 99, 121
claim to be fifth Veda, 98, 105
compared with Pūrvamīmāṃsā, 113, 122
continuity with Veda, 105
portrayal of the Vedas, 97, 100, 114
theistic nature of, 98, 100–2, 104–6, 123
as Veda, 97, 99
in relation to Veda, 98–100, 106, 116–23
Vedic imagery within, 99, 114–15
purāṇasaṃhitā, 98
purāṇaveda, 97, 122
Purāṇic infallibility, 105, 121
Pūrṇamāsa, 102
Purūravas, 108, 115, 186
puruṣa, 4, 9, 100, 101, 103
and *puruṣottama*, 100, 114, 120
Puruṣa Sūkta, 48, 89n. 25, 294
puruṣārthas, 99
puruṣottama, 4, 9, 100, 114, 120–21, 123
Pūrva Mīmāṃsā Sūtras, 282
Pūrva-Mīmāṃsā, 36–37, 99, 113, 122–23n. 1
pūrvaraṅga, 171, 173, 175, 177, 178, 187
and *nāṭyotpatti*, 179

Qur'an, Hindu criticism of, 242

Rahu, 112
Raja, C. Kunhan, 6, 283, 284, 287–89, 295, 296
Rājā (Soma), 113
Rajaśri, 187
Rājasūya, 116
Raka, 102
Rāma, 118
Rāmānuja, 10, 141, 150–51, 153–55, 262
Rambachan, Anantanand, 3, 5–6, 11
Rāmcaritmānas, 55n. 17
Rāṇāyanīya Sāma-Veda, 22
rasa, 172, 179, 180–81, 188–89
as *bhava*, 188
in Saivism, 188
in Sanskrit drama, 172, 179, 180, 181, 188–90
rathantara, 42

religion
importance to social reform, 263, 267
as intuitive, 258, 262, 263
and nature, 257–58
and science, 260–61, 269
search for "true" religion, 258
search for universality, 258, 261
speculations as to Indian origins, 207, 210, 214–15
Western history of, 218
religious knowledge, sources of, 257, 258–59, 262, 265, 267, 271
religious innovation, and canonical authority, 236–37, 238
Renou, Louis, 1–2, 9, 21, 24–25, 38, 56n. 20, 201, 236, 291
revelation, 257–58, 262, 270, 271
through biography, 265–66
and inspiration, 266, 268–69
and intuition, 263, 265, 271
Ṛg-Veda Saṃhitā, 9, 21, 22–23, 24, 30–31, 46, 70–75, 83, 95, 101–2, 106, 108, 111, 119, 125n. 20, 240–41, 247
and the "craft-theory" of poetry, 290
geographic origin, 23
and Sanskrit drama, 171
stories about its composition, 281, 290–91
supposed loss of, 207
transmission to the West, 216–19
universal dilemma of interpretation, 291
various redactions of, 21–23
Western idealization of, 215, 218–19
Ṛgvedabhāṣya, 283
Ṛgvedānukramaṇī, 283
rishi(s), 46, 55n. 13, 102, 103
modern interpretation of, 281, 282, 283, 285, 289, 293–95
and *śruti*, 37–38
Ritter, Karl, 214–15
ritual, 113–15, 118–19
and canon, 8
and devotion (bhakti), 9
Purāṇic, 107, 113, 115–16, 118–19, 129n. 66
and redaction of Vedic Saṃhitās, 24
and speech, 20, 23, 25

Rocher, Ludo, 98, 124, 204
Rohini, 113
Romantic mythologists, 212–16
Romantics, view of India, 209–10, 212–16
Rosen, Friedrich August, 201
Roy, Rammohun, 5, 11, 255, 256–59, 260, 261, 269, 270, 272
Ruci, 115
Rudra, 107, 111, 181
Rudrāgni, 107
Rudras, 73, 81, 88

Śabara, 253
sacred texts. *See also* canon, religious knowledge, Veda
  categories of, 36–37
  transformative nature of, 162
  scholarly approach to, 140, 156–65
  interpretation of, 139, 141
sacrifice, 7–8, 9–10, 75, 86–87n. 6, 123. *See also* ritual, *yajña*
  of animals, 116–17, 132n. 96
  in the Brāhmaṇas, 39–40
  as constructive, 182
  and creation, 39, 46–47, 49, 51–52
  and drama, 181, 184
  Purāṇic conception of, 97, 106–7, 113–20
  Purāṇic tale of origin, 115
  and theater, 174, 179–80
  and Viṣṇu, 102, 110, 113–14, 118
sacrificial fires, 71, 75
Said, Edward, vii, 283
Sainte Croix, Baran de, 204
Śaivism, 188
Śākala recension of the *Ṛksaṃhitā*, 21 22, 31
Śākalya, 22–23, 24
śākhas, 22
Śākuntala, 207, 209
Śālmalidvīpa, 113
salvation, 87–88n. 13
Sāma-Veda Samhita, 22, 47, 70–75, 84, 102, 115
sāman, 89n. 24
samanvaya, 146, 149
Samasyapurtis, 290
Saṃhitā(s), 3, 10, 20–21, 22, 25, 34, 36–37, 39, 102–3, 118, 126n. 32, 235. *See also* canon, Veda, *Ṛg-*, *Yajur-*, *Sāma-*, and *Atharva-Veda*
  and definition of Vedic canon, 20–22
  functions of, 30
  redactors of, 23, 24
Sāṃkhya, 114, 146
Sanskrit education, 284–85
Śaṅkara, 9–10, 100, 105, 141, 150–53, 154, 155, 157, 160, 258–59, 262, 269, 273
Śāṅkhayana, 21
Śāṅkhāyana Āraṇyaka, 76, 286
sannyāsins, 258
Sanskrit language, 29, 72, 284–85
  "divine" status of, 211
Sanskrit drama, 4–5, 207, 209–10
  consecration of, 175–76, 178
  hero in, 177, 178, 179, 187
  heroine in, 177, 178, 187–88
  and kingly succession, 184–85
  origins of, 173
  performative nature of, 183, 184, 189–90, 191
  relations with royalty, 185
  religification of, 176, 184, 191, 193n. 12
  religion in, 177
  and ritual, 173–78, 179–80, 182–83, 184
  role of *viduṣaka* in, 187, 188
  secularization of, 177
  triad in, 188
  universalism of, 173, 174, 179, 184
  Vedic imagery in, 181, 185–87
  Vedic origins of, 176–80
  Vedism of, 190–91, 171–72, 181–82, 189
Sanskrit poetry, Western conceptions of, 207–9
Śantiparvan, 100
Sarasvat, 41
Sarasvatī, 41, 178, 187
Sarasvatī, Dayanand, 5, 11–12, 87n. 9, 235, 238–48, 312. *See also* Hindu reform movement
Sarda, Harbilas, 240

Sarkar, Umesh Chandra
Sarvānukramaṇī, 281
sastrath (debates), 239–40, 242–43. *See also* Benares
Sastri, Subrahmanya, 259
Śatapatha Brāhmaṇa, 23, 27–29, 42, 43–46, 49, 50–51, 68, 70, 72, 74, 76, 79–80, 81, 87, 281
satya (truth), 68
Satyarth Prakas, 242, 246
Saunaka, 291
Sāvitrī, 102
Sāyaṇa, 245, 292, 293
  commentary on *Ṛg-Veda*, 217, 218
Schlegel, Friedrich, 5, 210–212
Schwab, Raymond, 204
scripture, 85–86. *See also* canon, sacred text
  authority of, 246, 257–258, 262, 266
  infallibility, 262, 270–271
  rejection of, 262, 264, 266
Sen, Keshub Chandra, 6, 11–12, 245, 262, 263–69, 270–71, 272
Shastabad of Brahma, 205
Shaster Bedang, 205
Shinto canon, 312
Sinīvālī, 102
Śiva, 110, 111, 129n. 63
  as guardian of dramatic cast, 178
  as lord of drama, 187
Skanda Purāṇa, 110
Skandasvāmin, 283
Smarta Brahman community, 105
Smith, Frederick, 2, 4, 9–10
Smith, Brian K., viii, 2, 3–4, 7, 19, 38, 48, 55n. 6, 56n. 19, 57n. 22, 58n. 28, 176, 183, 237, 241, 272, 309
Smith, J. Z., vii–viii, 2, 19–20, 31, 35–36, 86, 236, 237, 253, 271, 282, 311
Smith, W. C., 19
Smith, Barbara Hernstein, 309
smṛti, 110, 258
  and *śruti*, 36–37
social order, as primordial in origin, 68–69. *See also* caste, *varṇa*
social reform, 254–55
Soma
  identification with moon, 111–13
  as mind of Viṣṇu, 112
  as plant, 77, 79–80
  Purāṇic geneology, 112, 130
  Purāṇic interpretation of, 97, 102, 106, 111–13
  purifying power of, 111–12
  as ruler of plants, 112–13
  sacrifice, 27, 117, 118, 125–26
speech. *See also* mantra, Vāc
  Brahminical understanding of, 25, 28
  control of, 3, 8, 25–26
  and cosmic order, 40–41, 47, 50
  and creation, 180–81
  as an eight footed buffalo cow, 293
  geneology of, 103
  Mammaṭa's understanding of, 181
  and mind, 41–42, 60
  power of, 180
  and ritual action, 20, 23, 25
  role in cosmogony, 42–50
  and sacrifice, 25, 28
  in Sanskrit drama, 180–81
Spencer, H., 255
Spengler, Oswald, 222
Spivak, Gayatri, 296, 297
Śraddha, 119
śrauta fires, 108–11, 129
śrauta sacrificial system, 23, 25, 29, 30–31
Śrauta Sūtras, 295
Śrī, 177, 178, 187
Śrutaprakāśikā, 167n. 16
śruti
  and *smrti*, 36–37
  canon of, 36–38
Staal, Frits, 57n. 23, 125n. 18, 133n. 113
Sturm un Drang period, conception of the Veda, 210, 213
  intepretation of Veda, 5
Subalternist school of thought, 283
Śuci, 107
Sudarśana Sūri, 167n. 16
Sudevī, 112

Śudra(s), 91, 117, 258–59
Sudyumna, 119
śukra(s), 70
sūktas, 281, 286, 289, 290, 293
Śunaḥśepa, 289, 290–91
Sunderland, R. J. T., 269
Sūrya, 48–50, 70–73, 290
  chariot of, 120
Sūryasya Duhitā, 290
Svaha, 107, 110
Svāyambhuva Manvantara, 128n. 63
Svāyambhuva Manu, 115

Tagore, Debendranath, 6, 259–60, 261, 263, 272
Tattvabhusan, Sitanath, 262
Taittirīya Brāhmaṇa, 41, 50–51, 68, 76, 87n. 11
Taittirīya Saṃhitā, 21, 23, 26–7, 58n. 29, 76, 81, 126n. 32
Taittirīya Āraṇyaka, 76
Taittirīya Upaniṣad, 141, 142–55, 157, 160, 162–64
  Bādarāyaṇa's interpretation of, 147–49, 152
  Rāmājuja's interpretation of, 153–55
  Śaṅkara's interpretation of, 150–53
  Vedāntic interpretation of, 149–51
Tamil sangam poetry, 188
Tārā, 112
Tarkapancanana, Haracandra, 87n. 9
Tattvabodhini Patrika, 260
Tattvabodhini Sabha, 253
textuality, and canon, 10–11. *See also* sacred text
Thapar, Romila, 29–30, 283, 296
Thieme, Paul, 24, 29
Timm, Jeffrey, 32n. 3
Tiruvāymoli, 55n. 17
traya veda (Threefold Veda), 23, 39, 46–51, 58n. 26, 68, 73
trayī vidyā (Threefold Kowledge), 39, 42, 44, 45, 51, 58n. 26, 61n. 77
Trayī (as goddess), 102
Treta Yuga, 173
trigata, 178, 187
  as recretation of cosmogonic strife, 177
Trinitarian Christianity, critique of, 270
Trinity, 270
Tripura, 111
triṣṭubh meter, 75–81
Tuckerman, Joseph, 269
Tulsidas, 55n. 17
Tvaṣṭṛ, 119–20

Uddhava, 101–2, 126n. 25
udgatṛ priest, 71, 73, 84
Umā, 112, 181
Unitarian Christianity, influence on Brahmo Samaj, 269–71
universal religion, search for, 258, 261, 268, 272
Upanayana, 118
Upaniṣad(s), 36–39, 54n. 10, 103, 139, 235
  authority of, 260, 261–262, 273
  canon of, 141
  and perception, 267
  rejection of, 261–62
  scholarly interpretation of, 140
  Vedantic interpretation of, 141, 146, 161
  Western study of, 158–59, 162–63
Upavedas, 104
Urvaśī, 115, 186
Uśanas, 118
Uśas, 290
Uttara Mīmāṃsā Sūtra, 145–51, 154–56, 157

vāc (speech), 68, 83
Vāc, 40, 187. *See also* mantra, speech
  in the Brāhmaṇas, 25–26
  different levels of, 43–46
  goddess of speech, 2, 3, 8
  as "Mother of the Vedas," 41
  myths of her return to the gods, 28–29
  myths of her separation from the gods, 26–27
  and Prajāpati, 26–27, 40–47
  in *Ṛg-Veda*, 25–26
  role in cosmogony, 42–49
Vacaspati, 153, 166

Vahni, 108
Vaikuṇṭha, 106
Vaiśeṣika school of Indian philosophy, 36, 54 n. 9
Vaiśya
  connection with deities, 80–81
  connection with *jagatī* meter, 75–79
  cosmic association with, 73–74, 80–81
  and *Sāma-Veda*, 74–75, 84
Vaivasvata Manu, 119
Vajasaneyisamhitā, 21–22, 23
Vāmana, 114, 118
van Buitenen, 105
Varāha, 114, 130 n. 82
Vārkṣi, 112
varṇa, 48, 173, 174. *See also* caste
  and cosmic order, 73
  and meter, 75–76
  and sacrifice, 75
  and Veda, 4, 6, 12
Varuṇa, 88 n. 16, 119, 176
Vasu, 112
Vāsudeva, 118
Vasus, 73, 81, 88 n. 16
Vāyu, 48–50, 70–72, 79, 88 n. 16
Vāyu Purāṇa, 97, 107, 116, 123, 128 n. 63
Veda, 139
  accessibility of, 235, 237, 240, 241, 244–45
  authority of, 3, 4, 6, 12, 38–39, 67–68, 103, 123, 236, 237–38, 240, 253, 258
    questioning, 261, 258
    impact of Western contact upon, 254
  Brahmāṇical definition of, 37–38, 52
  canon of, 1–2, 12, 20, 22, 30–31, 35, 37, 68, 86 n. 9, 98–99
  issues of definition, 176, 191
  role in Hinduism, 237, 238
  universalism of, 235, 244, 261
  definition of, 235, 238
  as related to Christianity, 204
  and classics of Hellenism, 288, 290
  and contact with the West, 3, 6, 11–12
  and cosmic order, 68–69, 71–74, 82
  cosmogonic role of, 70–72, 75
  cosmogony, 37, 42, 45, 48–51
  as cosmologized, 3, 8, 12
  and definition of Hinduism, 19
  and drama, 171–72, 176–80, 290
  Enlightenment discourse on, 202–210
  as eternal, 84
  and fire altars, 142
  and Golden Age, 210, 214, 216
  gayatrī meter, 98, 102, 104
  hierarchy of, 74, 89 n. 24
  and history, 293–97
  human origin of, 271
  idealization of, 240
  identification with Prajāpati, 40
  identification with Vāc, 41
  interpretation of 6, 9, 99, 122, 257, 258, 287–293
    Brāhmaṇical, 4
    Dayānand, 4
    modern, 6
    traditional schools, of, 291
    Vedāntic, 4
    Western, 5, 6, 12
  image worship in, 239–40
  infallibility of, 4, 5–6, 97, 99–117, 102, 105–6, 123, 256, 257, 260
    rejection of, 261, 262–63, 264
  issues of definition, 204–5
  as "lost," absent text, 204, 205, 209
  and lower castes, 244
  manipulation of, 4, 5, 12
  modern Indian interpretation of, 288, 290, 292, 293–94, 295, 296
  as monotheistic, 235
  motives for Western study of, 221, 222
  and naṭional unity, 6, 12
  oral nature of, 7–8, 12, 19–20, 31, 121
  and orthodoxy, 97, 119
  performative nature of, 311, 314
  and poetry, 285, 288–91, 293, 294
  as purana, continually renewed, 97, 123 n. 1, 124 n. 2
  in relation to Purāṇas, 98–100, 116, 123 n. 1
  Purāṇic appropriation of, 4
  Purāṇic conception of, 97, 100, 114
  questioning uniqueness of, 258

and recitative tradition, 39–40
rejection of traditional views, 56n. 9, 258–59
religion, attempts to revive, 239–40
and ritual, 101, 102, 110, 113, 116, 122, 127, 132n. 98
Romantic discourse on, 210–16, 219
as "sacred word/knowledge," 38–40, 45, 52–53, 57n. 22
and sacrificial cult, 71, 75, 83–84
priests of, 71, 83–84
scholarly conception of, vii–viii
significance of modern study, 315
significance within cosmic order of Brāhmaṇas, 39, 43, 47–48
and social hierarchy, 3–4, 73
supposed primitive monotheism in, 203, 205
tales of origin, 115, 126n. 32
textuality of, 10–11, 39, 241–43, 312
as "three fold," 68, 73
as touchstone of orthodoxy, 236, 237, 248
transcendent nature of, 282
translated into Hindi, 240, 245
and *varṇa*, 68–69, 73–74, 83–84, 89n. 25
and Viṣṇu, 100–2
and *vyāhṛtis*, 69–71, 74
and Western scholarship, 203, 245–46, 295, 296–97
idealization of, 209, 216–17, 255–56
Indian criticism of, 283, 284–85, 287–88, 290, 292
and women, 244
Vedabhāṣyakāras, 292
Vedabhāṣyas, 292
Vedānta. *See also ātman, brahman*, Śaṅkara
and Brahmo Samaj, 260–61
and canon, 150
and exegesis of Upaniṣads, 140, 145–46, 156, 160
mode of interpretation, 141–42, 145–46, 151, 159
as school of "Vedic" exegesis, 4, 9, 36, 54n. 9, 100, 139
nature of argument within, 150, 155
Western conception of, 157–58
Vedanta Sutras, 240
Vedavyāsa, 102, 126n. 32
Videhas, 23
Vidura, 110
viduṣaka, Brahmin buffoon of the Sanskrit drama, 175, 177, 290
Vighnas, 173, 190
Vikramorvasiya, 171, 185, 186
Vīraśaiva, 55–56n. 17
Virjanand, 239
viś, 80, 84
Viśva Devas, 80
Viśiṣṭādvaita school, 151, 153
Viśñu, 98, 100–1, 102–3, 111, 112, 123
differentiation from Krshna, 101
equated with Veda, 100–1
and sacrifice, 102, 110, 113–14, 118, 130n. 82
Viṣṇu Purāṇa, 116
Viśvajit, 118
Viśvamitra, 295
Viśvarūpa, 119, 126n. 27
Vivekacūḍāmaṇi, 162–64
Voltaire, 5, 205–7
von Roth, Rudolph, 217, 284, 292
von Hallberg, Robert, 315
Vṛta, 119–20
vyāhṛti(s), 101, 69–71, 73, 81
essence of Vedas, 43, 46, 48–50, 52
Vyasa, 216

Weber, 22
White Yajur-Veda, 21–22
Whitney, 216
Wilson, H. H., 255, 291
women
access to the Vedas, 244
equality of, 254–55, 263, 267
Purāṇic view of, 102, 117, 119

yajña, 174, 176
and *nāṭya*, 179–80, 182–83
as *pūja*, 180
as re-creation, 182

Yajña (personified), 113, 115, 131n. 86
Yajñavalkya, 22, 23, 126n. 32
Yajñikas, 291
Yajur-Veda Saṃhitā(s), 21–22, 23, 70–75, 84, 102, 240–41
  and the flourishing of Brahmanism, 24–5
  geographic origin, 23
Yama, 289
Yama(s), 115
Yāska, 291, 294–95
Yoga school of Indian philosophy, 36, 54n. 9
Younger, Paul, 56n. 19
Yudhisthira, 116, 119